Literary Fiction

Literary Fiction

The Ways We Read Narrative Literature

Geir Farner

B L O O M S B U R Y

NEW YORK · LONDON · NEW DELHI · SYDNEY

Bloomsbury Academic
An imprint of Bloomsbury Publishing Inc

1385 Broadway	50 Bedford Square
New York	London
NY 10018	WC1B 3DP
USA	UK

www.bloomsbury.com

Bloomsbury is a registered trade mark of Bloomsbury Publishing Plc

First published 2014

© Geir Farner, 2014

Library of Congress Cataloging-in-Publication Data
A catalog reference for this book is available from the Library of Congress.

ISBN: HB: 978-1-6235-6484-1
PB: 978-1-6235-6024-9
ePDF: 978-1-6235-6025-6
ePub: 978-1-6235-6426-1

Typeset by Deanta Global Publishing Services, Chennai, India
Printed and bound in the United States of America

Contents

1   Introduction   1

2   What is Literary Fiction?   5

Attempts to define literary fiction   8

Intratextual criteria   8

Extratextual criteria   10

The embedding of real elements in fiction   10

A reader-oriented definition of literary fiction   12

Fiction with reservations   14

How to distinguish between fact and fiction?   14

Is the author of documentary fiction obliged to
     cite his sources?   16

The embedding of external facts: Conclusion   19

The embedding of fictitious elements in non-fiction   20

Narrative and fiction   20

3   The Fictional Communication Process   25

The question of genre   26

The levels of the communication process   28

Early theories of levels   29

Narratological theories of levels   31

The material text   35

The mental model of the action   35

The relationship between the mental model and the action   37

The cognitive content   40

What kind of content does literary fiction convey?   44

Identification   48

Popular literature   52

The cognitive content: Terminological alternatives   53

The truth of the message   54

The incompleteness of the mental model   55

The transparency of the model   57

The two aspects of the model   59
Why the term *mental model*?   62
One drawback of the terms *signifier, signified* and *referent*   66
Drama   67
Literary fiction as a speech mode   68
Possible worlds   69
What comes first, text or action?   71

4   The Cognitive and the Aesthetic Dimension   75
    Definition of the aesthetic   76
    The aesthetic dimension in art   79
    Does fiction have an aesthetic dimension?   80
    Does the text have an aesthetic function?   81
    Does the action have an aesthetic function?   82
    Does the mental model have an aesthetic function?   84
    Does the cognitive content have an aesthetic function?   87
    Does the interplay between the levels have an
        aesthetic function?   87
    Must fiction have an aesthetic dimension in order to be art?   88
    The cognitive function and consciousness   89
    Evidence of the cognitive function   90

5   The Delimitation of the Literary Work   93
    The text and the mental model of the action   94
    The message   99
    Drama and lyric poetry   101
    Ambiguous texts   102
    Reading in another order and repeated readings   104
    The simultaneity of the levels   105
    Other theories   107

6   Intention and Message   111
    The message as perceived by the receiver   112
    Different forms of communication   114
    The many faces of the author   115
    The message as perceived by the sender   115

Does the work always reflect the author's own views? 117
The relationship between the latent and the
    received message 119
To what extent is information about the author's
    intention available? 125
The expectations of the reader 126
The author's responsibility for the received message 127
Conclusion 129
Interpretative strategies 130

7   Problems Related to the Sender 133
The narrator and the narrative act 135
Käte Hamburger's theory 138
The nature of the narrator 139
The role of the receiver 140
Attachment 141

8   The Structure of the Action 143
The mental model and the action 143
What is the action? 144
The action as part of a larger fictional world 146
Problems with the definition of *story* 147
The author's influence on the action 150
The complexity of the action 152
The relationship between events and characters 154
Description of characters 156
Action-orientation and character-orientation as
    forms of selection 159
Attempts at simplification 160
The smallest meaningful elements of the action 161
How are these basic elements related to Propp's and
    Greimas's models? 164
The characters' mode of existence 168
Flat and round characters 170
The action as a vehicle for the message 175
Setting 175

9   Selection   177
    Theories about duration   177
    Selection   179
    Time and its content   181
    Quantitative selection   182
    Scene, summary, ellipsis, pause and stretch   185
    The problem *pause*   188

10 Voice   193
    Temporal relations   194
    Identity and level   201
    Terminological problems   204
    The significance of the author's choice of grammatical person   210
    The report of speech and thoughts   214
    Interference of the narrator   217
    Comments of the narrator   218
    Humour as a manifestation of voice   220
    Irony   223
    Other kinds of indirect communication   229

11 Viewpoint, Focalization   231
    Viewpoint or focalization?   231
    Viewpoint in non-fiction, film and drama   232
    Viewpoint in the novel and short story   233
    Omniscience and perception   234
    Position: Internal and external viewpoint   235
    Depth   237
    Breadth   238
    Stability   239
    Rewriting in the first person   240
    The point of view in the first-person novel   241
    The narrator's viewpoint: Double focalization?   243
    Is there always a viewpoint (or focalization)?   246
    Ambiguous viewpoint   248
    Viewpoint and voice   249
    Zero focalization?   252

Internal viewpoint and subjectivity   255
Viewpoint and identification   256
Conclusion   257

12 Frequency   259

13 Order   267

14 Suspense   273
    What is suspense?   273
    Various forms of suspense   274
    Suspense in *Effi Briest*   280
    Artificial suspense   282

15 The Functions of Literary Fiction   287
    Didactic literature and simplification   292
    Result- and process-orientation   292
    Non-cognitive functions   293

16 Evaluation   297
    To what extent is evaluation inevitable?   297
    How subjective is evaluation?   298
    Which aspects of the work are subject to evaluation?   303
    Evaluation criteria   307
    Evaluation criteria for the cognitive content   307
    Truth   308
    Importance   310
    Relevance   313
    Novelty and difference   313
    Entertaining effect   317
    Evaluation criteria for form alone and form and
        content as a whole   317
    Wholeness   318
    Complexity and simplicity   320
    Openness   321
    Criteria related to phatic function   322
    Professional competence   324

Criteria linked to time   324
Criteria linked to language   324
Extratextual factors   325
Who is entitled to evaluate?   326
Conclusion   327

17 Conclusion   331

Bibliography   335
Author Index   343
Subject Index   347

1

Introduction

In his *Literary Theory: A Very Short Introduction*, after a systematic discussion of the main issues of modern literary theory, Jonathan Culler concludes (Culler 1997, 119–20):

> Theory . . . does not give rise to harmonious solutions. It doesn't, for instance, teach us, once and for all, what meaning is: how much the factors of intention, text, reader, and context each contribute to a sum that is meaning. Theory doesn't tell us whether poetry is a transcendent vocation or rhetorical trick or how much of each. Repeatedly I have found myself ending a chapter by invoking a tension between factors or perspectives or lines of argument and concluding that you have to pursue each, shifting between alternatives that cannot be avoided but that give rise to no synthesis.

Theory, on this view, offers not a set of solutions but the prospect of further engagement. Theory is 'endless – an unbounded corpus of challenging and fascinating writings – but not only writings: it is also an ongoing project of thinking' (120). According to this conception of literary theory, the nature and function of literature will always remain an open question, and it is up to scholars to take their pick among the dizzying variety of more or less incongruous theories that compete for their sympathies. Culler implies that literature, by its very nature, resists theoretical analysis and understanding, but the cause of this resistance remains unclear. It may be that *literature* is an unstable concept whose nature and function are continually changing, invalidating any attempt to describe them, because every new description is rendered obsolete by the next innovation. Alternatively, the notion of *literature* may be stable enough, but our insight into how literature works is still too defective to permit a fruitful description of it. This book is meant as an argument for the latter alternative.

Admittedly, the means of literary expression have always been developing, but, nevertheless, the nature of literary fiction remains unchanged as long as its main structure concerns the presentation of fictional events. Instead of resigning ourselves to the belief that the nature of literature is too volatile or too paradoxical for rational understanding, I think it is fruitful to study the fictional work more closely to see if earlier research may have neglected something that might complete and to some degree reconcile existing theories.

Literary theorists have so thoroughly described the lower-level structures of the literary work (like events, characters, time, characterization, focalization and voices, speech representation and stylistic devices) that there seems to be little room left for improvement. However, the structuralist movement to which the substantial part of this progress is due has tended to exclude the cognitive aspects of literary communication, which are indispensable for any understanding of how literature functions. Limited by its solely linguistic perspective, classical structuralism regards the cognitive aspects of the work as irrelevant because they bear on its meaning, which is considered too subjective to be of scholarly interest. These constraints are typical of the work of Genette 1972 and 1983 and apply more or less to Chatman 1978, Rimmon-Kenan 1983 and Bal 1990. Instead of a general investigation of *what* fiction communicates and *how* it communicates it, literary theory at this stage tends to get lost in details of a lower order.

This structuralist resistance has not completely precluded cognition from being discussed in modern literary theory. On the contrary, there seems to be a growing interest in mimesis and cognition, even among modern narratologists (Herman and Vervaeck 2005, Phelan and Rabinowitz 2005, Herman 2007, Davies 2007, Abbott 2008, Fludernik 2009, Vermeule 2010). However, a more advanced description of the basic elements of fictional communication based on the distinction between *signifier, signified* and *referent* has yet to surface, and thus, literary theory has yet to satisfactorily explain fiction's cognitive influence on the reader.

This is due to multiple factors. Phenomenology, for instance, has tried to understand the literary work as a purely aesthetic phenomenon, leaving little room to consider its cognitive functions. A typical example of this is Wellek and Warren's *Theory of Literature* (René Wellek and Austin Warren 1954), in which the functions of literature are taken up early, in the third chapter, while literature's nature and basic communicative structure – which are essential for understanding these functions – are not discussed until the twelfth chapter. Many other internationally renowned works on narratology do not discuss these matters at all, such as Wolfgang Kayser 1948, Booth 1983 (1961), Genette 1972 and 1983, Chatman 1978, Rimmon-Kenan 1983, Stanzel 1985 and Bal 1990. Somewhat surprisingly, this also applies in part to Davies 2007 and Abbott 2008, who both discuss the functions of fiction from a modern cognitive viewpoint but neglect the literary communication process as such. Not even a modern cross-disciplinary approach like Herman 2009, which presents a broad variety of theories on narrative, language and communication, is entirely invulnerable to the foregoing criticism. A focus on the meaning of the literary work is characteristic of post-structuralist movements, such as deconstructionism, feminism, New Historicism, post-colonialism and cultural studies (see De Man 1989, 3–20), but these approaches overlook the ways in which meaning is conveyed structurally. Modern narratology takes an intermediate position, focusing on both meaning and structure, but its focus has shifted from fiction to narrative in general, thus neglecting the special complications related to fictional communication. All in all, literary theory has yet to explain *how* the fictional text is converted into meaning and *how* this process influences the reader.

Insofar as theory has concerned itself with the literary communication process and the function of literature, opinions have been sharply divided, indicating that the elementary theoretical foundations of literary theory and criticism still need clarifying. Indeed, given this state of affairs, it seems puzzling that modern literary theory invests so little in reaching a solution that can find wider acceptance among scholars. Modern linguistics, philosophy of language and linguistic psychology should have contributed to a clearer understanding of how fiction works. Instead, literary scholarship seems to be resigned to pursuing its traditional activities without a clear understanding of the basic structures and functions of its very object.

This state of affairs comes with a price, however. Many of the 'classical' problems that literary theory has been grappling with from Aristotle to our time, like *intention, function, evaluation, delimitation* of the literary work as such, *fictionality, suspense,* and the *roles of author and narrator,* along with such narratological problems as *voice, point of view* and *duration,* are still waiting for a satisfactory solution. These problems have persisted for such a long time that we seem to accept them as more or less irresolvable. Becoming accustomed to a problem does not, however, mean that it has ceased to be a problem and that it no longer adversely affects our work. The unsolved problems of literary theory increase the likelihood of misunderstandings and misjudgements, which is confirmed by the wide range of conflicting views among literary theorists. Ideological differences are inevitable, but when it comes to basic questions such as how fiction works, it must at least be possible to establish a clearer basis for discussion, even if a complete consensus is out of reach.

Because the basic problems of literary theory have met with little interest in recent decades, earlier research has left a number of loose ends. It may seem somewhat naïve or even arrogant to pick up threads which others have failed to complete, but as our horizon of understanding continues to grow with the development of society and science, new doors are opened which can throw new light on the theory of literature. Widely acclaimed theories (like Genette's theory of duration) may betray significant gaps when seen in new contexts, and previously rejected or discarded theories may attract new attention, turning out to be fruitful after all, or have to be rejected again, but on a new basis. Even if many theories are no longer regarded as relevant, it may be necessary to enter into a dialogue with them again. This is the case with Ingarden, Wellek and Warren, Hirsch, Genette, Bal, Greimas and many others. This book is meant to encourage new ways of thinking about some well-known problems of literary theory and reopen a debate that is much more important than the activities of modern theorists seem to imply.

2

What is Literary Fiction?

Is there a clear boundary between fiction and non-fiction? In colloquial as well as scholarly discourse, the distinction between the two has traditionally been taken for granted. Nevertheless, in recent decades, modern literary theorists have raised doubts over whether it is really possible to make such a distinction. These theorists include Gérard Genette in *Nouveau discours du récit* (Genette 1983, 11) and several other scholars mentioned by Dorrit Cohn in *The Distinction of Fiction* (Cohn 1999, 8):

> No doubt the most pervasive and prominently problematic application of the word *fiction* in recent decades has been to narrative discourse in general – historical, journalistic, and autobiographical – as well as to imaginative discourse. This inclusive denotation has been forcefully, even militantly advocated by numerous voices. I quote a few random examples: "the mere selection, arrangement, and presentation of facts is a technique belonging to the field of fiction" (Arnold Toynbee); "All accounts of our experience, all versions of 'reality', are of the nature of fiction" (Ronald Sukenick); "There is no fiction or nonfiction as we commonly understand it, there is only narrative" (E.L. Doctorow); "If it is true that narratives give us no reliable knowledge of what they purport to relate, they are all fictions, including those of history" (Wlad Godzich). It is important to realize that . . . this identification of narrative and fiction is weighted with considerable ideological freight. The motive force behind it is nothing less than the contemporary critique of the entire intellectual foundation of traditional historical practice – of the entire practice that is based on belief in the factuality of past events.
>
> This thesis has found its most eloquent and influential protagonist in Hayden White, for whom historical narratives are no less "verbal fictions" than their purely imaginative counterparts in literature.

This reluctance to discriminate between fiction and non-fiction may stem from a number of different considerations. Recent philosophy might, for instance, equate the subjectivity of truth with fictionality, pointing out that this subjectivity is an inescapable element in fiction and non-fiction alike.

A related phenomenon would be non-fiction's appropriation of techniques considered typical of fiction, especially in the documentary or non-fiction novel of the last 50 years or so. Monika Fludernik seems to base her definition of fictionality on both of these considerations, since in her view, non-fiction shares many techniques with fictional literature (Fludernik 1993) and fiction and non-fiction are both fictive constructs which are equally unable to replicate reality mimetically (Fludernik 1996, 40–1):

> All narrative (even on its minimal level of sequential report) is a fictive construct, a representation, and cannot reproduce "reality" in any mimetic fashion. Stories, lives, the products of conversation are all concepts of the human mind, the result of cognitive parameters which we bring to bear upon the flux of unknowable and indivisible being, upon our exposure to the world. The recent catch phrase which exposes historiography as "also fiction" since it employs "fictional techniques" – though important as an illustration of a developing historiographical self-awareness – needs to be handled with care lest it result in an indiscriminate equation of historical and novelistic texts. History is constructed discourse, and this discourse may "lapse" into fictionalizing tendencies, for instance by inventing items based on a construction of sequentiality unwarranted by documentary evidence. However, in so far as historical prose attempts to write "history" and not "specific human experience," it will tend to remain non-fictional in the framework that I have outlined. History, by definition, is that area of study which interprets, orders, analyses and attempts to explain human experience, but it does not set out to represent such experience.

Fludernik's definition of fiction seems pulled in two directions at once, because on the one hand, she regards all narrative fiction and non-fiction as a fictive construct that 'cannot reproduce "reality" in any mimetic fashion', and on the other, she pulls the rug out from under her own definition, warning us against exposing all historiography as fiction without any criteria for the distinction other than mere cautiousness. It is difficult to see how 'handling with care' can prevent 'an indiscriminate equation of historical and novelistic texts'. To confront this problem, Fludernik 1996 (39) proposes discarding the concept of fictionality altogether. She makes good on this proposal in Fludernik 2009 (59–60), where she contends that there is no distinction between fictional and non-fictional narrative: 'Narrative is fictional per se, not because it is "made up" or deals with fantastic occurrences, but because it is based on the representation of psychological states and mental perceptions'. In other words, instead of the distinction between fiction and non-fiction, she settles for one between narrative and analytical texts.

This confusion about fiction and non-fiction is reflected – and increased – by the fact that modern scholars tend to devote attention to *narrative* instead of *fiction*; even in the titles of their works, in fact, *narrative* is employed more often than *fiction* (Phelan and Rabinowitz 2005, Herman and Vervaeck 2005, Herman 2007, Abbott 2008, Herman 2009). In *The Cambridge Companion to Narrative*, the treatment of fictionality is reduced to a single endnote (Herman 2007, 35, n. 30).

Another strike against the fiction/non-fiction distinction has come from the authorial practice of embedding specific factual elements in the fictional world. David Davies (2007, 32–3) mentions *Reading in the Dark* by the Irish author Seamus Deane, which won a prize for fiction even though the publishers had originally commissioned the book as a non-fictional biography, before the author insisted it be published as fiction. A number of works by Philip Roth have been published as novels while featuring a protagonist named Philip Roth, thus constituting a kind of autobiographical literature that oscillates between fiction and non-fiction. According to Davies, the 'recent profusion of confessional writing, where literary techniques are used in the telling of "real" stories about people's lives', extends a tradition dating back to Truman Capote's *In Cold Blood* (Capote 1966). *In Cold Blood*, which details the brutal 1959 murders of a wealthy farmer from Kansas, his wife and two of their children, is considered a non-fiction novel, a factual 'true crime' account, despite the fact that Capote has 'changed facts to suit his story, added scenes which never occurred, and re-created dialogue' (Wikipedia), all of which usually indicate fiction.

In Norway, the distinction between fiction and non-fiction attracted new attention in 2009, when the historian Tore Pryser (Pryser 2009) accused the writer Kjartan Fløgstad of plagiarizing two of Pryser's books on Nazism (Pryser 1994, 2001). Pryser specifically pointed to two scenes and 28 minor characters in Fløgstad's novel *Grense Jakobselv* (Fløgstad 2009a) as lifted from his own books. Fløgstad, for his part, invoked the traditional right of fiction writers to borrow their material from as many sources as they wish without having to account for them (Fløgstad 2009b).

From all this, it should be obvious that any pretence of an unproblematic distinction between fiction and non-fiction is no longer tenable. While it is tempting to view this development as a discouraging step backwards, there is a way forward from the current impasse, as it is only a consequence of the past failure to define the notion of fictionality. Despite the abovementioned problems, I think that picking up where previous definitions left off will make it possible to distinguish fiction from non-fiction in a way that excludes transitional forms. In other words, we need a definition that accounts for the application of fictional techniques in non-fiction, for the embedding of specific factual elements in the fictional world and for the relationship between fictionality and subjective truth.

Attempts to define literary fiction

Attempts to distinguish fiction from non-fiction arguably date as far back as Aristotle (Cohn 1999, 9–10). Traditionally, fiction has been defined in relation to referentiality as *non-referential*. While non-fiction refers to reality and is expected to render the truth, fiction is a product of imagination which cannot be tested for truth or falsity. Nelson Goodman defines fictional objects as 'representations with null denotation' (Goodman 1988, 21); in other words, fiction consists only of signifier and signified, without any referent. More colloquially, the objects conjured by fiction exist only as mental entities. For instance, fire-breathing dragons are a product of human imagination and have no specific counterpart in the real world, and every enlightened person knows they are imaginary.

A definition of fictionality based exclusively on referentiality may be adequate for fiction in its broadest sense, but it does not fully account for the special conditions pertaining to literary communication. The author of a novel knows, of course, that what he has written is fiction, but this knowledge is of no use to the reader if he does not have it himself (throughout the book, I will write 'he' instead of the less wieldy 'he/she' when referring to persons who may be of either sex). To identify fiction, the reader has to be thus informed in some way or another. Such information may reach him through two possible channels, either intratextually, through symptoms of fictionality which the text itself exhibits, or extratextually, through statements from the author or other informed authorities outside the text.

Intratextual criteria

There have been several attempts to distinguish fiction from non-fiction by way of intratextual criteria. Most prominently, Käte Hamburger has shown how textual elements convey fictionality in many kinds of texts, especially in the third-person novel in which an omniscient narrator reveals to the reader the minds of other persons than himself (Hamburger 1968).

As the omniscient representation of thinking and feeling third-person subjects is a main feature in most third-person novels, it is a useful criterion for fictionality, but the drawback of Hamburger's definition becomes evident in fictional works that eschew markers of fictionality and imitate non-fiction. For instance, in the first-person novel, an internal viewpoint is normally linked only to the protagonist, the *I* of the text, not to other persons, making it impossible for the reader to distinguish it from the autobiography (as long as there are no other unrealistic features to betray its fictional status). Likewise, if the author of a third-person novel were for some reason to renounce the use of internal viewpoint in imitation of biography, it may be difficult to recognize it as fiction. Fictional works that lack symptoms of fictionality – like the first-person novel and third-person novels without internal viewpoint – should according to Hamburger's criteria be classified as non-fiction, which would be absurd since we *know* from extratextual sources that they are fiction.

Hamburger is of course aware of the fictional status of the first-person novel, and since her intratextual criteria cannot reveal it as fiction, she is obliged to delimit it from the non-fictional autobiography as *fingierte Wirklichkeitsaussage*: feigned non-fiction. However, in contrast to the third-person novel, the term *feigned non-fiction* is not based on intratextual criteria: only extratextual information (from the author or publisher) can tell us that the first-person novel is fiction. In special cases, third-person narratives may also lack features of fictionality, but Hamburger seems to forget this possibility. Such novels are rare, of course, but her account of feigned non-fiction feels incomplete without them. Not that it matters, because ultimately, intratextual criteria prove to be deficient as indicators of fictionality; Hamburger's distinction between fiction and feigned non-fiction is entirely artificial, both categories coalescing into the category of fiction on account of external information.

Therefore, as Hamburger's intratextual criteria for fictionality are only partially appropriate indicators of fiction, and are moreover made redundant by extratextual information, they are of little use for a definition of fictionality. Nevertheless, they are valuable in other important respects, because they reveal characteristic features of fiction that affect literary communication.

More than 30 years later, Dorrit Cohn tried to revive Hamburger's criteria (Cohn 1999, 8) in order to defend the traditional distinction between fiction and non-fiction against the above-mentioned attacks. But even though Cohn does base her argumentation on an impressive list of criteria for fictionality, elucidating them skilfully with textual analysis, and notwithstanding the useful light she sheds upon fictional techniques, her intratextual criteria are vulnerable to much the same objections.

To be sure, intratextual evidence can establish the fictionality of a substantial number of works, but it nevertheless leaves out works that mimic non-fiction, especially first-person novels, but also some third-person narratives that imitate biography in renouncing the internal point of view. The intratextual approach brings us no closer to a definition of fictionality because it turns the question on its head. A literary work is not fictional because it displays symptoms of fictionality. On the contrary, it displays such symptoms because it is fictional. Fictionality is of a higher order than its own symptoms and may occur without symptoms, as in first-person novels in general and in third-person novels without an omniscient narrator and internal viewpoint. Therefore, we need a definition that accounts for fictionality without resorting to intratextual criteria.

Extratextual criteria

The fictionality of a given work may be conveyed to the reader in various extratextual ways upon publication: by genre labels (e.g. *fiction, novel, short story, fairy tale, drama, etc.*), by an explicit assurance that the events and persons depicted in the story are not identical with real ones, and so on. Genette 1997 uses *paratexts* to describe this kind of extratextual information. The circumstances around the genesis of the book may even be lost, making it impossible to classify it as fiction or non-fiction (as with, for example, Icelandic family sagas).

Based on such extratextual sources, Thomas Roberts attempts to define fictionality as *fiction by intention* (Roberts 1972, 9): 'A book is fiction by intention if its writer has knowingly made it factually untrue but also warned his readers he has done it.' This definition accounts not only for the non-referentiality of the work in question, but also for the way this knowledge is imparted to the reader. The word *untrue* in Roberts's definition may not be strictly accurate (Lamarque and Olsen 1994, 53–4), but the point is clear enough: the fictional story is not identical with real events, and the reader, too, has to know it. If the author does not inform the reader that the story is not true, the result will be a fraud, not fiction. Roberts is therefore right to claim that the author must warn the reader. The criterion for fictionality, then, is not only the lack of identity between the fictional story and real events, but also a warning that no such identity exists.

The embedding of real elements in fiction

Roberts's definition presupposes that the text contains exclusively fictitious elements, and it remains adequate as long as every detail in a fictional work is pure imagination. But what if specific elements from the real world impinge upon the story, as is the case in a great many narratives that are indisputably fictional? In Virginia Woolf's *Mrs Dalloway*, for instance, the story takes place on a particular June day in 1923 in verifiable places in London (Woolf 2000). The real elements in a work of fiction may be few, like *Mrs Dalloway*'s references to London and World War I, or they may fill almost the entire text, as in documentary novels.

In many narratives, moreover, such factual elements can prove to be as reliable and valuable as the information given in non-fiction. There are many historical novels and fictional travelogues that provide useful and true information about the real world, like Tolstoy's *War and Peace* (Tolstoy 2006) and Conrad's *Heart of Darkness* (Conrad 1996). A novel can even present an exposition of the entire history of Western philosophy, as in Jostein Gaarder's *Sophie's World* (Gaarder 2007). Whether it is Virginia Woolf's verifiable information about London in June 1923, Gaarder's introduction to philosophy, or the historical elements in the above-mentioned *Grense Jakobselv* by Kjartan Fløgstad, according to Roberts's definition, all should be regarded as unreliable fiction. On the whole, the definition admits no possibility that novels could have a documentary function, since it does not admit that fictional works may contain elements that are identical with real events, persons or objects. This deficiency becomes especially evident with the rise of documentary novels whose story is closely linked to historical or biographical events. Is the modern documentary novel fiction in the traditional sense, or is it in fact a disguised non-fictional work? Clearly, our definition needs to account for the real facts that may be embedded in the fictional world, and explain the relationship between real and fictional elements, even when the real elements predominate.

Cohn 1999 (14) makes some useful suggestions along these lines:

> If the adjective *nonreferential* is to be meaningful, it must not be understood to signify that fiction never refers to the real world outside the text.

She explains the paradoxical presence of non-fictional elements in fiction by regarding references to the real world as an external framework around a fictional internal frame. We cannot, however, trust such references to the real world (Cohn 1999, 15):

> When we speak of the nonreferentiality of fiction, we do not mean that it *cannot* refer to the real world outside the text, but that it *need* not refer to it. But beyond this . . . fiction is subject to two closely interrelated distinguishing features: (1) its references to the world outside the text

are not bound to accuracy; and (2) it does not refer *exclusively* to the real world outside the text. . . . external references do not remain truly external when they enter a fictional world. They are, as it were, contaminated from within, subjected to what Hamburger calls "the process of fictionalization".

In other words, specific elements from the real world may be embedded in the fictional story, but as readers we cannot be sure that they are accurate. How do we adapt Roberts's definition to this information?

Roberts's definition of fiction consists of three propositions:

1. The events are not identical with real ones.
2. The author knows that they are not.
3. He informs the reader that they are not identical with real ones.

Evidently, the first item has to be changed. Using Cohn's wording, we can rephrase it thus: the events can – but need not – refer to the real world, and the reader cannot rely on their accuracy. This modification, however, affects the logic of the whole line of thought, so we have to adapt the two other items, too. The second proposition can easily be adjusted:

1. The events can – but need not – refer to the real world, and the reader cannot rely on their accuracy.
2. The author knows which elements are real and which are not.

However, now the third proposition presents difficulties, for it seems clear that the author does not tell the reader which elements are real and which are not. So what information does he convey to the reader? To be sure, he still informs the reader that the story is fiction, but this can no longer mean that the events are not identical with real ones. What exactly does it mean, then?

A reader-oriented definition of literary fiction

What is the author's real intention when he presents a mixture of verifiable facts and fictional elements as a novel? Does the label *novel* mean that he pretends that the verifiable elements are fiction? No, we would say, because then he would be lying. But the fictional framework leaves the reader with no way to distinguish between fact and fiction. These two factors must be reflected in the definition. Therefore, instead of regarding the label *novel* as a claim that every element is fictional, we should consider it *a request to regard* everything as fiction. A request is not as compelling as a claim and allows for the intermingling of facts and fictional elements. The point is that the author does not assume responsibility for the truth of the elements of his story; the label *fiction* expresses the author's relinquishing responsibility for the relationship between the elements of the story and specific elements (persons, objects, events) in the real world. There may or may not be a correspondence, but the reader cannot count on it. Consequently, *fiction* does not imply that every element in the book is fictional, only that the reader should treat them *as if* they were. Which parts of the story are fictional or real is the author's own business and none of the reader's.

From this we can formulate the following definition:

> Literary fiction means a text in which the reader is expected to treat the content as if it were fictional.

Contrary to Roberts's definition, which presupposes knowledge about the author's intentions, this definition is purely reader-oriented and does not depend on what the author knows and how faithfully he conveys his material to the reader. This definition exempts the author from any responsibility for the reality or fictionality of the elements of his story. Although the reader expects the fictional work to contain at least some fictional elements, the author may embed as many real elements as he wants to, as long as a minimum of fictional elements are left, which may in principle be very small. In other words, the label *fiction* means, first, that the author has no obligation to record specific real events or objects and that he does not have to base his story on historical sources. Second, however, this does not imply that he is forbidden from doing so, and no one has the right to accuse him of recording real events or objects.

This reader-oriented definition makes it necessary to distinguish between fiction as a literary genre and fiction as an ontological status. *Literary fiction* consequently takes on a somewhat different meaning from *fiction* in general. While *fiction* means 'signified without a referent', *literary fiction* denotes texts which contain a minimum of fiction, but may also include specific elements from the real world. Such loans from the real world are not marked in the text and can only be verified by authorities outside the work.

The insertion of specific elements from historical reality must not be mixed up with the occurrence of elements that *resemble* real events, persons or objects. As long as it is a question of likeness and not identity, such elements remain fictional, even if the resemblance is perfect apart from formal properties like name and address. This kind of fictionality is familiar from the example of the *roman à clef*. If the protagonist's name is Peter and he is a true copy of the historical person John, Peter is nevertheless fictional and never existed, however closely he may resemble the original model. Even if fiction turns out to be thinly disguised reality with an easily recognizable underlying truth, it remains fiction.

Fiction with reservations

While the reader can, with relative ease, distinguish the non-fictional philosophical content from the fictional elements in a novel like *Sophie's World*, the precise boundary between fact and fiction is murkier in historical and biographical novels. This leads straightaway to a problem, a seeming paradox. When a book is published as a documentary novel, it is, on the one hand, as fiction, exempted from the claim concerning veracity: the persons, objects and events it depicts do not have to be identical with real ones. On the other hand, as documentary, it is committed to the truth and is expected to record real facts: real persons, objects and events. This seeming paradox is, however, easily surmounted, because the things that are real and the things that are fictional are not the same. Some parts of the work are facts, while others are fictional. The protagonists and main events in the novel *Grense Jakobselv* are, according to the author, fictional, whereas a lot of other characters and events are historical facts borrowed from various sources about World War II, including books by the Norwegian historian Tore Pryser. Since readers who have only a general knowledge about the war can only guess at what is history and what is fiction, the documentary novel differs from ordinary novels in that the authorial contract with the reader is more complex: it is *fiction with reservations*.

How to distinguish between fact and fiction?

The problem, ultimately, lies in the ambiguity that these reservations entail. Fiction's exemption from the claim of truth creates a sharp distinction between fiction and non-fiction. Documentary fiction blurs this distinction, however, in claiming to be both true and fictional at the same time, without clear rules delimiting what is what. This ambiguity allows the author to reject any criticism by referring to the fact that the story is, after all, only fiction. If this is so, then the documentary novel turns out to be fiction, after all. But if the embedded facts are to have any utility value as facts, the reader has to know which parts of the text are real and which ones are fictional. How, then, can we reconcile the reader's need to distinguish between fact and fiction with a definition of fiction that on the contrary stresses the freedom of the author to report or disregard the truth at will?

In effect, the fictional context cannot guarantee for the reader the trustworthiness of the facts in fiction, even if they appear credible and can ultimately be confirmed as true. Ironically, he has to depend on his own prior knowledge in order to verify the information in the novel. On this view, the facts embedded in novels can in principle only tell him what he already knew. In practice, however, it turns out that readers can still learn something new from facts embedded in literary fiction, for even if they do not have complete knowledge about the subject, they are often sufficiently familiar with it to assess the probability of the information. Moreover, if the author has no obvious reason to deviate from reality, he will probably stick to the facts, and there is little risk of the reader being deceived. Virginia Woolf's portrayal of London around 1923 in *Mrs Dalloway* is convincing enough that readers with elementary geographical and historical knowledge are likely to take a chance on its veracity in the absence of any explicit guarantee from the author.

Of course, if the reader lacks prior knowledge, he runs a greater risk of being 'deceived'. For instance, the Flemish writer Herman Teirlinck (Teirlinck 1960–69b) transforms the tiny forest Zoniënwoud in Brussels into a very large forest in the novel *Het gevecht met de engel* (*The Fight with the Angel*). The target audience of Flemish readers would know enough about the Zoniënwoud to recognize Teirlinck's exaggerated description of it, but outsiders might take it literally and imagine Brussels as a city surrounded by enormous forests. This example shows how any trust in the author must be combined with prior knowledge. This combination enables the author to convey specific information about the real world *in addition to* the more general picture that the literary work paints of it.

The probability that the facts in fiction are true may be significantly augmented by external intervention. For example, the documentary text can be supplemented paratextually with information from the author, the publisher or other authorities. David Bradshaw's comments on *Mrs Dalloway* in the Oxford University Press edition (Woolf 2000, xi–lviii) help verify Woolf's picture of London. Likewise, the media publicity surrounding Kjartan Fløgstad's documentary novel has to a great extent increased the credibility of its historical facts.

An interesting question is whether verification can change documentary fiction's status as fiction. We may at once discard the possibility that a literary work can be completely verified, because neither in theory nor in practice it is possible to verify every single, minute detail. Hence verification is often only possible with respect to the rougher structures of the work. This is also the case when the author himself is responsible for the verification, as long as he does not verify every single word and thereby deprive the work of its fictional status. In other words, determining the veracity of Seamus Deane's *Reading in the Dark*, which had originally been commissioned as a work of biography, and Philip Roth's novels where the protagonist is named Philip Roth, would require us to verify every sentence in them, which can only be done by the authors themselves. If it turned out that Deane and Roth had stuck to the facts of their own lives without inventing a single detail (for instance, in order to enliven or concretize the story), their books would in fact be autobiographies and the label *novel* would be a lie, even if an innocent one. Then we could discuss the authors' motives for lying: perhaps a wish to preserve their own immunity, to illustrate a philosophical issue or simply to provoke. For future readers, however, these books would be biographies. In the absence of any such verification, the work continues to be a novel, and the reader must treat it as fiction, even if the incidental personal details of author and narrator (or character) seem to contradict its fictionality.

Insofar as external intervention can verify the fictional story or parts of it, this is not carried out by changing the work's overall fictional status, but by complementing the original fictional text with paratexts, which are additional non-fictional texts by the author, publisher or other authorities. The paratexts are not part of the original work, but create a new, semi-fictional work together with the original text. The documentary novel can stand on its own feet as long as we regard it as fiction, but as soon as it is used as a statement about reality, it has to be verified by this supplementary material. The fact that documentary fiction needs such explanatory comments clearly proves its fictional status.

Is the author of documentary fiction obliged to cite his sources?

What are the implications of our reader-oriented definition for the claim that authors of documentary fiction should cite their sources? As we saw in the debate over *Grense Jakobselv*, Fløgstad 2009b invokes the traditional right of authors to borrow material from all kinds of sources without being obliged to cite them, mentioning *War and Peace* as another historical novel that does not cite its sources. His main source, Tore Pryser, refers on the other hand to the Norwegian author Edvard Hoem, who has also used material from Pryser's research, but credits his work in footnotes.

Nothing can prevent an author from citing his sources, like Hoem, but it is a voluntary act with little established precedent. Authors who draw upon historical sources have not traditionally been required to state to whom they are indebted. Any fact from the real world, whether it dates from the past or the author's own time, is usually considered fair game. Critics, for their part, chiefly concern themselves with the work's literary merits – what the work does to the material – while disregarding the material's sources. Charges of plagiarism are usually only levelled at authors who copy sections from other fictional authors, passing them off as their own work. Has the modern documentary novel changed matters at all? Are documentary novels fiction in the traditional sense, or are they effectively disguised non-fiction, in which case it might be reasonable to expect the author to cite his sources?

Since readers cannot trust facts in documentary fiction in the same way as they can (or at least are supposed to) in non-fiction, these two modes of communication are necessarily distinguished from each other, and this boundary can only be crossed by transforming the fictional work into non-fiction through some form of external verification. Fløgstad's *Grense Jakobselv* must therefore be either fictional or a history book; as it happens, the author's claim that it is a novel and that the protagonists are fictional indisputably identifies it as fiction.

Because the documentary novel needs external verification, it retains its status as fiction, and this applies to all parts of the action, too, even if they are infiltrated by elements from the extratextual world. Instead of blurring the boundary between fiction and non-fiction, fictionality contaminates all references to the external world and makes them unreliable. The historical facts we could trust in Pryser's books or in other trustworthy historical sources must be verified in Fløgstad's novel to attain complete documentary value. Except for certain crucial facts that the reader feels safe to assimilate because they accord with his own prior knowledge, the reader can only incorporate those parts of the information into his knowledge which are already part of it.

Therefore, the documentary novel is only partially suited to the communication of facts. It supplies the reader with credible facts only insofar as he knows them in advance himself or because competent authorities can verify them. We can only trust the historical facts in *Grense Jakobselv* after Fløgstad himself, Pryser or other well-informed authorities have confirmed them, and even then we still do not know where to draw the precise boundary between the historically verifiable and the purely fictional. Fløgstad alone can tell, by commenting on the book, sentence by sentence. By now, it ought to be clear that the novel itself does not allow the reader to make full use of the historical material as historical facts. He is dependent on extratextual verification.

This makes the difference between the documentary novel and historiography clear: whereas the historical facts constitute a primary goal of a history book, the documentary novel uses them mainly as a vehicle for something else, something of a more general nature, like illustrating and explaining how young, gifted people are attracted to the National Socialist party. In this general context, it is completely irrelevant which parts of the story are real or invented. What matters is how the novel conveys a general impression of the conditions before and during the war so that the reader can better understand the dynamics of his own world, where war and the background of war are crucial elements. If Fløgstad happened to render one or more historical facts the wrong way, nobody would have the right to blame him for it as long as the historically false facts did not distort the general picture of war and its dynamics.

Fløgstad's purpose in embedding many historical facts in his novel is not primarily to inform the reader about specific facts concerning World War II, because in any case the reader cannot know to what extent he can trust them. The chief advantage of using historical material is that it increases the probability that the *general* picture that the fictional story draws of reality is authentic. The fictional elements, in turn, imbue this picture with the vividness of life. The author can invent gripping details and absorbing action sequences that are inaccessible to the historian, and add fictitious material based on his own general knowledge about people and the world. As a result, the general picture that the novel draws of reality is more uncertain than the one offered by historiography, but at the same time much more engaging and vivid. While the historian is confined to the historical fact of the matter and interpretations of it, the documentary novelist takes the reader into a rich virtual world where he can experience the war and its prelude through the minds of living characters with whom he can empathize.

The difference in goal and means implies a difference with regard to the necessity of references. Historiography requires scholars to dig up unknown historical facts, rewarding them with renown when they uncover new material. The historian is therefore expected to cite his sources so that proper credit is given to the scholar who did the pioneering work. Another important reason historians cite their sources is the scholarly necessity of substantiating their findings. Pryser's desire to be cited as a source is therefore understandable, but in the world of fiction, neither the discovery of new historical facts nor the substantiation of arguments brings renown. The novelist's goal is to give the reader a deeper understanding of how the human world works, not to convey particular historical facts, and insofar as he makes use of historical material, he does so in order to improve the reader's general understanding of the real world. On account of this, the fiction writer gets no credit for the historical facts that are embedded in the story, only for the total artistic context in which they occur.

The novelist, therefore, does not claim to be the originator of the historical material he is using and so does not deprive the historian of the credit he deserves. The novelist deserves credit solely for the creation of the fictional universe, where material from extratextual sources merges with free imagination into a fictional whole. The fiction writer Fløgstad is not obliged to cite his sources, and may take credit for having done thorough research and providing substantial historical material for his novel, but he cannot be accused of using Pryser's material 'in a way that makes people think it is his own' in the sense of trying to take credit for it as a historian.

The embedding of external facts: Conclusion

Although there are to some extent unwritten rules in documentary fiction that restrict any departure from historical facts, the author retains an indisputable right to invent and complete the limited available information about the historical world with his own imagination. Without extratextual help, the reader can never know to what extent the content is true, which is what makes it indisputably *fiction*. In this way the impassable boundary between fiction and non-fiction stays intact. This is not to say that documentary fiction is problem free; namely, in exploiting the freedom of fiction from referential restraints, it manipulates truth in a way the audience cannot check. What is clear, however, is that documentary fiction does not affect the theoretical distinction between fiction and non-fiction. In non-fiction as well, it may be necessary to verify the content, but there is no general need for verification as in documentary fiction, except when circumstances within or outside the text affect its veracity. The fact that truth and reality are subjective and relative does not blur the boundary between reality and fiction. The fact that reality cannot be perceived objectively, and that we may misremember on occasion or lie on purpose, makes the content of non-fiction relative and shows how difficult it is to deal with reality, but there remains nevertheless an inextricable bond between text and reality. There is no such direct connection between fiction and the real world, only an indirect one, in that the fictional world *more or less* resembles the real one.

The embedding of fictitious elements in non-fiction

A related problem arises when the author explicitly embeds fictitious elements in a non-fictional work. In the preface to his *Three Men in a Boat*, Jerome K. Jerome asserts that it is a record of events that really happened and that the characters are things of flesh and blood (Jerome 1975). So it is natural to conclude that the book is a non-fictional travelogue. But then the author adds that he has coloured the events. In other words, we cannot trust everything the book says, even if the main features are consistent with reality. Is the book then fiction after all, an autobiographical novel, or does it remain non-fiction?

The problem is that the author expresses himself equivocally; with one hand, he extends a guarantee that everything is true, while retracting it with the other. What are we supposed to believe? In practice, we are in the same situation as when reading a biographical novel: we know not only that the events more or less correspond with the historical facts, but also that it is impossible to draw a precise line between the fictional and the non-fictional elements. The difference between *Three Men in a Boat* and a documentary novel is that while the former purports to be non-fiction with a certain fictional colouring, the latter claims to be fiction with a significant number of historical facts. On this analysis, it all amounts to the same thing, the difference being just a question of terminology; Jerome could just as well have called his book a novel, adding that its content is in large part based on real events.

Whether fiction is embedded in non-fiction or non-fiction is embedded in fiction, the reader cannot distinguish between reliable and unreliable aspects unless the information is subjected to extratextual verification. Regardless of how closely documentary fiction is linked to factual reality, it will always need extratextual verification, and it is this feature that constitutes the chief barrier between fiction and non-fiction, as well as between the documentary novel and historiography.

Narrative and fiction

At the beginning of this chapter, we saw three arguments that have been raised against the fiction/non-fiction distinction. The first was the equation of subjectivity with fictionality, the second was the application of fictional techniques in non-fiction, and the third was the embedding of external references in fictional stories. With respect to the latter, we have already argued that the embedding of specific real elements in the fictional story poses no threat to the definition of fictionality. Now it is time to examine the two other arguments, which are partially related to one other.

As we have seen, several scholars equate the subjectivity with which the non-fiction author inevitably reports his story with fictionality. In court testimony, we are accustomed to the fact that different persons often give divergent versions of the same event (see Walsh 2005, 150–1), and it is easy to see why this subjectivity might also apply to historians and scientists. Nevertheless, subjectivity does not imply fictionality. A witness may give a biased or even wrong version of an event, but as long as he is not deliberately lying, his testimony is meant to report the truth, and this is also what his listeners expect. Language embodies the implicit convention that verbal utterances purport to be true as long as nothing else is explicitly signalled. They are automatically accompanied by a truth claim and are thus subject to verification or falsification. Even if a proposition is untrue, it is linked directly to reality by the fact that it primarily claims to be true, that is, to reproduce reality. Only the *claim* is of importance and suffices to establish a direct link to reality, and it is of no relevance whether the facts really correspond to the claim or not.

Fiction is not accompanied by any equivalent truth claim, and bears no responsibility for the relationship between the fictional world and *specific* elements in the real world. The extratextual label of *fiction* separates it from everyday utterances, exempting the author from the truth claim and conferring the right to mix reality and imagination at will. As mentioned above, this freedom from the truth claim does not mean that the novelist has no responsibility for the *implied truth*, the cognitive content, which is inherent in the structure of the work. A novel does not, in principle, purport to reproduce real persons and events; not even the special circumstances pertaining to documentary fiction change this condition. Therefore, in contrast to non-fiction, literary fiction (including the documentary novel) remains unconstrained by any direct link to reality owing to its freedom from the truth claim; the author takes by definition no responsibility for the relationship between the elements of his story and specific real elements. A direct connection between documentary fiction and reality can only be established by extratextual verification and would in any case only be valid for the verified paragraphs, not the work as a whole. Hence, a clear boundary between fiction and non-fiction can be established on the basis of the differing truth claims, which are expressed by extratextual information in fiction and by implicit extratextual convention in non-fiction. This difference, moreover, is not affected by the subjectivity of the sender.

The extratextual information attached to fiction and non-fiction also explains why the use of fictional techniques in non-fiction does not affect the distinction either, in contrast to Fludernik's principal argument for rejecting the fiction/non-fiction distinction (Fludernik 1996, 40–1):

> All narrative (even on its minimal level of sequential report) is a fictive construct, a representation, and cannot reproduce "reality" in any mimetic fashion. Stories, lives, the products of conversation are all concepts of the human mind, the result of cognitive parameters which we bring to bear upon the flux of unknowable and indivisible being, upon our exposure to the world.

To illustrate the artificial devices with which non-fictional narrative is constructed, she refers to reproduction of speech (Fludernik 2009, 65):

> If . . . we look at the direct speech the narrator uses to address her/his narratees and the actual words the characters exchange, it seems as if these were represented iconically, mirroring the actual utterances in the world of the novel in the same form. Language reproduces language verbatim.
>
> The impression that this is the case is wrong, as spoken language can never be faithfully represented in writing. Even in conversational narrative, direct speech is often different from the real thing, sometimes even entirely fictive, although we expect it to be authentic.

In the paragraph she refers to here, she writes (Fludernik 1993, 435):

> I have argued . . . that even direct speech representation in a real-life context cannot be identified with verbatim recreation of original discourse. In oral narrative direct speech passages . . . are frequently invented *ad libitum*. This applies even more stringently to the "direct quotation" of thoughts, particularly somebody else's, and it becomes transparently obvious in hypothetical, negative or interrogative clauses and, generally, in modal environments:
>   . . . it would be so wonderful if you were here – we would leap around in this glorious park and say *isn't it just wonderful* . . .

Even if we grant the impossibility of reproducing real events verbally in a completely objective way, this does not demolish the boundary between fiction and non-fiction. Being at the mercy of subjectivity, the non-fiction sender must settle for the available means, even though they may not be accurate. The subjective version of the truth is at least preferable, if the alternative is no communication at all. Since such subjective interpretations purport to render the truth, they are linked to reality in a way that meets the conventional truth claim. As I have repeatedly pointed out, fictional texts do not purport to render facts in a comparable way, because the only link between fiction and reality is indirect and consists in likeness. Historical non-fiction is related directly to reality through the sender's intention. It is irrelevant how subjectively the non-fictional text actually reproduces its object as long as the sender's intent is to be loyal to the truth.

3

The Fictional Communication Process

The enormous difficulty in reaching solutions to the basic problems of literary theory that everyone can agree upon is, of course, due to the fact that literature primarily takes place in the reader's mind, and cannot therefore be objectively studied the way that external scientific objects can. The only concrete experience that readers have in common is the text as a material object, which different readers are likely to perceive in approximately the same way. As soon as we make any effort to analyse the semantic meaning of the text, the process disappears into the mind of each individual reader, beyond the reach of objective observation. The study of the reader's mental reception of and reactions to the material text is only possible through introspection, verbal exchanges between readers and behaviourist methodology, all of which tend to work against intersubjective consensus. By foregrounding the linguistic aspect of literature and applying linguistic methods, formalism and structuralism have tried to pull the literary communication process out of its mental hiding place and make it objectively accessible, but by doing so, they miss important processes in the mind of the reader. Although Paul de Man expresses it in quite different terms, this is arguably the gist of his famous article, 'Resistance to Theory', in which he expresses his scepticism with regard to structuralist theory (de Man 1989).

In theories based on the relationship between *sign, reference* and *referent* (or *signifier, signified* and *referent*), the cognitive function of literature is more likely to be taken into account, as in Nøjgaard 1996, who provides a theory of literary function. But Nøjgaard barely considers the indirect way in which narrative fiction conveys its content. The brief theory of function that he proposes brings nothing new, only the old dichotomies between *enlightenment* and *entertainment, cognitive value* and *experiential value* (Nøjgaard 1996, 284–8). The discussion remains where it was in 1949, when Warren and Wellek contented themselves with the *dulce et utile* of Horace in their famous *Theory of Literature* (Wellek and Warren 1954, 30–1, 37). To point out that literature has a cognitive as well as an entertaining effect is a rather superficial description of its functions, which leaves out the literary communication process producing these effects and says little about the nature of cognition and entertainment.

Modern literary scholars show an increasing interest in the cognitive aspect of literary communication, but are still neglecting the details of the communication process itself (Phelan and Rabinowitz 2005, Herman and Vervaeck 2005, Herman 2007, Davies 2007, Abbott 2008), which are indispensable for a complete understanding of the various aspects of literary fiction. A deficient understanding of the literary communication process leads to ambiguity in various fields of literary theory, such as the delimitation of the work as such, intention, interpretation, the sender issue, duration and evaluation. In this book, I propose a detailed model of the fictional communication process which I hope can shed new light on the crucial problems of literary theory.

The question of genre

Research on literary function has been hampered by, among other things, the fact that scholars have been rather narrow in their selection of examples. Both Russian formalism and New Criticism have taken their examples primarily from lyric poetry or colloquial speech. Their conclusions suffer from this unbalanced starting point, as they tend to neglect the special problems pertaining to other genres. In particular, they neglect epic and drama, both of which demand individual treatment because of their indirect modes of communication. Colloquial speech is a fundamentally different form of communication than fictional literature, as is lyric poetry to a certain extent, in which fictionality as well as story and linguistic clarity may play varying roles.

Lyric poetry, moreover, is a more ambiguous genre than epic and drama; its referential status may be fictional or non-fictional and is often rather uncertain. It is usually published without any referential labels that might reveal its relationship with reality, and apart from poems that are obviously fiction because of intratextual criteria (e.g. Goethe's *The Sorcerer's Apprentice*, Goethe 1985) or non-fiction because of extratextual information (e.g. Tennyson's *The Charge of the Light Brigade*, Tennyson 1938), its referential status is more or less uncertain. Between these obvious extremes lie a large number of poems whose relationship to reality is less clear-cut. Although non-fiction may share communicative similarities with fiction, it is distinct from fiction because of its clear reference to real objects. The fact that storyline in poetry may be partially or completely replaced by an abstract content is also an important difference from drama and epic.

Verbal messages may, of course, be unclear or ambiguous, and much lyric poetry is already characterized by intentional linguistic ambiguity and scarcity of information on a textual level. In these cases it is difficult for the reader to make out the motive or story. The brevity of many poems often increases the obscurity by precluding any clarifying context. This is in contrast to the novel and drama, which normally have ample opportunity to convey a relatively unequivocal idea of the action. When interpreting novels and dramas, we seldom have difficulty understanding the structure of the action itself. The problem is rather to understand what more the action has to tell us.

Because literary scholars have devoted so much time to non-fiction and lyric poetry, research has primarily focused on direct communication and non-fictional indirect communication, in which semantic clarity and ambiguity have been the main issues, while the peculiar kind of ambiguity linked to indirect fictional communication has been neglected. In this respect, it is revealing that in *Is There a Text in this Class?* (Fish 1980, 149–50), Stanley Fish regards interpretation as more or less a problem pertaining to the interpretation of words and not to *the events* that the words mean, and he does not distinguish between the interpretation of the text itself (the signifier) and the action (the signified or the referent).

The present book is mainly about literary fiction, because this is where the confusion is most profound, but in some contexts it may be useful or interesting to include non-fiction. In this book I define *literary fiction* as epic literature in the traditional sense (novels, short stories, epic poetry, sagas, fairy tales) and drama. Lyric poetry will only partially be considered in this project; its relation to fictionality is problematic as storytelling plays a varying role in lyric poetry. Moreover, lyric poetry often tends to complicate language intentionally, which is a key difference from most fiction.

In literary studies, the term *literature* is often reserved for works deemed worthy of criticism, so-called 'serious' literature. As evaluation is by its very nature subjective and relative, I prefer to expand the term to include all sorts of literary fiction, regardless of its supposed value. 'Non-serious' literature, from 'escapist' literature down to jokes, works according to the same principles as its serious counterpart. This conception of literature accords with Nelson Goodman's notion of the aesthetic as a value-independent category (Goodman 1988, 255). Peter Lamarque and Stein Haugom Olsen, on the other hand, argue in *Truth, Fiction and Literature* that escapist literature ought to be excluded as non-literary, admitting nevertheless that a work can be added to and subtracted from the canon according to critical evaluation and revaluation, and thereby unintentionally confirming the close relationship between serious and escapist literature (Lamarque and Olsen 1994, 434–5).

For practical reasons, this book will deal mainly with novels and short stories, and other genres will be mentioned only as needed or for practical purposes.

The levels of the communication process

Literary scholars have tried to explain the literary communication process by means of various models. For the time being, we restrict our analysis to texts that are written down and read on the page, coming back to theatrical performance later. A common descriptive model is Ogden's semantic triangle, which discriminates between *symbol, reference* and *referent* (Ogden and Richards 1969, 10–11). A sign (symbol) symbolizes a thought (reference), which refers to an extra-linguistic referent.

In recent usage, the term *referent* has been retained, while *symbol* has been replaced by *signifier* and *reference* by *signified*.

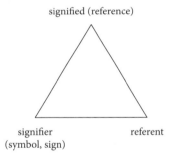

This triangle is indispensable for understanding literary communication, but it needs elaboration in order to be useful for analysing the fictional communication process. The problem is that the reference of the fictional text remains obscure: is the fictional *action* signified or referent, and is the *message* conveyed by the action, signified, referent or something else? And what then is the essence of the fictional action?

Roman Jakobson's communication model, with a *sender* and a *receiver* at each end of the diagram, and the *message* in the middle supplemented by *context, channel* and *code*, does not solve the problem either (Jakobson 1960):

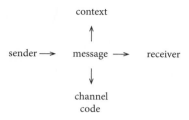

To be sure, Jakobson's model introduces sender and receiver, but these were, of course, also implied in the triangle model. The triangle model itself has been reduced to two vague key words, *message* and *context*. The term *message* is evidently meant as a synonym for *signifier*, whereas *context* stands for *signified* or *referent*. In discarding the distinction between signified and referent, Jakobson's model is a step backwards compared to the semantic triangle.

Early theories of levels

Roman Ingarden's phenomenological theory of layers (or levels) constitutes a key step towards a deeper understanding of the fictional communication process (Ingarden 1968; Falk 1981, in which Ingarden's theories have been treated thoroughly). It has also left traces in modern literary theory, particularly in Wolfgang Iser's reader-response theory (Iser 1974). Ingarden's model (Ingarden 1968, 10, 55–6) contains four layers, which he regards as *structures of the work*, not as *levels of the reading process* as Iser calls them later. His four layers are (1) *the phonetic layer* (the speech sounds), (2) *the meaning units* (words, sentences), (3) *the represented objects* (the action) and (4) *the schematized aspects* (the way the reader conceptualizes the action):

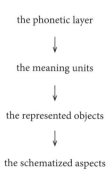

The first two layers correspond to the signifier, of which they constitute subordinate components, whereas the last two layers correspond to the signified, although Ingarden has an eye to the referent as 'the intentional object'.

In Ingarden's theory, ultimately, the relationship between signified and referent is as obscure as in Jakobson's. The four layers Ingarden proposes are in fact only two, consisting of *text* and *action* (story). The phonetic sounds form the words and sentences and constitute together a whole, the signifier or, in other words, the material text. The next two layers are merely different aspects of the action (story) and their connection with the signified and the referent is obscure. *The represented objects* designates only the action (story) in the schematic shape in which it is conveyed to the reader, while *the schematized aspects* refers to the way the reader supplements it with his own imagination, using his own personal experiences in the real world to make the fictional world more concrete and vivid. This is for instance what happens when the reader equips Mrs Dalloway with individual features borrowed from his own real acquaintances or the portrait on the front cover of the book.

Ingarden's layers, moreover, do not elucidate the cognitive aspect of literary communication. He rejects this as irrelevant, characterizing readers who are tempted to establish referential correlations between the represented world and the real world as naïve (Falk 1981, 112, 160). According to Ingarden, the function of the literary work consists in a purely aesthetic contemplation of the interplay between the constituents of the four layers, which are effectively only two and far from clearly defined. In the end, Ingarden's model does not contribute any new understanding of the cognitive communication process.

The formalists and structuralists also happen to operate with layers, or rather levels, which may vary in number and go under different names. Russian formalism distinguishes between *fabula* and *sjuzhet*, while E. M. Forster has *story* and *plot*. The pair *action* and *intrigue* has a corresponding function. In a way, it may seem as if the relationship between the two levels consists in one level functioning as a raw material to be processed by the other level. The *sjuzhet*, *plot* or *intrigue* processes the *fabula*, *story* or *action* in a superficial way, for example by presenting them in a different order from the original chronological one. In practice, the terms are far from clear. In *A Glossary of Contemporary Theory*, Jeremy Hawthorn characterizes them as a minefield of confusing vocabulary because these terms are used in a multitude of partially conflicting senses (Hawthorn 2000, 336–8). None of these pairs distinguish clearly between signifier, signified and referent.

Narratological theories of levels

A clear distinction between story and the way it is reproduced in the text is provided by the structuralist Gérard Genette, who considers the previous dyads out of date (Genette 1983, 10–11). He does not furnish any arguments for this statement, but he is probably thinking of the sort of confusion pointed out by Hawthorn. Genette, however, avoids breaking completely away from tradition and recycles old terms as a springboard for his new definitions. He redefines the term *récit* (narrative or story) as the *text* or *discourse*, and uses *histoire* (story) for the events that the text conveys (Genette 1972, 71–2). Although he does not explicitly say so, we can infer by the way he treats the various structures of the text (or discourse) that he considers the discourse (i.e. the text) to be the way the story is represented. But instead of being content with the pair *story* and *discourse*, he opts for a triad: *histoire, récit* and *narration*, or *story, discourse* and *narration*. As we will see, of these *narration* is particularly unclear, though the entire triad is obscured by the more or less synonymous alternatives he employs to define the three levels: (1) *récit* (the discourse) is defined either as the signifier, the statement, the discourse or as the narrative text itself; (2) *histoire* (the story) is the signified or the narrative content and (3) *narration* (narration) means the creative act of narration, including the real or fictional situation in which it takes place.

In adopting Genette's triad, Shlomith Rimmon-Kenan unquestioningly translates them into *story, text* and *narration* (Rimmon-Kenan 1983, 3). Monika Fludernik also endorses Genette's triad, but wants *narration* and *discourse* classed together as *narrative discourse* (Fludernik 2009, 2). In this respect, she comes close to Seymour Chatman's simplification: 30 years earlier, he had omitted narration and restricted himself to a dyad between the *story* that expresses what is told and the *discourse*, or how it is told (Chatman 1978, 19). Mieke Bal (Bal 1990, 19–22) does not conceive of narration as a level, but operates nevertheless with three levels: *text* (Dutch *tekst*), *narrative* (*verhaal*) and *story* (*geschiedenis*). This would resemble Genette's triad if *narrative* were identical with narration, but according to Bal, the narrative is the content of the text whereas the story is the content of the narrative (Bal 1990, 19, 22). Consequently, her terms seem to correspond to *signified, signifier* and *referent*, in which the *text* is identical with the *signifier*, the *narrative* with the *signified*, and the *story* corresponds to the *referent*. However, the resemblance becomes uncertain as soon as she tries to fill in the details. Because the reader must 'construct the structure of the text', Bal's text seems to be *signifier* and *signified* at the same time: when we read a text, we construct its meaning, that is, the *signified*, which according to

Bal's model should be the *narrative*, not the text. Bal goes on to explain that the story may exist in various versions, which indicates that it is a kind of framework, a skeletal story, or what many scholars would call a *plot* (Herman 2007, 43). In this sense, the story is of a more general nature and does not merge with the referent, which is linked to one specific chain of events, the action (exactly how fictitious action can be the referent is an issue we will return to shortly). So the narrative and the story must both be classified as signified, but what happens to the referent then?

It is telling that Bal only mentions the triad in the introduction to her book, focusing afterwards merely on the relationship between narrative (or text) and story (or narrative). In practice, therefore, her three-way model comes down to a binary relation, but unfortunately, it is now entirely unclear on which sides of the diagram the text, the narrative and the story belong. Are text and narrative together signifier with the text as signified, or is the text signifier with narrative and story as signified? And how are narrative, story and text related to the discourse?

The depth of the confusion around these narratological terms is illustrated by H. Porter Abbott (Herman 2007, 40–1), who returns to the triad, but substitutes *plot* for *discourse*. He also applies the term *discourse*, which could become confusing if not for his main goal, which is to chart the inconsistent attempts of other scholars to define these terms rather than formulate his own set of adequate definitions. He concludes that *narration*, *discourse* and *plot* have proven to be slippery terms, and that the definitions given by different scholars conflict with each other.

Indeed, we have seen how plot, story, narrative, narration and discourse are used in different senses by different scholars. What has prevented them from arriving at definitions everyone can be happy with? In comparison, the controversy between scholars as to whether the three-way distinction between narration (narrative act), discourse (or text) and story (action) should be merged into the binary distinction between discourse (or text) and story (action) is of less importance. In theory, *the narrative act* (narration) remains distinct from the text, but this applies mainly to oral texts produced and passed on by a narrator before an audience, face-to-face. Such a live performance will include extratextual devices that influence the communication process, such as mime and vocal modulation. In such cases, narration must be distinguished from the text itself as an extratextual factor. The distinction between the extratextual and intratextual properties of an oral performance of a text is, however, not necessarily clear; some vocal modulations are clearly unique and individual, such as those expressing the feelings of the speaker, whereas others are necessary properties of spoken language, like phonemes.

Modern fiction, on the other hand, is conveyed to the reader by way of a written text, which leaves out all extratextual elements. The voice of the narrator in written texts cannot compensate for the supplementary information a live narrator conveys through gesture and voice modulation. The narrator of a written text may read the text aloud while writing it and accompany the narrative process with shifting facial expressions, but of course this is not mirrored in the text.

The only information the reader receives about the narrator and the narrative act is what he can infer from the text. Because the text comes into existence simultaneously with narration, it is part of the narrative act and at the same time a result of it, as the only testimony of the finished narrative process.

The text produced during the narrative act and the text that is eventually published merge completely, and because the narrative process is only accessible through inference from evidence in the text, it is merely a theoretical entity without relevance for the understanding of the fictional work. To be sure, the narrative act leaves substantial traces in the text, such as selection, voice, focalization, frequency, duration, order and style, but these are narratological and stylistic phenomena that are covered by the term *discourse.*

The *discourse* is the way the narrator reproduces the action (story). The rendering is coloured by the language of the text, and as a consequence, the narrator's temporal, spatial and mental relation to the elements of the action is recorded in the text. He cannot write without revealing his identity in relation to his characters (first-, second- or third-person narrative), nor can he conceal his temporal relation to the events (present, past or future tense). His selection of details in the text, the viewpoint from which the characters are perceived and the way he renders speech and thought all express his knowledge and choices. Comments, judgements and irony express his opinions and attitude towards his objects. The order of the events in the text and frequency (repetition, iterative summary and singulative rendering of elements) are choices he makes in order to influence the reader's reactions. The discourse is therefore unavoidably an expression of the narrator's personality and intentions; even if the narrator makes not even the slightest mention of himself, the text reveals his existence and influence in many different ways.

From this we may formulate the following conclusion: narration consists of the text *and* additional extratextual information, and is therefore theoretically separated from the text, forming a greater whole. But the extratextual component of narration is inaccessible except through inference from the text. The text, however, to some extent covers the narrative act since it contains evidence of narration in its discourse. Neither in theory nor in practice can the complete narrative act be of relevance, and as the term *discourse* fulfils the role of the term *narration* in all possible respects, there is really no practical reason for keeping the term *narration*. Of course, narration is a theoretical entity, but since it is of no relevance for written fiction, the triad of *narration, text* (or *discourse*) and *story* (or *action*) should, in accordance with Chatman and Fludernik, be reduced into a dyad consisting of only *text* and *story*. This leaves us with the pair *text* (or *discourse* or *plot*) and *story* (or *action*).

The foremost problem of modern narratology is the multitude of more or less synonymous terms used to designate different things. The terms refer effectively to one and the same notion – an obscure mixture of text and story – without a clear boundary separating the different component notions. The term *text* may mean the signifier, but also the signified. If you 'fail to understand a text', this can mean that you do not understand either the meaning of particular words, or the content that comes into being only after you have understood all the words. You may, for instance, understand what a character is doing but fail to understand why. *Story* implies signifier, signified and even referent all at once: 'A writer writes a story' (signifier = text); 'In this story, a man commits suicide' (signified); 'The story I am going to tell happened many years ago' (the referent). *Discourse* may mean text (signifier), but also the way the signified is structured. *Narrative* does not discriminate between text and story, and *plot* may refer to the story or only the skeleton of a story.

Even the seemingly simple binary relation between *story* and *discourse* is deficient, because it does not account for the relationship of these two terms to signifier, signified and referent. Is the discourse signifier or signified? Is the story the signified of referent? Since text, story and discourse are inseparable, the distinction between them may seem superfluous, but only a clear terminology will enable us to fully understand how fictional communication works.

Genette's attempt to create order by recycling old terms is unsuccessful because of the inherent ambiguity of these terms, which are ill-suited to define the complexities of the literary communication process. Their ambiguity, together with their close relationship, lead to overlap and confusion when we try to distinguish one term from the others. In order to solve this problem, we have to introduce new, unambiguous terms. The levels of the fictional communication process must be described in a more transparent way, with terms that are better equipped for theoretical as well as for practical use. The new terms must be based on the semantic triangle, while also taking into account additional distinctions that have thus far drawn little or no attention.

The material text

The first level of the communication process is the *signifier*, the sign, which, with respect to the work as a whole, means *the material text*. The notion of a *text* has been used in various senses. It may mean a typographic or phonetic phenomenon or the work as a whole (see Hawthorn 2000, 357–8). Bal 1990 (18) defines the text as a confined, structured whole of linguistic signs. In Klaus Brinker's more specific definition, a text is a confined sequence of linguistic signs that are coherent in themselves and signal as a whole a recognizable communicative function (Brinker 1992, 16–17). Both definitions concern the material text and do not include the realization of its semantic potential. The material text means the visual impression the text makes on the reader before he starts to decode the language. A Chinese text is therefore a text to me even if I do not know any Chinese.

The material text is composed of two layers: the written (mostly typographic) text and the oral text that the written text conveys. The written text is of a lower, more ambiguous order compared to the oral one; for instance, it does not render sentence intonation and stress. Most texts nowadays are written or printed and are hence subject to these limitations. Oral versions may be produced by recitation, but they remain second order since they are based on an interpretation of the written text. For our purposes, nevertheless, it should not be necessary to distinguish explicitly between the written version of the text and the oral interpretations of it. I am therefore going to treat them both as one level: the *text*.

The mental model of the action

The duplicity of the text as a sign is a complicating factor in the definition of *text*. It is, on the one hand, a purely physical phenomenon, but on the other, it is a vehicle for a mental content, the *signified*. However, it is no more identical with the signified than the postman is identical with the letter he puts in the mailbox. So what is the signified? In spite of anti-psychological theorists like Gottlob Frege, Roman Ingarden and Algirdas Julien Greimas, it is difficult to deny that the signified is a mental phenomenon (Ingarden 1968, 12; Greimas 1966). Ogden and Richards conceive of the signified (which they call *reference*) as a thought (Ogden and Richards 1969, 11), while Ingarden contradicts his own anti-psychologism in referring to the reader's decoding of the text as a mental activity and representation (Ingarden 1968, 36–7, 59).

The social psychologist Ragnar Rommetveit regards the signified as something mental, specifying however that it does not consist of an image or copy of the object (Rommetveit 1972, 55–70). The exact nature of the signified is not important to our investigation. The important thing is that the linguistic signs are converted in the mind into representations of the referent (the objects at issue).

The signified of a fictional text is a comprehensive collection of notions, a complex conception of more or less coherent events: the *fictional action*. The signified is in other words simply a *mental model* of the fictional action. The kind of material that comprises this mental model is, again, irrelevant here, but I can offer some suggestions. The mental model of the fictional events (the fictional action) that the text conveys is no longer a linguistic phenomenon. When it reaches the reader, it liberates itself from the language that conveyed it, just as the caretaker who is asked to fetch chairs only remembers the content of the command, not its wording. Language is the silent servant nobody notices (Rommetveit 1972, 55). We can remember the action of a novel, even in detail, without being able to repeat verbatim how it was formulated. Rommetveit mentions an experiment in which bilinguals were dictated a list of words, randomly distributed between the two languages, which they had to memorize. When they were asked to repeat the words they had heard, they often switched from one language to another without being aware of it and said, for instance, *horse* when it was *cheval* that had been dictated, or *chaise* when it was *chair*.

What this shows is how the mental model of the action is not made up of words; it renders the action by means of something other than words. It is not easy to pin down what this non-verbal material is. When we imagine something, more or less clear sense impressions, words, feelings and intuitions flicker through our mind. To ask about the material of the mental model is the same as to ask about the material the mind uses to save our memories. The only thing that is clear is that the mental model is not linked to particular words or a particular language. Even little babies are capable of thinking causally and abstractly long before they can speak, and some animals seem to have concepts and be capable of limited abstract thought. The mental model is a comprehensive, complex and coherent notion, a schema without individuality, and insofar as it appears individual, it is because we fill in the schema with our own memories and associations, which Ingarden calls *schematized aspects*. But this individualizing supplement to the model of the action (the signified) is an entirely personal contribution which varies from reader to reader.

The term *mental model* refers only to the mental model (of the action) that is shared by all readers. This mental model is, however, not the only mental model linked to the literary communication process. All kinds of thinking somehow involve the use of mental models. The reading process as an isolated phenomenon, as well as its cognitive effect on the reader, occurs by means of mental models. For our purposes, I will therefore confine the term *mental model of the action* to the 'image' of the action shared by all readers.

The relationship between the mental model and the action

One advantage of the model concept is the possibility of comparing the mental model with other kinds of models, for example film, architectural models and ship models, in order to better understand how it works. Models are merely practical replacements for something that is not available itself. The ship model does not give access to the object it represents, the ship itself. Similarly, the mental model of the action stands between us and *the fictional action*, with which we will never come into contact because it is fictional and exists therefore by definition only as a mental model. By distinguishing between the action and the mental model of it, we express clearly that the action is not identical with the *signified* (the mental model of the action), but rather only with the *referent* to which the signified (the mental model) refers. As referent, the action is fictional, and according to what we have already said about fiction, this means that it neither exists nor ever existed in the extratextual world. So on the one hand, the referent does not exist, while on the other hand, it does, as the fictional entity that the model represents – a model has to be a model of something. Although there are no such things as ghosts and ogres, we can imagine how they might be by creating a mental model of their appearance and behaviour.

This paradoxical situation is related to the way our imagination works. Although we are able to imagine fictional objects, our imagination is always based on the real world, much in the way that acrobats and tightrope walkers always have to take into account gravity and the ground. We are simply not able to imagine a world where absolutely everything is different from our own, and thus tend to think in analogies to our world. The reader and the author automatically project the general picture they have of the real world onto the fictional world. Moreover, the projection comprises the circumstances of the communication itself; because non-fiction has a referent in the real world, the novel must have a corresponding referent in the fictional world. The fictional action of which the mental model is a model comes into existence as a fictional entity, because it is inconceivable that the model does not render something. As a consequence, the model opens an entire fictional world to the reader, created according to the same principles as the real world, as a projection of the reader's prior knowledge about the real world and non-fictional communication. On account of the analogy with the real world, the reader imagines the fictional action as part of an entire universe.

It is essential to distinguish between the action itself and the mental model of it: there are crucial differences between them if we hold the action to be the referent and the model the signified of the text. To a great extent, the distinction between *action* and *mental model* corresponds to the traditional narratological distinction between *story* and *discourse*. So why not employ these traditional terms instead of the less current term *action* and the entirely new term *mental model*? The negative implications of *discourse* will be given a more thorough discussion later, but for clarity's sake, a brief explanation of my choice may be in order at this point. While the term *mental model* is straightforwardly related to the signified, *discourse* is especially liable to cause misunderstanding, as it straddles the boundaries between the signifier and the signified as a result of its close association with the material text.

As already alluded to, the term *action* is not new, drawing on a long tradition in German, Dutch and the Scandinavian languages. According to normal usage, it refers to the referent, the events. The word *story*, too, exists in the Germanic languages, but compared to *action* it has a different as well as broader meaning, referring at once to the signifier (the text) and the signified (the model), whereas it is less suited to denote the referent. The difference between *story* and *action* becomes apparent when we use them in concrete sentences. We can say that the author writes or creates the story, referring respectively to the text (signifier) and the mental model of the action (signified). As for the action, the author can only create it, not write it: he invents the events (referent) by creating the mental model of it (signified). On the other hand, we can talk about the characters of the story (signified, perhaps referent?) as well as of the action (referent). In this book, I will consistently prefer *action* to *story* and use it to mean *referent*.

In literary theory, as Hawthorn (2000) demonstrates, the term *story* has been used in various and partially contradictory senses. By using the term *action*, which has the advantage of being less used and hence less abused, we avoid unnecessary misunderstandings.

Some scholars have shown interest in whether the text (and consequently, the inherent mental model) precedes the action (story) or vice versa (Culler 1981, 169–87; Genette 1983, 11; Abbott 2008, 20–2). According to Culler, the genesis of text and story is an ambiguity that cannot be resolved. Genette, on the other hand, points out that the action's coming to life is simultaneous with the author's writing the text, whereas to Abbott, who takes no clear stance, the fact that stories can be adapted is an argument for the pre-existence of the story. The priority of the genesis between the text/mental model and the action may seem unimportant, but it brings Abbott to wonder whether the distinction between story and discourse is a real distinction at all, since all we ever know of the story is what we get to know through discourse (in Herman 2007, 41). To prevent further misunderstanding, it may be useful to look a little more closely into the matter, but we will have to postpone this discussion until after we have acquired more knowledge about the model and the next level of literary communication, the cognitive content.

A comparison between the novel and biography may shed useful light on the relationship between mental model and action. In kinship with the novel, the material text of a biography transfers a mental model to the mind of the reader. The biographical model also reproduces events, with the difference that these events have really happened. The referent of the novel is (with the modifications discussed in Chapter 2) not identical with specific real events, whereas the referent of the biography can be verified as real. The reader of a biography is entitled to consult extratextual sources that can verify the mental model of the portrayed person. The reader of a novel has no such right and is even in some sense lucky if extratextual aid is available; often, he is warned not to seek any correspondence at all between the action and real events. Documentary and biographical novels constitute exceptions to some extent, but even then within certain limits, as we have seen. The usefulness of a biography's mental model lies in its informing us about existing persons, in the way for instance that reading about the Finnish painter Helene Schjerfbeck's hip injury can help us better understand her art. The practical value of the information is especially pertinent when the lives and personalities of living persons – politicians, for example – are revealed, whose careers may be shaped or spoiled on account of biographical material.

The mental model of the action of a novel, on the other hand, is meaningless as information about specific real persons and events, again with the exception of documentary fiction. Septimus's suicide in *Mrs Dalloway* informs us only about a non-existent person and has no value as specific information. If I looked up from a novel my wife had not read, announcing that one of the characters had misappropriated funds, she would throw me a suspicious glance. On the other hand, she would listen attentively if I read about a prominent politician from the newspaper. But if fiction does not provide trustworthy specific information about the real world, then what is it that attracts so many readers to it?

The cognitive content

The answer lies in the cognitive function of literary fiction. The fictional world is constructed according to the same pattern as the real world and resembles it. On account of this likeness, the fictional events shed useful light on the general structure of the real world; they exemplify essential patterns in the real world, as can be seen in the example of Henrik Ibsen's The Wild Duck (Ibsen 2006 [1884]).

In this drama, the naïve, weak, untalented Hjalmar Ekdal lives a happy home life with his sympathetic wife Gina who earns the household income and encourages him in his work on a nebulous and wholly imaginary 'invention'. His kind and loving daughter Hedvig contributes to his happiness at home. This happy existence is, however, based on many unpleasant secrets of which Hjalmar is ignorant: Hedvig, for instance, is not his daughter, and his marriage has been arranged by Hedvig's real father in order to legitimize the child. Then his boyhood friend Gregers Werle shows up, obsessed by the idea that everybody will be happier if they know the absolute truth. When he reveals the shocking past to Hjalmar, who is not strong enough to bear it, he ruins Hjalmar's life. Gregers realizes too late that if you deprive an ordinary person of his illusions, you make him unhappy.

Hjalmar Ekdal is a fictitious creation, but real life is full of people in the same situation. The reader conceives of the fictional world as a parallel to the real world; he expects the conditions in the former to conform to conditions in the latter, with the two worlds shedding light on one another. The likeness that the reader expects is not specific but general. The elements of the fictional world must follow the laws and principles of the real world, and patterns in the fictional world must mirror patterns in the real one. It is not a question of the fictional events being identical with specific real ones, and the author may deviate from the norms of reality as long as the deviation is not thematic, that is, part of describing patterns in the real world. Marie-Laure Ryan refers to the imitative potential of literary fiction as the 'principle of minimal departure' (Ryan 1991, 51): 'This principle states that whenever we interpret a message concerning an alternate world, we reconstrue this world as being the closest possible to the reality we know.' Likeness does not have to be complete and the action not necessarily realistic, as long as it is sufficient to illustrate important general patterns. That is why there is room for symbols, allegories and other devices that deviate from the realm of possibility in the extratextual world in the service of some informative content. This applies, for example, to Antoine de Saint-Exupéry's *Le petit prince*

(*The Little Prince*), where a host of fantastic events are staged in order to exemplify general aspects of human behaviour.

This cognitive exchange between fiction and reality is also called *mimesis*, which, however, is not a clear term (Hawthorn 2000, 78–9). The concept of *mimesis* implies that fiction somehow imitates the extratextual world and that on account of this likeness, the receiver can use the fictional events *as if* they were real so that the *general* knowledge he extrapolates from the fictional action is also valid for the extratextual world. In other words, the patterns of the fictional world provide insight into the patterns of the real world, conveying information on reality in this indirect way.

The transmission of cognitive understanding occurs in principle in the same way we learn from our own experiences in the real world. The fictional action is an experience that we add to our real experiences; both provide general knowledge about reality. From the elements of the action, we infer the laws and norms that pertain to the extratextual world, making abstractions and generalizations, building a general understanding of how reality works and how we should react in various situations. *Mrs Dalloway* exemplifies how a doctor's lack of empathy makes the psychical problems of his patient (Septimus) worse and drives him to suicide. Harriet Beecher Stowe's novel *Uncle Tom's Cabin* does not explicitly state that racism and slavery are inhuman; it shows it by means of a sort of 'virtual' reality (Stowe 2010).

The fictional story shows us how other people think, feel and react in various situations, exemplifying causality and values. The understanding of the real world that the reader acquires through his interpretation of the fictional action goes under several more-or-less adequate names: *message, cognitive content, theme, Weltanschauung, worldview, fundamental idea, ideology, implied author, author's intention, moral of the story*. Personally I prefer terms like *cognitive content, message* and *indirect information*. The cognitive process occurs automatically whether the reader wants it or not. A baby whose fingers are burned by a candle learns quickly that fire is dangerous, without having to reflect on it. The ability of human beings to extrapolate and generalize remains intact when they face fictional events.

There is however an important difference between our own experiences and the fictional events of a novel. While our own experiences come to us unsorted, in an almost endless variety of detail, the novel's action has been filtered of irrelevant material into a more manageable quantity of details. The author invites us into a guided tour through a limited landscape, which, of course, makes it much easier to process the material.

The special thing about fictional texts is that, in contrast to non-fiction, this kind of communication is based on concrete examples (the events), while abstractions and generalizations are to a great extent left to the reader. Even when the author seems to remain completely objective, however, he necessarily selects and omits elements and may even leave out important information. The author can easily lead his readers astray by giving them biased information.

To be sure, the various ways we process our experiences are not necessarily less biased than the structures the author imposes on the fictional world; our unconscious, for instance, filters out information it considers irrelevant or harmful. The key difference between the experiences we meet in the novel and those we face in our own real world is mainly a question of who is in control: the author or ourselves. Both alternatives present advantages and disadvantages, depending on the qualities of the person processing the material. The cognitive content (the message) that the reader extrapolates from the mental model of the action is as much a factor of the background and personal qualities of the reader as of the author-imposed structure of the action and the mental model of it. The message is, in other words, a result of an interaction between the mental model of the action and the mental qualities of the reader.

Over time, literary theory has attached varying significance to the various components involved in literary communication, vacillating between author, text, reader and extratextual context. M. H. Abrams bases his classification of literary theories on these very distinctions, differentiating between mimetic, pragmatic, expressive and objective theories (Abrams 1889, 3–4) according to their foregrounding of, respectively, extratextual context, reader, author and text. According to reader-response criticism, literature cannot be understood apart from both text and reader (Iser 1974). In this book, I will try to show how literary communication involves all the above-mentioned factors, but that the interaction between reader and text plays an indispensable role, a subject which will be examined more thoroughly in Chapter 6.

As mentioned above, there also seems to be a growing interest in mimesis and cognitive functions among modern narratologists (Herman and Vervaeck 2005, Phelan and Rabinowitz 2005, Herman 2007, Davies 2007, Abbott 2008, Fludernik 2009, Vermeule 2010). Scholars who deny the cognitive effect of fiction, such as Ingarden, seem to have all but disappeared. Instead of denying the importance of cognition, modern scholars have attempted to understand the communication process itself and its effects on the reader. The linguistic tradition has not, however, completely loosened its grip. Some scholars are still trying to defend the autonomy of the text on a linguistic basis. In *Fictional Truth*, Michael Riffaterre asserts that fictional truth is only a question of linguistic perception based on rhetoric, not on any likeness with reality (Riffaterre 1990, vii–viii):

> Fiction establishes its *truth* status by the way language turns back upon itself, tautologically, to accomplish the expectations it sets up. The narrative need not be judged true because it corresponds to an external image of the world, but because it is consistent with the linguistic usages current in a given social context, at a given moment in time.

Riffaterre denies 'that words carry meaning by referring to things or to nonverbal entities' (3):

> . . . exterior referentiality is but an illusion, for signs or sign systems refer to other sign systems: verbal representations in the text refer to verbal givens borrowed from the sociolect, but such verbal givens are actually present in the text, explicitly or implicitly, as presuppositions.

In 'The Pragmatics of Narrative Fictionality', Richard Walsh finds it difficult to uncover the theoretical flaw of theories such as Riffaterre's, according to which narratives are constructs whose meanings are internal to the narrative system (Walsh 2005, 150–1), and he resorts to complicated, pragmatic arguments to repudiate them. The problem however lies in the linguistic basis of such autonomist theories, which derives from a Saussurean conception of meaning that does not comply with reality. Saussurean linguistics regards meaning as a formal system of differential elements. In this view, the meaning of a word, for instance *man*, is not defined by its reference to entities in the external world but only by its internal reference to other words: *woman*, *boy* etc. This non-referential conception of literary communication is not in line with psychological research and does not account for non-linguistic thought processes (Rommetveit 2005, 55–70). Language is a complex activity based on semantic-associative networks, in which all the components of the semantic triangle – text, mental model and the external world – are always interacting. The relevance of the mental model is apparent when we, after reading a report on a real event, are able to reproduce it in our memory, even though we no longer remember the text itself. The fact that such a non-fictional report refers to the reality it renders is obvious. The fact that fiction also refers to reality is not as obvious, and explains Riffaterre's attempt to reduce the referentiality of fiction to linguistic devices, but as we have seen, this referentiality is indirect, through likeness.

What kind of content does literary fiction convey?

For years, scholars have been discussing the nature of the cognitive content conveyed by literary fiction. There is a general consensus that fiction imparts a kind of general understanding of the real world, but what this understanding consists in is controversial. Lamarque and Olsen (1994, 135) mention strategic and conceptual skills, factual and general knowledge about the extratextual world, and the expansion of the reader's sensory and conceptual world.

In principle, theorists may have different opinions as to the kind of subjects fiction deals with – history, society, psychology, philosophy, ethics, morality and so on – but this is in fact no real disagreement. The different subjects do not preclude one another. In fact, one problem in literary theory has been the foregrounding of ethics and morality at the expense of the remarkable range of other subjects literary fiction takes up (Anderson 2006, 6, 112, 122). Fiction, ultimately, can impart knowledge about any subject according to the structure of each particular work. The unbalanced emphasis on the philosophical, ethical and moral dimension of fiction has probably hindered a cognitive understanding of literature, in addition to excluding a multitude of other important issues.

In this connection, it is useful to distinguish between different kinds of knowledge. Gilbert Ryle and Dorothy Walsh discriminate between *knowing what*, *knowing how* and *knowing what it is like* (Walsh 1969, Ryle 1971). The last kind of knowledge pertains to how it feels to experience certain situations and events, and is a kind of virtual experience. To read about important events in the lives of people with whom we identify engages us emotionally and affects us much more strongly than a purely intellectual exercise. The virtual experience need not be dramatic in order to be interesting, of course; descriptions of natural beauty, gastronomic pleasures or sex may awaken memories and longing in us as well. Lamarque and Olsen do not find it very valuable to know how it is to be in a given situation, but conclude all the same that it is just that kind of knowledge that creates our values. In *Mrs Dalloway*, for instance, the numerous impressionist descriptions of the urban environment of London pay homage to street and park life as an aesthetic and social experience.

David Davies conceives of the cognitive content as learning by means of thought experiments (Davies 2007, 157–63, 170–81). Insofar as the author does not slavishly transpose factual events into fictional action, as in autobiographical novels, he depends more or less on thought experiments to build up a coherent and meaningful story. Freedom from facts enables him to use the fictional model to test out alternate consequences of different choices. In science fiction, for instance, authors often test alternate political systems and the effects of technological innovations (Orwell's *Nineteen Eighty-Four* [Orwell 2008], Huxley's *Brave New World* [Huxley 1977],) or reflect on how people may react in extreme situations (Wyndham's *The Day of the Triffids* [Wyndham 1954]), H. G. Wells' *The Days of the Comet* and *The Invisible Man* [Wells 1985 and 2001]). It would be possible to write a novel about what would have happened if Hitler had won the war, if someone felt so inclined. Under the cover of an experiment, novels with a historical frame can deviate from historical facts unpunished, as in the novel *Siegfried* by the Dutch author Harry Mulisch, where the author lets Hitler have a son (Mulisch 2001).

The cognitive content does not necessarily consist in definitive answers and complete knowledge; it may consist in preliminary cognitive processes and questions. Some works deliver complete solutions that need only to be accepted or rejected, while others only serve to indicate a problem. Even in works with a clear message, there will be many phenomena and events that fit into no obvious pattern and require supplementary information to be meaningful. In *Mrs Dalloway*, our knowledge about the various characters is far from sufficient to answer the fundamental questions posed by the action. We know too little about Clarissa, Richard, Peter and Sally to decide which of the latter three Clarissa should have chosen as a partner, or if she should have made an entirely different choice altogether. The novel tells us more about how difficult such choices are and how hard it is to live with those choices than about what is the right choice. The cognitive benefit for the reader consists as much in the kind of impressions he receives as in a ready-made philosophy.

The sheer amount of cognitive content is often missed in literary scholars' analyses of fiction, which often overlook the profusion of trivial information that every action contains. That is, the greater part of petty everyday patterns of behaviour are taken as a matter of course by more experienced readers, but may be new and important to the young and uninitiated. Such patterns may be social conventions, common responses to various kinds of social interaction, ways of establishing social contact, simple causal relations, sexuality and so forth. When such trivialities occur in accordance with our expectations, they escape our notice, and we consequently neglect their corroborative influence and their value as new information for the young. For some readers only parts of the story are interesting because the rest is already familiar to them. For others of a different experiential background, even the smallest details may be of interest, according to age, gender, sexual orientation, social, cultural and political affiliation.

We have already mentioned that in certain cases, with certain reservations, fiction may also convey specific knowledge about the real world, but we do not primarily expect or seek factual information from fictional literature, even though such information is obviously useful. What attracts most readers is the portrayal of interpersonal relations. The cognitive content or message stimulates the reader's mind in a comprehensive way; in addition to pure facts, it comprises values and norms, it involves the conscious as well as the unconscious mind, intellect and emotions, and as a process, we register it as thoughts, intuition and feelings.

The cognitive process initiated by reading fiction is usually understood as learning. This can involve knowing what, knowing how and knowing what it is like; facts, values and norms; trivial information and everyday patterns of behaviour; social conventions, common responses to various kinds of social interaction, ways of establishing social contact, simple causal relations and knowledge about sexuality; questions; thought experiments; and finally, to a certain extent, even specific knowledge about the real world. Learning is an essential aspect of human nature and inevitably constitutes a dominant part of literary communication. Even anti-cognitivists cannot deny that, although they can dispute its relevance to the literary experience. This is a discussion we will come back to later, but for now we can note that the process that some scholars call *learning* may be more compatible with their conception of the reading process than they think.

The reader's experience of the fictional action has two aspects: the experience itself and the learning process. Because the experience is fictional, it has in principle no pragmatic value. A description of lush grass does not induce hay fever. Nevertheless, it may prompt the reader to reminisce about previous encounters with grass. A passage about sexual intercourse may excite the reader as much as a sexual situation in real life, and the joy or grief of a fictional character may evoke corresponding feelings in the reader. The common factor across all these scenarios is the likeness between the fictional and the real world. Although the fictional world has no immediate pragmatic impact on the reader, it concerns him because he is aware of parallels to his own world that may affect his life pragmatically. If he pities the fictional protagonist, his pity is aimed not at the fictional character, but at all the real people who have been, are or are going to be in a similar situation. These people may be complete strangers, close relations or even himself. The same pertains to the grass and to sex: they concern him and affect him emotionally because they represent real things that may sooner or later have an impact on his own life. In this way, the fictional action offers the reader (or the audience in a theatre or cinema) virtual experiences that have value in themselves. This value is not aesthetic, except when the experience is itself clearly aesthetic, such as the contemplation of a sunset. It is experiential and may, of course, be one of the reasons why we read fiction.

However, the experiential way of reading does not preclude the cognitive way, and vice versa. Moreover, there is strong evidence to indicate that the cognitive function is of essential value for the reader (see Chapter 4). In practice, the two functions merge, making it impossible to distinguish clearly between them, and since both are crucial constituents of the reader's experience, it is probably not important either. Even an anti-cognitivist inevitably absorbs knowledge when reading, and because the learning process is to a great extent unconscious, it is easy to mistake the learning process for the experience of the fictional action.

The cognitive impact of fiction also has another aspect. Fictional action allows us to peep into the lives of other people, and watching others is an activity that attracts nearly all human beings. Since fictional characters resemble real people, it is as fascinating for us to watch them as to watch real people. This function is not aesthetic in Genette's use of the term (Genette 1999, see Chapter 4), because the spectator is more concerned with the activity of the people he watches than with their appearance. In film and theatre the physical appearance of the actors may, of course, hold an additional interest, which may be aesthetic, but this aspect is less relevant in literature, where the reader has to supplement the inevitably inadequate description of physical attributes with his own memory of similar properties.

Perhaps the role of peeping in fiction is valuable in itself, but if we proceed to ask why, it is tempting to assume that there is a cognitive motivation behind it. Observing other people is a continual source of information on countless aspects of human life, and although we may say much of this information is redundant because it repeats what we already know, what it does is confirm our own vision of human existence while also improving and extending it. This kind of learning is inconspicuous, because it is so rich and complex that it is difficult to discern simple structures that can be formulated as clear themes and theses. The writer can facilitate this learning by way of a purposeful selection of elements, prioritizing certain cognitive content at the expense of other content. But even though the author has to economize words, omitting an infinite amount of detail, some writers render the fictional action in a way that reveals no clear message, as is the case with the *nouveau roman*. However, even the *nouveau roman* carries an implicit message; after all, the idea that the world offers no messages and that we are on our own if we want to discern the meaning of life is still a message.

The message of the *nouveau roman* is bound to be more complex than that, as the text inevitably represents human activity which constitutes information in itself, for example, the insight that this kind of activity belongs to human life. The activity described can also be understood in terms of value, as something negative or positive.

The distance between the fictional virtual world and the reader's empirical reality protects the reader against pragmatic consequences. However intensely he empathizes with the fictional characters, the fictional events leave no specific traces in the reader's extratextual world; there is no change in the external environment, only in his mind, in the shape of expectations, hope, fear, new understanding and new questions. This feeling of safety from the consequences of the events may perhaps be regarded as a kind of aesthetic distance, but *fictional distance* is a more appropriate term.

Most readers consume a substantial amount of fiction during their lives, and if we multiply the cognitive impulses they receive from each book with the number of books they have read, it turns out that every reader receives a large quantity of experiential material from literary fiction. The significance of this supplement to the reader's own experiences should not be underestimated.

By virtue of the indisputable cognitive impact of literary fiction, it seems to follow that both author and reader consider cognition to be a main function of fiction. Cognition may be intended by the author and expected by the reader, but because the cognitive process occurs unconsciously in many readers, this function may easily escape notice among author and reader alike. This lack of a conscious intention or expectation does not imply that no such intention or expectation exists. Indeed, the evaluation of literature is to a great extent unconscious and the author as well as the reader would miss something if the cognitive content of the work did not accord with their intentions or expectations. The author would feel that he had failed, without quite being able to explain why, and the reader would equally feel that something was missing. The very existence of literary criticism and literary research reveals the need to make our unconscious reactions to literature accessible to consciousness.

Identification

One of the chief advantages of fiction, whether it is a play, poem or novel, is the author's unique licence to invent necessary information in order to generate identification and empathy. Identification does not, of course, mean that the reader believes he *is* the character with whom he identifies, only that he shares the strong bond of common interests with the character. This feeling has no pragmatic foundation, since fictional characters, of course, have no interests which may affect the reader in a pragmatic sense: the hero of a novel is unable to tell the reader whether his wife is cheating on him, whether their children steal from the store, or to give the reader compliments when he is most in need of them. The fictional character's importance is merely as an example of how a human being can be, what he may experience in the real world, and how his choices can affect his own life and that of others.

When the reader identifies with a fictional character, he regards that character's experience as representative of himself and his own life in the real world. In many ways the character functions as a guinea pig that the author sends out into the big, uncertain world to show the reader what may happen to him under similar circumstances. The fictional character is sent into a minefield of obstacles and pitfalls to show the reader where it is safe and where dangerous. The narrative action is a game, a kind of virtual reality, which shows the reader how certain values work in practice. Fiction represents the reader's values, resources and possibilities, testing their consequences in different settings so that the reader can better choose his goals and means when he faces conflicts, challenges and problems in the real world.

Because the fictional character represents the reader's own interests, the reader is not only intellectually but also emotionally involved in the character's destiny. The reader follows his victories and defeats with the same concern as if he had been in the fictional battle arena himself. If the character fails, it represents a defeat for the ideals, hopes and expectations of the reader as well. If he succeeds, it is a promising victory for the reader's own future. The reader's empathy for the fictional characters is in some ways comparable to the football fan's identification with his favourite team and the strong feelings a football match can evoke in the crowd. After all, the psychological mechanisms are the same, except that the parallels between the lives of fictional characters and those of readers are much more perspicuous and better explain the reader's emotional engagement.

Identification with and emotional investment in a fictional character can be established in various ways. As identification consists in a feeling of similarity and common interests, it is only natural that empathy and identification come about through *likeness*. The reader is apt to sympathize with characters that share his own views, values and interests. However, other factors may also contribute to the reader's identification, especially *temporal* and *spatial proximity* to the character. Film obtains this effect by means of close-up photography, allowing a close look at a character's facial features and expressions. The novel can obtain a similar effect with detailed, evocative, intimate descriptions of the characters.

Why does physical proximity increase the feeling of identification and emotional involvement? Why does the nearness of another person affect us so strongly? Social psychology has dealt with the invisible boundaries other people must not cross in everyday interaction (Brown 1965, 80). In everyday conversation, we do not permit very close facial contact with our interlocutors, and this is due to more than the fear of bad breath. From a purely evolutionary perspective, it may be that this kind of proximity deprives us of control and makes us vulnerable to physical attacks. But whatever the reason might be, this aversion prevents all but our closest relations inside our boundary of intimacy. When the camera or the mental model of the action shows us a character so closely that it feels within our boundary of intimacy, we are confronted with a choice: whether to regard the person as an unwelcome intruder or regard him as a close friend. If we like the person, we probably tolerate the blunt introduction, accepting him as a close acquaintance and adapting our feelings correspondingly. The impact of the cinematic or literary close-up can be compared with what happens if a complete stranger embraces us without warning at a party. If we like the stranger and do not regard him or her as a threat, we may accept this unconventional way of introduction. The boundary of intimacy does not pertain only to physical nearness but also to other kinds of intimate contact, such as talk about one's own body or deepest secrets.

A person's being *at the centre of attention* for an extended time may also lead to identification and emotional involvement. A single character who dominates a film or a novel is usually regarded as the protagonist. We easily conceive of dominant objects as important, because they occupy so much time or space, taking up our attention at the expense of other objects and colouring our experience whether we like it or not. This applies not only to the people we encounter in real life but also to fictional characters, given the fictional world's analogies with the existing world.

Another way to make the reader identify with a fictional character is to establish him as a narrator speaking about himself with the first-person 'I', as with lyric poetry, dramatic monologue and first-person novels. In non-fictional poetry and poetry with an unclear fictional status, the identification is, of course, increased by the feeling of personal contact with another human being, a real person talking to *you* and confiding in *you*. In fiction, no one is talking directly to the real reader, who is only a witness to a one-way dialogue between the narrator and the narratee (the fictional receiver), but the character's dual role as character and narrator distinguishes him in a way that encourages identification.

The author can also bring about identification by leaving the reader alone with a fictional character who dominates the scene, as in Ernest Hemingway's *The Old Man and the Sea* (Hemingway 1999). To be alone with another person forces us to look at him differently. It makes us more tolerant and understanding, because we have no choice, meaning that the other person has to be rather unsympathetic to be rejected.

Access to a fictional character's sense impressions, thoughts and feelings is also a device the author can employ to make it easier to empathize with that character. In the novel and in narrative poetry, the author can employ *internal viewpoint* (focalization) to reveal the characters' minds to the readers. For one thing, internal point of view augments their knowledge and understanding of a character. For another, it draws readers' attention and brings them closer to the character. This is why focalization (point of view) affects the reader's sympathy or aversion to the criminal in crime fiction. Seeing a character from the outside (external focalization or viewpoint), not knowing what he perceives, thinks or feels, does not necessarily mean that he becomes less sympathetic than if he were seen from the inside, because the author may compensate for this with some of the other devices to bring about identification and sympathy. The author can also influence the reader's sympathy through selection and by equipping the character with particularly sympathetic features.

One proof of our identification with the fictional characters is the strong emotions we display when something happens to them. Our suspense is to a great extent due to our desire for the protagonists to succeed, since their success confirms our own hopes of happiness and success. The sorrow we feel when they fail is in fact concern about our own future.

We have seen that several factors may contribute to identification and empathy:

1. spatio-temporal closeness to the character
2. an extended focus on the character
3. access to a character's sense impressions
4. access to a character's thoughts and feelings
5. the reader and the character's shared situations
6. the reader and the character's shared values and interests
7. a first-person narrator
8. being left alone with a character who dominates the work
9. internal viewpoint

We are more easily influenced by the values and worldview of a fictional character with whom we identify; identification implies respect for and confidence in the other person and makes us more open to his ideas and opinions. In social psychology this kind of influence is called *the consistency principle* (Brown 1965, 610–11).

Popular literature

The author's indirect mode of communication – presenting the reader with the fictional action (through the mental model) instead of conveying the cognitive message directly – foregrounds the action (the story) and makes the cognitive process easier to overlook. This is a key reason why some scholars remain sceptical about literary fiction's cognitive function. Nevertheless, the main function of literary fiction is the communication of general information about the existing world. Fiction's other functions – such as passing the time, relaxation, entertainment, activating certain feelings, therapy, stimulation of the imagination and so on – are secondary functions based on the primary cognitive function.

Popular literature also conveys a cognitive content, even if we do not usually associate it with learning and information. But it is the cognitive content that makes popular literature entertaining because it provides the reader with pleasant information about what he can expect from reality. Literature entertains us and provides a mental break through information that evokes such good feelings as joy, hope, suspense and pleasure. As human beings we want a good life and are attracted to information that feeds our hope of a happy existence. Since we regard patterns that repeat themselves as natural laws, seeing people succeed who are representative of our own situation provides a boost to our sense of optimism. The more often we witness people who resemble us succeeding, the stronger the belief that it will soon be our turn. Therefore, popular literature by and large depicts human success, sacrificing hard truths on the altar of entertainment. In its depiction of success, it tries to convince the reader that the real world is easier to handle than it in fact is, and the reader unconsciously ignores the reality that true success is seldom as attainable as it appears in popular literature. Hence, reading allows the reader to escape the challenges of the existing world and becomes *escapism*. It encourages the reader to underestimate problems and wait passively for happiness to come to him. Popular literature becomes entertaining by luring the reader into an existential lie that makes him optimistic and glad, although given the human mind's limitless capacity for contradiction, the reader may well believe the lie and see through it at the same time.

Literature that does not convey any kind of cognitive content is rare. It is difficult to write a text that conveys meaning units that cannot be interpreted to yield information in some rational way. Even meaningless syllables may be interpreted as an expression of protest, for instance against language as an institution or against rationality.

The cognitive content: Terminological alternatives

The insight into the problems of the real world that the reader extrapolates from the fictional action has been designated as *message, cognitive content, theme, Weltanschauung, worldview, ideology, implied author, author's intention* and *moral of the story*. The term *moral of the story* should be discarded because it overstates the importance of morality in literary communication, making it easy for anti-cognitivists to dismiss any cognitive approach to literature as moralizing. *Weltanschauung, worldview* and *ideology* are also too narrow, leaving out other kinds of information inherent in the mental model of the action. Ethics, ideology and worldview are of course essential in many literary works, but the cognitive scope of fiction is much wider than that, comprising the many different kinds of knowledge an audience might be interested in. *Theme* has gained much currency, but the drawback is that it refers primarily to the subject of the communication and does not reveal what is said about it (Beardsley's *thesis*). One of the main themes of *Uncle Tom's Cabin* is slavery, but mentioning this theme alone does not give us much information about the cognitive content of the book. *Implied author* and (*author's*) *intention* refer to the cognitive content without limitations, but foreground the author at the expense of the reader. I prefer to reserve these terms for contexts in which the author's role in the communication process is of relevance. This leaves us with the terms *cognitive content, message* and *indirect information*, among which I will alternate depending on the situation.

In Norwegian, the scholar Rolf Gaasland has proposed *norm* (Gaasland 2001, 185–90), which is practical on account of its succinctness but may be confused with the sociological and political meaning of the word. In English the neutral term *message* should do fine. Compared to *cognitive content, message* may seem more restricted, leaving the impression of conveying just one thing. However, its succinctness will make it useful, especially when we need to employ such compounds as *latent message* and *received message*. When we use *message*, we must always bear in mind that a message can be complex, as the message of literary fiction always is. The message that most people associate with *Uncle Tom's Cabin* is that slavery should be abolished and that all races are equal, but another important message is that women ought to have more influence in politics (Tompkins 1985). These principal messages are, however, based on a complex pattern of subordinate messages, and in fact, there are probably as many messages in this novel as there are sentences. Every detail of the story is loaded with information about human life and reality. This does not mean that all this information is equally interesting and pertinent to literary criticism, but it indicates that the cognitive scope of literary fiction should not be underestimated. We should also bear in mind that the content of the message may comprise all the aspects of human existence, not only the philosophical, ethical, moral, political, religious, psychological, sociological and scientific aspects. For instance, aesthetic aspects like hedonistic pleasure or the beauty of nature may also be important, while pragmatic activities and values are other possible themes.

The truth of the message

It is a common supposition that in order to be valuable to the reader, the cognitive content or the message must reflect the general structures of the existing world in a truthful way. It must give a true picture of the norms, laws and values that rule events in the extratextual world. Since the action is fictional, the reader can only check the truth of the message by comparing it with his own prior knowledge, rejecting anything that does not fit in.

Lamarque and Olsen 1994 (434–5) take a somewhat different view. They agree that a learning process takes place, but deny the relevance of determining the truth of fiction's cognitive content in relation to the extratextual world. They regard truth as a scientific matter that has to be verified empirically, and identify this as the chief difference between literary communication and science, history and philosophy (410, 438). In their analysis, *mimesis* means the communication of universal themes, and other information is a by-product without relevance to literary evaluation (398–9, 455). Notwithstanding their thorough discussion of other theories and their explanation of how we identify literary themes, their concept of *theme* remains obscure. Referring to Monroe Beardsley's use of *theme* and *thesis*, they content themselves with the statement that their notion is somehow broader than Beardsley's. To Beardsley, a *theme*, such as pride, fate or slavery, is 'something that can be thought about' (Beardsley 1981, 404), while *thesis* is 'something . . . that can be called true or false', for instance, 'Slavery must be abolished.'

Lamarque and Olsen's theory differs from others with respect to the restrictions it imposes on the communicative content of literature. This is due to their value-based definition of literature: to be interesting, the cognitive content must be related to universal themes while illustrating the subject in a sufficiently advanced way, through an interesting literary form (434–6). Lamarque and Olsen admit that the difference between their own theory and those of others is partially terminological, but assert that their alternative better satisfies the traditional claim that literature must take up a universal theme to be 'good and grand' (438). Their term *theme* seems to me a step backwards from Beardsley's much clearer definition, and tends rather to obscure how literary fiction works. However, in spite of their narrow conception of cognitive content, their theory nevertheless supports a cognitive approach to literary fiction.

The incompleteness of the mental model

It goes without saying that the author must limit the length of the text so that it does not become fatiguing for the reader. How long a text can be before it tires or bores the reader depends on the content and the personality of the reader, but one thousand pages seems to be an upper limit, with 200–300 pages being usual. The author must therefore omit an infinite amount of events and details that could have been included in the action, retaining only the most essential material for the reader. But in his effort to save the reader's time, he faces another and much greater problem than the need to reduce the text's length. This problem is related to verbal communication.

One feature of models, of course, is that they reproduce their object (the referent) with some element of deficiency. The ship model is significantly smaller than the original and leaves out a lot of detail, while film is two dimensional, constrained by camera angle and shot-length and can only render visual and auditory impressions. The mental model of fictional action is likewise deficient compared to the object it represents, and some of these deficiencies are due to the features of verbal communication. Language is not capable of reproducing the individual features of its objects. Words symbolize concepts, and a concept is just a class comprising any object that meets certain minimum requirements. The word *chair* refers to any real or imaginable object with a back and four (or three or five) legs intended for one person to sit on. When words refer to an individual, they do not evoke any individual image of it, only a general concept of it based on the general properties that delimits the class. 'The chair I sit on when eating' refers to a particular chair, but the representation it evokes in a receiver's mind who has never seen it is general and lacks colour, shape, size and individual properties. The incapability of language to render individuality is the reason why the mental model is bound to be meagre, dominated by gaps. If a text says, for instance, 'A man appeared in the doorway', we have no idea how this man and his surroundings look or his manner of approach. An infinite amount of details are effectively left out. To be sure, most of these are of no or little relevance to the action, but a comparison to the real world would at once reveal innumerable gaps.

It may seem absurd to talk about such gaps in the mental model; if only the model really exists, how can anything be lacking? In analogy with the existing world, there has to be a fictional action to which we can compare the mental model, because a model must be a model of something. The action comes into existence as a projection of the mental model of it. As long as the text does not explicitly tell us otherwise, we expect the fictional world to be fitted out with properties similar to those of the real world. If the text does not mention the colour of a character's hair, for example, this is a gap in the model. Like the hair of real people, that of fictional characters must too have a particular colour; we just do not know which. When we read, 'He was killed by being pushed out of a sixth floor window', we understand that the character died from the fall, even though the fall is not stated explicitly, because we are all acquainted with the law of gravitation and how it may affect the human body. The reader attributes to characters, events and setting all the general properties he knows from the real world. The author need not waste time and energy rehashing them all explicitly in creating the mental model. All readers are supposed to master filling in these sorts of gaps, and therefore this activity can be seen as an intersubjective part of the communication process.

Ingarden 1968 (56) and Iser 1974 are aware of the gaps that verbal communication entails, but it is not clear whether they regard the material readers must supply as intersubjective or essentially private phenomena. The first kind of supplement (like the law of gravitation) may be regarded as authorized by the author, while the other (imagining a character as blue-eyed when the text does not mention any colour) is a private matter that cannot be used to support a particular interpretation. In Chapter 5, we will meet with other types of supplements.

Because the action is available only through the mental model, it is impossible to ascertain whether the model renders it truthfully. An unreliable narrator can only be exposed if he contradicts himself. If he lied without leaving any traces in the text, the reader would never discover it, and the act of lying would therefore not be part of the fictional world. What the reader either cannot know from the text itself or cannot infer from the likeness to the real world does not exist in fiction. A lie in real life may have pragmatic consequences if it is not found out, whereas an untraceable lie in fiction would have neither internal consequences for the action nor external import for the world of the reader, and would therefore be totally irrelevant. The impossibility of revealing internal untruth does not however exclude other kinds of internal comparison. The likeness between the fictional and the existing world enables a comparison between the elements of the model and those of the fictional world to see what the model has included or excluded. The author's selection of elements influences the ideological content of the work. As we have seen, the likeness between the fictional and the existing world also allows the reader to check how truthfully the fictional action renders the *general* structures of the existing world.

The transparency of the model

Since models are merely a substitute for an object not available to us, the object itself is our chief concern, which is expressed in common usage. For instance, if we look at a model of a given sailing ship that is still in commission, we may say: 'It's too bad that so many of the old sailing ships have disappeared, but luckily we still have this one.' Here we obviously mean the ship itself, not the model in front of us. The model becomes transparent: we see right through it to the intended object. We register it as a physical object only if we are considering it as an object of study in itself, in order for instance to learn the craft of model ship building, or if its physicality becomes in some other way conspicuous, with cracks due to age, a dusty surface, perhaps a red wine stain.

Mental models are similarly transparent. When a rape victim describes the rapist to a policeman, the policeman directs his attention to the rapist as a real person, not to the mental model that the description evokes in his mind. The mental model of a fictional action is also transparent in the sense of being easily looked beyond to the events it renders. Even though we only come into contact with the model, we think only of the action, for instance when we say that we find a novel's action boring. But what we find boring is not the action itself but the action as it appears in the model. And we empathize with the characters and experience the events without thinking of the fact that we experience the fictional world through a model, which in addition is a very selective one.

It is worth mentioning that the more frequent term *story*, which is used as a synonym for the action, is more related to the text and the model than to the action itself, and therefore, it is possible to say, 'The story is boring in spite of the exciting action.' This would mean that the model presents the events in a bad way.

Although we tend to experience the fictional world without noticing the mental model, one small bit of evidence points to the fact that even laypeople are aware of the existence of the mental model: the use of the present tense when recounting fictional events. Even if a novel is in the past tense, the reader retells the story in the present tense: 'Septimus cannot cope with his mental illness, and driven by callous doctors, he commits suicide.' Only a naïve reader would say, 'Septimus could not cope with his mental illness, and driven by callous doctors, he committed suicide.' Then it would sound as though the action were a historical fact. The present tense does not refer to the action as an external reality (referent), but to the mental model, which is present in the mind of the reader.

In non-fiction, the referent is also conveyed to the reader by means of a mental model, and real events that are told in the past tense are often retold in the present tense, not because the past tense has lost its temporal function, but because the present tense refers to the mental model. The Wikipedia biography of Oscar Wilde and the much shorter biography on Wilde's official website both tell us that Wilde was accused of homosexuality and imprisoned (Wikipedia):

> After a series of trials, Wilde was convicted of gross indecency with other men and imprisoned for two years, held to hard labour.

And (website):

> Oscar was . . . arrested and convicted of gross indecency and sentenced to two years hard labor.

Both articles tell the facts in past time, as they refer to a real event in the past, but if we were to compare the two passages, it would be natural to use the present tense:

> In both articles Oscar Wilde is convicted of gross indecency.

The present tense here refers to the mental model of the event, the model being at hand as part of the reader's experience in the present time. It might be tempting to substitute *text* for *mental model*, but this would be misleading. Taking the above example, no one can be convicted in a text, only in the mental model it conveys. Hamburger does not consider the use of the present in non-fiction, thus missing an important counterargument against her epic preterite.

The two aspects of the model

If we want to understand the various structures employed by the author to convey the action (style, composition, metaphors and narrative structures), it may be important to first discriminate between the text's own structures and those of the mental model and then to further break down the mental model into its two structural components: (1) the original structure of the action, which is in principle independent of (2) the simplified structure that the mental model imposes on the original structure of the action.

The original structure of the action is the primary source of general insight into the extratextual world. Following the analogy with the real world, the original structure of the fictional action must be given in advance, just as Oscar Wilde's life is a fact that cannot be changed by someone writing a biography about him. The selection of material in the biography does not modify the events themselves; it only determines which aspects of the events are to be rendered. A real event is given in advance and cannot be changed without deviating from the truth. Biography has no freedom to manipulate real events even if it might be more interesting or dramatic to do so. The author of fiction, on the other hand, creates the fictional events and may draw material from an infinite range of possibilities. Fiction thus allows a distinction that is out of the question in non-fiction.

When the novelist or playwright has invented a concrete coherent action with all necessary details, a mental model of the original structure of the action is the result. However, because everything is fiction, he has a cooling-off period that is denied to the non-fiction writer: without changing the main structure, he can adapt the original structure of the action in order to improve the action as a communicative whole, and he can add supplementary elements that do not affect the course of the action itself but influence the reader's understanding and reaction to it. Such adjustments as introducing symbolic elements and allusions, using characters as spokespersons for the author's own ideas or modifying the order of the events may all be done without affecting the total context.

Based on their different functions within the action we can distinguish between the *indispensable constituents of the action*, which cannot be changed without altering the main structure of the action, and *facultative (optional) free elements*, which do not affect the main structure. Free elements may be integrated or coalesced into the indispensable constituents of the action; the main point, however, is that the indispensable constituents of the action are indispensible by definition, while the free elements may be omitted without affecting the action. Since such changes normally occur in the planning and writing phase, the readers will never know about them unless the author introduces them in a later edition.

Ironically, we are obliged to illustrate the author's possibilities of manipulating the original action (the complete action, as it was before being rendered) with an example from autobiography. Naturally, as non-fiction, autobiography and biography are required to render facts without manipulation, but there are exceptions in which the manipulation can be discerned by comparing the autobiography with other sources.

In an article about Rousseau's *Confessions*, Jean Starobinski tells us how Rousseau changed the chronological order of two episodes for thematic reasons (Starobinski 1970). The background is that Rousseau was employed as a servant by a noble family and was in love with their daughter. In the episode that originally came first, he has the bad luck one day to spill water on the girl when pouring water in her glass, and the second episode has him impressing the whole family by explaining the Old French motto on the family escutcheon, thereby winning the admiration and respect of the young lady. In the altered version, both episodes take place on the same day and in chronologically reverse order, with the protagonist spilling the water because he is excited and nervous from the positive attention he received earlier that day. Two events having nothing in common are suddenly causally related to each other and take on the more profound meaning that success may easily be followed by humiliation.

As *Confessions* is an autobiography, Rousseau should in principle not be permitted to deviate from the original order of events, however slight an impact it has on the truth. It may seem awkward to choose an autobiography as an example of the author's ability to modify the action, but it is the only way we can compare an altered version of the action to the original account. In our example, the free or optional (facultative) element is the order of two events. For the action as a whole, the order in which the two events take place matters little; the original order illustrates the ups and downs of life as much as the rearranged version. The new order of events, however, highlights the pain caused by failure when defeat follows triumph.

The author's selection of indispensable and free elements is an *external (extratextual)* activity and is part of the creative process. In addition, an *internal (intratextual)* selection takes place as part of the communication process, where the action is forced into the text and the mental model. That is, when reproduced verbally, the as-yet complete and 'unabridged' action is subjected to heavy 'abridgement', an infinite amount of elements and details are omitted, and it re-emerges full of gaps in the form of a mental model. These gaps are not a feature of the action, but of the model.

The mental model is a structure which is imposed on the action's own structure without changing it; its typical features are devices like point of view (focalization), voice, duration, selection, frequency, order and metaphors, which together with the structure of the action, influence the reactions of the reader. In analogy with the real world and non-fiction, the authorial external selection and the model's internal selection are strictly separated in theory, but in practice it is not always possible to determine whether certain elements have been omitted by the author in the creative process, or form an ellipsis in the model, that is, an omission performed by the fictional narrator (who, of course, has in turn been created by the author). If the childhood of the protagonist is left out in a novel, this is a conspicuous gap in the mental model of the action. If the model shows the protagonist's childhood without indicating any traumatic occurrences, the reader cannot know whether this is because the childhood was a happy one or because childhood difficulties are suppressed in the model. If we did not have the historical order of the episodes in the life of Rousseau, we would never have discovered that his autobiography renders them in reverse order.

Viewpoint, voice, duration and *frequency* are kinds of *selection*, and together with *metaphors* and *tropes,* they are linked to the level of the model, while *order* and stylistic elements like *rhyme* and *rhythm* are related to the textual level. Order and stylistic elements nevertheless also affect the impact of the model. The specific structure of the model (excluding the action's original structure) is what is traditionally called *form.* The structure of the model is a *form* imposed on the action. Although modern literary theory seems reluctant to distinguish between form and content, it may be useful to conceive of form as the interplay between text (signifier) and mental model (signified). In principle, any change in the text's structure entails a corresponding change in the structure of the model. The substitution of a synonym for a given expression is sufficient to alter the mental model, because even synonyms carry different connotations and affect how the model impacts the reader. Goodman believes that substituting a synonym for a single word in a text creates a new work, which makes it impossible to translate literary works since the translations themselves are other works (Goodman 1988, 209).

As it is inconvenient to talk about the text and the mental model every time we refer to their interplay, I will often mention only the mental model, with an implicit understanding of the text's impact on the model and on the reader's reactions to the model. The action and the mental model of it are the two means at the author's disposal to influence the reader, and by analysing these structures, one can to a certain extent reconstruct the author's intention (see Chapter 6).

Why the term *mental model*?

The model of the communication process that I have proposed above offers a clearer distinction between the elements of the process than the traditional distinctions of narratology do. I have already discussed the bi- and the tripartitions proposed by the structuralists. Genette's *récit*, *histoire* and *narration* proved to be only a bipartition (Genette 1972, 72) which leaves Genette with the same two levels as his formalist predecessors – the action itself (story) and the presentation of it (text or discourse). In the way it regards the narratological categories of point of view (focalization), voice, duration, frequency and order as ways of presenting the action without changing the action itself, this bipartition is in many respects functional and corresponds to my own distinction between text/mental model and action. Discriminating between the action's original structure and the text/ model-imposed structure on the action enables us to study how the author influences the reader's reactions, by means of not only the action as such but also devices independent of the action.

However, if we compare the dichotomy of the narratologists with the semantic triangle, it becomes obvious that their distinction between *text (discourse)* and *story* does not account for the distinction between *signifier* and *signified*, or to use my terms, between the *material text* and the *mental model of the action*. While their *story* obviously refers to the *referent*, the term *text* or *discourse* straddles the boundaries between *signifier* and *signified* (the *material text* and the *mental model of the action*). Since text and mental model are inseparably linked, this distinction may seem unnecessary, but it is indispensible to a complete understanding of how the communication process works, just as much as it is when we interpret a text. In the case of the latter, we often seem unaware of whether it is the text, the action or mental model of it we are interpreting. But there is a fundamental difference between the interpretation of an ambiguous word or expression in a text (in order to reconstruct a corresponding element in the mental model of action) and the interpretation of an obscure element in the mental model of the action or in the action itself (to obtain a more complete picture of the action or extrapolate some insight into life in general). This may call for further explanation.

Interpretation on the level of text focuses on the comprehension of language. In this respect we must distinguish between semantic and stylistic ambiguity. Semantically, words and expressions can be ambiguous. The language of novels is generally relatively unequivocal, because the text is long enough to give sufficient room and context for clarification. Lyric poetry, on the other hand, tends to be too short to supply clarity, which is why it affords more examples of linguistic ambiguity. In *Is there a Text in this Class?*, Stanley Fish cites two divergent interpretations of Milton's twentieth sonnet, 'Lawrence of virtuous father virtuous son', depending on one's interpretation of the ambiguous verb *spare* (Fish 1980, 149–50).

Beyond the direct semantic sense of a word, linguistic elements can also be used to create meaning in a broader sense. *Rhyme* and *rhythm, enjambment*, the choice of *parataxis* or *hypotaxis*, the *order of elements in the text* and the like all contribute in various ways to elaborating the semantic meaning of the text and influencing the reader's interpretation of the action. The choice of rhythm may, for instance, have an *iconic* (metaphoric) function and symbolize feeling and movement, and the order in which the elements of the action are rendered affects the reader's emotional as well as intellectual attitude. Parataxis may intensify the reader's empathy with children, for instance, by using short, simple main sentences and childish logic to illustrate their way of thinking.

Interpretation on the level of the action focuses in particular on a psychological, sociological, philosophical, moral and ethical understanding of the action's elements. In addition to providing a more perspicuous overview of the events as such, the interpreter tries to extrapolate information about human life in general and all problems related to it. *Mrs Dalloway* supplies one example in which the action itself is open to interpretation, in the question of whether Clarissa is unstable or even suicidal. The crux of the matter here is whether the text provides sufficient evidence of depressive and suicidal tendencies (Woolf 2000, xix–xx). Another example in which the action demands amplification is the meaning of Peter's large pocket knife in this novel (Woolf 2000, xxii). Why is he always playing with it? As a reminder of his masculinity, because he feels threatened, or both? Beyond these specific moments, the novel affords more general opportunities for interpretation, such as the lessons to be drawn from the story of Clarissa and Peter's relationship. From it, we may conclude, for example, that a multitude of conflicting considerations make it extremely difficult to choose the right partner.

When we interpret the specific structure of the mental model (as a model), the original structure of the action is no longer at issue, only the way the action is presented in the model. We interpret the author's choice of non-action-related devices, like point of view, voice, duration, selection, metaphors and symbols, in terms of how this choice is dictated by the message he is trying to convey to the reader. In his introduction to *Mrs Dalloway*, David Bradshaw interprets the red and white roses, which Richard brings home to Clarissa, as a symbol of death (Woolf 2000, xx–xxi):

> Septimus's affliction is expressed in similar terms and both he and Clarissa are at once homicidal and suicidal, with the perilousness of Clarissa's life underscored by her husband's gift of red and white roses. "Richard's first duty was to his country" (p. 94), so it is entirely proper that the roses he has chosen are in the same two colours as the cross of St George, the patron saint of England. But red and white flowers are also "omens of death".

Neither Clarissa nor Richard shows any sign of interpreting the flowers as an omen of death, so it is Bradshaw's personal interpretation of the model that the bunch of flowers are a hint from the author that Clarissa is suicidal. Whether that was really Woolf's intention is, of course, an open question. In this case, the interpretation of the model hinges a discussion of whether the colour of the roses has only an intradiegetic significance, as an example of the interaction between Richard and Clarissa, or an extradiegetic function, as a symbol of death. The interaction between characters is the subject of the interpretation of the action, whereas the flower's symbolic aspect, as long as it is not perceived by the characters, belongs to the interpretation of the mental model as such.

The terminological ambiguity that stems from a failure to differentiate between the levels of literary communication is a common thread in the theoretical works and the practical analyses of literary scholars. In his analysis of the abovementioned episode from Rousseau's *Confessions*, Jean Starobinski interprets the action as it is expressed in the mental model by drawing on his own prior knowledge of human life, society and history. But one moment he presents this as an interpretation of the text, the next as an interpretation of the action (Starobinski 1970, 158, 161, my translation):

> It is now time to examine our own way of commenting on this page by Rousseau. I have tried to reveal its network of social and emotional relations by subjecting it to a stylistic analysis. Having first identified the significant parts of the text, I have tried to describe them according to the vocabulary that is at our disposal today: I have just empirically applied current words and concepts from psychology and social philosophy.

> The interpretation scene [a scene in the action where the protagonist interprets the motto of the family escutcheon] as I have interpreted it myself . . .

The first quotation is not an interpretation of the text but, on the contrary, an interpretation of the action. The second is, indeed, an interpretation of the action, as Starobinski himself indicates.

The ambiguity also runs through Wolfgang Iser's theory of interaction between text and reader, which does not distinguish between text interpretation and action or model interpretation. He quotes Virginia Woolf's comment that Jane Austen 'stimulates us to supply what is not there. What she offers is, apparently, a trifle, yet is composed of something that expands in the reader's mind and endows with the most enduring form of life scenes which are outwardly trivial' (Iser 1974). Iser continues:

> What is missing from the apparently trivial scenes, the gaps arising out of the dialogue—this is what stimulates the reader into filling the blanks with projections. He is drawn into the events and made to supply what is meant from what is not said. . . . The "enduring form of life" which Virginia Woolf speaks of is not manifested on the printed page; it is a product arising out of the interaction between text and reader.

One moment Iser speaks of what is missing from the *scenes*, which are part of the mental model of the action, while the next he refers to the interaction between text and reader, presupposing that text and mental model are identical. Although gaps in a text are generally accompanied by corresponding blanks in the mental model of the action, with a gap in the text entailing a gap in the action, this correspondence is not automatic. As demonstrated by our example with the laws of gravity, a gap in the text does not necessarily imply a gap in the model. Moreover, as we have seen, the problems related to text interpretation differ from those linked to the interpretation of the model, which in turn are different from the difficulties we encounter when interpreting the action as such.

In these examples, the ambiguity has no obvious negative consequences, but the lack of differentiation contributes to the illusion that the ambiguous notion of *text* may be used without further ado in any situation. Traditional terminology's confusion over theories of duration, which will be discussed in Chapter 9, should be enough to dispel this false idea. The lack of clarity also prevents any investigation of those aspects of the interplay between text, model and action that are left out by the dichotomy between *text* (or *discourse*) and *story*.

One drawback of the terms *signifier, signified* and *referent*

In contrast to the dichotomy, the trichotomy of *signifier, signified* and *referent* corresponds perfectly to my terms *text, mental model* and *action*, so a good question is what point there can be in introducing the new terms when the old ones seem to be adequate. The drawback of *signifier, signified* and *referent* is their abstractness, which best suits them for abstract contexts, such as the introductory chapter in books on literary theory. In the further elaboration of theory, these terms are absent, as if the distinction were no longer necessary when scholars get to work on the real problems. This has led to the stagnation of many problems in the field of literary theory.

Of my terms, *mental model of the action* is especially important, as it is more easily intelligible than *signified*. *Signified* means simply *meaning* and does not indicate the ontological form meaning takes. If we specify that *meaning* consists in the mental representation of fictional events, it is easier to relate it to something more concrete, but only the notion *mental model of the action* makes us conceive of a coherent whole, like a film. Models are something we have a lot of direct experience with, and the representations the text evokes in our minds are in fact a model of the fictional action.

After the mental model has been transferred to our mind, we can save it for later use, independently of the text, provided we can remember it. The fact that the mental model can be detached from the text in this way proves that it is not identical with the text and that the text is merely a vehicle. To be sure, as a vehicle, the text leaves characteristic traces in the model – the effects of rhyme, rhythm, order and so on – but this is comparable to the traces goods bear of the mode of transport.

An essential advantage of *mental model* is that it allows us to discriminate between two aspects of the signified: the mental model and the cognitive content inherent in it. The meaning of the text is achieved by both the mental model and the cognitive content, which *signified* by itself cannot account for. *Mental model* and *cognitive content* divide the signified into two new levels, a distinction necessary for the delimitation of the literary work as such and for the understanding of how literary fiction works as a vehicle for information.

The entire term, *the mental model of the action,* is somewhat unwieldy on account of its length. One solution might be to shorten it into *action model.* At any rate, it is not to be used interchangeably with less precise terms like *plot, text* or *discourse.* In certain situations, it may be practical to refer directly to the *action*. When we are interested in the properties of the model as a model – for instance when studying formal aspects like viewpoint, voice, duration, frequency, order and style – the full-term *mental model of the action* is indispensable. As for *text*, the interplay between text and model often obviates any specific mention of it, as long as the correspondence between them is unproblematic. For the same reason, it makes practical sense to use *extra-* and *intratextual* even if it is the mental model that is meant and not the text as such.

Drama

The drama's way of communication is especially interesting for the study of the mental model. The mental model that forms the primary meaning of the dramatic text can be transferred to the stage as a theatrical performance. This transfer requires a comprehensive filling of the model's gaps. The deficient mental model of the action is replaced by a material model on the stage, replete with a full range of details and individuality. The reader is transformed into a spectator who perceives human beings of flesh and blood moving and talking on a stage that can be very detailed and realistic. But in spite of the individuality of the elements, the audience is not facing the fictional action itself any more than the readers of a novel are. The performance remains a model of the action, just as the model ship is not the ship itself. This finds confirmation in the fact that the characters are merely parts played by actors and that the stage is not the open world in which real events are taking place. This becomes particularly evident when an ample old diva sings the role of a slender young girl or when an adult actress plays the title role of *The Little Prince*. In such cases, it is the transparency of the physical model that saves the performance from becoming a fiasco: looking right through the corpulent diva or adult actress of the physical model, the audience conceptualizes them as respectively the slender young girl and the small boy of the fictional action.

There are many ways of staging a play, and a given theatrical performance is just one of many possible ways of realizing the mental model that the dramatic text *means*. The transformation of the mental model into a performance by filling the necessary gaps is based on an interpretation of the action and the mental model of it as well as on the subjective creativity of the stage manager, the actors, the scenographer and the technical staff. If we regard the theatrical performance as an independent work of art, it is the product of teamwork among the playwright, stage manager, actors and technical staff.

Goodman compares the theatrical performance to a musical work, in which the performance represents the work as a member of a *compliance class*: a performance maps onto the class of performances that are identified as the work (the compliance class) when the score (the text) complies with the performance (Goodman 1988, 143–4, 210). Goodman's definition of *compliance* allows for a good deal of discussion over what counts as sufficient compliance. For drama, compliance is ensured by observing the dialogue and the stage directions are observed. In spite of varying scenography and stage management, *The Wild Duck* by Ibsen retains its identity wherever it is performed.

Literary fiction as a speech mode

The freedom of fiction from referential constraints distinguishes it as a particular mode of communication from the *factual mode* we are accustomed to in everyday life, which is inexorably burdened with an absolute truth claim. We expect fiction to render truth, too, but only indirectly. It may be useful to compare the fictional mode with two other modes of communication that exist besides the serious one: *humour* and *irony*. Drawing upon considerable research, Michael Mulkay verifies that laughter and humour permeate everyday life to a much greater extent than previously presumed. Furthermore, not only is laughter aroused by humour, but laughter is also an important factor when it comes to creating a humorous atmosphere (Mulkay 1988). He goes as far as to define humour as a particular speech mode in contrast to the 'normal' serious speech mode. Whereas the serious mode of speech requires truth and conceptualizes the world as consistent and coherent, the humorous mode of speech is a sanctuary in which it is allowed to represent the world as complex and contradictory (213–14). Laughter and smiling must be understood in relation to social processes: they are not only a result of humorous stimuli and the experience of humour, but also a signal that the communication is taking place in the humorous mode, where the rules concerning truth, consistency and relevance are quite different (110). Almost anything said in the humorous mode is exempt from responsibility; under cover of humour, you can take up taboo subjects and often do not even have to disguise or sanitize them. All you have to do is laugh after the statement, say you were only joking, and in that way you get by saying things that cannot be said in other circumstances.

The ironic mode of speech has a lot in common with humour. It consists in saying something entirely different from what you mean to say, but in such a manner that the receiver nevertheless gets the message. Like humour, irony presupposes signals in the text or context informing the receiver about the intended speech mode. While humour renders the content harmless by branding it as insincere ('just a joke'), irony maintains the sincerity of the content, but its indirect form shields one from responsibility. The innocent surface structure elicits a pass from the critical element in our psyche, the superego, allowing the underlying structure – the real message – to slide through. This content-obscuring technique corresponds in principle to the technique that Freud illuminates in his analysis of the tendentious joke (Freud 1958). The tendentious joke disguises the taboo content – something sexual, for instance – with an innocent surface structure that the superego lets pass, allowing the id to enjoy the forbidden deep structure.

The fictional mode enjoys the same freedom from truth as the humorous mode, but only with respect to specific real objects and events. In contrast to humour, we expect literary fiction to contain *general* truth. Literary fiction and irony both employ an indirect way of communication, using surface structure to convey underlying structure; while irony is based on opposition, however, literary fiction is based on similarity.

Possible worlds

Different observers may have different conceptions of the existing world according to their subjective perception and interpretation of the real facts. Such subjective conceptions of the existing world may be regarded as different worlds. The version of reality defended by one person can be seen as a world of its own in contrast to the subjective worlds (versions) of others. Equally, any imagined modification or alternative to the real world may be called another world, and can be either a *possible* or an *impossible world*. This is roughly the basis of the theory of possible worlds, which has seen a certain rise in popularity in recent literary theory (Ryan 1991; Herman and Vervaeck 2005, 150–1; Phelan and Rabinowitz 2005, 47–8; Herman 2007, 71; Abbott 2008, 167–8; Fludernik 2009, 107). The theory of possible worlds purports to explain the relationship between fiction and reality, starting with the claim that the fictional text establishes a fictional world which is different from the real world. The fictional world is linked to the existing world by a degree of likeness that varies according to the information explicitly provided in the text. The fictional world is similar to the existing world as long as there are no significant deviations which the author would need to report to the reader (the crux of Ryan's principle of minimal departure).

Although the theory of possible worlds is compatible with the conception of the literary communication process I have outlined in this chapter, one drawback is that the term *possible worlds* foregrounds the referent at the expense of the signified (the mental model). Hence, it understates the more fragile basis of the fictional world as a projection of the mental model of the action, a projection that draws on a similarity to the existing world. We must always bear in mind that all the elements of the fictional world that are not explicitly mentioned in the text (or shown on the stage or on the screen) can only be reconstructions based on parallels with the real world; in other words, the reader can reconstruct them in accordance with the patterns of the real world. If a novel, film or theatrical performance does not reveal the childhood of a character, we nevertheless know that he was born and grew up and so on. In texts, the lack of specificity (the gaps) is, of course, increased because language can only communicate by means of general concepts and is incapable of recreating individuality.

The fictional action and the infinite fictional world of which it is a part are accessible to the reader only through the mental model of the action, which may be supplemented by information from the parallel real world to form a more complete world. Because of the likeness between the fictional and the real world, the fictional action is part of an entire world notwithstanding the fact that the model only explicitly provides facts pertaining to the action itself. The rest of the fictional world in its infinitude is only relevant as a framework, ready to be activated if for some reason the reader finds it (or, more likely, just parts of it) useful. When we speak of the *fictional world*, it is important to be aware whether we mean the fictional universe as a whole or merely the part of it that pertains to the events described in the text.

The term (*fictional*) *world*, which is linked logically to the referent, cannot replace *mental model* (or *signified*) even if the transparency of the mental model tempts us to speak directly of the referent, for there are essential differences between the two. The mental model of the fictional action consists of a limited amount of explicit facts and is full of gaps, whereas the fictional world is in principle complete but only implicitly, by way of general facts that can be inferred from the parallel real world. It is especially when the existing world is at issue that certain expressions, like 'Those two live in completely different worlds', can cause confusion, as the world they live in is objectively the same; the difference lies in their mental models of the world. In fact, one ought to distinguish between *the mental model of a possible world* and the *possible world itself*, in accordance with the distinction I have already made between the fictional action and the mental model of it.

What comes first, text or action?

We have described the reading process in terms of four levels: (1) *the fictional action*, (2) *the text*, (3) *the mental model of the action* and (4) *the cognitive content (the message)*. This ordering brings up the question over what comes first, the text (and, consequently, the inherent mental model) or the action (story), a discussion we had to postpone until we had a better grasp of these terms. Now it is time to take it up again.

As we have seen, the action, being fictitious, has no existence as such. It exists only in the minds of author and reader as a projection of the mental model. However, this projection can only be a mental model, too, so in fact, we face two models: the primary mental model of the action to which we are already accustomed and a secondary mental model of the action, which is the referent of the primary model. The mental model of the action is not identical with the mental model we have of the referent itself, and this difference becomes evident when we try to imagine the referent independently of the signified, as a complete entity, free of gaps. The primary mental model is deficient and is characterized by narratological devices (viewpoint, voice etc.), whereas the secondary model is our conception of the action as it would be if it were real. It is the difference between the primary and the secondary model that enables us to reveal the influence of the narrator, which is expressed through narratological and stylistic structures. The secondary mental model (our conception) of the action as a (hypothetically) real thing is fresh and untouched, as the elements have not yet been subject to any authorial rendering. Of course, we cannot imagine every single, specific element out of this infinitude, but only sketch a very general picture of them based on our general knowledge of the existing world. We do not know the details of Clarissa's childhood in *Mrs Dalloway*, but we know she must have had one, and based on our general knowledge about late-nineteenth-century middle-class English life in the countryside, we can guess roughly how it must have been. This vague model of her childhood is not part of the primary model, in which it is a gap, but is an indispensable constituent of the secondary model, which tries to render the original whole from which the primary model has taken its details. This original whole only exists, of course, as a projection of conditions in the real world, where any report of events is based on a complete reality that can at least theoretically be retraced.

In the light of these facts, the fictional action turns out to have three sources: (1) the general features of the existing world, (2) the text and its inherent (primary) mental model of the action, and (3) the imagination of the author. The fictional action's dependence on the real world implies that the action has a kind of prenatal existence in the real world. In this sense, the action precedes the text (and the mental model of it). If the author imagines the action (i.e. the model of it) in his mind before he writes it down, it is equally prior to the text. So the mental model of the action can precede the text and is, in fact, independent of the text. On the other hand, if the author creates the action (i.e. the model of it) while writing, text and action (i.e. the model of it) are simultaneous. Then, the action comes into being simultaneously with the text, as a projection of the mental model that the text *means*, accompanying the text/mental model like a shadow.

If we rule out the action's latent prenatal existence in the general structure of the existing world, we see that the method of the author determines whether the action comes before the text or vice versa. The precise order is of no importance as long as we discriminate between the action itself (represented by a secondary, more comprehensive model of the action), the primary (more limited) model of the action, and the material text. This indispensable distinction saves us from unnecessary misunderstandings, and furthermore answers Abbott's question (in Herman 2007, 41) about whether the distinction between story and discourse is a real distinction at all, since all we ever know of the story is what we get through discourse. Given the parallel between the fictional and the existing world, it is not true that the discourse (text and model) is all we know about the story (action). The likeness between the two worlds allows us to compare the reduced model of the action with the complete reality that it renders in spite of the fact that both model and action are fictional entities. This comparison is important for our understanding of the ideological impact of the fictional work.

One confusing consequence of the action (i.e. our secondary, more comprehensive mental model of it), being as it is a projection of the primary mental model of the same action, is the reversibility of the relationship. The more comprehensive concept of *action* is secondary to the more restricted concept *model of the action* because the model creates the action by rendering it. But in accordance with the conditions in the real world, we compare model and action as if the action were primary, conceiving of the blanks of the model as deficiencies compared to the 'complete' fictional world of the action that is the referent.

We should now be able to set up a diagram of the literary communication process:

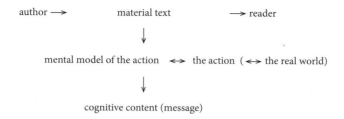

The three levels *text, the mental model of the action* and *the message* each function as a surface structure of the next level, which then constitutes an underlying structure. The message is, consequently, an underlying structure in relation to the mental model and the action.

But where do we locate the discourse in this diagram? Since it is how the mental model mediates the action, it is identical with the specific structure of the mental model. We have distinguished between the original structure of the action that furnishes the raw material for the mental model and the new structure that the model imposes on the original structure. *The discourse* is therefore the structure that the model has independently of the original structure of the action, or the structure through which it presents the action. The chronology of the action cannot, for example, be changed, but the specific structure of the model can present the chronological events in a non-chronological order, beginning with the end of the story for instance. The specific structure of the model is therefore identical with the *discourse*, while the action's original structure is the *story (action)*. We must still bear in mind that *discourse* may cause confusion because it does not distinguish between the text and the mental model, and *story* tends likewise to be associated with the text.

4

The Cognitive and the Aesthetic Dimension

Although literary scholars normally take care to define their technical terms to avoid misunderstanding, the word *aesthetic* is a conspicuous exception. Scholars seem to take it for granted that their audience knows what the term means whenever they use it, for example, Ingarden 1968; Iser 1989, 9; Nøjgaard 1996, 278–80; Davies 2007. After centuries of impassioned discussions about the nature of the aesthetic, however, philosophers and scholars have yet to agree on a definition, which of course explains why scholars feel compelled to leave the term undefined (Gérard Genette 1999; Eagleton 1990). This nevertheless has led to confusion and misunderstanding when it comes to the aesthetic aspect, for example, in understanding how fiction works.

Through the ages literary theorists have held widely diverging views regarding the function of literary fiction; some of them foreground its aesthetic aspect while others take a more cognitive approach. For the phenomenologist Roman Ingarden, for instance, literature has a purely aesthetic function, and he rejects the cognitive aspect as irrelevant (Ingarden 1968, 84–5), dismissing the attempt to establish referential correlations between the fictive and the real world as naïve. On the other hand, a cognitive attitude to fiction is characteristic of David Davies's discussion of aesthetics and literature (Davies 2007, 157–63, 170–81). Offering hypotheses about the extratextual world, fiction furnishes empirical information, even though this information needs to be tested against 'the unarticulated knowledge of the world, upon which the reader's intuitions of rightness are based' (162).

Among Scandinavian theorists, Morten Nøjgaard (Nøjgaard 1996, 279–80) takes a relatively cognitivist view, thinking that aesthetic experience in literature is more related to cognitive values than in the other arts. To what extent the cognitive aspect in his opinion supplants the aesthetic one, however, is not quite clear, because he partly contradicts himself. On the one hand, he regards the aesthetic experience as one of the two main criteria for literary value (288), while on the other, he rejects the individual aesthetic criteria as false (279–80, 285–8), leaving him with the vague criterion of 'the quality of the pleasure' (288), which we are told depends completely on the reader's momentary needs and ability to perceive. The Norwegian theorist Erik Bjerck Hagen questions whether there can be any criteria to distinguish aesthetic experience from other kinds of experience (Hagen 2003, 13–14, 114–15). In many modern schools of literary theory, a cognitive attitude seems to be implicit, such as in Marxism, feminism, post-colonialism and cultural studies.

A general agreement on the role of the aesthetic aspect in literary communication is impossible as long as the term is not adequately defined. In spite of countless attempts throughout history, we still do not have a workable notion of aesthetic experience that would make a constructive discussion of the functions of fiction possible (Genette 1999, Eagleton 1990).

One factor behind this state of affairs may be the fact that the concept has mostly been left to philosophers, whose abstract, general style of thinking cannot accommodate a concrete discussion of how fiction works. It may also be that their concept of the aesthetic applies only to arts other than literature. In *The Aesthetic Relation*, Genette tries to improve earlier definitions from a literary point of view, clarifying in many ways the aesthetic experience and providing a good definition of art, but he does not succeed in throwing new light on the role of the aesthetic in fiction (Genette 1999). This may be due to the fact that his thorough structuralist understanding of literature does not comprise the literary communication process as a whole in which structural elements like *mode, voice, duration, frequency* and *order* take part. To understand the role of the aesthetic in fiction, we must understand the communication process in which the aesthetic aspect is to be included. In this chapter, I shall draw on the conception of the literary communication process elaborated in the previous chapters.

Definition of the aesthetic

The words *aesthetic* and *aesthetics* are used with varying references. In one situation they refer to a philosophical discipline, in the next to the closely related concept of *art*, then suddenly it is a question of beauty, taste or a peculiar attitude towards an object. For the most part, no one feels it necessary to specify what he really means by the word.

A typical example is Nøjgaard's use of *aesthetic* as an adjective (Nøjgaard 1996, 279–80). He says that we always evaluate the literary work in relation to either its cognitive value ('the statements inherent in the work are true or false') or its value as an experience ('the statements inherent in the work give rise to pleasure or displeasure'), but classifies both values as aesthetic judgements.

Accordingly, he also regards cognition as an aesthetic activity, which seems to give rise to a contradiction straightaway. However, the paradox is due to the fact that the word *aesthetic* has two different meanings. When used in the term *aesthetic judgement*, the adjective refers to a philosophical discipline and may be replaced by *literary* or *artistic*, whereas Nøjgaard obviously has another meaning of the word in mind than *philosophical discipline*, that is, the quality of an experience. He associates this experience with pleasure and displeasure, which he regards as synonymous with the experience of beauty and ugliness, or what is traditionally called *aesthetic experience*. What Nøjgaard probably means to say is that, on the one hand, we expect (non-aesthetic) cognition as well as an (aesthetic) experience of beauty or ugliness when we read fiction, and on the other, both are qualities that belong to the discipline of literature. With this formulation we avoid the ambiguity which led to the apparent paradox.

Ludwig Wittgenstein (1967) compares the sort of ambiguity we encounter in a word like *aesthetic* to the different kinds of likeness that link the members of a family together. There are various similarities between the individual members of the family, but none of them shares a particular feature with all the others. Similarly, the word *aesthetic* is a collective term for phenomena that are interrelated in many different ways but share no single feature with all the other members of the group. The link between the different members may be more or less casual, making it difficult to find a definition that takes all the members of the family into account. This is the very conundrum the history of aesthetics confronts us with. Contrary to Wittgenstein's many examples of 'language games', many of the references of the word *aesthetic* are rather vague, with a great potential for misunderstanding. Moreover, its various meanings have changed throughout history; traces of past usage coexist with new senses, causing further adding to the confusion.

Genette's *The Aesthetic Relation* attempts to define the aesthetic experience as a special emotional response ('the aesthetic appreciation') linked to the particular attention you direct towards an object when you are concerned only with its superficial aspects, not with its function (Genette 1999, 6–7, 222). Similarly, to Jan Mukařovsky, the aesthetic function isolates an object, concentrating on its shape and arousing aesthetic pleasure (Mukařovsky 1970). Genette, however, clarifies his definition with examples from everyday life, taking as his point of departure the following anecdote about Courbet working on a landscape. Courbet was painting a distant object without knowing what it was; when he dispatched an assistant to find out, he was told that it was a pile of sticks. Genette's point is that Courbet in this case cares neither about the identity nor about the function of the object he is painting, only its aspect, its contours and colours: 'What does it look like?' This kind of disinterested attention, to Genette, is aesthetic.

This definition will suffice in simple, straightforward situations, like when we enjoy a sunset without wondering what tomorrow's weather will bring or thinking that another day is over, or when we appreciate the shape of a stone we find on the beach. But the definition also allows for kinds of experiences that Genette does not accept as aesthetic. He denies, for instance, that enjoying a glass of wine can be an aesthetic pleasure, arguing that this is a physical experience, but it differs from the sunset and the stone only in the sense organ being activated. The sunset, stone and wine are all physical phenomena, and taste is just as much a mental experience as visual sensation. Why should only visual and aural impressions be linked to aesthetic experience? Are wine tasting and perfume testing aesthetic experiences of a lower order than listening to music? Couldn't embracing and physical nearness be aesthetic pleasures, according to Genette's definition?

The reason Genette excludes smell, taste and touch seems rather to be historical, for these are senses that have traditionally been ignored in aesthetics. Originally, however, the word *aesthetic* meant perception in general, including all five senses, and there is no reason why we should not extend its meaning again. It is the only way to go if we want an airtight definition, and it would also be a logical parallel to the development of the concept of art, which has gradually opened up to handicraft, design, even gourmet cuisine.

Most people are able to understand aesthetic experience as long as it is linked to perception, but is an aesthetic attitude possible with respect to abstract and mental phenomena, too? Can a thought or a feeling be 'beautiful' for its own sake? Are we able to look into our own mind and contemplate our thoughts and feelings in the same way as when we enjoy a sunset or music? Genette does not broach this basic question, and it remains uncertain how we should distinguish our emotional reaction to the content of the thought or feeling from the reaction when we consider the thought or feeling apart from any pragmatic considerations.

It becomes even more difficult to sort out the aesthetic attitude when objects arouse other attitudes at the same time, for example, of a more practical kind. Architecture is one area in which it is easy to distinguish between utility and aesthetics, as there is no close connection between the exterior appearance of the building and its practical purpose. A building may be beautiful but hopelessly impractical, or ugly but very useful. And the precise boundaries between aesthetic, erotic and personal qualities become murkier with respect to a potential partner. Is it any single one of these that creates the impression of beauty? Research indicates for instance that our sexual ideals of beauty are primarily based on biological criteria (Grammer 1993, 297–327). As a potentially aesthetic object, literature is extremely complex and, moreover, composed of both physical and mental elements, so it is almost impossible to discern any one clearly aesthetic aspect in our reactions to it.

Although aesthetic experience is of an emotional sort, some scholars regard it as value-neutral, so that it may comprise both positive and negative experiences (Genette 1999, 79). This definition excludes *the beautiful* as a synonym for *aesthetic*, so that looking at an ugly painting or listening to disagreeable music would both be aesthetic experiences. Others think that aesthetic experiences are per definition positive (Beardsley 1981, 501–2), that is to say, 'beautiful'. The two definitions of the aesthetic can be reconciled if we subordinate Beardsley's definition to Genette's value-neutral one, but we must then explicitly distinguish Beardsley's narrower term as a *theory of the beautiful*.

Whether the aesthetic reaction to an object is positive or negative, however, it is difficult to distinguish it from other emotions, like our feelings after the accomplishment of a difficult task (for instance solving a complex mathematical problem), the sight of an impressive building or watching a 'beautiful' goal being scored. The overwhelming pleasure some feel when contemplating a mathematical formula may be an experience of beauty, or simply admiration, recognition or pride of the sort one might feel before a bookshelf he has just finished building. In this situation, there is a mixture of feelings: relief over finishing the work, satisfaction with the new piece of furniture, pride in one's own technical skill, and, possibly, aesthetic pleasure if the bookshelf has a beautiful design. There is probably no clear borderline between the pure aesthetic feeling and other, related feelings, and we can only distinguish among the obvious extremes. However unclear the aesthetic experience may be, perhaps the combination of positive (or negative) feelings and an isolating attitude towards the object is sufficient to distinguish it from more practically oriented experiences.

The aesthetic dimension in art

So far we have concentrated on spontaneous aesthetic relations that are not linked to any human intention. When a person produces an object with the intention to achieve an aesthetic effect, the product is a work of art (Genette 1999, 222). In order for something to be a work of art, it suffices that the receiver believes there is an aesthetic intention. At the same time, in addition to the aesthetic function, the work of art may also serve a practical function, as in architecture, figurative pictorial art and literature. According to Genette, only a scintilla of aesthetic intention is required to classify it as a work of art (Genette 1999, 219). Although this definition of art leaves room for non-aesthetic functions, it presupposes that art objects have an aesthetic dimension. But is this a matter of course? Must an artefact achieve an intentional aesthetic effect in order to be classified as art, or can it be art even if the creator has not intended any aesthetic effect? Is it the aesthetic factor that links all the different kinds of art together, or is it a case of family resemblance that links together many – but not all – family members?

At this point, we need to distinguish between two different senses of the word *aesthetic*: on the one hand, as in *aesthetic attention/attitude/ experience* and, on the other, when it indicates an artefact's belonging under the philosophical discipline *aesthetics*, that is, *art*. Henceforth, to avoid confusion, I will restrict the adjective *aesthetic* to the aesthetic experience, or alternatively mark it with (1), whereas objects linked to aesthetics will be referred to as *art* and *artistic* or marked with (2). To claim that fiction has an aesthetic (1, 2) function is ambiguous. It can mean that fiction belongs to art in general or that it has an aesthetic (1) function (as experience). If all forms of art share an aesthetic (1) minimum as Genette assumes, the two different senses coincide to a certain extent, but if fiction should turn out to lack Genette's aesthetic minimum, in spite of its status as art, the ambiguity becomes important, because then the question is whether the *aesthetic* (2) discipline of literature has an *aesthetic* (1) function or not. Consequently, we get two discussions: First, does fiction have an aesthetic (1) function or not? If not, then second, can fiction lack the aesthetic (1) dimension and still remain art?

Does fiction have an aesthetic dimension?

To discuss this problem, we first need to differentiate between intentional and spontaneous aesthetic (1) experiences. Spontaneous aesthetic experiences may principally occur in any field of human activity. It suffices that a person isolates an object from its possible practical contexts, concentrating merely on its exterior aspect as an object of perception. We cannot rule out the possibility that the reader adopts an aesthetic attitude to the different elements of the reading process, but it is difficult or even impossible to verify or disprove such aesthetic effects, due to the subjectivity linked to them. A reader may get caught up in a particular word or sentence and perhaps enjoy the interplay between sound and meaning in the way others enjoy a sunset, and although I am unable to feel the same way about it myself, I can hardly disprove that a text can elicit such an aesthetic (1) response.

In literature, however, such spontaneous aesthetic reactions do not occur systematically enough to be regarded as a function peculiar to it. The aesthetic (1) response would either have to be intended by the author or at least shared by many readers. In order to ascribe an aesthetic (1) function to a work of fiction, the aesthetic dimension must apply to more than contingent elements of it. We would not, for instance, accept isolated parts of a melody to be separate works of music even if they each have an aesthetic quality in themselves, or call a car a work of art because there is a lithography by Edvard Munch in the backseat. When Genette requires an aesthetic minimum, he hardly means to imply that a non-fiction work becomes art by virtue of containing a single good metaphor. The aesthetic minimum in literature must be sufficiently dominating and systematic to characterize the whole, just as a building has an aesthetic aspect as a whole in addition to its pragmatic functions. Therefore we have to ask: Do fictional works on any level contain significant structures that are meant to produce or are capable of producing an aesthetic effect, like colour and form in painting or melody and rhythm in music?

Does the text have an aesthetic function?

Let us start on the lowest level of the communication process, the material text. We have already mentioned that the material text consists of a material typographic level and a phonetic level. The phonetic level is originally composed of phonemes, which are abstract concepts waiting for the reader to realize them as individual sounds with his personal pronunciation of the text. From an aesthetic point of view, it is possible to conceive of the printed text as an abstract drawing and of the spoken text as music. The printed text may then give the reader aesthetic pleasure much like calligraphy would, but the aesthetic effect would in this case be merely incidental, not intended, because the identity of the literary work is normally not linked to a particular typographical expression. Whether a novel is printed in Arial or Times New Roman may have some aesthetic impact, but is irrelevant to the reader's experience of the novel.

The sound patterns are to a greater extent predetermined by the author, but this only applies to the abstract phoneme level. The individual realization of the oral text is left to chance according to the reader's dialect, idiolect and voice. The properties of phonemes and prosody take on more importance in lyric poetry, where such properties as rhyme, rhythm and onomatopoeia are exploited intentionally; however, such acoustic ornaments still have primarily a semantic function, creating a special atmosphere or having iconic functions. Experimental attempts to reduce the lyric poem into pure sound devoid of semantic content do not prove that pure sound has a substantial aesthetic function in literature in general, just as it is not an essential feature of wine glasses that one can play them like musical instruments. As readers we do not expect the phonetic aspects of the text to take centre stage, nor do we believe acoustic effects to be a dominant part of the author's intention. On the contrary, I think most of us enjoy the musical qualities of language only as a subordinate effect that accompanies its semantic functions. After all, a recital of verses composed of meaningless syllables would hardly draw a big audience.

Alliteration, rhyme and the abundance of certain vowels or consonants in verse are not primary aesthetic qualities that we can enjoy independently of any meaning. It is only as semantic elements that they gain relevance. The use of the spondee (a metrical foot consisting of two stressed syllables) in the first, second, third and seventh lines of the first stanza of the English national anthem and the dactyl in the fourth, fifth and sixth lines have primarily a semantic function, connoting solemnity and importance:

> God save our gracious Queen
> Long live our noble Queen
> God save the Queen
> Send her victorious
> Happy and glorious
> Long to reign over us
> God save the Queen

The predominantly semantic function of rhyme and metrics in poetry does not conflict with the clearly aesthetic function that the same devices have in rap music, where the rhythmic qualities of the lyrics are emphasized by the musical accompaniment with drums and other instruments. The difference between rap and conventional poetry consists in the intention of the sender and the expectations of the receiver: rap emphasizes the aesthetic aspect of the communication, while conventional poetry foregrounds the cognitive.

Does the action have an aesthetic function?

The next level of the communication process is the mental model of the action with its two subordinate levels, *the original structure of the action* and *the specific structure of the model*. We will first attend to the former.

To what extent can the action be experienced as something purely aesthetic? Events of the kind depicted in fiction consist of various elements which might have an aesthetic effect if we perceived them physically. However, they do not come to us as living individuals of the extratextual world, only as concepts without individuality. As a result, they have no aesthetic effect of their own. The general representation evoked by the word *chair* is no aesthetic experience, in contrast to the perception of a real, concrete beautiful chair, of which not even a thorough description could substitute in terms of aesthetic effect. The author may, however, resort to devices, such as embedding emotive words in the description, in order to involve the reader's own aesthetic experiences with chairs. But in that case, it is not the described object that elicits the aesthetic response in its own right, but the beautiful chairs the reader has seen himself and with which he compares the concept of *a beautiful chair*. Normally, literary texts cannot replicate aesthetic experiences; however, the author has recourse to evocative words that revive the reader's own aesthetic experiences, in effect parasitizing the memories of the reader. Some objects elicit an aesthetic response in so many people that the aesthetic response has merged with the notion of these objects as an intersubjective emotive factor. This applies to everything human beings generally regard as beautiful, whether it be artefacts like jewellery and Greek sculptures, or natural phenomena like roses and sunsets. The poem *Wanderers Nachtlied* by Goethe is such a vivid evocation of nightfall that only the most insensitive could fail to relive the atmosphere of a previously experienced twilight:

Über allen Gipfeln	Over all the hilltops
Ist Ruh,	is calm.
In allen Wipfeln	In all the treetops
Spürest du	you feel
Kaum einen Hauch;	hardly a breath of air.
Die Vögelein schweigen in Walde.	The little birds fall silent in the woods.
Warte nur, balde	Just wait . . . soon
Ruhest du auch.	You'll also be at rest.

It is not certain that one relives any one particular twilight hour; it may simply be an intuitive combination of all the twilight hours of one's life, which together form a concept that merges with the text's notion of twilight and lends the concept emotional richness.

When the author draws on such intersubjective experiences of beauty, the aesthetic attitude of the reader is automatically involved. In this case, the aesthetic effect is intentional and constitutes an indisputably aesthetic element of the work. However, no more than the currants of a currant bun are representative of the ingredients of the dough, the embedding of such aesthetic motives does not imply that the action in itself has an aesthetic function. It is self-evident that an aesthetic motive, whether in a poem or a novel, produces an aesthetic experience, just as a painting of a sunset can evoke the same feeling as the original sunset. But the fact that the sunset has been painted on the canvas by a conscious mind implies that the painter is trying to convey a message. He wants to tell something by means of the sunset, perhaps no more than that sunsets are beautiful. Consequently, the painting conveys a cognitive content, an invitation to look for sunsets or at least to take the time to contemplate it when we run into one. So in addition to the aesthetic component of the original sunset, the painting also has a cognitive component. In this case there is an essential difference between the aesthetic experience and the rendering of it. If admiring a sunset inspires you to see more sunsets, this is no message from the sunset, only a reaction to the experience, whereas the painting by virtue of its existence alone is a message about the sunset it recreates. It is at once an experience and a sign. In this way aesthetic motives are part of a superior cognitive perspective, where they are thematized and become part of the cognitive content.

If the action of a literary work is not capable of eliciting an aesthetic response in its own right, as is the case in *Mrs Dalloway*, then this action as a whole is not an aesthetic object. To conceive of Septimus's tragedy or Clarissa's regrets and doubts as aesthetic objects, one would have to either be emotionally stunted or confuse an admiration for the novel's successful structure with aesthetic pleasure. Human behaviour in fictional action does not attract aesthetic attention any more than it does in everyday life. Except for passages rendering objects that are aesthetic in their own right, aesthetic pleasure is not the reason why readers are carried away by the action of a novel or a drama. The reason lies rather in its cognitive function, even though other functions may also have their role as well.

Does the mental model have an aesthetic function?

In spite of the current view that discourse and style are aesthetic phenomena, the mental model of the action is primarily a means of conveying a cognitive content; it is just a vehicle to convey the message. Its structure deviates clearly from that of the fresh, untouched action, which it can only render in a deficient manner. The structural limitations of the model compel the author to choose between different narratological and stylistic options – selection, duration, point of view, voice, frequency, order, metaphors, tropes and various other stylistic devices – all of which primarily have a semantic function, influencing the reader's reactions to the action. A constant internal viewpoint affects, for instance, the reader's sympathies, while the order in which the events are presented controls his attention and expectations, highlighting or obscuring connections and contexts. Metaphors and tropes can have an explanatory function or influence the reader's focus by presenting objects in an unfamiliar way; this is what Shklovsky (1990) calls *defamiliarization* (a cognitive device that frees the reader of his customary automatic reactions to the object and shifts the focus to the object's very nature, making him perceive consciously, see Ingarden 1968, 72–3, 84).

According to the prevailing view, style is a purely linguistic feature, and would seem to have little to do with our new concept of *mental model*. The traditional narratological terms of *discourse* or *text* are generally preferred over style, because discourse and (especially) text are closely associated with language and blend in nicely with a linguistic conception of style. In reality, this harmony is deceptive and tends to conceal the essential distinction between language and its meaning, between signifier and signified. One cannot change the signifier without somehow changing the signified. There are innumerable individual ways to shape the language of a text, but every linguistic feature is echoed in the inherent mental model. It is impossible, strictly speaking, to write about the same thing in different ways, because each change affects the mental model of the action and the reader's reactions. Even synonymous expressions have different connotations which entail corresponding alterations in the mental model. For example, if you use passive instead of the active voice ('she was hit by a car' instead of 'a car hit her'), you foreground the object at the expense of the subject, and the noun *lady* carries other social implications than *woman*. In lyric poetry, rhyme, metrics and enjambment draw attention to particular words and often also have an iconic function. This shows that the structure of the mental model, including style, plays a cognitive role. Can it also have an aesthetic function?

The mental model of the action comprises the structure of the action as well as the structure that renders the action. It is difficult to isolate the structure from the object it contains without its being influenced by the object itself. Is it possible to enjoy the narratological and stylistic features of a fictional work for their own sake? When we drink a glass of wine, we usually direct our attention to the qualities of the wine instead of the glass, but nothing prevents us from shifting our attention to the glass. The glass is, however, a solid, separate object in its own right, whereas point of view, voice, duration, frequency, order, selection, metaphors and tropes and style are abstract notions, and it is difficult to imagine that one can enjoy them for their own sake, apart from their communicative function. It is more probable that they attain their value through the interplay with the action and the cognitive content. This value is cognitive, not aesthetic. One cannot praise the use of the first person, the present tense, anachronies or a special metaphor *for their own sake*, because that would imply that a story in the first person would be superior or inferior to a story in the second or third person, that the present tense would have a higher or lower aesthetic value than the past tense, that anachronies would be more or less valuable than historical faithfulness or that metaphors would be more or less preferable to direct description. It is hard to imagine anyone reading a novel only for the sake of narratological and stylistic devices, in complete disregard of the fictional world as such.

It seems more likely that we appreciate narratological and stylistic features because of their function in the communication process. We do not appreciate the use of the first person or the present tense in a novel for their own sake, but because these choices are well-suited for mediating the cognitive content to the reader. Likewise, if someone appreciates a metaphor, it is not due to its beauty as a verbal expression, but because of how well it expresses the underlying meaning. The primary communicative role of the mental model and its close relationship to the cognitive content (the message) are evidenced by the expectations of readers and critics, who would pounce to criticize the work if the structure of the action, the mental model or the text in any way interfered with their reception of the cognitive content (as they interpret it). Of course, the predominance of the cognitive function does not preclude an additional minor aesthetic function, but any such function would be difficult to prove; the mental nature of the model makes it all too easy to mix it up with other qualities, as when, for example, the communicative adequacy of the mental model is mistaken for an aesthetic quality.

Of course, the mental nature of the model of the action also makes it difficult to repudiate the possibility of the model having an aesthetic effect. Instead of basing our arguments solely on introspection, we must also draw on external facts, like statements from authors, readers and critics about their intentions and expectations. However, although such statements confirm the importance of cognition in fiction and despite the fact that statements in favour of an aesthetic conception of discourse and style may be based on theoretical fallacies and misinterpretations of introspective observations, we cannot completely rule out that the mental model has an aesthetic aspect. This is not, however, important, as long as we acknowledge cognition as the major function of the model.

Does the cognitive content have an aesthetic function?

The highest level of the communication process is the cognitive content, and ironically, this may also theoretically have an aesthetic aspect. What this would mean is that the reader perceives the information he extrapolates from the mental model of the action as aesthetically appealing or repulsive. Here we face the same problem we had with respect to the aesthetic function of the mental model. It is difficult to distinguish aesthetic impulses from other impulses at such an abstract level, and to determine whether the author has intended to elicit an aesthetic response from the cognitive content and whether readers in general comply with this intention. It would only be relevant to assign an aesthetic function to it if it were a recurrent feature of fictional literature, intended and expected by author and reader respectively. But it is unlikely that the abstract information inherent in literature elicits an aesthetic response from readers in general. That would imply that the readers of *Uncle Tom's Cabin* would attribute aesthetic qualities to its anti-slavery and feminist messages, which seems as improbable as a student scrutinizing his algebra book for the beauty of its content.

Does the interplay between the levels have an aesthetic function?

We have been searching for an aesthetic intention on the different levels of the literary communication process without finding any convincing indication of it. However, according to Ingarden (1968, 72–3, 84), the interplay between different levels is a polyphonous aesthetic experience, which is the main function of literary art. Is it possible that the interplay between the levels produces an aesthetic effect that none has on its own? In this context, a comparison with musical polyphony may be useful. In a symphony, the individual parts have an aesthetic value of their own, and although the interplay increases their value considerably, it is possible to enjoy them separately. In contrast, the levels of the literary communication process have little or no individual aesthetic value, which makes it doubtful that their interplay should attain an aesthetic value. After all, another difference between a symphony and fiction is the fact that the parts of the symphony are all equivalent, so no part is the vehicle for another. If you omit one, something might perhaps sound a bit off, but the music goes on. The levels of the literary communication process are arranged hierarchically, which brings communication to a halt if you remove one of the basic levels, since the higher levels then fail to materialize. Everything indicates that the author has intended the text, the mental model and the action to be vehicles for the cognitive content and nothing else. For instance, the only value of the action, as fiction, is as an imitation of the existing world, and the reader pays close attention to it only as long as he feels he derives cognitive benefit from it. His sole objective is to receive the cognitive content; the lower levels of the communication process are of interest solely as vehicles for the cognitive content. There is nothing to indicate that typography, sound or the mental model (the discourse) continues to reverberate in the mind after delivering the next level. This is akin to losing interest in the postman as soon as he has delivered the letter we were waiting for. It is as absurd to compare the literary communication process to a polyphonous musical work as it is to regard a relay race as polyphonous. Although the levels of the reading process are almost simultaneous, making it difficult to discriminate between them temporally, they still form an obvious cause and effect chain, whereas polyphony is simultaneous and not hierarchical.

I have tried to show that cognition is a major function in literary fiction and that aesthetic aspects play little or no role in the communication process. Fiction's cognitive function is no longer controversial, whereas denying aesthetic aspects in fiction still is. Here we must remember that the aesthetic qualities attributed to fiction have largely been based on a meaning of the word *aesthetic* that refers to art in general (aesthetic [2]) and has nothing to do with the aesthetic experience (aesthetic [1]). Only after clearing up this misunderstanding will we be able to make an unprejudiced analysis of possible aesthetic aspects of the literary communication process.

Must fiction have an aesthetic dimension in order to be art?

If we detach the term *aesthetic* from the philosophical discipline of *aesthetics* and use it in Genette's sense (with the abovementioned modifications), the aesthetic component disappears from literary fiction or plays at most a minor role. Here I disregard the cases in which aesthetic objects are embedded in the action in order to call forth an aesthetic response. The idea that literature must have an aesthetic function is a myth based on an inaccurate analogy with those arts that have an obvious aesthetic aspect. In this respect I am on collision course with Genette's definition of art, which requires at least a minimum of intended aesthetic appreciation. Since, as we have seen, literary fiction often lacks this minimum, it cannot be art according to Genette's definition. But in spite of Genette, all language users conceive of literature as indisputably art. After Wittgenstein's notion of family resemblance, literature is not required to have the aesthetic aspect shared by all the other arts; it has many qualities that link it now to one, now to another of the other arts – features that can explain why we associate literature with art. Such features may be the relaxed, detached situation of the reader when reading, the demanding form of literary works, the author's status in society as a creative person and so forth.

Beardsley provides five criteria in his definition of the aesthetic experience (Beardsley 1982, 288): (1) orientation towards an object, (2) having the air of being freely chosen, (3) emotional distance from the object, (4) active discovery of connections etc., and (5) a sense of integration between oneself as a person and the object of interest. According to Beardsley, not all of these conditions have to be satisfied for an experience to be aesthetic. These criteria apply to art in general but are also valid for literature: (1) the reader's attention is focused on the work, (2) no practical considerations disturb him, (3) he is distanced from the work, the information he receives having no specific reference (only general) or 'return address' obliging him to have consideration for the sender, (4) the work invites him to interpret and reflect, and (5) it may give him a feeling of integration, although the last item is somewhat obscure. Indeed, Beardsley's definition is far too vague to be useful. It seems rather that he bases his definition on the literary experience instead of on aesthetic situations, so instead of defining the aesthetic experience, he defines aspects of reading fiction. Such misunderstandings occur easily as long as literature is considered an aesthetic object in line with painting, sculpture and music.

The cognitive function and consciousness

An equivocal conception of the aesthetic is in part why Ingarden and others assign it a major role in literature. Another explanation may run as follows. When the reader uses the literary work as a source of general information about the existing world, the reception of information largely occurs unconsciously. The reader must concentrate on the structure of the action in order to extrapolate general patterns about the extratextual world, and because the cognitive process is largely unconscious, he retains the impression that the fictive action interests him for its own sake, and fails to see its cognitive function. The literary learning process is not unconscious per se but occurs at such a low level of consciousness that the reader does not usually reflect on what he is doing. He is therefore only likely to notice the mental model of the action and the emotions and associations it evokes, when it is the cognitive process that is the real cause of the emotions. Nevertheless, he is affected by the cognitive process. When we observe the things that happen in our own lives, we are not conscious of being subject to a learning process either, but it alters our knowledge and understanding of the world all the same.

We may compare the reader's unconscious relationship to the cognitive process with the relationship people have to food in affluent parts of the world: we eat for enjoyment and forget that food's original function is to keep us alive. Were it not for the bathroom scales' unpleasant reminders or the news about third-world famine, we might forget entirely that food is more than a source of enjoyment. Similarly, we forget that reading novels or going to the theatre makes us wiser, and in many ways it is much easier to overlook the cognitive process than to forget the nutritional necessities provided by food.

In spite of their analysing the action and establishing themes and theses, all of which are incontestably cognitive activities, literary scholars and critics are per se no more conscious of the cognitive function of fiction than lay people are. Perhaps they do not recognize this cognitive activity because they regard the themes and theses as intratextual, immanent phenomena, which makes them unwilling or unable to see the indirect reference to the extratextual world. It could also be that on account of their ambiguous notion of the aesthetic, they consider thematic analysis an aesthetic activity; something like this is probably why Ingarden denies that literature has a cognitive function.

Evidence of the cognitive function

Even if the cognitive process is unconscious, it can be traced in the mind as emotions that reflect the reading process's capacity to meet the reader's various needs: his need, on the one hand, for entertainment and leisure activity, and on the other for information about the real world. These emotions manifest themselves as various forms of suspense, satisfaction, frustration, approval and rejection, and this range of feelings occupies the reader so completely that it at least contributes to passing the time and – if the emotions are on balance positive – serves as entertainment. However, these feelings are not due to any aesthetic experience (with the exception of effects caused by embedded aesthetic elements); instead, they are derived from the provision of general information about the existing world, which yields pleasure because it seems useful or creates optimism. Information that strengthens our faith in the future, confirming our highest wishes and needs, provides a rush of positive emotions. As noted in Chapter 3, seeing people we identify with success boosts our optimism, since we are inclined to regard things that repeat themselves as a law. The more we witness the success of others, the stronger our belief that it will soon be our turn. Popular literature (for instance, in an American context, Horatio Alger novels) exploits this by primarily depicting human success, often at the expense of the truth because it simplifies problems and suggests unrealistic solutions. Although serious literature makes us confront unpleasant issues and evokes negative feelings, this too has an entertaining effect, not by creating a feeling of pleasure but by gripping us in other important ways: politically, psychologically, morally, intellectually and so on. The emotions evoked by the reading process tend to draw attention away from the cognitive content that causes them, and one might easily think that they are the end goal of reading. In reality, they are merely a measure of the extent to which the real end goal, the cognitive content (the message), is reached.

The fact that the cognitive influence is largely unconscious explains, of course, why it is so easy to overlook it; its emotional symptoms are more easily detectable on the surface. But we have seen how the structure of the work clearly indicates a cognitive function, along with other evidence outside the work that is related to the author as well as to the reader. In private conversation, readers betray their cognitive mentality when they answer the question, 'What is this literary work about?', by often giving a summary of the action, without noticing the difference, while at other times they indicate a theme or even a thesis. Even calling something a love story or a social drama evidences abstraction and generalization, which are cognitive activities.

Furthermore, the very practice of literary research and criticism reveals an obvious orientation towards a cognitive understanding of fiction. Cognitive criteria prevail in the examples provided in John Jørgensen's monograph on evaluation (Jørgensen 1971), although aesthetic criteria also seem to be represented. *Truth*, along with synonyms like *veracity*, *probability* and *realism*, is such a cognitive value criterion. In this case, truth does not refer to any identity between the action and specific real events but to the likeness shared between the thematic elements of the action and corresponding elements in the extratextual world. This similarity is a condition for learning something about the structures and relations of the real world. In order to conform with reality, it is less essential for the surface structure of the action to be realistic as long as the underlying structures are, for instance in symbolic and allegorical literature or works employing auxiliary structures to convey a true message. *The Little Prince* is an example of both.

More evidence of the cognitive attitude comes from scholars' use of the truth criterion to denigrate popular literature. If popular literature is to be shunned because the picture of reality it offers is false, then we have based our judgement on cognitive considerations. *Importance* or *universality* – other terms used against popular literature – are also value criteria; as mentioned above, Lamarque and Olsen hold that literature must have a universal theme to be 'good and grand' (Lamarque and Olsen 1994, 434–5).

Moreover, if one scrutinizes aesthetic criteria, one discovers that they, too, are directed towards the cognitive aspect. *Complexity* and *unity* are two examples of traditional aesthetic criteria for literary value. The criterion of *complexity* can refer to the structure of the action as well as that of the mental model. According to this criterion (which Nøjgaard 1996, 285–6, rejects as false), a complex structure of action (story) or mental model (discourse) is better than a simple one. The reason for this criterion could be the conviction that more proficiency is needed to master a complex work. Another reason might be the belief that complex events are more interesting than simple ones, for example because it is easier to understand simple relations than complex ones. The first reason applies to the structure of the action as well as to that of the mental model, while the second pertains only to the action. The action is the very basis of the insight that the reader extrapolates, but we have also seen that the mental model (the discourse) contributes to the cognitive content by influencing the reader's reaction to the action.

The claim concerning unity also has a cognitive function that has to do with saving time as well as with communication as such. Irrelevant elements take up valuable time and confuse the reader, who thinks they have a function and tries to interpret the whole in a way that makes them fit in. It is an old convention that informative presentations should contain only pertinent elements, and classical theory has transferred this rule to literary fiction. The criterion is debatable, but in our context it is useful because it betrays a cognitive attitude to fictional literature.

Finally, Nøjgaard mentions another piece of circumstantial evidence for the cognitive function of fiction: we speak of works of the other arts as beautiful or ugly, which are aesthetic properties, whereas we call literary works interesting or boring, which are cognitive qualities.

5

The Delimitation of the Literary Work

Contrary to most other disciplines, literary studies has not yet succeeded in delimiting its object in a way that has found general acceptance. There is not even so much as a consensus about the kind of objects the notion of *literature* should comprise. If we link the concept only to written texts, drama again blurs the boundaries with opera, pantomime, film and cartoons. Another exception must be made for oral tradition, as well as for diaries, letters, travelogues, myths and essays politically politically, not to mention non-fiction. Fictionality invites us to consider even jokes as literature. A further complication is the link between the definition of literature and value, as many scholars reserve the term *literature* only for serious literature, excluding popular literature (Lamarque and Olsen 1994, 255, 426–7).

The distinction between literature and non-literary phenomena is, however, too comprehensive a subject to be included in this investigation. This chapter will be dedicated to the interaction between the reader and the literary work. In scholarly as well as in everyday contexts, we speak of the *work* and have some intuition about what it means, but despite various attempts to define the concept, the issue is far from settled.

In his attempt at a definition, I. A. Richards does not even venture to distinguish the reader's experience from that of the author (Richards 2001, 211). He proposes four possible definitions:

> The superstition which any language not intolerably prolix and uncouth encourages that there is something actual, *the poem*, which all readers have access to and upon which they pass judgment, misleads us. . . . We may be talking about the artist's experience, such of it as is relevant, or about the experience of a qualified reader who made no mistakes, or about an ideal and perfect reader's possible experience, or about our own actual experience.

In the end, he opts for a definition of the work 'as a class of experiences which do not differ in any character more than a certain amount, varying for each character, from a standard experience. We may take as this standard experience the relevant experience of the poet when contemplating the completed composition' (Richards 2001, 212–13). What is a standard experience and to which levels of the reading process does it refer?

We find an equally obscure concept of the work in the reader-response theory advanced by Stanley Fish. Fish 1980 (167–8) thinks the reader creates the text (work) in interpreting it; the work is not a single entity common to all readers but rather contingent entities that vary from reader to reader. Nevertheless, text interpretation is not entirely contingent, as it is governed by the individual reader's belonging to *an interpretative community*. The members of a given social group share more or less the same worldview and tend to interpret texts along the same lines, applying a common set of interpretative strategies that they have learnt as members of that group. According to Fish, interpretative communities preserve a kind of unity in preventing the work from splitting up into too many different works.

Fish's interpretative communities are not, however, sufficient to stabilize the work as a common entity, because the members of such a community do not form a stable, uniform group. There will always be movement and overlap between different interpretative communities, blurring the boundaries between them and disrupting their homogeneity. Even if every interpretative community were completely homogeneous, this would not prevent the splitting of the work, as each community would have their own set of interpretations and every interpretation would be another work. Shakespeare's *Hamlet* would be as many different works as there were readers or spectators.

E. D. Hirsch is probably the most renowned representative of the opposite opinion. He maintains that the work is a constant entity and that we must distinguish between an invariable and a variable part of the reading process (Hirsch 1967). This view is endorsed by scholars such as Umberto Eco (Eco 1996) and Jan Mukařovsky (Mukařovsky 1970). We may call those scholars *subjectivists* that argue that the work is subjective and relative, and the Hirsch faction *objectivists*. I will try to show that the disagreement between the two groups may be based on an equivocal conception of the reading process.

The text and the mental model of the action

Intuitively, we conceptualize the literary work as a constant, recognizable entity shared by all readers, a conception confirmed by common usage. This is what allows a conversation like the following:

> Peter: "I have just finished *Cakes and Ale* by Somerset Maugham. I think
>   it is an interesting novel."
> Mary: "I've read it, too, but I found it a little boring."

Two different people who have read *Cakes and Ale* obviously think they were reading the same novel or the same work, but their reactions were different, and they express this through contradictory evaluations of the book. Their relation to this novel is characterized by a mutual experience (the same work) as well as by a non-mutual one (different reactions). To delimit the work we must distinguish the part of the reading experience that is shared by all readers from those that are not. Therefore, we must sort out the constituent parts of the experience in order to test which of them readers have in common and which they do not.

The model of the fictional communication process we developed in Chapter 3 must form the basis of our attempt to define the work. We originally distinguished between four levels, but for the definition of the work it is not necessary to discriminate between the action and the model of it, as they may be considered one level in this context. It is sufficient to distinguish between three levels: (1) the material text, (2) the mental model of the action and (3) the message (the cognitive content).

To what extent are the text, the model and the message common to all readers? At minimum, it is evident that the visual text is shared by all readers, and in practice, the oral version it conveys is also the same, to such an extent that it should not be necessary to distinguish between the visual and the oral text. We can safely consider the text an experience common to all readers. This is the basis of Nelson Goodman's definition of the work as the text (Goodman 1988, 207–8).

However, if we only consider the text without considering its semantic aspect, we have a problem. To be sure, it seems satisfactory to regard the text as the work as long as two users who share the same mother tongue talk about having read the same novel. We can, it seems, substitute the term *text* for *novel* without any consequences: 'I have just read the text of *Cakes and Ale*.' 'Yes, I've read it, too.' Nevertheless, if we replace one of the speakers with a foreigner who has only learnt to pronounce the words without understanding them, nobody would say that he had read the text in the sense of comprehending it. Having read a text means something more than mechanically reproducing the sounds. You have to understand the words and sentences, or in other words, you must be able to receive the mental model of the action, the signified. Nobody has read a novel until he has conceptualized the mental model. Because the mental model of the action is inseparably linked to the text, it is something the readers have in common just as much as the text on which it is based. However, we must take care not to confuse the mental model with all the other mental activities that are also part of the reading process. To delimit the mental model evoked by the sentence, 'He sat down on a chair,' we have to strip our conception of this event of any individualizing depiction of the subject and the chair, as well as of any subjective notion of how the act of sitting down is performed; such details are subjective supplements and cannot be part of the mental model as we have thus far understood it. Of course, the individual details with which the reader supplements the original model create a new and more extensive mental model of the action, but in this book, I apply *mental model* in its restricted sense, as the mental model shared by all readers. The mental model of the action is by definition the idea of the events that all readers have in common. Consequently, Septimus's suicide and Clarissa's interest in Peter are indispensible parts of the mental model of the action in *Mrs Dalloway*, while the sexual tendencies of Septimus and Clarissa fall outside the model, depending on speculation that will differ from reader to reader.

The term *mental model* accounts primarily for the *explicit* elements of the action, but also includes *implicit* elements that all readers fill in identically because they share the same prior knowledge. This applies, for example, to the law of gravitation, geographic and historical facts, general knowledge about human beings and so forth. In other words, the mental model consists not only of explicit elements but also of implicit ones, as long as they are the same across all readers.

Defining the mental model as that part of the reading experience that is shared by all readers distinguishes clearly, in principle, between the mental model and the reader's further interpretation and elaboration of it, but in practice, the boundary may be less precise due to the implicit elements of the model. While the explicit elements are unquestionably part of the model, the boundary between intersubjective and subjective implicit elements is not always as easy to pin down; indeed, it may be open to debate whether particular elements are a legitimate part of the mental model. Let us look at a couple of specific examples of this.

We are already acquainted with Bradshaw's analysis of *Mrs Dalloway*, in which he argues that Clarissa is unstable and may be suicidal. The crux of the matter here is whether the examples we find in the text are sufficient evidence of depressive and suicidal tendencies (Woolf 2000, xix–xx). Although Bradshaw succeeds in finding a surprising amount of circumstantial evidence in the mental model itself, which may be hints from the author, the evidence offered by action itself is less conclusive (7, 157):

> She felt very young; at the same time unspeakably aged. She sliced like a knife through everything; at the same time was outside, looking on. She had a perpetual sense, as she watched the taxicabs, of being out, out, far out to sea and alone; she always had the feeling that it was very, very dangerous to live even one day.

Then (she had felt it only this morning) there was the terror; the overwhelming incapacity, one's parents giving into one's hands, this life, to be lived to the end, to be walked with serenely; there was in the depths of her heart an awful fear. Even now, quite often if Richard had not been there reading *The Times*, so that she could crouch like a bird and gradually revive, send roaring up that immeasurable delight, rubbing stick to stick, one thing with another, she must have perished. She had escaped. But that young man had killed himself.

Bradshaw bases his conclusions mainly on a parallel between Clarissa and Septimus, whom she never meets but only hears about at her evening party at the end of the action, where his suicide is mentioned. Admittedly, the model of the action seems to link the two associatively (through references to birds, for instance). It is not, however, certain that all readers would agree that Clarissa's fear of death really means that she is suicidal, even though the sentence 'She had escaped' implies that she has felt the threat. Although there is plenty of evidence to corroborate Bradshaw's interpretation, there remains sufficient doubt to exclude it from the mental model.

In contrast to this, *Three Men in a Boat* by Jerome K. Jerome contains an example of an interpretation that is unquestionably intersubjective (Jerome 1975, 7):

> There were four of us – George, and William Samuel Harris, and myself, and Montmorency. We were sitting in my room, smoking, and talking about how bad we were – from a medical point of view I mean, of course.
>
> We were all feeling seedy, and we were getting quite nervous about it. Harris said he felt such extraordinary fits of giddiness come over him at times, that he hardly knew what he was doing; and then George said that *he* had fits of giddiness too, and hardly knew what *he* was doing. With me, it was my liver that was out of order, because I had just been reading a patent liver-pill circular, in which were detailed various symptoms by which a man could tell when his liver was out of order. I had them all.

Here we meet three young men who think they are very ill indeed, but every normal reader sees through the irony, exposing them as hypochondriacs. The irony is accentuated through exaggeration ('I had them all') and behaviour that would be familiar to readers as typical of hypochondriacs. Therefore, the inference of hypochondria is intersubjective enough to be considered an integrated part of the mental model of the action.

The boundary between intersubjective and subjective inferences is, of course, subject to individual judgement. One indication that an interpretative supplement should not be regarded as part of the model is a lack of consensus among readers, as disputed elements fall outside the framework of the mental model. In *Mrs Dalloway*, Clarissa's motives for not marrying Peter or for being attracted by Sally give room for speculation (did she marry Richard owing to his money or position and did she have lesbian inclinations?), and as speculation, they do not belong to the mental model.

So far, we have only considered ambiguities in the mental model and the action. What about ambiguities in the text, such as obscure metaphors? In such cases, we risk some readers choosing one interpretation and others a different one. What relationship do such ambiguities have to the work? A typical example is Milton's twentieth sonnet, 'Lawrence of virtuous father virtuous son', which we already saw mentioned in Fish's theory of interpretative communities (Fish 1980, 149–50, Milton 1968):

Lawrence of virtuous father virtuous son,
    Now that the fields are dank, and ways are mire,
    Where shall we sometimes meet, and by the fire
    Help waste a sullen day; what may be won
From the hard season gaining; time will run
    On smoother, till Favonious reinspire
    The frozen earth; and clothe in fresh attire
    The lily and rose, that neither sowed nor spun.
What neat repast shall feast us, light and choice,
    Of attic taste, with wine, whence we may rise
    To hear the lute well touched, or artful voice
Warble immortal notes and Tuscan air?
    He who of those delights can judge, and spare
    To interpose them oft, is not unwise.

Fish points out that the word *spare* in the penultimate line has generated controversy, since it can be read as *leave time for* as well as, as *refrain from*. 'In one reading "those delights" are being recommended—he who can leave time for them is not unwise; in the other, they are the subject of a warning—he who knows when to refrain from them is not unwise' (150).

Context ensures that such problems seldom arise on crucial points, but when they do, the ambiguity is part of the model, and the model is simply deficient on such points. It is comparable to a novel whose ending is left open: when the action stops abruptly, any further development is simply not part of the mental model of the action. The point is that we only regard the conceptualizations of the action shared by all readers as identical with the model. Contradictory interpretations that arise from verbal ambiguity are therefore not part of the model, which remains open on such points.

The dramatic text has the same potential for ambiguity as the novel, but the ambiguity only pertains to the side text (stage directions and the like). Ambiguous words and constructions in the main text (the dialogue) are elements in the fictional world and contribute to the representation of characters and events. The same applies, of course, to the direct speech in novels. When the drama is performed on the stage, the text is transformed into three-dimensional physical action and the spectator faces what is in principle an unambiguous model of the action. We can discuss how readers comprehend the written sentence, 'He sat down slowly on the chair', whereas in the theatre there can be no doubt about how slowly he sat down because everyone sees it with his own eyes. This does not imply that theatre is exempt from verbal ambiguity on the level of the dramatic text, but rather that the director, scenographer and actors fill in these gaps for the spectator.

Both text and model can be defined as the work since they are shared by all readers. Moreover, certain properties of the mental model of the action, such as the order of events, rhythm and rhyme, are primarily linked to the text (language), but only make sense in relation to the mental model. Therefore, it is necessary to include both text and mental model in a delimitation of the work.

The message

What is the relationship between the cognitive content and the work? Is the message constant enough to be regarded as part of the work? When fictional works are subject to conflicting interpretations, it is not usually because the text itself is equivocal but because the receiver uses the mental model of the action to enhance his understanding of the existing world, trying to interpret the behaviour of the characters and the interplay between the various factors of the action in a psychological, sociological, philosophical or ethical perspective. Different interpretations arise from each reader's extrapolation of the cognitive content. Each reader may have his own ideas about why Clarissa did not marry Peter or have a lesbian relationship with Sally and about what lessons can be drawn from these situations. Since the message depends on not only the structure of the mental model but also the individual background and qualifications of the reader, it is an effect of and a reaction to the work (i.e. the symbiosis of text and model) and is not shared by all readers. Therefore, it cannot be part of the work.

We can compare the work and the cognitive content to the conditions required to plant a seed. When it has been sown, the results depend both on its genetic properties and on its external conditions pertaining to soil, light, temperature and water. Under different conditions, the same seed may give birth to different plants that share only a common genetic background. Similarly, differences of personality and background entail a splitting of the work into different reader experiences. The fictional core of the communication, the mental model of the action, remains unchanged, but the reality-oriented interpretation of it, the cognitive content, varies from reader to reader. Among the different levels of literary communication, we can now identify the text and the mental model of the action as the work, whereas the cognitive content, the message, must be excluded from it. I do not mention the action in this context, as it is just a projection of the mental model and is hence closely related to it.

In *Theory of Literature* (Wellek and Warren 1954, 142–7), Wellek and Warren discuss whether the mental experience of the reader can be a possible candidate for *the work itself* (in their words, 'the poem itself'). After dismissing the written and oral text as candidates, they also reject the reader's mental experience, arguing first, that if the reader's mental experience were the work, there would be as many works as there are readers, and second, that the work exists whether it is experienced or not. The first argument fails because Wellek and Warren do not discriminate between the mental model of the action, which is shared by all readers, and the message, which is an effect of the mental model and varies according to readers' backgrounds and personalities. By defining the work as those parts of the experience that all readers have in common (the text and the mental model of the action), we prevent the *work* from slipping away into an endless profusion of readers' experiences. We pin the work down as something that all readers have in common so they can say that they have read the same work.

Wellek and Warren's second argument, that the work exists independently of being experienced, is no real argument. Verbal statements are impossible without a consciousness to decode them, because encoding and decoding go hand in hand; the sender has to understand what he is writing. Therefore, the work is at least experienced by the author.

We have seen that the reader's cognitive benefit from reading depends on the interplay between the mental model and his personal qualities, so it is not identical with the model. This also implies that the various perspectives into which the reader can put the action are not part of the model but an effect of it that belongs outside the work. Any angle from which you can see the action, whether psychoanalytic, sociological, Marxist, historical-biographical, feminist or post-colonial, is a way to extrapolate information from the action and is not part of the work itself. That does not mean, however, that these approaches are irrelevant to understanding the work; often the structure of the work even invites us to look at it from a particular angle. *Uncle Tom's Cabin*, for instance, encourages a feminist interpretation in addition to the traditional anti-racist interpretation (Tompkins 1985, 122–46).

Based on the distinction between text, mental model and message (cognitive content), we can elaborate our understanding of the communication process by distinguishing between four types of interpretation:

1. transformation of the text into a mental model of the action (shared primary meaning)
2. filling in gaps in the mental model with intersubjective knowledge (shared primary meaning: implicit material, like the law of gravitation)
3. filling in gaps in the mental model with subjective knowledge (individual primary meaning: for example, understanding interactions between characters on the basis of a given psychological theory)
4. application of the mental model to improve one's own worldview (secondary meaning: for example, changing or reinforcing one's own values and understanding of cause-effect relations)

Types 1 and 2 fall inside a framework shared by all readers and are part of a final version of the mental model that can be defined as the work itself, while type 3 is an extension of the mental model and falls outside the shared framework. Type 4 is the information the reader extracts from the action (and the model of it). A reader interpreting the behaviour of the doctors in *Mrs Dalloway* as a manifestation of professional culture (instead of, for instance, individual callousness) is an example of type 3, filling gaps with subjective knowledge. We cannot assume that all readers would agree, so this interpretation cannot be considered part of the work. If a reader concludes that it is very difficult to choose the right partner or that one should follow one's feelings when choosing a partner, these are examples of messages, which fall under type 4.

Drama and lyric poetry

As we have seen, drama is a special case because the actors and producers create the performance by filling the gaps of the mental model that is based on the written text. The written version of the drama does not affect the delimitation of the work, since all readers share its mental model of the action just as they share the novel's mental model. However, from the moment the play is performed on the stage, the delimitation of the work becomes more complicated. If we regard the theatre performance as an independent work of art, it becomes a cooperative project between author, director, actors and other theatre personnel. To what extent can different performances of Ibsen's *The Wild Duck* be said to be the same work?

Goodman compares the theatre performance to a musical work, in that the performance represents the work as a member of a *compliance class* (Goodman 1988, 143–4, 210). A performance is representative of the work (falls inside the class of performances that we identify as the work) when it complies with the text. Goodman's definition leaves room for individual judgement: what is sufficient compliance? For the drama, compliance is ensured if the theatre group follows the dialogue and the stage directions. Different performances of *The Wild Duck* retain their identity as realizations of the same work despite varying scenography and staging as long as they respect Ibsen's dialogue and the stage directions. The dramatic work is therefore shared by all possible and actual audiences with the exception of the individual features imposed by each particular performance on the original mental model of the action. The physical appearance of the actors and the stage are not part of the work itself, apart from general descriptions given in the text, like age, gender, hair colour and so on. When the title character of Saint-Exupéry's *The Little Prince* is played by a woman instead of a little boy, the audience understands that the female actor is meant to represent a boy.

So far, we have stuck to fictional literature. What about non-fictional literary genres? What we have already said about the novel (apart from the special features pertaining to fictionality) also applies to diaries, letters and biographies, all of which have action. The work is the combination of the text and the mental model of the action. As such, the status of the work is not affected by the fact that non-fictional literature provides information about specific historical facts in addition to general information about the existing world (the message). Lyric poetry bears an ambiguous relationship to non-fiction, since it bears no label to indicate its status, apart from genres that are obviously fiction (like ballads) or non-fiction (like occasional poetry). Its status in relation to fiction and reality is therefore more or less uncertain, but this does not affect the definition of the work.

Ambiguous texts

So far, I have assumed that the text has been clear enough as a verbal expression to draw a satisfactory picture of the action. But some texts use such ambiguous language that the receiver is unable to reconstruct a clear model of the action (or of the abstract content if there is no action). Whereas epic and dramatic texts are more likely to reproduce the action clearly, certain kinds of lyric poems prove more resistant. This sort of poetry, which is typical of modernism, transfers a mental model so deficient that it is meaningless without a comprehensive interpretation in which the reader substitutes different expressions for every ambiguous expression in order to test out what fits best into the mental model as a whole. This means that he must also anticipate the potential cognitive content, because the model that provides the most plausible message is perhaps more likely to be the right one. In such cases, is it still possible to define the work as the combination of text and mental model, given the latter is so open and obscure? Yes, it is, but the material that readers have in common consists as much of unsolved riddles as comprehensible elements. In such cases, the work is no more identical with the conflicting interpretations than in other cases; it is the semantic basis that all readers have in common, or in other words, the common riddle everyone is confronted with. If the interpretation of the text or the model is so evident that all the receivers share it, it seems plausible to consider it a part of the work. Such interpretations amount to intersubjective filling of gaps.

What about literary genres that lack action? Some literary works, like essays or poetry with a general or abstract content, do away with action entirely, leaving only general statements about extratextual reality. In such cases, the author conveys his message directly, but even then ambiguities may arise, especially in modernist poetry (Simpson 1972, 276). Take, for instance, D. H. Lawrence's poem, 'As Far as I'm Concerned' (Lawrence 1977):

> The feelings I don't have I don't have.
> The feelings I don't have, I won't say I have.
> The feelings you say you have, you don't have.
> The feelings you would like us both to have, we neither of us have.
> The feelings people ought to have, they never have.
> If people say they've got feelings, you may be pretty sure they haven't
>   got them.
> So if you want either of us to feel anything at all
> You'd better abandon all idea of feelings altogether.

In this poem, the lyric subject, whom we can probably identify with the author himself, says directly what he thinks, without the intervention of events or action. Nevertheless, what the speaker really means to tell us is subject to interpretation. Why does he make all these statements about his own feelings and those of his receiver (who is not identical with the reader) and people in general? By feelings, he could mean love, because that is a common meaning when we say we do or do not have 'feelings'. If we could be sure that all readers construe 'feelings' as love, we could perhaps agree that it is a poem about love. Then we would perceive a conflict between the speaker and his silent conversation partner, in that the speaker does not return the love that his conversation partner purports to have. Moreover, the lyric *I* asserts that neither the person he is talking to nor anybody else ever feels love, even if they say they do. But there seems to be some hope: if the listener stops carping about her expectations and visions of love, maybe they would feel something similar to love. It might be that the *I* and the *you* both feel attracted to each other, but the *you* combines his or her feelings with expectations or demands that the *I* resents. These expectations or demands must be clear to the couple but are a mystery to the reader. Even if the interpretation of the feelings as love seems plausible and may find wide acceptance, 'feelings' could also mean solidarity with people in distress, a certain political affinity, or any number of things.

Therefore, we have to take into account that works that communicate directly, without taking the detour via an action (story), may be equivocal, too. Then the work is limited to the structures that all readers have in common, and all the controversial elements fall outside the notion of *the work*.

Reading in another order and repeated readings

Two possible objections to defining the work as the text and the mental model of the action involve, first, the reader's possibility of reading the text in a different order than the one in which it is written, and second, repeated readings. To what extent is the original order of the text an obligatory property of the text and of the symbiotic model? Can texts be read in another order or be reread and still be considered identical with the version linked to the first reading or to the normal order of reading? If we read *Mrs Dalloway* for the second time, or for the first time after prematurely peeking at the ending, are we then reading another work? The answer is no, we are not. To some extent, the problem is akin to what happens when we meet someone for the first time and afterwards get to know him better. We identify him as the same person every time we see him despite knowing increasingly more about him. Similarly, the text and the mental model of the action remain the same independently of reading order and frequency. Of course, the different order in which the elements of the action reach the reader influence his reactions, and similarly repeated readings shed new light on the action. But rereading *Mrs Dalloway* or reading it in a different order would neither change the events nor the narratological properties of the text and the mental model, like point of view, selection, voice, frequency and style, which would remain intersubjective. And to some extent, as a potential influence, even the original order of the text remains intact.

Defining the work as the combination of text and mental model and separating it from the cognitive content (information) sheds valuable light on the dichotomy between autonomy and heteronomy. For instance, by now it should be clear that neither the intention of the author nor the cognitive benefit of the reader is part of the work itself, only effects of it, the author's intention and the reader's cognitive benefit being respectively an intended effect and a realized effect of text and model. Admittedly, the author's intention determines the structure of the mental model, but is no more part of the model itself than the car designer's intention is part of the car. If, for instance, the car designer's intention is to create a car that has low maintenance costs and pollutes little, this wish is likely to be reflected in the car's structure, but it is not certain that the car will actually realize this intention. Similarly, it is far from certain that the ideological wishes of the author will actually be fulfilled by the reader, who may extract information from the model that is very different from what is intended by the author.

The simultaneity of the levels

It is easy to overlook the distinction between the mental model of the action and the reader's further use of it in the form of private associations, interpretation and cognitive benefit. This is due to the fact that we experience reading (or the theatre performance) as a complex whole, in line with what Ingarden describes as a polyphonous experience. There is no temporal boundary between the four levels of the reading process. At the same time as we perceive the text and decode it into a mental model, we interpret the mental model both as a manifestation of the action and as a model and extend all the levels of the experience with private associations. This merging of the different components of the reading process (or theatre experience) into a simultaneous, apparently homogeneous experience helps explain why it has been so difficult for literary scholars to discriminate between them.

In order to distinguish between the different levels of the experience, the scholar must concentrate consciously on one level at a time. This is akin to the way a conscious listener can separate and follow the individual melodic parts in a symphony, either managing to hear them separately and together at the same time or having to hear the symphony several times in order to concentrate on one or two parts. When reading, it is possible to concentrate on the typographic picture without involving the meaning of the signs. When reading aloud, we can listen to the quality of the sounds alone or concentrate on the action (as it is presented by the model), suppressing any tendency to create private associations or to interpret the action. And when we conceptualize 'clearly' the mental model that is shared by all readers, we can watch ourselves extrapolating general knowledge about the extratextual world, perhaps even scrutinizing our private associations one by one. Even though private associations are only of private interest, they contribute to the colouring of the total experience and may be phenomenologically interesting (Ingarden 1968; Falk 1981; Iser 1974); it is not clear, however, what role such free associations play in relation to filling gaps as Ingarden conceives it.

So far I have based the delimitation of the work on the presupposition that all readers decode the text in the same way and arrive at the same mental model. Perhaps it is time to consider some wiggle room for minimal deviations. After all, it is not certain that two different readers will understand every word in *exactly* the same way when it comes to the finest nuances. They may at times have slightly different connotations, and one of them may misunderstand a word here and there. There is always recourse to a dictionary to reveal such mistakes and confirm or dismiss the readers' experiences as right or wrong. In this case, one of the readers has read the same work as the other, but misunderstands the text in some respect. The problem is more serious when the dictionary cannot reveal any fault, for instance, when one reader considers a word vulgar and the other does not. Here we face two options: either to accept minimal differences as negligible and ignore them, or to regard the text as a *score* (in Goodman's sense of the word). In the latter case, we regard the mental model of the action as a performance that falls inside the framework of the work, which becomes a *compliance class*. The mental model is then shared by all readers in the same sense as two different pianists' performances of Beethoven's *Moonshine Sonata*. This sort of relativity does not diminish the importance of distinguishing the mental model from the receiver's further transformation of it into a cognitive content. As for the mental model, it is a question of minimal variations, whereas the variations in the cognitive content may be substantial.

Taking Goodman's notion of compliance classes further, one might be tempted to ask if it is also possible to define different readers' experiences as members of the same compliance class, which then would also be identical with the work. As long as the cognitive content can be traced back to and be supported by structures of the text and the mental model, the experience may be intersubjective enough to be defined as a performance that has the text and the mental model as a score. In some cases, where the mental model has a very clear, evocative structure, agreement about the gist of the communication may be widespread enough that this part of the cognitive content could be regarded as part of the work. Since such cases are exceptional, however, this has little bearing on our general concept of the work. As soon as some readers disagree about the interpretation, the disputed part of the experience falls outside the work.

Other theories

What sets the above description of the reading process apart is the concept of a *mental model* as a connecting link between the material text and the cognitive content (the message), and furthermore, the differentiation between different levels of interpretation that link the text to the final cognitive content. This differentiated description allows a more precise distinction between fixed and variable parts in the reading process. As mentioned in the introduction to this chapter, the fixed-variable distinction is common to many theories; nevertheless, my model of the reading process is the first to specify what the fixed and variable consist in. None of the other theorists takes into account the mental model of the action, nor do they differentiate between levels of interpretation.

Mukařovsky 1970 distinguishes between the material and the aesthetic object. The aesthetic object changes with time and society and therefore corresponds to the cognitive content that is an effect of the work. The material artefact, on the other hand, is fixed and corresponds to the material text before the reader has transformed it into a mental model. However, Mukařovsky does not take the mental model into account, thus omitting the crucial link between the text and the cognitive content and ultimately leaving the boundary between the fixed and variable parts unresolved.

Defending the relevance of the author's intention, E. D. Hirsch proposes a distinction between *meaning* and *significance, interpretation* and *criticism*, which seems to be an improvement on Mukařovsky's distinction (Hirsch 1967, 7–8):

> *Meaning* is that which is represented by a text; it is what the author meant by his use of a particular sign sequence; it is what the signs represent. *Significance*, on the other hand, names a relationship between that meaning and a person, or a conception, or a situation, or indeed anything imaginable.

Interpretation leads to *meaning*, and criticism entails *significance*. While the meaning of the work is fixed, its significance is subject to change.

Hirsch's example is the author who changes his attitude to his own work in the course of time, such as Arnold's public attack on his *Empedocles on Etna* (7). One problem with Hirsch's dichotomy, however, is that he does not allow for different literary expressions' making use of different forms of communication, each of which entails a different sort of interpretation process. In order to distinguish between the different levels of the experience, the scholar must concentrate consciously on one level at a time. This is akin to the way a conscious listener can separate and follow the individual melodic parts in a symphony, either managing to hear them separately and together at the same time or having to hear the symphony several times in order to concentrate on one or two melodic parts.

When communication is direct – for instance in statements like 'The sky is blue', 'The chair I'm sitting on is rickety' and 'Honesty is the best policy' – the surface structure of the utterance is identical with the underlying structure. In indirect communication, the surface structure (the mental model of the action) only serves as a vehicle for an underlying structure (the real content, or the information). Hirsch fails to consider that indirect communication entails more levels of meaning and interpretation than direct communication, and overlooks the importance of the mental model of the action (the signified) as an example and a basis for further interpretation. To be sure, he is not far from our distinction when discussing the example of biography (141):

> Interpretation corresponds to the understanding of a man's life as it was lived and experienced, while criticism corresponds to the placing of that life in a larger system of relationships. It is one thing to trace the life of Marlborough and another thing to discuss the significance of his life with respect to European political history.

Here he at least differentiates between two aspects of the action, which correspond to the mental model of the action (the man's life) and the subjective filling of gaps (placing that life in a larger system of relationships). However, he does not mention the further extrapolation of information about the world in general that characterizes fiction's indirect mode of communication.

Hirsch's example of Wordsworth's 'A slumber did my spirit seal' reveals a broad concept of *meaning*. He mentions two contradictory interpretations that do not concern the comprehension of the text itself (the transformation of the text into a mental model) but an assessment of the situation that the text depicts. This takes us to a secondary level of interpretation that pertains to values and information. Nevertheless, Hirsch considers both interpretations to centre on *meaning*, and consequently the only question is which assessment is right (227). Although Hirsch adheres to 'objective' interpretation, in practice his notion of *meaning* includes both the subjective filling of gaps (his biographical example) and the cognitive content, which overloads the notion of *meaning* and renders it useless. The combination of *meaning* and *interpretation* does not account for the distinction between the mental model and the message. Moreover, according to Hirsch's practice, the combination of *significance* and *criticism* accounts neither for the difference between the message and the author's attitude to it nor for the interplay between model and message.

However, even if we disregarded Hirsch's own equivocal use of these terms, they would still fall short in being made to cover too many concepts at once. Their ambiguity can be seen as deriving from Frege's *Sinn* and *Bedeutung*, which Hirsch draws upon (212). The dichotomies between *meaning* and *significance*, *interpretation* and *criticism* contribute as little to the distinction between the different levels of interpretation as Mukařovsky's dichotomy between *material* and *aesthetic object*.

Similarly, Umberto Eco's trichotomy between *the intention of the author*, *the intention of the text* and *the intention of the reader* fails to account for the reading process (Eco 1994, 64). Eco is aware that the text's intention is transformed into the reader's intention on its way to the reader and that it is only indirectly accessible through a hermeneutic circle, which is based on isotopies in the text (i.e. the context). But the three types of intention can all comprise the mental model as well as the cognitive content (message); insofar as they only refer to the cognitive content, which is their most usual sense, he does not take the mental model into account. The *text's intention* is perhaps what comes closest to the mental model, because it pertains to the interplay between the mental model and the message that the reader extracts from it, foregrounding the structural features of the text (and consequently, of the mental model) that determine the reader's interpretation.

I have tried to show that the text and the mental model it transfers to the reader are the same for all readers and can therefore be identified as the work itself. The work is invariable, with respect to both different contemporary readers and future generations of readers. But as long as scholars keep using *the work* to express both the constant (text and mental model) and the variable (the readers' individual reactions to and use of the mental model), the work will remain in limbo between the two aspects.

The distinction between the unity of text and mental model (including the intersubjective filling of gaps) on the one hand and the message (including subjective filling of gaps) on the other offers a bridge between the theories that regard the work as a variable entity (Richards, Fish) and those that conceive of it as invariable (Mukařovsky, Hirsch, Eco). A consensus would depend on the former's acceptance that the text and the mental model are shared (to a sufficient extent) by all readers and on the latter's equal acceptance that the cognitive aspect may differ from reader to reader. To this end, all scholars must share a minimum of confidence in the communicative power of language; if not, there will still be room for controversy. But our distinction makes it at least easier to discuss the communicative power of language without talking at cross purposes. I see no conflict between the objectivist theories of Mukařovsky, Hirsch, Eco and my own definition of the work.

I have based my definition on the readers' experience of the work as something invariable, and I have defined the work as those parts of the reading process that are common to all readers. The difference from previous definitions consists in an attempt to isolate and identify the invariable elements by means of the terms *mental model* and *cognitive content*. We have seen that the reader's addition to the primary mental model consists of various implicit elements that are mediated explicitly by the text, some of which are intersubjective, others subjective. Consciously or unconsciously, the author expects the reader to provide the intersubjective supplements, which become part of the model and the work, whereas the subjective elements that the reader adds to the mental model fall outside the work, even if they are linked to the model (by free associations or interpretation). In practice, this means that the work has a core that is sufficiently consistent and constant for the readers to share the same experience, while outside the boundaries of this core, there is a gradual transition from intersubjectivity into complete subjectivity. It is in this space (outside the core) that the reader's reactions to the action and the mental model of it (as cognitive stimuli) belong.

6

Intention and Message

When we discussed the fictional communication process, we devoted our attention to the interaction between the reader and the work, putting the role of the author to the side for the time being. In this chapter, we are going to take up the role of the author's intention in the communication process. The discussion over the relevance of this intention can be traced back to the publication of Wimsatt and Beardsley's 'The Intentional Fallacy' (Wimsatt and Beardsley 1954, 3–18), which dismissed authorial intention as irrelevant to literary analysis. It argues that if the author has succeeded in conveying his message, it is apparent from the work itself, so you need not look for evidence outside the work. Moreover, it is pointless to look beyond the text itself, because it is impossible to know the author's intention with certainty, and the meaning of the text changes, even for the author. The writer does often not know his own intention or may forget it.

Anti-intentionalism was advanced by not only the New Critics but also structuralists and post-structuralists like Roland Barthes (Barthes 1977, 142–8) and Michel Foucault (Foucault 1981), who both declared the death of the author. Anti-intentionalism has been attacked primarily by E. D. Hirsch, who holds that the objective of literary interpretation must be to reconstruct the original meaning of the text, that is, the intention of the author (Hirsch 1967). P. D. Juhl improves and elaborates Hirsch's arguments (Juhl 1980).

In *A Glossary of Contemporary Literary Theory* (Hawthorn 2000, 175–6), Jeremy Hawthorn points out that the question of intention has aroused little scholarly interest in the last three decades leading up to 2000. Lately, however, the issue has gained international relevance again as a result of a renewed interest in the implied author (Booth 2005, 75–88; Nünning 2005, 89–107). The controversy has nevertheless not yet been resolved, and the question of authorial intention's relevance to literary analysis is still open. But how wide is the gap between intentionalism and anti-intentionalism, and can it be bridged?

The long debate over intention has suffered from certain weaknesses. For one thing, the selection of material for investigation has been too narrow to be representative of fiction in general. Both Russian formalism and New Criticism base their analyses mainly on poetry, while Hirsch and Juhl also take examples from everyday speech. However, everyday language is a different form of communication than fiction, and so is poetry, to some extent, since it may be non-fiction and even lack a story.

In general, literary theory has not sufficiently accounted for all the different ways of communication. It is essential to distinguish between direct and indirect communication, for instance. Direct communication states the cognitive content overtly, coalescing surface with underlying structure ('The earth is round'; 'I've only just arrived'; 'Could you pass me the butter?'), whereas indirect communication disguises the underlying structure in its surface structure. When someone says, for instance, 'Many have tried before you without succeeding', what is implied is, 'You won't succeed either'; the parables of Jesus and the action in novels, fairy tales and plays are further examples of indirect communication. The mode of communication is partially related to genre, since the indirect method often characterizes novels and plays, while everyday speech and certain kinds of poetry rely on direct communication.

Finally, the understanding of the fictional communication process has suffered from a lack of indispensable distinctions. If the debate about intention is ever to reach a conclusion, a more sophisticated conceptual structure is needed. In this chapter, I will try to show that the theoretical distinctions made in the previous chapters may throw new light on the role of the author in literary communication.

The message as perceived by the receiver

We have seen how the cognitive content can go by many names, and in this chapter, for practical reasons, I will resort to the short-term *message*.

Indirect communication by means of a fictional action entails another kind of uncertainty than the one linked to direct communication. Instead of telling the reader directly what he thinks about the world and life in general, the author presents a package of concrete examples that the reader must interpret himself. This indirect way of communication matches that of Jesus' parables; just as his disciples were often perplexed by the parables, it may be difficult for the modern reader to understand what the fiction writer really means.

Since the text and the mental model of the action are fictional, they have no value on their own. They become meaningful only when the reader begins to use them to shed light on his own world. The message – the worldview inherent in the text – is not realized until the reader 'develops' it through a process of interpretation. Reception theory and reader-response criticism have shown how the reader's individual background impacts the cognitive effect of reading. In order to extrapolate the message, the reader has to draw on his own resources – intelligence, knowledge, personality, situation and so forth – and these factors affect his reactions to the work as much as the structure of the action and the mental model.

The reader's attempts to understand the background of the action and how its elements affect each other are therefore subjective, for example when it comes to understanding why Clarissa married Richard instead of Peter or why Richard cannot speak with his wife about his feelings. Some readers may think Clarissa was attracted by wealth or social status, while others may blame it on a need for security; still others may view it as a pre-emptive flight from a happiness (with Peter) she might risk losing later. Each particular interpretation leads to a different message.

I will refer to the cognitive content the reader extracts from the work as the *received message*. While the text and the mental model of the action are shared by all readers, the received message varies from reader to reader, a fact that finds confirmation in different scholars' conflicting interpretations of the same work. I will use *latent message* when talking about the original, 'virginal' message inherent in the structure of the action and the mental model before being extracted by the reader.

There are several possible intratextual criteria that can confirm that the received message conforms to the latent message. One such criterion is, for instance, that the interpretation leading to the best coherence between the elements of the mental model is the right one. But it is not necessarily certain that the writer, in constructing the text and the mental model, has succeeded or even wants to succeed in integrating everything into a coherent whole. Iser, for instance, considers it a sign of good quality that not all elements fit in (Iser 1974). All such intratextual criteria for the agreement between the received and the latent message are unreliable (Juhl 1988,148–9), and when anti-intentionalists hold that it is evident from the work itself whether the author has succeeded in conveying his message, this argument is as relative as Hirsch's belief that one can extrapolate the intention of the author from the work.

We have seen that the structures of the action and the mental model favour certain messages, and it may seem as if the reader is a defenceless victim of this influence. However, the reader can avoid this by calling upon his knowledge about the medium (literary studies) and about the existing world (psychology, sociology, philosophy and so on), hence seeing through the various means of persuasion the author employs.

Different forms of communication

If the ex-husband of a divorced mother calls, asking her to change the date for a visit of their children, nobody would object that this is direct communication between two persons. It is also direct communication if a person explicitly gives another person advice. On the other hand, if a divorced woman tells her new boyfriend about the bad habits of her ex-husband (implying that he should not make the same mistakes), she is communicating indirectly. Indirect communication differs from direct communication in presenting the receiver with a surface structure from which he is supposed to extract a message. The surface structure requires interpretation, and therefore different receivers may take away different messages. That is why indirect information is much less reliable than direct information, even if direct communication may also be subject to varying interpretations due to verbal ambiguity.

The above examples of direct and indirect communication are all non-fiction, and because of their reference to the real world, the receiver's interpretation of them has pragmatic consequences. Although the recently divorced woman's statement only applies directly to her ex-husband, it will affect her new suitor's life if he fails to glean the intended lessons from the behaviour of his predecessor. Fictional communication is also indirect and equivocal, but lacks these sorts of pragmatic consequences for the receiver. Ultimately, it is up to the reader of a novel or the audience of a play whether they will consider the author's intention or not. Moreover, the literary message's fulfilment of intellectual or emotional needs is not comparable to the direct effect that non-fictional messages have on the receiver's life. The advisory function of the message does not create any real interpersonal relationship between the reader and the author.

Because the debate about intention has drawn so much attention to everyday speech and poetry, scholars have mainly focused on the kind of communication that is predominant in these modes. Hence they tend to foreground verbal ambiguity (see Wimsatt and Beardsley 1954, 10; Fish 1980, 147–8; Hirsch 1967, 31, 212–13; Juhl 1980, 205, 232), while neglecting the special kind of ambiguity that arises in fictional communication: the ambiguity of the action and the mental model. Their insufficient treatment of the indirect communication that is characteristic of fiction has prevented a deeper understanding of the interaction between writer, work and audience.

The many faces of the author

One possible objection to the term *intention of the author* might be that the writer or author of the work is an ambiguous entity. Due to the various influences the author has been subject to from birth (personal experience, parental influence, the impact of literature, politics, philosophy, psychology and so forth), his mind is complex and may contain internal contradictions. As an answer to such difficulties, Wayne Booth's *implied author* refers to the censored and purified personality that the author shows to his readers in the shape of the latent message (Booth 2005, 75–88).

The mental complexity of the author becomes more conspicuous when the work is a result of direct cooperation with others, which can be expressed explicitly by indicating the names of the helpers in the acknowledgements. The extreme form of such cooperation is collaborative authorship, like the Swedish common-law husband and wife team Maj Sjöwall and Per Wahlö, who have written many detective novels together. Harold Love discriminates between different kinds of authorship: precursory authorship, executive authorship, declarative authorship and revisionary authorship, according to the role different people may have in the creation of a book: providing an important source, writing the text, being featured as author on the title page or making amendments to the text (Love 2002, 40–50, Fludernik 2009, 15).

Whether the complexity is due to contradictions in the mind of the author, external influence or cooperation, the mental model of the action may contain material that points in different ideological directions, leading to an inconsistent message. Internal inconsistencies come in addition to the polyinterpretability that the mental model of the action entails. To be sure, inconsistency is no argument against the relevance of the author's intention. If the author's intention is inconsistent, it may confuse the receiver and confront him with difficult choices. But readers of fiction are not in any fateful pragmatic situation – receiving orders in the military, for instance – in which ambiguity can have serious consequences. Inconsistencies in the fictional message can even serve as a stimulating challenge. If the influence of the author or authors is inconsistent, it remains nevertheless an influence.

The message as perceived by the sender

In creating the structure of the mental model of the action, the writer acts as an implied adviser. He influences the reader's understanding of the extratextual world by bringing together the structure of the mental model and the reader's own mental background. For instance, *Uncle Tom's Cabin* attempts to evoke indignation in the reader over slavery and racial discrimination. It is usual to assume that the author has a conscious or at least unconscious message that he wishes to convey and which he, consciously or unconsciously, integrates into the structure of the mental model. The author's intention may be to convey thoroughly developed opinions or it may confine itself to presenting basic facts as sign-posts for further discussion.

Ultimately, the reader cannot take for granted that the message that the author integrates into the work really represents *the author's own views*. The author's message is not always clear and may in theory even be omitted entirely, for instance if he presents a random collection of events, leaving the reader to find meaning on his own. The author may also miscalculate the effects of his structures, and end up investing the work with a different message from the one he originally intended. He may also manipulate the structure of the work in order to deceive the reader. In such cases, the latent message deviates considerably from the author's own views. If the deviation is due to an error, the intended message is identical with the author's own views, while the latent message is what diverges. If the deviation is due to a deliberate evasiveness, the intended message is identical with the latent message, but inconsistent with the author's own views.

Consequently, we have to discriminate between the following different shades of meaning in the word *message*: (1) *the author's own views*, (2) *the intended message*, (3) *the message that is actually dispatched*, which is identical with *the latent message*, and (4) *the received message*. While the author's own views, the intended message and the received message are all in principle verifiable, in that you can interview the author and the reader, the dispatched, latent message is at a non-verifiable intermediate stage, and can only be partially verified by comparing it to the author's own views, the intended message and the received message.

The intended message, the dispatched, latent message and the author's own views express all the intention of the author. Normally there is no difference between them, and they are in fact synonyms. Usually it is sufficient to apply the term *the author's intention* (or *the author's message*) in all three senses.

The notion of *intention*, however, is broader than *message*. It refers to the writer's objectives in general and may pertain to things other than the message. An example would be the goal of making money off one's book, in which case the cognitive content that is inevitably inherent in the action would not necessarily express the author's own views, but views that are more conducive to maximizing sales. The term *intention* has a further drawback compared to *message*. If after publication the writer discovers that the mental model of the action expresses different views than the ones he had in mind when he created it, *intention* is not an appropriate term for the message his text conveys. It is natural to use the term *intention* when referring to the message that the writer intends to convey during composition, but not the message he finds only later as a reader of his own text, as this message was not the one intended.

Eco uses the term *text intention* (Eco 1994,64), which gives the impression of a whole message included in the text (or the work) like the passengers of a bus. But the message is no more present in the text than the figures patients see in a Rorschach test are present in the inkblots. The dispatched message inherent in the intersubjective structures of the mental model of the action becomes meaningful only when the reader interprets it in accordance with his own worldview. The term *text intention* is hence better rendered as *latent* (or *inherent*) *message*.

As for Wayne Booth's *implied author* – the self that the author presents to the reader via the latent message – it is unnecessarily focused on the writer as a person; the mental model of the action renders only those of the writer's views that are of any relevance, whereas his physical existence and real-life personality are irrelevant. If we want to express the distinction between the latent message and the author's own views, it is more appropriate to substitute *latent message* for *the implied author*. The term *latent* (or *dispatched*) *message* is more accurate and does not involve more of the author than is relevant to the communication process.

Does the work always reflect the author's own views?

One of the reasons why the anti-intentionalists want to discard the author's intention is that the author is often not consciously aware of his own intention, so we can only know it by extrapolating it from the work itself. There is, however, an ample body of fiction in which the author is usually not expected to air his own views. Popular literature, for example, is hardly ever held up as a reflection of the author's passionately held worldviews, not necessarily because he does not have any, but more likely because he does not bother to impart them to the reader. As popular literature must entertain in order to sell, it must have a message that appeals to a wide audience. Such messages are generally optimistic, minimizing the problems of life and raising a bright view of the world in their place. Instead of his own views, the author integrates a more commercially attractive message into the mental model. If he does this deliberately, then that also amounts to a conscious intention behind popular literature, but with the difference that there is a discrepancy between the latent message and the author's own views, since the author is guilty of a kind of lie. When the latent message does not represent the author's own views, the received message cannot, of course, represent them either, and information about the views of the author cannot shed light on the latent message.

In addition to the popular literature's discrepancy between the latent message and the author's own worldview, there may theoretically be cases where the author does not have any message in mind, not even unconsciously. He has just put together a random selection of events, without any rational aim. Even in this case, the reader would be able to make some sense of the action, given the surprising ability of human beings to discern connections and coherence in apparent chaos. This is what enables us to make out the shapes of objects and living beings in the clouds, and what leads to a multitude of creative interpretations in, for example, modernist literature. But in the case of the randomly assembled story, it would be misleading to speak of the author's intention even if the action somehow still contained a latent message and a corresponding received message. The author would still be the creator of the text, and as such responsible for its effects, but his involvement with the message would be left completely to chance, just as a painting produced by accident by the pallet falling on the canvas the wet side down would not be an expression of any intention. It would be absurd to ask the writer what his text is meant to express in such a case.

However, this hypothetical exception is not a sufficient argument against the relevance of the author's intention in other cases. Nevertheless, the circumstances concerning the message in popular literature constitute such a comprehensive exception that they must be included in the discussion. If the latent message is random or contradicts the author's own views, then it is plausible to regard the mental model of the action (and, as a consequence, the work) as independent of the author, whereas a consciously intended latent message encourages the reader to look for a connection between the mental model (i.e. the work) and the intention of the sender. The first case might be used as an argument in favour of anti-intentionalism, the second in favour of intentionalism. One can object that only the author himself knows when the latent message does not conform to his own views, and the reader cannot be affected by what he does not know, but as most readers have a certain general knowledge about genres, this prior knowledge creates expectations. For instance, readers do not expect popular literature to express the views of the author, in contrast to serious literature.

The relationship between the latent and the received message

Hirsch points out that there is a consciousness behind every text whose existence you cannot deny by claiming that the text has a meaning of its own. However, this pertains only to the relationship between the author and the text/the mental model of the action. Nobody would deny that the text and the mental model of the action have an author. The issue is whether the reader must link the text and the mental model to a particular message from the author. It is in this respect that Hirsch's failure to distinguish the work (text and mental model) from the message leads to problems. The author is evidently the sender of the text and the mental model of the action, conveying to the reader a collection of fictional events. On the other hand, his role as sender with respect to the message is much more obscure. Does the reader perceive the mental model of the action as an expression of the author's intention to convey a message, or does he perceive the author's voice as restricted solely to the text and the mental model of the action, leaving to the reader to make of them whatever he likes? In other words, does the reader sense that the author is reaching beyond the mental model (the collection of examples), pointing towards a particular message? Hirsch does not account for the reader's choice in this situation.

Juhl has a clearer conception of the communication process, pointing to several forms of reader behaviour which prove that the reader is continually aware of the author's intention (Juhl 1980, 58–9, 62–3). Allusions and certain types of irony are incomprehensible if they are isolated from the author's intention. For instance, in *The Wild Duck*, Ibsen allows Hjalmar Ekdal to display his naïveté and egocentrism in such an exaggerated way that the audience immediately grasps the ironic attitude of the playwright towards his character. Even structuralists refer to other works by the same author in order to substantiate their interpretations, effectively revealing that they find knowledge of the author's intentions useful (Juhl 1980, 238).

Juhl, moreover, regards interpreters' interest in the author's language as an indication of the relevance of the author's intention (148–50). However, language here is the same as the level of the text, which is the basis on which the reader reconstructs the mental model of the action. Juhl is obviously thinking of the communication of the mental model as part of the author's intention, which is of course undeniable to the reader; however, since the mental model is shared by all readers, it is not this level of the communication process that is at issue in the debate about the author's intention, but rather the next level, that of the cognitive content inherent in the mental model.

The author has two intentions; to convey the action (represented by the mental model) to the reader through the text, and to convey an abstract message, the cognitive content, through the action (represented by the mental model). As we have seen, the former intention is not problematic, because at this level, the communication is direct and all readers receive the same model of the action. It is the latter intention, concerning the indirect communication of the cognitive content, which is at issue. Juhl's confusion of the two intentions is evidently due to an incomplete understanding of the levels of literary communication. The distinction between the levels of text, model (or action) and message is, once again, indispensable.

However, there is one more piece of evidence that shows literary scholars' conscious or unconscious interest in the author's intention: their interest in symbols embedded in the text. In a previous chapter, I mentioned Bradshaw's interpretation of Richard's red and white roses as a symbol of death and as evidence of Clarissa's suicidal inclinations. Bradshaw does not conceal his belief in the relevance of the author's intention and frequently quotes Woolf's own statements about her works (Woolf 2000, xxix). Nevertheless, the author's use of symbols does not prevent the reader from disregarding the dispatched or latent message.

In non-fictional communication, the message is accompanied by a clear return address and there is a clear pragmatic relationship between sender and receiver. If you receive a letter from the tax office regarding taxes due, the content of the letter affects your life directly. You can also contact the tax office to tell them they are in error. Or if you read a history book, its content alters or confirms your knowledge about events that have contributed to the creation of the social, economic and political world you live in, and this knowledge affects your attitude to real people in the past or in your own society.

In fictional communication, on the other hand, the action is a world of its own: a collection of examples that normally have no value as information about the real world or its author. However, the resemblance to the real world enables the reader to use the fictional material just as he uses his own real experiences, and he can extrapolate general insights about life from the action without knowing anything about the writer's intentions. There is no relevant return address and no pragmatic danger. Therefore, the reader faces a choice that is not present in direct communication: he can disregard the original message with impunity, completely ignoring what the author wanted to tell him through the action (represented by the mental model). This might be what the anti-intentionalists have in mind when they argue that the message is evident from the work itself. They are right that the reader cannot be compelled to take the author's intention into account. But on the other hand, as we shall soon see, the reader's freedom does not mean that the author's intent is irrelevant or that the author's views do not affect the received message.

The reader's ability to reconstruct the model of the action without help from the author reduces the author's control over the received message. The indirect mode of communication that characterizes fiction can be compared to a mirror. When we look at ourselves in the mirror, the quality of the reflected image depends on the structure of the mirror's surface, the material it is made of and its shape. The interplay between the mental model of the action and the reader's mind reflects the latent message, but the mental model's structure and the reader's own background and qualities affect the surface of the 'mirror' so that the received message gives a correspondingly distorted picture of the latent message. The reader must therefore allow for a certain divergence between the message he extrapolates himself and the messages other readers receive. The degree of the deviation depends on various factors: the structure of the mental model and the action it renders, the structure of the cognitive content and the author's and reader's horizons of understanding. Any similarity between the author's and reader's backgrounds and qualities are, of course, important, and because the message is complex and touches upon many different topics, the latent and the received message may overlap to a varying degree.

Another important factor is whether the author offers ready solutions or leaves problems unresolved. Some authors, for instance realist authors, are more consciously aware of what they want to say in a given text than others are, like impressionists or surrealists. The author's intention is easier to recognize in *Uncle Tom's Cabin* and *The Wild Duck* than in Beckett's *Waiting for Godot* (Becket 2008) or Pirandello's *Six Characters in Search of an Author* (Pirandello 1995). In addition to the multitude of interpretations that are due to characteristics of the text or the reader, we have seen that the author is also an important variable, split into the author's own views, the intended message and the actual latent message, not to mention contradictory partial messages arising from contradictions in the mind of the author. All these factors affect the likelihood of the authorial intention's reaching the reader.

As we have seen, an important anti-intentionalist objection to the relevance of the author's intention is that one cannot know anything certain about it. Hirsch, on the other hand, holds that most authors believe that their intention reaches the reader or at least has a good chance of doing so (Hirsch 1967, 18). Here it is essential to take into account the nature of the object that is subject to interpretation. Are we interpreting a directly formulated statement about reality, a non-fictional poem or a fictional story? Is the action itself or only the ambiguous word subject to analysis?

If the object of interpretation is an ambiguous word in a non-fictional text, a telephone call to the sender will probably resolve the issue, provided he is available. If, on the other hand, the question concerns a particular message from the action of a novel or play, it is not certain that the author himself is aware of the cognitive scope of the story he has created. Both Hirsch and Wimsatt are right, each in his own way, depending on the kind of text being offered up for interpretation. Even if the reader uses all available internal and external evidence, he cannot come closer to the intention of the author than the individual properties of the text and the quality of the evidence allow. I will illustrate this with the example of *Mrs Dalloway*, which affords a wealth of both extratextual and intratextual information.

In his analysis of *Mrs Dalloway*, Bradshaw refers repeatedly to Virginia Woolf's own statements, for instance her diary entries where she states that her work in progress is meant as a study of insanity and suicide and that Septimus is meant to be seen as Clarissa's double (Woolf 2000, xix, xxi). This extratextual evidence plays a substantial role in Bradshaw's interpretation of Clarissa as suicidal (xx), and encourages him to interpret intratextual elements of the novel as further evidence. This intratextual evidence consists in superficial similarities and coincidences that link Clarissa and Septimus together, such as the narrator's comparison of the two with birds (Woolf 2000, xxxviii), and Clarissa's momentary fear of death combined with a subsequent feeling of having escaped death in contrast to Septimus (Woolf 2000, 157). We have already mentioned Bradshaw's suggestion that the Richard's red and white roses for Clarissa are a symbol of death indicating her suicidal inclinations. Bradshaw could also have conceivably used Woolf's own suicide as an argument, but does not, although this biographical fact may have influenced his conclusions.

The evidence Bradshaw uses to substantiate his interpretation is partly extratextual (Woolf's statements) and partly intratextual, including extradiegetic devices (the narrator's use of symbols and correlations: the roses, associating Clarissa and Septimus with birds) as well as one intradiegetic element: Clarissa's momentary fear of death. Notwithstanding its diversity, Bradshaw's evidence is not sufficient to establish an indisputable interpretation of the author's intentions, as Woolf's own extratextual statements and the intratextual evidence themselves allow for different interpretations. As for Woolf's own statements, we cannot assume that she meant the parallelism of insanity and suicidal inclinations between Clarissa and Septimus to be complete. She may have simply regarded Clarissa as a parallel to Septimus because they are both unhappy. If the fact of Woolf's suicide had been brought up, it would have been more plausible to draw a parallel between Woolf and Septimus than between Woolf and Clarissa. Perhaps Septimus represents

Woolf's fear of committing suicide, while Clarissa represents her hope of escape, which would make Clarissa a parallel to Woolf and a contrast.

The intratextual evidence is similarly inconclusive. The correlations linking Clarissa to Septimus encourage the reader to draw parallels between them, but as we pointed out above, this parallelism may simply come down to unhappiness. The red and white roses do not prove anything either. Although the combination of red and white flowers is an omen of death according to the dictionary of superstitions Bradshaw quotes, this superstition is hardly so widespread that Woolf may be expected to have shared it, and nothing indicates that Clarissa and Richard associate the roses with death. Bradshaw's association of the roses with death hence seems a little farfetched. These colours can just as well be interpreted in terms of innocence and love, white signifying the platonic innocence of Clarissa's marriage and red her yearning for love. Another interpretation might be that red symbolizes the vitality of Clarissa, Peter and Sally, whereas white refers to the stiff, lifeless Richard. Even in such a relatively stable context as *Mrs Dalloway*, symbolic elements may be open to a great number of interpretations.

Bradshaw could have confined his interpretation to a parallel between Septimus and Woolf with respect to suicidal inclinations and restricted the parallel between Clarissa and Woolf to unhappiness, considering Clarissa's will to survive as a contrast to Woolf's actual suicide. Most readers would probably accept such an interpretation as an expression of the author's intention (meaning 'the author's own views'), in contrast to his interpretation of Clarissa as a woman with an unstable mind and suicidal tendencies. The latter is too subjective to be generally accepted, in spite of the solid body of extra- and intratextual evidence on which it is based. On the other hand, Clarissa's momentary fear of death may seem to confirm Bradshaw's interpretation, but it is the only intradiegetic element that does. There is nothing else in Clarissa's behaviour that indicates that she is suicidal in the normal sense of the word; her momentary fit of fear may be little more than a brief existential insight into the perils of life, which most of us experience in the course of our lives without having to be suicidal.

The question over whether Clarissa is mentally unstable and suicidal is essential to the message. The essence of the message in *Mrs Dalloway*, as far as Clarissa is concerned, seems to be linked to her ambivalent marriage and the existential situation this entails. If Clarissa really was continuously on the verge of suicide, it would make sense to impute this to her marriage, which would emphasize the importance of her past choice of partner. At the same time, this would highlight Richard's responsibility as a husband, increasing his culpability; at the same time, Clarissa's own passivity would become less innocent, and her apparently harmless behaviour would become more suspect. Instead of being an instance of an innocent upper-class wife, Clarissa would turn into a candidate for suicide. Then we would get the impression that suicidal inclinations can be present without exhibiting symptoms, although this is contradicted by Septimus's behaviour. However thoroughly we scrutinize the text and Woolf's extratextual comments, there is room for doubt and multiple interpretations of Clarissa's behaviour. The novel remains relatively open in this respect, and it is left up to the reader to interpret according to his own knowledge about human beings.

Despite the multitude of possible interpretations, Hirsch and Juhl insist that only one can be correct, while anti-intentionalists are open to many and consider all incompatible interpretations equivalent. We should now have knowledge enough about the workings of fiction to throw some light on this basic disagreement. The conflict arises from the fact that the fictional action is both a link in a communication process and an experience that can be used independently of the intention of the sender. The reader can choose freely between these two options, adopting either an intentionalist or an anti-intentionalist stance. He may even combine them: the reader may take the fictional action as an experience apart from the author's intention, while also trying to make out the author's intention as a supplement to his own private interpretation. The strategy each reader settles upon, however, makes a difference and has consequences.

If we foreground the mental model's function as a vehicle for a latent message, the author's own views can help us get more useful information out of the work. How useful this help will be depends on the qualities of the author. If he is more insightful than us, finding out his views will augment our cognitive benefit. If he is not, it may still be useful to know them, because the more interpreters there are, the greater the chance of finding the most productive interpretation. Instead of the author, other interpreters might help us, but the author has an advantage over the others: as the work's creator, his interpretation is more likely to be the key to understanding the work and its cognitive potential. There are two reasons why it may be useful to search for the optimal coherence between the elements of the work: first, the interpretation that makes the pieces fall into place in the most convincing and systematic way may be the cognitively most productive, and second, the reader is concerned with the work as a coherent organism and wants all of its elements to fit in, just as when he solves a crossword puzzle. Whether the interpretation that makes most of the pieces fall into place is necessarily the best one is, however, debatable.

It is also possible to foreground the value of the fictional story as a human experience per se and disregard the intention of the author. Then we have to search for a message on our own, without the aid of the author. In this case, we do not consider the author a useful authority and do not care whether his message can lend coherence to the structures and make them more meaningful. If we attempt to find some optimal coherence (for cognitive or artistic reasons), we do it on our own or look to other interpreters for support. In that case, the intention of the author may, in fact, come in handy as an interpretation among others, despite the reader's autonomist stance. The search for optimal coherence can still have a cognitive or artistic objective.

The difference between the intentionalists and the anti-intentionalists, in other words, lies in the fact that intentionalists permit the use of extratextual information about the author to augment the cognitive benefit, in contrast to the anti-intentionalists. Moreover, even if they choose not to make use of extratextual information, their focus on the author's intention may influence their interpretation, making them more determined and persevering so that they can derive more from the cognitive content. Hence, the intentionalists have a certain advantage over anti-intentionalists, who are confined to the information inherent in the mental model of the action. On the other hand, the extratextual influence of the author may be a handicap if it makes the interpreter blind to other interpretations. Consequently, it matters which option one chooses, both approaches having their pros and cons, but neither the inclusion of the author's intention nor the exclusion of it is inferior to the other. It is a question of goals and means.

To what extent is information about the author's intention available?

The fact that literary works give rise to incompatible interpretations in practice may be regarded as an argument for the anti-intentionalist stance that there is never one right interpretation but several equivalent ones. Juhl nevertheless raises a good counterargument: being ignorant of which interpretation is the right one does not preclude there being only one right interpretation (Juhl 1980, 237–8).

If the reader receives a message that is incompatible with the intended message, the intentionalists contend that communication has failed. However, it is a peculiar feature of fictional communication that the receiver is generally unaware of any failure and is unable to complain. If someone commissions a portrait and finds that it does not resemble the portrayed person, he has a choice between rejecting the painting and accepting it if he nevertheless likes it as a piece of art. The reader has no such option, because he does not know what he has missed, and does not even know he has been deceived in some way. The only way to discover this is to compare the received message with the intended message, which must be available. If the communication fails, then the intentionalists are not much better off than the anti-intentionalists. In most cases, both are left with a message whose origin is unknown to them or at least uncertain. Nevertheless, the possibility of communicative failure is not a sufficient argument against intentionalism, for if one exploits all available intra- and extratextual material, it is in many cases possible to establish what is most likely the interpretation of the author.

Although Hirsch considers knowledge about the author's intention necessary for understanding the work, he does not clearly state the extent to which it is necessary to draw upon extratextual information (Hirsch 1967, 224–5). Hirsch also regards the text as the main evidence of the author's intention, but in cases where this is not so (as in Wordsworth's 'A slumber did my spirit seal', where Hirsch quotes two conflicting interpretations by Brooks and Bateson), he allows recourse to knowledge about human beings in general as well as about the author (Hirsch 1967, 68). Drawing upon Husserl, Hirsch calls this extratextual knowledge *horizon*, without explaining further what this horizon consists in and how the reader acquires it. If the reader really decides to draw on extratextual information, it nevertheless makes sense to dig up all available material, acquiring as much information as possible about the background of the latent message. Such external material may include dictionaries, comments by the author and by people who knew him, historical and biographical material, comparisons with the author's other works, the literary, cultural, political and philosophical currents that shaped the author's time and so on. Juhl allows for this kind of external help, but warns us at the same time to tread carefully (Juhl 1980, 68). In drawing upon extratextual sources the critic risks attributing to the work intentions there is no evidence for in the text/the mental model.

The anti-intentionalists are of course right in pointing out that extratextual information is never watertight, but if it corroborates a particular interpretation, it is better than total uncertainty. The anti-intentionalists' demand for certainty is therefore no argument against the application of extratextual material or against the inclusion of the author's intention.

The expectations of the reader

The reader's interest (or lack thereof) in the intention of the author does not have to be a conscious choice. Several external factors influence him, like expectations and prejudices engendered by genre, epoch, environment or circumstances pertaining to publication, sale and library due date. For instance, we expect serious literature to express a message, which we often identify as the author's intention. On the other hand, we are seldom equally concerned with the ideological purpose behind popular literature. This is of course why the latter is often not considered literature at all. Lamarque and Olsen 1994, for instance, reserve the term literature for canonized literature (434–5). Apart from the work's status as serious or popular, its affiliation with a particular literary current may influence the reader's expectations with respect to authorial intention. He may be more likely to expect a naturalist or realist work to express a clear intention than one that is surrealist or modernist. Differences in social and cultural background may also play a role, as do differences in theoretical background, like that between intentionalism and anti-intentionalism.

The author's responsibility for the received message

How responsible is the author for the received message in view of the fact that he is, strictly speaking, the author of only the work itself (the text and the mental model of the action), whereas the message is merely an effect of the work? To what extent is he responsible for this effect?

Because the mental model has a substantial influence on the received message, it is reasonable that he is at least responsible for this part of the communication process. Although the received message is a rather unstable entity, both readers and society tend to hold the author (as a historical person) co-responsible for the received message; in the same way, if an adult does not think of the dangers of letting a child play with a plastic bag, he is still responsible if the child is suffocated by it. Because the author creates the structure of the work, we expect him to know enough about its effects on the reader to have some responsibility for the received message. This responsibility must not be confused with the naïve mistake of attributing to the author views expressed by the fictional narrator or characters. The message is after all based on the work as a whole and is not identical with isolated statements.

All the same, however, the author's responsibility is limited. If the child in the above example puts the plastic bag in the microwave and ends up damaging the oven, we would probably not blame the adult for not predicting this possibility, even if he deserves blame for not watching the child. The author cannot be blamed for unreasonable interpretations. An example of this is when slaveholders in the American South interpreted the Bible as justifying slavery, in which case we would not hold the writer(s) of the Bible responsible for this wrong interpretation.

The author's responsibility also comes into play if he has mistakenly or on purpose expressed another message than the one he intended, even though the responsibility is somewhat different. Then he is not responsible for the mistaken views per se, but must still account for the mistake or lie that included them in the work. I have already mentioned popular literature, where the reader is less likely to regard the latent (dispatched) message as an expression of the author's worldview, but even here the reader can hold the author accountable for including it in the text. You cannot blame the drug dealer for producing the drugs, but you can arrest him for selling them.

Since by definition fictional works do not mirror the author's intention clearly, it is difficult to prosecute an author for the message of a novel or a drama. There can only be a moral, ethical or political responsibility, areas in which we judge on a more subjective basis than in court.

A symptom of the tendency to hold the author himself accountable for the latent (dispatched) message is the use of the author's name when mentioning the authority responsible for it. Three different types of literary comments serve to illustrate this:

1. Stowe was a strong opponent of slavery.
2. *Uncle Tom's Cabin* works as an argument against slavery.
3. In *Uncle Tom's Cabin*, Stowe is a strong opponent of slavery.

The first sentence refers to the author such as we know her independently of the work. The second refers only to the received message, while the third refers to both the received message and the author as the person responsible for the received message, assuming the intended and received message coalesce. The fact that the name of the author is attached to the message is proof that readers tend to regard the received message as an expression of the author's own views. However, the phrase 'In *Uncle Tom's Cabin*' in the third sentence specifies that the statement pertains to the author as we meet her in the work, represented by the latent (dispatched) message. We could extend the third sentence thus:

> In *Uncle Tom's Cabin*, Stowe is a strong opponent of slavery, an attitude that she also expressed clearly as a historical person.

In this version, the author's name clearly links the different versions of the message (the views of the author and the latent or received message) to the same identity.

Despite the uncertainty entailed by the multitude of possible interpretations, the reader identifies the received message with a message the author (as a historical person) dispatches or aims to despatch, and he senses a communicative connection between himself (as receiver) and the author (as sender).

Conclusion

The distinction between the text, the mental model of the action, the action and the message enables us to discriminate between *direct* and *indirect communication* and distinguish fictional communication as a special form of indirect communication. The ambiguity in *the author's intention* splits into *intention* and *message*. The message splits in turn into *the author's own views*, *the intended message*, *the latent message* (or *dispatched message*) and *the received message*. It is also essential to distinguish between *the author's intention* and *the author's responsibility*, as well as between *the reader's expectations* with respect to the author's intention. Moreover, we must differentiate between the action as a means of establishing the intended message and as an experience independent of the author's intention. We can sum up these conclusions thus:

1. Various factors, such as genre and literary movement, determine whether the reader perceives the mental model as communicating a particular authorial message or not. The fact that the reader automatically links the received message to the author's name indicates that he regards the latent (dispatched) and the received message as versions of the same message.
2. It may be difficult to make out the author's intention, but the problems are not insurmountable. By analysing internal and (if relevant) external facts, one can make out the author's intention with a degree of probability that is inevitably subject to debate but at least at a rational level.
3. One can benefit from the work without knowing what the author is intending, but the inclusion of the author's intention may affect and perhaps enrich the received message. The reader's eventual choice is a question of personal preference, but his choice influences the received message.
4. The structures of the action and the mental model of it are put together to give certain messages a head start. The reader may try to evade

this influence with his knowledge about the communication medium (literary studies) and about the external world (psychology, sociology, philosophy and so on), that is, through insight into the various factors of the process of influence.

Interpretative strategies

As the aspects of the fictional communication process are so complex and accompanied by so many reservations, readers and scholars alike face a wide choice of strategies. Each of them, in its particular way, may shed light on the work and communication:

1. The reader may want to know as much as possible about the author as a historical and biographical person. Even though the received message cannot be an unequivocal mirror image of the writer's views, the impression it gives of his interests and views is clear enough to have biographical value. In addition, it may be useful for criticism to consult historical and biographical sources. In this case, the focus is on *the author as a human being*.
2. Even if the reader is not interested in biography, he may want to discern the author's intention as exactly as possible. In this context, historical and biographical facts as well as a thorough analysis of the interplay between the structures of the work may be useful. The focus here is on *the communication as such* and the *dispatched (latent) message*.
3. If the reader is inclined neither to find out about the writer as a human being nor to uncover his original message, he may still be interested in obtaining optimal benefit from the work. Historical and biographical facts may still be useful to the analysis of the structures of the work. The focus here is on *the reader's personal benefit*.
4. The reader may choose to forego any connection between the author's intention and the work, regarding the work as an autonomous world he can exploit according to his own wishes. This strategy excludes historical and biographical sources, and does not look for connections and traces that can indicate the author's intention. In this case, the focus also is on *the reader's personal benefit*. This stance permits the reader to more easily make independent and original interpretations, but at the potential cost of failing to see valuable information.

Apart from the last strategy, the reader may combine the different kinds of focus with extratextual knowledge, but he may also have to or choose to restrict himself to the work itself. An immanent method of analysis does not preclude a transcendent focus. Overlapping and transitional forms between the four approaches are possible with respect to both the application of extratextual knowledge and the inclusion of an extratextual focus. It all depends on the reader's interests and access to information beyond the text.

7

Problems Related to the Sender

The insight that the novel (short story, fairy tale and epos) has a narrator that is not identical with the author probably dates back to antiquity, but in German literary theory, for instance, it finds expression in Wolf Dohrn's *Die künstlerische Darstellung als Problem der Ästhetik* (Dohrn 1907), followed closely by Käte Friedemann's *Die Rolle des Erzählers in der Epik* (1910, Friedeman 1965). In the rich scholarly tradition of the twentieth century, the narrator-author distinction has been taken for granted, even by narratologists. Insofar as objections have arisen, the conflict has never concerned the distinction between the author and the narrator itself, only the nature of the latter.

In 1958 Wolfgang Kayser advanced the idea that the third-person novel 'is narrated by itself', which found support from Käte Hamburger, who developed an entire theory in which she denied the existence of a narrator in third-person novels (Kayser 1958, 82–101; Hamburger 1968). Hamburger depersonalizes the narrator of the third-person novel, substituting the term *narrative function* (*Erzählfunktion*) for *narrator*. She bases her conclusions on a straightforwardly logical set of observations:

1. As fiction, the action of the third-person novel does not belong to the author's historical reality, so the author is not a sender in the same sense as the sender of the first-person novel. From Hamburger's definition, it follows that the sender must belong to the world he is telling about. Since the author of the third-person novel does not belong to the world of the fictional characters, he cannot, therefore, be the sender of the statement (115), and the verbal tense of the third-person novel does not refer to the temporal position of the author.
2. The characters of the third-person novel are often represented as subjects, which means that the reader has access to their thoughts and feelings in spite of their being third-person characters (72–3).
3. Certain deictic adverbs and pronouns like *today*, *here*, *now* and *this* can refer to the relationship between internal (intradiegetic) elements (on the level of the action): 'Tonight the king wanted to play the flute' and 'Yesterday the manoeuvre lasted eight hours.'

These observations lead Hamburger to infer that the third-person novel has no sender (*Aussagesubjekt*), that its verbal tense has no function and that phrases like 'I', 'we', 'our hero' and so forth, which seem to indicate the existence of a fictive narrator, in reality refer neither to the author nor to any fictional narrator (65, 67, 72–3, 83, 115). Hamburger uses *epic preterite* to refer to the allegedly functionless tense of the third-person novel, most frequently the past tense.

In Chapter 3, we saw that readers who recount passages from a novel normally apply the present tense even if the text is written in the past tense. Hamburger brings up this shift in tense, regarding it as proof that verbal tense has no function in fiction.

Modern literary theory has carried forward Hamburger's theory of the epic preterite, for instance, Monika Fludernik, who adopts it a little waveringly (Fludernik 2009, 51):

> As Käte Hamburger explains in *The Logic of Literature* (1957), the past tense form used in German narratives is not a "genuine" past tense. It simply serves to mark out a text as fictional. On the basis of F. K. Stanzel's work and subsequent studies of the use of tenses, we must conclude that the deictic function of such past tenses is, if not cancelled out entirely, then at least extremely limited. In other words, the past tense which normally fixes a "here and now" pertaining to the speaker in relation to an event situated in the past loses this function of referring to past time pure and simple and adopts the function of signalling fictionality . . .
>
> But, of course, such a narrative [a story filtered through the consciousness of a character] is not possible in real life so that the fictionality of such narratives does not necessarily derive from the use of the epic past tense. In fact, the reverse is probably true: the preterite gives the impression of being fictional because it occurs in a text that is obviously fictional.

The status of the narrator is closely linked to the definition of fictionality, and to be grasped fully, it requires a clear borderline between fiction and non-fiction. The blurring of the boundaries between fiction and non-fiction that pervades part of modern literary theory obscures the nature of fictional mediation and the existential role of the narrator. Postmodern literature's practice of embedding non-fictional elements in fiction or vice versa works in the same direction. Often, we are faced with a narrator in a novel who bears the name of the real author and seems to be identical with him in every biographical respect. Are we, then, dealing with the real author or a fictional character?

The narrator and the narrative act

Although *author, narrator* and *writer* originally refer to different stages of literary production (creation, telling and writing), they have more or less become synonyms, designating the creator of a text. The author of a biography combines the role of creator, writer and narrator, and there is no reason to distinguish the terms from each other. Only in fiction does the *narrator* cease to be identical with the *author* or *writer*, while the two latter terms are synonyms. The distinction between narrator and author is necessary because fiction has a far more complex communicative structure than non-fiction. The fictional action does not belong to the author's (and readers') own empirical world, and when the author tells the fictional story, he indicates its fictionality by publishing it as a novel, as *fiction*. The label *novel* or *fiction* is extratextual like the author and reader.

Although the novel often contains unrealistic elements that reveal its fictionality (such as insight into the minds of third-person characters), it claims intratextually to recount events from the empirical world, paradoxically denying that it is fiction. This paradox is due to a convention providing that the sender believes the content of his statement to be true unless he tells the receiver otherwise. Since the author does not inform the reader intratextually that the action is fiction, he creates the illusion that it is real. As a consequence, the reader receives events (the action) that are fictional from an extratextual point of view, while they are non-fiction from an intratextual point of view. On account of its fictionality, the text belongs simultaneously to two different worlds, the internal fictional one and the external empirical one. In the empirical world, it is marked as fiction, while in the fictional world it is presented as reality. The text is the same; only the extratextual label is different. How does this textual duality affect the role of the sender? Who is telling what?

Henceforth, I will refer to the extratextual aspect as *the external text*, which is opposed to *the internal text*. From the vantage point of the external text, the author is its sender, since it is he who says directly or indirectly, 'The story I am telling is fiction.' However, once he signals fictionality, he relinquishes any claim to be the sender of the internal text. The sender of that text claims (according to convention) that his story is true and that the events he is telling about have really taken place. From the reader's perspective, the person who regards the action as fiction must be another person than the person who takes it as reality. Logically there must be two authors, one who creates the fictitious events and one who narrates them as a story about reality. In addition to the real author, the fictional narrator comes into existence as a projection of the text, a projection resulting from the above-mentioned convention of the sender believing his text to be true as long as he does not explicitly deny its veracity.

To avoid confusion, literary theory has named the novel's two senders *author* (or *writer*) and *narrator*. The author is a historical person belonging to the existing world, whereas the narrator is a fictional person and belongs to the fictional world. As a projection of the fictional world, he is as much a creation of the reader as of the author. According to the logic of the language of which they are both users, the author knows in advance that the reader will experience the action as if narrated by a fictional narrator, so the narrator is a product of the system, an inevitable part of the author's creative act that neither author nor reader controls. Only when the narrator is already there may the author develop him further into a more explicit person, lending him the capability to comment, express opinions and judgements, be ironic and talk about himself. In this way, the narrator is subject to artistic exploitation.

The narrator, in other words, is a logical consequence of the fictional text. More than an artistic device or a useful element for analysis, he is logically inevitable and cannot be omitted whatever we might think of him. As soon as a work is announced as fiction, the sender splits into author and narrator.

As human beings, we are not able to imagine a statement that has no human sender. Therefore the narrator has to be a person. The fictional text is not only in itself a testimony of the fictional narrator (someone has to give utterance to the text), but it also contains more specific traces of him: elements that inform us about his temporal, spatial and sometimes intellectual and emotional relationship to the narrated objects. Such traces are verbal tense, personal pronouns, deictic adverbs and pronouns (*now*, *today*, *here*, *this* and so on), comments, judgements, the narrator's statements about himself and verbal expressions with an emotive, phatic, conative or poetic function (Roman Jakobson's four functions of language that reveal the narrator's existence most conspicuously, expressing respectively the speaker's feelings, desire to establish contact with the receiver, volition and selection of linguistic devices). The conspicuousness of the narrator may vary, but however unobtrusive he is, the text always reveals its speaker through verbal tense (or temporal adverbs in languages that lack tense) and, of course, through the very existence of the text itself. If the text says, 'Peter sat down', the past tense situates the action in the past of a speaker who must belong to the same fictional world as the action. As the fictional event does not belong to the author's past, it must belong to the past of another speaker, the fictional narrator.

By not being entitled to render the fictional events in the past tense the author betrays that he does not belong to the fictional world he is telling about. For instance, Virginia Woolf could never have said, 'The doctors drove Septimus to suicide.' She would have had to use the present tense ('The doctors drive Septimus to suicide'), or else it would have looked like she believed in the existence of her fictional characters. As we already know, this present tense does not refer to the fictional action but to the text and mental model of it, which are present tense in the reader's mind: 'In the story (i.e. the mental model), the doctors drive Septimus to suicide.'

If the text is written in the present tense, as many modern novels are, the present tense may be understood as the historical present referring to the narrator's past, but the reader may at times interpret the present tense literally. In this case he would conceptualize the narrator as on the spot like a reporter, commenting on the events as they happen. As we shall see, the narrator does not have to be realistic. Even Alain Robbe-Grillet's *nouveau roman La jalousie* has a narrator, even though he renders the events as if through the lens of a film camera (Robbe-Grillet 1957). Someone has to report these events, even if he restricts himself to rendering the perceptual memories of the protagonist.

This also pertains to documentary novels and novels where author and narrator seem to be identical, as long as the elements of the action require verification to become real facts, which, as we have seen, is the very nature of fiction. The author Philip Roth *is not* identical with the protagonist who bears the same name in a novel he has written, even if they *may* be identical. As long as they appear in a novel, the reader can never distinguish truth from falsehood, and it is this doubt that distinguishes the fictional character from the real person. To be sure, the reader may presume that they are identical, which is often sufficient to make documentary literature relevant as information about the real world, but the borderline between fiction and non-fiction remains intact, as does the distinction between author and narrator.

By now, it should be obvious why I have preferred *action* to the current narratological term *story*. The ambiguity of *story*, which may refer to the text as well as the events, leaves it straddling the borderline between reality and fiction, author and narrator. *Action*, on the other hand, refers only to the fictional events and stays firmly on the narrator's side of the line. The author *creates* the action that the narrator *tells*, but both the author and the narrator *tell* the story, the author telling it as a *fictional story* (the novel) and the narrator as a *true story*. To the author, the story is real, as a physical manuscript he can hold in his hands, and at the same time fiction, as the mental model of the fictional events (the action). To the narrator, the story is real both as manuscript and as events. The narrator is part of the story told by the author, but not of the story he tells himself (even if, in a first-person novel, an earlier stage of himself can participate in the action). In other words, the story told by the author is the entire novel, comprising (1) the author as speaker and the real manuscript that is his statement *in the existing world* (the extratextual level), (2) the fictional narrator as a speaker and the fictional manuscript that is *his* statement *in the fictional world* (the intratextual level), and (3) the fictitious action (the intratextual level).

Käte Hamburger's theory

With this account of the genesis of the fictional narrator, we are in a better position to discern the weaknesses of Käte Hamburger's theory of the epic preterite (fictional past) and absence of a speaker in the third-person novel. As we have seen, Hamburger bases her theory on the fact that the fictional action of the third-person novel does not belong to the past of the author (Hamburger 1968, 115) and that the past tense of the text therefore does not refer to his past. Logically, this should entail that the preterite refers to no sender, creating a vacuum that renders the verbal tense functionless. In a way, therefore, Hamburger is right, but she fails to see that the very logic that removes the sender and renders the verbal tense functionless also forces the reader to fill the vacuum with a new sender, the narrator. We cannot imagine a text without a sender; texts do not exist in a vacuum. Texts require a human sender with a past to which the past tense can refer. If the sender is logically absent and the preterite refers to no one's past, the logic of language fills the vacuum.

This automatic creation of the narrator is sufficient to explain the observations on which Hamburger builds her arguments. Deictic adverbs and pronouns like *today*, *here*, *now* and *this* can refer to the viewpoint of third-person characters, because as an inexorable part of the fictional creation, the narrator has access to their minds and discloses to the reader the world as they see it. As for readers' use of the present tense even when speaking of a text written in the past tense, it also fails to support Hamburger's argument. In Chapter 3, we saw that this use of the present tense refers to the presence of the mental model of the action, not to any alleged atemporality of the preterite. Furthermore, contrary to Hamburger's theory, such references to a narrator as 'I', 'we', 'our hero' and so forth are not empty phrases, but really indicate the existence of a fictive narrator.

In other words, the third-person novel has a narrator just as its first-person novel counterpart, and the verbal tense has a normal temporal function in referring to the temporal relationship between the narrator and the fictional action. Hence, Hamburger's *epic preterite* is based on a logical mistake, and its continued use is justified neither in literary theory nor in linguistics.

The nature of the narrator

The fictional narrator, as part of the fictional world and like the fictional action a product of the author's imagination, benefits from the same constitutional freedom from referential constraints as the fictional action and is not restricted by the rules governing non-fictional authorship. The biographer and the historian cannot furnish the reader with more information about the subject than their sources permit. They cannot, for instance, relate what happens in the minds of others apart from what these people have disclosed themselves. People can forget or lie, however, so the reader cannot be absolutely sure that the information the author has acquired is true. In fiction, on the other hand, the author invents all the information he wishes to share with the reader, so there are really no constraints. As a projection of the text, the narrator is not only created by the text but also formed in accordance with the information it offers. If the model of the fictional action comprises information about the inner life of third-person characters, the narrator becomes automatically omniscient. In fact, the reader is not allowed access to the minds of the characters *thanks to* the omniscient narrator. On the contrary, the narrator becomes omniscient because the thoughts and feelings of the characters are accessible to the reader. Only afterwards does it look as if the omniscient narrator has supplied the reader with the otherwise inaccessible information.

Even in first-person novels, the narrator may be omniscient, although it does not occur very often and then mostly unobtrusively. An example of this is *Moby Dick* (Melville 2005), in which the first-person narrator Ishmael tells us what Captain Ahab experiences in private. Käte Hamburger regards this as a flaw in the novel, contending that the omniscient third-person representation of thinking and feeling subjects in a first-person novel is like oil and water, but the reader is more interested in information about the prominent character Ahab than in the thematically irrelevant omniscience of the narrator. Only the action of *Moby Dick* is of thematic value to the reader, who is grateful for all the information about it he can get. The impossibility of this information having reached the narrator is insignificant in comparison to the information's value. Hamburger considers the first-person novel a mirror image of autobiography, overlooking the fact that fiction's constitutional freedom from referential constraints also applies to the first-person novel, as long as it conveys a content that serves the interests of the reader.

Although narrative fiction nowadays always reaches the reader in written form, this does not automatically mean that the narrator communicates with his narratee (the fictional receiver) in writing. In this respect, it is useful to distinguish between overt and covert narrators. Completely covert narrators do not, of course, inform the narratee about the circumstances pertaining to the delivery of the text. The written text simply is there, and it is up to the reader to imagine how it came into being. Overt narrators do not necessarily explain the genesis of the text either, but some may tell the receiver that they are writing, like the narrator Serenus Zeitblom in Thomas Mann's *Doktor Faustus* (Mann 1967). However, the written text may also be the product of an obscure person who in some obscure way has overheard the narrator's story. For example, in Albert Camus' *La chute* (*The Fall*, Camus 1976), an oral version of the story appears in writing for unknown reasons. The narrative situation is a bar conversation in which only one of the speakers' voices is rendered. How the conversation ends up in a book is never revealed. The writing narrator in *La chute* is evidently not identical with the speaking narrator, but he belongs to the fictional world because he reproduces the conversation without comment, presenting the story as something real. So the fictional narrative process may consist in a speaking narrator's thoughts being reported in some supernatural way to a fictional writing narrator.

The role of the receiver

The real author addresses a real reader, and because of the parallel between fiction and reality, the fictional narrator must also address a fictional receiver, the *narratee*. Like the narrator, this narratee is a projection of the text, of the fictional communication. Whereas the fictional events are fiction to the real reader, they are real to the narratee, who is part of the fictional universe. The real reader is only a spectator watching the one-way communication between the fictional narrator and the narratee, and he does not actually take on the role of narratee even if he identifies with it. The real reader sits behind the narratee, listening together with him to the monologue of the narrator. It would not disturb him in the least if the narratee were explicitly exposed in the text as a different person from himself, for instance as a participant of the action, as in second-person novels like Michel Butor's *La modification* (Butor 1957).

As long as the narratee is only a passive receiver, he does not modify the structure of the work and is of little relevance. It is analogous to pouring water in a glass; the water assumes the shape of the glass, so we speak of the shape of the glass, not the 'shape' of the water. Similarly, only when the narrator gives us explicit information about the narratee does the latter become thematically pertinent.

Scholars such as Iser who use the term *implied author* have also, of course, reserved a place for an *implied reader*. The implied reader is, however, just an inevitable complementary supplement to the implied author. Both are expressions of the latent message, which can only be realized through the author's or reader's interpretation of the work and is not an independent entity. It is not the implied reader who contributes to the interpretation of the work but the real reader's qualities as a human being. For our purposes, even if the narratee or implied reader affects the structure of the work, their functions are already covered by other terms (latent message, received message), and therefore I see no reason to elaborate on them here.

Attachment

Susan S. Lanser seems to address the problem of the implied author in her essay, 'The "I" of the Beholder: Equivocal Attachments and the Limits of Structuralist Narratology', which links the question of the narrator's identity or non-identity with the author to the reader's experience (Lanser, 207–19). However, Lanser turns out to be concerned with something quite different. Her focus is on the reader's feeling of coming into contact with the real author in particular passages of the text, hearing his voice through that of the narrator or one of the characters. In this way, the text takes on a peculiar duality: through the fictional surface we get a reference to the real author, his real voice resounding through the voice of the fictional narrator so that the reader reads the text fictionally and referentially at the same time. Lanser calls this special contact between reader and writer *attachment*: the author is attached when his voice comes through the text and detached when the fictional world takes over again. It is characteristic for attachment and detachment that readers routinely 'vacillate' and 'oscillate' between referential and fictional modes of reading. Attachment, then, only occurs in parts of the text. This distinguishes attachment from implied and biographical authorship, as well as from 'the commonplace practice of reading texts in relation to the historical person who wrote them, which attaches to the author the *whole* of the text'.

Lanser suggests five terms related to attachment: *singularity, anonymity, identity, reliability* and *non-narrativity*. By *singularity* she means the presence of one rather than many voices on the highest diegetic level of the text, which singles out lyric poetry as especially subject to attachment. *Anonymity* on the part of the narrator means that the narrator has no name to distinguish him clearly from the author and hence disrupt the attachment. *Identity* encompasses all (perceived) social similarities between a narrator and an author: name, gender, race, age, biography, beliefs and values, or occupation as a writer. *Reliability* is the reader's determination that the narrator's values and perceptions are consistent with those of the author, and *non-narrativity* refers to the narrator's comments and intradiegetic dialogue.

It may be difficult to understand what Lanser means by *attachment* as long as the term is used to rule out the implied author and the biographical person who has written the book. Moreover, she does not tell us why attachment is a relevant subject for literary theory. However, the distinctions we introduced in relation to the author's intention might help us better understand what Lanser means.

By excluding the implied author, Lanser signals clearly that attachment goes beyond the latent message, so she must mean the author's own views, which, however, are often identical with the latent message. Her insistence on *identity* and *reliability* as terms of attachment shows clearly that attachment is related to the author's own views. In other words, the reader sometimes has the feeling or illusion of perceiving the author's own views through the voice of the narrator or one of the characters. Lanser's purpose in drawing our attention to attachment and detachment is obviously not to foreground the distinction between the latent message and the author's views, and she does not discuss whether or how often they may coalesce. But if she is interested in the author's own views, why does she rule out the biographical and historical person who is inseparably linked to them? The prevalence of attachment in lyric poetry indicates another possibility. Is she is more interested in the voice of the author as a manifestation of interpersonal contact than for the message it conveys? If that is the case, her notion of attachment comes close to a social function of literature that consists in establishing a feeling of personal contact between reader and author, making the reader feel less alone in the real world. In previous chapters, I have called this phenomenon the *phatic function*. This feeling of personal contact is particularly strong in confessional poetry and intimate, personal, lyric poetry. It is difficult to know whether Lanser's concept of attachment really refers to phatic function, but if this is her intention, it is an interesting contribution to the understanding of the various functions of literature.

8

The Structure of the Action

In narratology, interest in the action (story) itself has varied over the years. The prominent narratologist Gérard Genette (Genette 1972 and 1983) has not, for instance, been interested in the structures of the action (the story) as such, only in the way it is reproduced in the text (the discourse). On the other hand, the action has received a lot of attention from other structuralists and narratologists (Propp 1968, Greimas 1966, Todorov 1973, Chatman 1978, Rimmon-Kenan 1983 and Bal 1990).

The mental model and the action

What is the *action*, or *story* as narratologists prefer to call it? When we were dealing with the four levels of the communication process, we identified the action as the referent in the semantic triangle, while the mental model of it was the signified. We have seen how the action (the referent) comes into existence as a projection of the mental model (the signified) thanks to the model's analogy with the real world. If we want to compare the mental model with the action it renders in order to see how truthfully it reproduces the action, the action itself is not directly available. It exists only by virtue of the parallel between the fictional world and the existing world, but because of this parallelism, we can infer from the existing world how the fictional action must be, filling in the gaps of the mental model with inferences or educated guesses. Ernest Hemingway, for instance, conveys the cognitive content not only through dialogue and action, but also through elision; he often omits the thoughts and feelings of his characters and some relevant physical details, leaving the reader to complete the blanks with his own prior knowledge of the world. According to Carlos Baker, 'Hemingway referred to his style as the iceberg theory: in his writing the facts float above water; the supporting structure and symbolism operate out-of-sight' (Baker 1972). The elements 'operating out-of-sight' are the general knowledge about the world and human life which Hemingway shares with his readers and which his concise style depends upon. This prior knowledge fills in the gaps, allowing the reader to establish a sufficiently coherent picture of events in order to extrapolate useful information about his own world.

Although the action as *referent* is part of a physical world (in analogy with real events), it is only accessible to us through a mental model, primarily the explicit mental model we are already acquainted with but also a secondary, more general mental model of the world in general. Our extratextual, general knowledge about the real world helps us establish a similar general model of the fictional world, which supplements the limited primary model of the action. All in all, we have to account for three different mental models: (1) an intratextual (primary) model based on the text, (2) an equally intratextual (secondary) model of the fictional world in general, which is based on a comparison with (3) the reader's extratextual model of the real world. In the first place, we receive the concrete representation of the fictional action from the text (the primary mental model of the action). Second, we obtain a general notion of how the original action 'must have been' before being reduced into text (the secondary mental model of the world in general). Finally, there is the reader's general knowledge about the existing world.

As we take in the author's selection of elements and details, we compare the signified (the text-based mental model of the action) with our general conception of the extratextual world, not with the referent itself (the action). The thoughts and feelings of Hemingway's characters are left out of the text (i.e. the text-based model of the action), but after comparing the text (the text-based model) with our general model of the real world, we realize that their thoughts and feelings have been left unstated. In other words, the thoughts and feelings of these characters are only implied in the text/model, whereas they exist in our general conception of the action, as general notions without details.

What is the action?

The action is the process of change and development in the conditions of the fictional characters, comprising both changes in their external environment and in their own bodies and minds. The content of the action may range from minimal alterations (like natural aging) to radical changes in the characters' existential situation, but in fictional literature, there is a tendency to prioritize dramatic changes, which are usually the result of conflicts between characters: one character cannot satisfy his own needs without affecting or interfering with someone else's. Most literary action implies some sort of conflict; the antagonists may include human beings, other sorts of living creatures, objects or even the environment as such.

However, literature can also be almost actionless, primarily in lyric poetry, whose brevity often restricts it to idylls and static situations. Conflict-free novels and plays are rare, though not unheard-of. In 1916, not far from the horrors of the trenches, the Flemish author Felix Timmermans (Timmermans 1950) published the conflictless novel *Pallieter*, whose title character is a miller who enjoys the simple pleasures of life, especially nature and the company of others. The book's descriptions of life's small pleasures are so lively that it became a great success and was translated into many languages despite its lack of conflict.

Apart from this example, conflictless action is more or less an ingredient in modern experimental literature. Alain Robbe-Grillet's short story *La plage* (*The Beach*) only describes some children walking on the beach without hinting at any conflict or change (Robbe-Grillet 1966). The only change consists in their movement along the beach and the lapse of time. In Robbe-Grillet, this kind of story may be seen as a protest against the traditional plot with its conflicts and dramatic events, which are not typical of most people's lives. His story instead depicts life as most people experience it, as a set of perceptions without strong conflicts: 'The world is neither meaningful nor absurd. It just *is*' (Robbe-Grillet 1963, 21, my translation).

The same approach characterizes his novel *La jalousie* (*Jealousy*), which gives a detailed description of a character's memories of events that appear trivial until we learn they are a suspicious husband's analysis of the interaction between his wife and a neighbour (Robbe-Grillet 1957). In this novel, conflict sneaks in through the back door.

Although there are examples of fiction without conflicts, conflicts are the norm, ranging from the simple problems of everyday life to dramatic crises. From a cognitive point of view, both conflicts and static situations are interesting, because they teach us about cause and effect or about values. Both kinds of information contribute to our understanding of human life in terms of challenges as well as solutions. In popular and serious literature alike, there is an overrepresentation of strong conflicts and extreme events in comparison to the quiet routines and events of everyday life. If the reader consults literature to learn more about the extratextual world, it may seem strange that he looks for it in the extraordinary behaviour exhibited in books. Although dramatic events rarely concern common people, however, they are still an aspect of life that may happen to us, and as such we need information about them. Furthermore, dramatic events may shed useful light on less dramatic forms of human interaction. The exaggeration and over-dimensioning of human behaviour and its consequences makes it easier to see the mechanisms at work in them. Finally, another motive for magnifying and distorting reality may be for pure entertainment. Even serious readers are hardly insensitive to the emotional rush afforded by suspense.

The action as part of a larger fictional world

Owing to the deficiencies of language, the fictional work is unable to render the entire fictional world with its infinite amount of elements and details, so in the mental model, the action appears in a radically reduced version. A similar reduction occurs in biography, which can only render a minimal part of the biographical person's life, even if the sources allow for much more. On account of the similarity between the fictional and the real world, the fictional action is part of a limitless world of detail. How can we delimit the action from this endless context? Is the referent of the novel everything that has taken place in the fictional universe since the (fictional!) big bang?

In principle, the answer is yes, but in practice, the reader identifies the action with a small, very limited section of the endless whole of which it is a part: the section of the universe he deems relevant. What is relevant is, of course, subject to interpretation and belongs to the interpretative process, but normally the reader contents himself with the elements that are closely related to the fictional events explicitly mentioned in the text. In *Mrs Dalloway*, the action is confined mainly to London and Bourton (Clarissa's childhood home in the countryside), with the rest of the world excluded as irrelevant, apart from some short passages about India and World War I in Italy. In spite of the novel's interest in the female protagonist's activities, her everyday life (grooming habits, meals etc.) is to a great extent left out without the reader missing them. The mental model of the action only renders explicitly those aspects of everyday life that shed light on the relationship between the characters and on their values and needs.

The manner in which World War I is included in the novel is an interesting example of how the deficient mental model of the action is capable of appropriating supplementary information from the fictional universe which parallels the extratextual world. With the exception of a few lines (Woolf 2000, 73) that hint rather superficially at the war's horrors, it is mentioned only as the root of certain problems, like Miss Kilman's interrupted education and Septimus's mental illness. Septimus's mental condition and suicide are a dominant subject in the novel, and are valuable insofar as they tell us about how a mentally ill patient is affected by his condition, the national health service and the social environment. However, it is also thematically important that his mental disease is an effect of the war, because first of all this information highlights the injustice of the victim's fate, and second, it is a strong argument against war in general. In *Mrs Dalloway*, the political aspects of the war are not at issue (even though they are implicitly part of the fictional world), but rather the experiences of the soldiers in the trenches. To fully comprehend Septimus's psychological wounds of war, the reader must already know something about the hell the soldiers went through in the trenches. When the novel was published in 1925, readers knew in detail the atrocities of war through literature, media and personal contact, and Woolf undoubtedly expected them to transfer this knowledge to her fictional character's situation. She intended the reader's general conception of World War I to serve as a supplementary framework for the understanding of the mental model of the action. Insofar as all readers know what the modern experience of war implies, this implicit prerequisite is part of the work itself.

We can distinguish between three different levels of the action thus: (1) the directly accessible, deficient action expressed by the mental model, (2) the limited, not directly accessible but nevertheless complete section of the fictional world that is relevant to the action and (3) the infinite remainder of the fictional world that is not relevant to the action.

Problems with the definition of *story*

When we treated the different levels of the literary communication process in Chapter 3, we saw that structuralist scholars use the term *story* in different and partially conflicting senses. One reason for this terminological confusion is that scholars frequently use the term without clarifying its relationship to the semantic triangle. Genette tries to adapt his terminology to the triangle, defining *story* as the *signified* (Genette 1972, 72), but as we shall see, this only increases the confusion.

To explain the flaw in Genette's definition of the story as the signified, we need the distinction between *the material text*, *the mental model of the action* and *the action*, which is an exact parallel to the triad *signifier*, *signified* and *referent*. The point of the narratological distinction between *text* (or *discourse*, in Chatman and Genette's usage) and *story* is to enable the scholar to study how the text (discourse) modifies the story: how the text/discourse by means of selection, duration, viewpoint, voice, frequency, order and style presents the story in a new shape without affecting its original facts. Transposed into our own terms (*the material text, the mental model of the action* and *the action*) and the parallel semantic triangle, this means that the material text (the signifier) converts the action (the referent) into a mental model which differs from the original complete action by having retained only a limited selection of its infinite detail.

According to the logic of Genette's own theory, the story has to be identical with *the referent* (the action) and cannot be defined as *the signified* (the model of the action) that modifies it, so Genette's definition of *the story* as *the signified* is in conflict with his own logic. As we have seen, the signifier (the material text) determines the signified (the model of the action) so that they are completely correlated, and there is no question of the signifier modifying the signified. If the term *the story* were really equivalent to the term *the signified*, it would be meaningless to study the differences between them. The application of voice, for instance, is identical in signifier (the material text) and signified (the model of the action): if the text contains the sentence, 'I woke up one morning', the application of the first person is maintained in the mental model, as the letter 'I' *means* the first person. On the other hand, the first person of the signified (the mental model) that unifies one of the characters with the narrator constitutes a selection compared to the referent (the fresh, untouched action), in which the humans are still neutral in terms of grammatical person as long as none of them has yet been selected for the role of narrator.

Genette's confusing attempt to define the story as the signified exposes the drawbacks of the abstract terms of the semantic triangle as well as those of the originally more or less synonymous *text, discourse* and *story*. Genette's use of *text* to mean *mental model* is so confusing that even Genette himself mixes it up with the material text (the signifier) and mistakes the pair *signifier* and *signified* for the pair *signified* and *referent*. The synonym of *discourse* is probably less apt to be confused with the material text, so for scholars who dislike the admittedly inconvenient *mental model of the action*, Chatman's *discourse* is preferable to Genette's and Rimmon-Kenan's *text*.

Story is ambiguous in one more crucial respect. Several scholars regard the story as a skeletal structure that can be replicated in different works, like the stories of Romeo and Juliet, Faust or Tom Thumb (Bal 1990, 18–19; Abbott 2008, 21–4). The fairy tales of different countries are often so strikingly similar that it seems reasonable to identify them as the same story. If the likenesses are due to cross-cultural transmission of an original tale, it seems even more logical to regard the similar tales as variations on a single story. Does this mean that the mental model conveyed by a given text can have several referents? Here, a comparison with the non-fictional story may be instructive.

In the existing world, an event may be recounted in different versions because different witnesses interpret the incident their own way. Their stories differ even though they stem from the same event. There is only one referent, but several mental models of it (signifieds). The author of a novel does not relate something he has witnessed (except if he is writing an autobiographical novel, a special case we dealt with in Chapter 2). He invents the referent (the action or story), and there are no other witnesses to his imagination, so he is the only one to report the referent, and the story he tells has only one version, his own. In other words, there can only be one referent (story or action) and one signifier/signified (text/mental model) in fiction. As the referent and the signifier/signified are created simultaneously, it follows that the fictional referent cannot have more than one signified. If the author changes his text/mental model, he inevitably creates a new referent (story or action). Hence, the action of a fictional work is a unique, individual entity that belongs to this work alone, and it cannot be shared by other works.

How, then, do we explain the cross-cultural spread of one story? The answer lies in distinguishing among the various meanings of *story*. A story that occurs in different versions is not a *referent* (particular events) but a *signified* (a mental model) that serves as a source for new signifieds. When a story is recycled, it is not repeated literally, but only part of it, a skeletal structure. *Story* in this sense does not mean the original events themselves, only a radically simplified, abstract model of it. Simplification and abstraction can ultimately reduce the original action to such an extent that it could apply to almost any novel or drama. When Gottfried Keller, working from Shakespeare's *Romeo and Juliet*, wrote his own version of the 'same' tale, the short story *Romeo und Julia auf dem Dorfe* (Keller 1953), he only retained the general pattern of young lovers who commit suicide because of the enmity between their families. All the other elements are totally different from the original: the setting, the characters and the background of the conflict between the families. Keller did not copy the *action* of Shakespeare's drama, only an extreme abstraction of it. As we see, the term *story* also lends itself to designating the *source material*, which only adds to its considerable ambiguity.

In contrast to the ambiguous *story*, *action* is naturally associated with the referent, so to avoid the above-mentioned problems I prefer to replace *story* with the less ambiguous *action*, which I define as identical with *the referent*. However, I still find *story* useful as a synonym, mainly in situations where its association with the signified is not likely to cause misunderstandings.

The author's influence on the action

In spite of the likeness between the fictional and real world, the fictional world deviates from the real one in one important respect. The existing world faced by the individual is in principle an infinite chaos of events and details before it is organized by a human mind. This chaos only gets processed and modified when perceived by a human mind. Because of the inner qualities with which the individual is endowed through heritage and environment, the mind functions as a filter; as we have seen in the chapter on intention (Chapter 6), every outside impression that passes through it is filtered and interpreted. However, the world the reader encounters in literature is already processed and filtered by another consciousness. The author has selected the content according to his own worldview and his own conception of relevance, in an attempt to be neutral and objective or convey a subjective view on the world. Whatever the motives, the author's subjective conception of the world stands between the reader and the original, untouched world on which the story is based, as has been thoroughly discussed in previous chapters.

All fictional action is based on ingredients from the existing world, but its freedom from referential constraints gives the writer licence to manipulate and modify the material he takes from this world. In theory, there is no limit to how radically the author can change the empirical foundation. In transforming the general information into an individual fictional story, not only can he choose his material freely from the general patterns of the real world (he is, after all, often inspired by real events), but he can also distort the fictional elements so that they deviate from real patterns. He can create witches and ogres, future societies and little princes that live on asteroids in space and move to other asteroids with the help of migratory birds. The freedom from referential constraint also extends to the fictional narrator, who can be endowed with unrealistic features like omniscience and the ability to go on telling the story after death. Ultimately, the fictional action may deviate so radically from the patterns of the existing world that it becomes entirely incomprehensible, thus losing its cognitive content. In practice, the author's freedom is constrained by various considerations, depending on his intentions with the work. The author's manipulation of the material he borrows from the extratextual world must be in proportion to the influence he wants to exert on the reader. For example, if he wants to convey insight into the conditions and values of the existing world, the structure of the action must contain this kind of latent information. This, of course, restricts the writer's freedom. The fictional world cannot deviate from the real one in any respect that disrupts the cognitive content.

If we assume the author wants to convey some cognitive content, he has a choice between different ways of rendering the material he borrows from the existing world:

1. *Reproductive rendering* of the action: the author copies coherent real events so that the fictional world is as identical with the real one as verbal communication permits (in autobiography, for example). This technique ensures complete veracity.
2. *Combinative rendering* of the action: the author mixes elements from one chain of real events with those of another one, creating a new story (in documentary novels, for instance). The action is still based on real facts, but the combination of the elements endangers the veracity of the story to a certain extent.
3. *Deductive rendering* of the action: the author invents a story independently of real events but according to general patterns he has extrapolated from his own experiences or learnt in other ways (in realistic novels, for example). The action still resembles real events, but because it is based on theoretical knowledge, the authenticity of the subordinate elements is uncertain, in contrast to the theory-based skeleton they flesh out.
4. *Intuitive rendering* of the action: based on intuition, the author invents a story independently of real events (in realistic novels and symbolic novels, for example). The action may still resemble real events, but because it is based on the author's unconscious worldview, the authenticity of the subordinate elements as well as the theory-based skeleton they flesh out is uncertain.
5. *Alternative rendering* of the action: the author invents a story that contrasts with real events or a dominant conception of the general patterns of reality. The action may conform to the general structures of reality in other respects. The intention is to show alternatives to actual events or ingrained convictions (for instance utopias, dystopias; the novel *Siegfried* by the Dutch writer Harry Mulisch, who imagines Hitler as the father of a son [Mulisch 2001]).
6. *Auxiliary rendering.* The author invents action that conflicts with the general structure of reality or with actual events and facts, but the deviation is not thematically relevant and is only intended to facilitate the communication of another message. The underlying action is then conveyed by symbolic or allegorical structures (the medieval play *Everyman*) or non-symbolic auxiliary structures (*The Little Prince*).

7. *Non-veracious rendering.* The author can invent an action that conflicts with the general structure of reality or with actual events and facts, and the deviation is thematically relevant (in escapist literature, for instance).

Compared to the limited ways of influencing the reader that are available to non-fiction, the freedom from referential constraint greatly augments the author's influence.

The complexity of the action

The action is a complex collection of specific examples of human behaviour that the reader can study and interpret in order to obtain a deeper understanding of the interaction between humans and their environment in the extratextual world. It is the vehicle for the latent message. The way the mental model renders the action (through selection, viewpoint, voice, frequency, order and style) is not sufficient to create a message, although it influences the message that the reader ultimately extrapolates from the action. The author's selection of viewpoint does not, for instance, alter the structure of the action, only the perspective from which it is seen and hence the information that this perspective makes available. A constant one-sided internal viewpoint, for instance, gives the reader direct access to the perceptions and experiences of one character, to the exclusion of the direct perceptions and experiences of other characters. Because the structure of the action is of primary importance for the cognitive process, it is the first object we should study in order to understand the potential impact of the work on the reader.

Literary action is not a homogeneous phenomenon, however. Our corpus of literature consists not only in the countless different actions that already exist in all national literatures, but also, strictly speaking, in all those that have yet to be written. This means that the theory of literature must allow for new types of actions to come. Since literary fiction attempts to communicate information about the extratextual world, the fictional world is, in principle, as complex as the extratextual one. Moreover, the author's freedom to create divergent patterns increases the diversity. It is therefore as difficult to classify the elements of the fictional action as it is to classify the elements of life itself. Although fiction largely restricts itself to those aspects of reality that pertain to human and interpersonal problems, the enormous variety of human behaviour patterns attested to in psychology, sociology, criminology, medicine, anthropology, ethnography, ethnology, philosophy, comparative religion and history indicates that literary action cannot be reduced into a simple, clear typology.

Furthermore, the above-mentioned fields adapt their typologies to their own needs, and we cannot assume that they can account for all the aspects of human life that occur or may occur in fictional literature. On the other hand, these fields offer knowledge that can save literary studies from doing the same work all over again, and there is no reason why the literary scholar should not benefit from this promise as long as it helps him understand the literature's effect in general or in particular works.

Of course, it is debatable whether we can understand the literary world through methods that apply originally to the empirical world. Because of the author's freedom from referential constraints, we have already seen that the fictional world and the real world follow different rules. As long as it does not affect the cognitive message, the author may manipulate the action, dramatizing, concentrating, intensifying and distorting it at will. Within certain boundaries, our expectations of fictional characters are different from what we expect from real people. The reader must distinguish between the surface structures of the action and its underlying structures. The surface structures may be completely unrealistic, as long as the underlying structures comply with reality. In allegorical literature (e.g. Bunyan's *The Pilgrim's Progress*; Bunyan 2009) and symbolic literature (Swift's *Gulliver's Travels* or Carroll's *Alice in Wonderland*; Swift 1998, Carroll 1996), the surrealist surface action disguises an underlying realistic representation of human interaction, conveying profound insight into human problems and values. Although the author distorts the action mostly to make it easier for the reader to grasp the message, such devices are not always meant to facilitate comprehension. Shklovsky's famous article, 'Art as technique' (Shklovsky 1990), points out how defamiliarization can intensify attention and perception.

When studying literary action, in other words, we must discriminate between meaningful underlying structures and surface structures that are not meaningful in their own right but convey meaning indirectly or lay the ground for meaningful structures. Only the meaningful structures are meant to correspond to reality's own structures, and can therefore be analysed with the same methods as real events. The non-meaningful auxiliary structures are, on the other hand, subject to literary methods of analysis and should not be involved directly when we study the latent cognitive potential of the action. In *The Little Prince*, the boy's age, living conditions and ways of getting around and the ability of animals and plants to speak are only auxiliary constructions without thematic function. It is the interpersonal relationships between the characters and their attitude to existential problems that constitute the theme.

The relationship between events and characters

What is the best way to describe the thematically relevant structures of fictional action? One traditional way of classifying the elements of the action is to distinguish between *characters* and *events*, which, although useful, may pose problems. Handbooks of literary theory tend to treat characters and events separately (Chatman 1978, 43–4, 107–8; Rimmon-Kenan 1983, 6–7, 29–30.; Bal 1990, 92–3, 135–6; Herman 2007, 66–7; Fludernik 2009, 44–5, and to a lesser extent in Herman and Vervaeck 2005, 55; Abbott 2008, 130), implying that characters and events are independent of each other. Through the centuries, scholars have discussed whether character or action is more important. Aristotle, the Formalists and some structuralists subordinate characters to action (Chatman 1978, 110–11; Abbott 2008, 130–1). Tomashevsky even asserts that 'the hero is scarcely necessary to the story. The story as a system of motifs can entirely dispense with the hero and his characteristic traits' (Chatman 1978, 111–12; Tomashevsky 1965, 293). Nevertheless, there seems to be a growing consensus that character and action are inseparable (Chatman 1978, 113; Rimmon-Kenan 1983, 35–6; Herman and Vervaeck 2005, 55; Abbott 2008, 131). Drawing from Hrushovsky, Rimmon-Kenan suggests that the predominance of characters or events may primarily be a question of the reader's interests (Rimmon-Kenan 1983, 36). Although it seems evident that 'there cannot be events without existants' (Chatman 1978, 113), Rimmon-Kenan points out that the forms of the interdependence between character and action remain to be analysed (Rimmon-Kenan 1983, 35). That is what we shall try to do now.

We are normally able to isolate character and action as if they had little or nothing to do with each other. We speak of a character's qualities and environment as something static. Take the following example from *Max Havelaar* (Multatuli 1860):

> The Controller Verbrugge was a good man. If one saw him there in his blue clothing, with embroidered oak and orange branches on the collar and the cuffs, it was hard to mistake the type which is common among the Hollanders in the Indies – a kind of man who is very different from the Hollanders in Holland. He took his ease as long as there was nothing to do, and he was remote from the organising zeal which is in Europe called industrious, but he was industrious when work was needed – eager to give information and to help, hospitable – well-mannered but not stiff – candid – honest and righteous, without being a martyr to these properties – in short, he was a man who, as it is said, would fit in

anywhere, although one would not consider naming the age after him, which he did not desire.

In this passage, the character is described in terms of static qualities, not as an active agent; even the activity ('saw him there') that accompanies the static description is passive. The description is far more detailed than what is necessary for the reader to benefit cognitively from the action: this mental model of the action informs the reader about more than the relevant events in the strictest sense, showing him that the people behind the events have more complex personalities than evidenced by their actions and indicating their potential of reacting differently to other situations.

Folktales seem, on the contrary, to foreground events and take little interest in characters, as shown in Grimm's description of Snow White:

> After a year had passed the king took to himself another wife. She was a beautiful woman, but proud and haughty, and she could not bear that anyone else should surpass her in beauty . . .

> Now, Snow White was growing prettier and prettier, and when she was seven years old she was as beautiful as day, far more so than the queen herself. So one day when the queen went to her mirror and said,

> "Looking-glass upon the wall,
> Who is fairest of us all?"

> it answered,

> "Queen, you are full fair, 'tis true,
> But Snow White fairer is than you."

> This gave the queen a great shock, and she became yellow and green with envy, and from that hour her heart turned against Snow White, and she hated her. And envy and pride like ill weeds grew in her heart higher every day, until she had no peace day or night. At last she sent for a huntsman, and said, "Take the child out into the woods, so that I may set eyes on her no more. You must put her to death, and bring me her heart for a token."

The text focuses on the action and only mentions Snow White's qualities insofar as they are necessary to understand the action, primarily her beauty.

However, our capacity for separating characters and events in this way does not imply that they exist in isolation in the extratextual world. However a character is involved in the action, the events affect his life. Whether he is a passive onlooker or an active participant, the small world he is part of changes. It is therefore impossible to isolate the characters completely from the events. This applies even if we seem to direct our attention only towards the properties of the characters or the action. For example, if we characterize the action as dramatic or relatively uneventful, we refer to the changes in the relationships between the characters and not to an abstract chain of events without agents. Structuralists who are only interested in the structure of the action still must implicitly include the characters performing the actions. Agents and actions are inseparable in the existing as well as in the fictional world, so if we want to say anything about the characters, we automatically bring in the action. But what relationship is there exactly between the descriptions of characters and the action?

Description of characters

Characters can be described through four different types of information: (1) *inner qualities* (personality, background, attitudes, views, inclinations), (2) *appearance*, (3) *the physical objects they surround themselves with* and (4) *physical and verbal actions*. What, then, are the functions of these four types of information in relation to the action?

Of course, the characters' actions are most closely related to the action of the book; what they say and do in fact *constitutes* the action. Our inclusion of the characters' actions in the characterization of them indicates just how inextricably events and characters are interwoven. What a person says and does is registered by his social environment, which sees statements and actions in relation to each other and process them into abstract patterns, creating expectations with respect to the person's future behaviour, or in other words, an inventory of his inner qualities. This process may be conscious or unconscious. On account of our inclination to sum up a person's previous behaviour into abstract, general patterns (e.g. *kindness* as the sum of several generous acts in combination with the absence of negative behaviour), there is a close relationship between the characters' actions and what we regard as their inner qualities. The inner qualities of human beings are only a potential, a readiness to behave in a particular way in particular situations. Kindness, presence of mind or language proficiency means only that a person is predisposed or able to do nice things, react quickly or speak a given language.

When the author (through the narrator) explicitly describes a character's properties, as in the excerpt from *Max Havelaar*, the static description postpones the continuation of the action, and its relevance to the events is not immediately clear. To understand the interplay between description and action, we must be aware of the difference between verbal reproduction and direct perception. When we perceive directly, we register the nature of the events and the perceptual appearance of all involved elements, and in addition, we are aware of the thoughts and feelings that this experience evokes. A text that renders these events will inevitably leave out an enormous amount of elements and detail and, moreover, it presents the elements scattered in space (across the pages) and consequently also in time. Every detail is attached to a particular place in the text that separates it spatially and temporally from the elements with which it constituted an inseparable whole in the perceptual world before they were fragmented by language.

When the author/narrator characterizes a fictional character by an abstract inventory of properties, the information is meant to help the reader understand the action. Knowing about a particular character's qualities helps the reader understand his behaviour and his part in the events, whether or not the behaviour confirms or contradicts the expectations inherent in these qualities. If a character we know to be kind unexpectedly performs a bad act, the presumed kindness becomes a mitigating circumstance, and the reader does not condemn it as strongly as he otherwise would have. In *Max Havelaar,* the narrator presents Verbrugge as a good man, and when Verbrugge later betrays Max Havelaar in a critical situation, the combination of presumed goodness and betrayal conveys the message that no one can be trusted in a crisis, not even decent people.

The external characteristics of a person and the physical objects he surrounds himself with are also related to the action. We can distinguish between two possibilities in this respect: (1) the characteristic is due to some kind of action or is liable to influence the action, and (2) the characteristic is incidental and is not causally related to the action. We will now consider both of these possibilities.

In the fairy tale of Snow White, the short description of the young girl has a clear causal function in the action. Her white skin and black hair are manifestations of beauty, and it is this very beauty that triggers the action, provoking her stepmother's jealousy and desire to kill. The description of the stepmother's beauty and arrogance is another necessary cause of the action.

On the other hand, the causal function of description is not always so evident. In Somerset Maugham's *Cakes and Ale*, the narrator spends an entire page describing the character George Kemp, who seems to be of minor importance to the action (Maugham 1948, 67–8). The essence of the description is that George dresses and behaves in a flashy way that is met with contempt in the village. His attempts to be a good fellow villager by being friendly and helpful is of no avail: 'His efforts at sociability were met with blank hostility.' New descriptions keep adding to this first one (69, 82, 93, 221). When some small incidents indicate that George is having an affair with

Rosie, the novel's heroine, the reader receives the information with disgust and refuses to fully accept it. Only at the end of the action, do we realize George's important role, having always been a nice, sympathetic person. This revelation comes as a surprise to the reader, after having seen nothing but other characters' prejudice against George, which even the narrator echoes. The seemingly unimportant descriptions of George prove to be of great relevance to the action, foregrounding the crucial issue, the message: how snobbishness and prejudice prevent people from discovering and appreciating good qualities in others. George's flashiness is a causal element that might have prevented Rosie from seeing his sympathetic personality, but she does, revealing a clear-sightedness and lack of prejudice that contradict her frivolity and compel the reader to reconsider his own prejudice against her unconventional way of life.

Not all personal features have a causal function. Many descriptive elements, including details of the characters' appearance, serve merely to help the reader visualize the action and augment his identification with the characters. The detailed description of George gives the reader a thorough basis for understanding and endorsing the prejudices of those around him.

However, descriptions of a character's appearance may also have another function, which it shares with other forms of description. In 'The Reality Effect', Roland Barthes draws attention to certain descriptive elements in realistic literature that seem to have no function at all (Barthes 2006). As an example he points to a barometer in the sitting-room of Madame Aubain in Flaubert's *Madame Bovary*. Barthes holds that realistic authors' use of such elements is based on a misunderstanding of the relationship between signifier, signified and referent. He ascribes this mistake to the naïve belief that 'useless details' give the reader the illusion of coming into direct contact with reality (Barthes 2006, 234):

> Semiotically, the "concrete detail" is constituted by the *direct* collusion of a referent and a signifier; the signified is expelled from the sign, and with it, the possibility of developing a *form of the signified*, i.e., narrative structure itself. . . . This is what we might call the *referential illusion* . . .
>
> This new verisimilitude . . . proceeds from the intention to degrade the sign's tripartite nature in order to make notation the pure encounter of an object and its expression.

In *How Fiction Works*, James Wood rejects this account as an expression of Barthes' antipathy towards realism, and shows how even apparently useless details may serve a characterizing function (Wood 2008, 64–6). However, if we take Barthes literally, his argument is based on a wrong conception of the semantic triangle, because the reader has no access to the referent, which would have to be a fictional version of the physical world. Only the mental model of the action, the signified, is accessible to him, and it seems implausible that Barthes would attribute so little intelligence to realist writers as to think they would believe themselves able to convey a piece of the physical world by means of trivial elements in the text. However, we need not take recourse to the semantic triangle to explain why 'useless detail' in a realistic novel can create a reality effect. 'Useless' details are traditionally rare in fiction because the author omits them, whereas they occur in abundance in the real world before it is subjected to authorial selection. Insofar as the realist author really permits 'useless' detail in his novel, it may reinforce the reader's impression of facing reality itself insofar as the text creates an illusion of being unfiltered like reality itself. This does not imply that the reader believes he is perceiving the real world itself, only that he has the impression that the text renders a more complete (and consequently, more realistic) picture of the referent than other texts. The author pretends that he has not subjected the mental model of the action to any ideological filtering, giving the feigned impression of objectivity.

Sometimes details that may be useless per se become functional due to the reader's prejudices (which the author might share with him). For instance, the dark colour of a character's skin may provoke the reader's disdain, while blue eyes and blond hair may inspire undeserved trust. In *Cakes and Ale*, the blue eyes of the frivolous Rosie (Maugham 1948, 60) have, according to traditional prejudice, the connotation of innocence, which seems to contradict her promiscuity, but on the other hand, her blue eyes fit perfectly with the innocence of her promiscuous behaviour. Maugham's message is to warn readers not to condemn the behaviour of others before they have considered all relevant information. In Rosie's case, promiscuity becomes not an offense but an expression of generosity and a different cultural code.

Action-orientation and character-orientation as forms of selection

It is possible that the tendency to separate action and characters may in fact be an obscure attempt to distinguish between two forms of selection. The foregrounding of the action at the expense of describing the characters may imply a more superficial approach to the theme, whereas a thorough introduction of the characters may lead to a deeper understanding of the world. In *Cakes and Ale*, the detailed description of the narrow-minded bourgeoisie and the liberal Rosie is a prerequisite for understanding and assessing Rosie's unconventional behaviour (Maugham 1948, 38–40, 74, 151–4, 155, 159). The description of the characters reveals the crucial social and cultural conflicts that characterize Victorian and early post-Victorian society and increases the reader's intellectual and emotional involvement in the action. In comparison, the information about the characters of the folk tale is far too sketchy and one-sided to involve the reader in a comparable manner. The hero or heroine, for instance Snow White, is described in terms of only one function in the action and is part of a much simpler social system than Rosie. *Snow White* presents an uncomplicated conflict between good and evil that throws light on individual moral problems, whereas *Cakes and Ale* elucidates complex forms of social interactions. The difference between a folk tale and a novel like *Cakes and Ale* is less a question of preference for action or characters than a question of interest in particular aspects of the events.

Attempts at simplification

Based on the distinction between character and action, various attempts have been made to discover general patterns in fictional action. In his famous analysis of Russian fairy tales, Vladimir Propp differentiates between 31 functions (types of action) and 7 character types: the *villain*, the *donor*, the *princess* and *her father*, the *dispatcher*, the *hero*, the *helper* and the *false hero* (Propp 1928). His classification is tailored to Russian fairy tales and is therefore less suited for other literary genres, or even other types of fairy tales, like realistic fairy tales.

Based on Propp's seven character types, A. G. Greimas has tried to make a more universal list of character types or *actants*, of which he lists six: *sender*, *object*, *receiver*, *helper*, *subject* and *opponent*, all of whom interact with each other (Greimas 1966, 174–85 and 192–212). To illustrate the various forms in which these six actants can appear, Greimas lists a variety of thematic motives that may influence the action: all kinds of love, admiration, feelings of responsibility, religious or political fanaticism, greed, envy, vengefulness, avarice, pride, hate, peace, freedom, the impulse for change, patriotism, fear and so on (Greimas points out that the list is meant to be neither complete nor systematic).

Bremonds's system of bifurcation is another form of simplification, where the action is divided into new bifurcations at each point of the story that offers new options. In this way the action is schematized in a diagram that shows realized as well as non-realized alternatives (Bremond 1973; Rimmon-Kenan 1983, 22–3).

The purpose of compressing the action into such a simplified skeleton is to find a basic structure, the smallest meaningful elements of which the action is composed. The idea seems to be that just as natural science reduces substance into molecules and atoms, the larger elements in literature are better comprehended in the light of the smallest elements. Such a scientific attitude has dominated the linguistic conception of verbal utterances up to the semantic level and has gained access to literary theory through semiology. To what extent, however, is such an atomistic approach useful in a literary context? What are the smallest meaningful elements in fictional action?

The smallest meaningful elements of the action

The smallest entity our senses can distinguish in the real world is *detail*, which belongs to the realm of phenomenology. A detail at the lowest level is an object, quality or relationship that we distinguish as something elementary. A detail may be a chair, the colour of the chair or the position of the chair in relation to its environment. But whatever the detail, it must be related to time and space if it is to be intelligible; the chair must be situated in space and time. Therefore, the smallest meaningful building block of action is not detail, but a *static situation* like the appreciation of a sunset or the pain during a dental visit. The criterion is that nothing important changes during the event and that it is conceived of as a homogeneous entity. The main ingredient of the experience of the sunset is perception itself, which is static, while the change caused by the disappearance of the sun is considered irrelevant to the static activity. The spectator himself is subject to no change.

The duration of a situation may vary. It may be a quick look at the sky, the appreciation of a good meal, a walk in the forest, a holiday spent in the sun or even a long bout with depression. Then the meal, the walk, the holiday and the bout with depression are all conceived of as static entities. However, the term *static* is relative. A tennis match, for instance, is usually dynamic and full of action, but one may also regard it as a whole and conceive of the suspense as a static situation. In this case, it is not each particular element of the match that counts, but the totality of its various elements. When such situations are accompanied by other situations, the order in which they take place is of little importance. You can go for a walk in the forest and play tennis afterwards or vice versa without the order of the events being essential. The relationship between such static elements is loose and I will call them *facultative* or *free*.

In *Mrs Dalloway*, there is an abundance of free static elements when the characters contemplate life in the city or recall particular experiences from their lives. An airplane writing letters in the sky and the question of whether a particular car is carrying royalty have no other function in the action than showing life in London and the values of ordinary people.

In a cognitive context, the static situation exemplifies possible kinds of content that can fill our lives, and sheds light on value by showing what we want to experience or avoid.

The situation can be logically linked to other situations to form a greater, more dynamic entity. One such connection is *cause* and *effect*. Gulliver ostensibly incurs the disfavour of the Lilliputians through his offensive way of saving the king's castle from fire (by urinating on it), but the deeper reason is the envy of Lilliputia's powerful citizens and the burden his enormous size presents for the country's food resources (Swift 1998). The causal chain forms an inseparable unity, where every event is indispensable to the whole. In isolation, each event may be regarded as a situation (the fire extinguishing, the envy, Gulliver's meals and the food suppliers' exasperation), but related to the whole, each situation is a *causal element*.

In a cognitive context, the causal chain exemplifies how things are interrelated and influence each other. Causal chains are also linked to value, as their impact can be negative or positive, encouraging or discouraging particular patterns of behaviour. Evidently, the understanding of cause and effect is crucial to the struggle for life, and causality is a frequent theme in fiction.

A special case of causality is the relationship between end and means. The end leads to the selection of an appropriate means, which in its turn entails the accomplishment of the end. This kind of causal chain starts, for instance, when a character has a particular need, sets out to satisfy this need, and finds a means to reach this end. Often the means becomes a goal in itself that exacts another means in order to be reached, and so on. Cause and effect, goal and means usually play a decisive role in fictional action.

Situations may also require a particular chronology even if there is no causal relation between them. We are born, go through childhood, adolescence, adulthood, old age and death without any of these stages being an obvious cause of the next one; they are only stages succeeding each other in a genetically determined development. Unlike other events, their order has been determined once and for all. You cannot become a child again after you have grown up. I will use *consecutive elements* to talk about elements whose chronological order has been predetermined in this way. Septimus's hallucinations in the park in *Mrs Dalloway* are a link in a development that culminates in a suicide; as such they are consecutive elements, not causal, because the hallucinations are not the cause of the suicide, only symptoms of the disease.

By distinguishing between causal and consecutive elements, I deviate from Eberhart Lämmert's terminology in *Bauformen des Erzählens*. Lämmert uses *consecutive* as a synonym for *causal* in his description of different connections between elements of the action (Lämmert 1967, 43–4), thus missing, in my view, an important distinction.

Insofar as the order of consecutive elements is predetermined, we can, as human beings, only adapt ourselves to it as best we can. We cannot avoid growing older, but we can adapt by keeping mentally and physically fit and by choosing suitable activities. But because we can choose between different strategies of adapting, it is useful to receive information about the challenges that a particular development entails and how to respond to them, which is just what literature provides.

A situation, causal chain or developmental sequence may be associated with other elements with which they have no necessary connection, elucidating each other by contrast or likeness. Lämmert calls this type of connection *correlative*, and *correlative element*s throw light on each other by being in some way comparable. From a cognitive point of view, correlative elements may, for example, weaken or reinforce the impression of a pattern depending on whether there is contrast or similarity. Two relatively similar events confirm a particular causal connection if both end in the same way, whereas they contradict it if they end differently. In *Mrs Dalloway* Clarissa's happy memories from youth in the countryside with Peter Walsh as well as her vivacious friend Sally (to whom she was attracted sexually) (Woolf 2000, 28) have a correlative function, contrasting with her colourless life with her husband Richard in London.

To recapitulate, we can distinguish between four types of basic elements: *free static, causal, consecutive* and *correlative elements*. To a great extent, these elements represent our interpretation of the existing world, and on account of the fiction-real world parallel, they are important to our interpretation of the fictional action. Causal and consecutive connections consist of free static elements that are part of a logical chain, whereas a correlative relationship can consist of any structures that are in some way comparable.

Since the free static element (the situation) is the building block on which the other structures are based, causal and consecutive elements have a more or less ambiguous function. Depending on context, they may have an independent value as a situation in addition to their causal or consecutive function. The war flashbacks in *Mrs Dalloway* are too short to serve more than the causal function of providing background to Septimus's psychosis. On the other hand, the many episodes about Septimus's contact with doctors are far more detailed, and in addition to being important causal elements in the plot (the doctors' cynicism drives him to suicide), they are by themselves interesting examples of how doctors' behaviour can affect patients. Apart from Septimus's plot line, causal elements play a remarkably subordinate role to the free static, consecutive and correlative elements in *Mrs Dalloway*. The novel consists mainly of situations that exemplify the content of the characters' previous and present lives, providing the reader with a basis for comparison. The mainly facultative and correlative relationship between the elements reflects the thematic intention of the author, which is linked to values rather than to causality. The topic is not primarily *why* Clarissa has chosen Richard over Peter or Sally, but rather the evaluation of the two or three alternatives.

How are these basic elements related to Propp's and Greimas's models?

If we now return to Propp's functions and study them in the context of our four basic elements, at first glance his functions seem like situations (free static elements). The following list is based on the Vladimir Propp Wikipedia page:

1. *Absentation*: a member of a family leaves the home (the hero is introduced).
2. *Interdiction*: an interdiction is addressed to the hero ("don't go there," "don't do this").
3. *Violation of interdiction*; the interdiction is violated (villain enters the tale).
4. *Reconnaissance*: the villain makes an attempt at reconnaissance (either villain tries to find the children/jewels etc., or intended victim questions the villain).
5. *Delivery*: the villain gains information about the victim.
6. *Trickery*: the villain attempts to deceive the victim to take possession of victim or victim's belongings (trickery; villain disguised, tries to win confidence of victim)
7. *Complicity*: victim taken in by deception, unwittingly helping the enemy.
8. *Villainy or lack*: villain causes harm/injury to family member.
9. *Mediation*: misfortune or lack is made known (hero is dispatched, hears call for help etc.; alternative is that victimized hero is sent away, freed from imprisonment).

10. *Beginning counter-action*: seeker agrees to or decides upon counter-action.
11. *Departure*: hero leaves home.
12. *First function of the donor*: hero is tested, interrogated, attacked etc., preparing the way for his/her receiving magical agent or helper (donor).
13. *Hero's reaction*: hero reacts to actions of future donor (withstands/fails the test, frees captive, reconciles disputants, performs service, uses adversary's powers against him).
14. *Receipt of a magical agent*: hero acquires use of a magical agent.
15. *Guidance*: hero is transferred, delivered or led to whereabouts of an object of the search.
16. *Struggle*: hero and villain join in direct combat.
17. *Branding*: hero is branded (wounded/marked, receives ring or scarf).
18. *Victory*: villain is defeated.
19. *Liquidation*: initial misfortune or lack is resolved.
20. *Return*: hero returns.
21. *Pursuit*: hero is pursued.
22. *Rescue*: hero is rescued from pursuit.
23. *Unrecognized arrival*: hero unrecognized, arrives home or in another country.
24. *Unfounded claims*: false hero presents unfounded claims.
25. *Difficult task*: difficult task proposed to the hero (trial by ordeal, riddles, test of strength/endurance, other tasks).
26. *Solution*: task is resolved.
27. *Recognition*: hero is recognized (by mark, brand, or thing given to him/her).
28. *Exposure*: false hero or villain is exposed.
29. *Transfiguration*: hero is given a new appearance (is made whole, handsome, new garments etc.).
30. *Punishment*: villain is punished.
31. *Wedding*: hero marries and ascends the throne (is rewarded/ promoted).

In fairy tales, these units are strictly speaking not free static elements, but links in a causal or consecutive chain that have no value in themselves as situations. The hero's return, marriage and so on are not meant to exemplify interesting experiences that are valuable in themselves. The entire causal or developmental chain is the theme, and when Propp divides it into single units, it is not because the causal or developmental chain as a whole is common to all fairy tales; only parts of it are. Propp could conceivably have presented a lowest common denominator, but in a manner similar to

Wittgenstein's family likenesses, he instead lists ingredients of which all the members of the family have some – but not necessarily all – in common. Such an inventory of family likenesses allows for a more comprehensive picture of the individual works than a lowest common denominator. Propp's units are not primarily minimal units, but units that are big enough to be meaningful and small enough to be common to a sufficient number of fairy tales.

The list hence gives an impression of the various motives (types of events) that recur in fairy tales, one of which is the confrontation between hero and villain, a battle in which the hero always comes out victorious. Other motives are when the hero breaks a prohibition, thus incurring unpleasant consequences, or must pass one or more tests in order to obtain a magical agent, or when a false hero claims to have performed the deed but is exposed, or when the hero is rewarded with marriage or the throne. Although Propp's story units are formulated in rather general terms, their primary role in the fairy tale world distinguishes these skeletons of action from other literary genres. Otherwise they appear in many kinds of suspense literature, for example action and spy literature. Propp's model can easily be adapted to modern suspense literature by substituting more general notions like *reward* and *technical means* (like the technical wonders James Bond is equipped with) for the assumption of the throne and magical agents.

To some degree, Propp's units of action are indicative of the cognitive content of the action. The hero's ability to surmount his problems is an escapist hint to the reader that the character he identifies with succeeds in the end, while the accumulation of obstacles announces that there is light in the tunnel even if all looks dark. The rest of the cognitive content is not, however, linked to elements that are reflected in the model. Although folktales have no complex cognitive content, their action elucidates some value in that the characters represent certain types of qualities: wisdom and foolishness, courage and cowardice, intelligence and stupidity, good and evil and so on. In *Snow White*, the heroine's success is due to a combination of beauty, innocence and kindness, while the beautiful but evil stepmother is punished for her vanity, envy and evil, so cognitively, this fairy tale argues that good leads to success and evil to disaster.

Propp's model does not encompass such aspects and can seem somewhat superficial in this respect. Moreover, his distinction between action units and character types is not a real distinction. In his action units, the characters are inevitably present as subjects and objects of the action, which is revealed by his frequent application of agent nouns, terms designating the person who performs a particular action: donor, dispatcher and helper. This cast of characters is hence only a condensed manifestation of the action.

The connection between characters and action becomes even more conspicuous in Greimas's simplified actantial model, whose *sender, object, receiver, helper, subject* and *opponent* all refer to *actants*, who are linked to the action by way of verbal nouns or as subject and object of a verb. The *sender* is the dispatcher (e.g. the king) and the *subject* is the hero, who is going to save the *object* (the princess) from the *opponent* (the villain) aided by the *helper* (person or thing) in order to receive his reward as *receiver*. This expresses the interactive relationship between the *actants* so clearly that Greimas can dispense with action units, as action and characters completely merge in his model. By implicitly expressing the action as a relationship between the characters, this model represents a further simplification of Propp's separate models for characters and action. Greimas's model acquires even more flexibility in that an actant can be covered by several characters. There may, for instance, be several helpers and tools, and a character may be subject, object and receiver at the same time; if he has a split personality, he may even be his own opponent. In the final model, the action consists of a person who has a goal and applies means to achieve it, but is hampered by one or more obstacles that he has to surmount, achieving in the end a result which may be a reward.

As it happens, it is difficult to find a story that does not somehow fit this description. It may even express the essence of human existence in general. If we strip Greimas's model of its linguistic terminology, we are left with the banal insight that we all have needs we try to satisfy in some way, that there are obstacles we have to surmount and that we may succeed or fail. Simplification and classification make it easier to orient ourselves in our field of study and sort the essential from the inessential, so although Greimas's model is undoubtedly valid, it is so general that it is of little advantage. To be sure, in order to give an impression of the diversity of contexts into which these six actants can be put, Greimas adds a long list of driving forces that can influence the action: love, admiration, political or religious fanaticism, pride, envy and so on. But instead of adding to our understanding of what characterizes different forms of action, Greimas's model ends up diverting our attention from the crucial issues.

While Greimas aims for a simplified pattern into which one can force all kinds of stories, Bremond is interested in the individual pattern of each story: the movement of a plot strand from crossroad to crossroad, with all its possible bifurcations creating a long chain of choices that have been made. This model of the action throws light on choice as a crucial literary motive and theme and touches on important cognitive aspects like causality and value.

Although it is certainly possible to find meaningful ways of simplifying and classifying the structures of the action, there is no reason not to apply methods from other human sciences like sociology, psychology and so forth. It must be a principal goal of literary analysis to understand how the fictional action affects or can affect our understanding of our own world. This implies, first, that we understand the internal structures of the fictional world: why the characters act as they do and how their behaviour affects their interaction. Second, it implies that we transfer these concrete experiences to our own general conception of the existing world, including our own value system. As the fictional action is constantly open to new readings, the reader's cognitive benefit from the same text can more or less be extended and improved as he becomes more familiar with it. Simultaneously, his understanding of it profits from his own extratextual development as a human being. This dynamic hermeneutic process is far too complex to fit into oversimplified models. This does not mean that that simplification and abstraction are not useful or even necessary tools in this process, but we must be careful not to forget the rich diversity that is one characteristic of fiction's cognitive impact.

The characters' mode of existence

A recurring question concerns whether fictional characters are mere constructions in the text that can only be understood within the world of the text, or whether they are imitations of people in the existing world who have mental lives of their own independent of the text (Rimmon-Kenan 1979, 1–2, 185–211; Chatman 1978, 118). James Wood quotes William Gass's extreme opposition to the latter mimetic conception of the characters:

> What is Mr Cashmore? . . . Mr Cashmore is (1) a noise, (2) a proper name, (3) a complex system of ideas, (4) a controlling perception, (5) an instrument of verbal organization, (6) a pretended mode of referring, and (7) a source of verbal energy. He is not an object of perception, and nothing whatever that is appropriate to persons can be correctly said of him.

Wood deeply disagrees with Gass's scepticism, regarding it as 'a dandyish flippancy, a refusal to be taught by literature about other people'.

Rimmon-Kenan opts for a compromise between these two views (1983, 33). She thinks they represent two different aspects of narrative fiction: as part of the text, the characters cannot be detached from 'the construction', while as part of the action, they exist apart from their textual context. She quotes Chatman (Chatman 1978, 118) on the point that we often retain a lively memory of fictional characters even after forgetting the text. She argues further that as abstractions in the text, the names of the characters often function as labels for a feature or a particular constellation of features that are characteristic of real people (for instance, 'He's a Hamlet'). Rimmon-Kenan's compromise is adequate enough to reconcile the opposing views, but it does not explain the fictional characters' mode of existence. What does it mean to exist as constructions in the text?

The question of whether fictional characters are only textual constructions or imitations of existing people is resolved when we distinguish between how they are rendered in the mental model of the action and their existence in the action itself. In this connection, we must be aware that the characters cannot exist in the text itself, which consists exclusively of phonetic sounds. They can only exist in the mental model of the action, and in the action itself, they exist only as fictional projections of the model, because a model has to be a model of something. As projections they do not become flesh and blood; they remain models, although we conceptualize this new model as complete, in contrast to the mental model of the action, which we conceptualize as deficient. Because of the likeness between the fictional world and the real world, we expect the model of a particular fictional character to represent a 'real' individual, complete in all respects that real persons are.

A comparison with biography should make the point even clearer. When we read about a real person in a biography, the mental model we construct of him does not give a complete picture of his appearance and personality, but we know that he is a complete person even if we cannot provide the missing information. This knowledge is itself a model, and although it is as deficient as the first one, it differs in containing the missing supplementary information that the real person to whom it refers possesses. The problem is only that we do not know the person. However, no one would claim that the lives of historical figures are restricted to facts that can be substantiated by historical sources.

The limitations of our knowledge apply as much to fictional as to historical figures (especially if they are dead and the available information is scant); in both cases we have to rely on inferences and guesses. The difference between biography and fiction is that biography often allows us to get the missing information by either meeting the still living person or resorting to historical sources, both of which are out of the question with respect to a novel. Nevertheless, we imagine fictional characters as complete human beings. The eyes of a fictional character have a colour even if the text never mentions it. The reader's impression of the characters is subject to the limitations that the mental model entails in the shape of 'deficiencies' and omissions (authorial selection), but this does not mean that they are flat as paper or reducible to phonetic sounds. It may seem pedantic to insist on the difference between the text and the mental model, as they are two sides of the same coin, but the disadvantage of associating the characters with the text instead of with the mental model is that one gets the impression that they exist merely as print on paper. In the mental model of the action they are precisely as clear and alive as we can imagine human beings, as clear and alive as the historical figures of a biography. To be sure, the reader's visualization of historical figures in a biography may be nourished by historical sources (like photos and film recordings), whereas the characters of a novel or play must settle for the reader's general knowledge about the empirical world. However, the sources from which the material is derived are of no relevance for the reader's imagination. We visualize Saint-Exupéry's fictional little prince as clearly and vividly as the picture we have of the historical Attila the Hun.

The aspects of the characters that are omitted in the novel are nevertheless implicitly included in the action (as projections) due to the fiction/existing world parallel. What makes the characters' mode of existence seem problematic is not whether they are complete human beings or not, but the fact that the mental model conceals substantial parts of their existence. Whether we like it or not, we simply cannot imagine people who are not equipped in accordance with the same principles as real people in general. We can imagine ogres and Martians, but not a person that has not been born (or at least somehow created), or a person without a past. If the text leaves out information about a person's past, we assume nevertheless that he has had a previous life.

Flat and round characters

The reader's impression of the characters depends, on the one hand, on the selective way they are presented in the mental model of the action, and on the other, on their implied qualities in the action itself. This distinction is important for grasping the difference between *flat* and *round characters*, E. M. Forster's terms that have proven so resilient over the years (Forster 1927). The metaphorical aspect of these terms introduces various connotations related to flatness and roundness. *Round* connotes a greater, more complete content than *flat*, and flat characters are therefore defined as having only one or a few features, of which one in particular is dominant. Therefore it is easy to remember flat characters; they are predictable, never surprising the reader with new and unexpected behaviour. Often they are caricatures that do not develop over the course of the action. Round characters are complex, have many personality features and are less predictable. They are open to interpretation and give you a feeling of intimacy, of being real persons, and they develop in the course of the action.

Rimmon-Kenan (1983, 40–1) points out the following flaws in these terms:

1. The term *flat* suggests something two-dimensional, devoid of depth and "life," while in fact many flat characters, like those of Dickens, are not only felt as very much alive but also create the impression of depth. 2. The dichotomy is highly reductive, obliterating the degrees and nuances found in actual works of narrative fiction. 3. Finally Forster seems to confuse two criteria that do not always overlap. According to him, a flat character is both simple and undeveloping, whereas a round character is both complex and developing. Although these criteria often co-exist, there are fictional characters which are complex but undeveloping (e.g. Joyce's Bloom) and others which are simple but developing (e.g. the allegorical Everyman).

To this, Rimmon-Kenon adds that a static personality may come about as a result of psychological trauma, which would in itself constitute an interesting personality trait in a flat character. According to her, this problem can be solved by classifying the characters as points along a continuum rather than according to exhaustive categories. One continuum would indicate the complexity or simplicity of a particular character, and another, the extent to which the character develops or stays the same. The third would indicate how much of the character's feelings and thoughts are revealed to the reader. This notion of continuum, which Rimmon-Kenan borrows from Joseph Ewen (Rimmon-Kenan 1983,41–2), reflects essential aspects of the information that the author gives about characters in the mental model.

But to what extent does this description reflect the distinction between the action and the mental modal of it? Do the terms *flat* and *round* only refer to how the characters are rendered in the mental model, or do they refer to the characters' personality traits in the action itself? In the first case, the terminology is an expression of the degree of selection, while in the second it is meant to describe different types of human beings. In other words, it is possible that a character is *round* in the uncut fictional action, but rendered as *flat* in the manipulated mental model of the action, and vice versa. Neither Forster nor anyone after him seems to have considered this distinction.

Of the three dichotomies *simplicity* vs. *complexity*, *change* vs. *constancy* and *external* vs. *inner life* (thoughts and feelings), only the first two can refer to the version of the mental model as well as to that of the action itself, while the last one is a question of viewpoint (focalization) and can only be related to the mental model.

The words *simple* and *complex* are ambiguous. We associate simplicity with such different properties as low intelligence, one-sidedness, frugality, extroversion, openness and clearness (and therefore predictability), joviality, straightforwardness, willingness to cooperate, harmoniousness and so forth. *Complexity* may mean a difficult personality, a personality full of contradictions, but also versatility, introversion, creativity, initiative and so on. However, in the context of Forster's terms, *simple* must mean a character who displays few aspects of his personality, while a *complex* character displays more of his personality. Since the picture we get of the character through the mental model has been filtered through the mind of the author, it is not evident that a simple character has to be simple in the action itself. Just as a biography may draw a simplified, biased portrait of its object, a novel may also render its characters in a deficient way in comparison to how they 'are' in the action itself, according to our knowledge about real people. The degree of simplicity or complexity is therefore due to selection, and there is a contrast between how the character is rendered in the mental model and how he is supposed to be in the fictional action (that is, in principle, complete).

From his experience with non-fictional communication, the reader is familiar with selection and knows that mental models can only reproduce a heavily cut version of the referent (the action) so that there is always a certain incongruence between signified and referent, between mental model and action. The representation of characters in the novel is merely the tip of the iceberg (to recall Hemingway's theory). The reader cannot know for certain what is hidden beneath the surface, only infer it or guess it on the basis of his own general knowledge about the existing world. Whether a character who is rendered as a simple personality is also that way in the action is not always evident from the text. Therefore, the reader takes care not to interpret the simplicity that a character displays on the level of the mental model as proof that he is really meant to exemplify simplicity. The reader does not necessarily interpret the character's simplicity as part of the cognitive content (i.e. as part of the theme). When fairy tale characters display only the few features of personality that are needed to convey the simple message, the reader does not interpret this simplicity as evidence that they lack other personality traits.

Just because Snow White does not exhibit a rich and profound personality does not mean she is not a fascinating, multifaceted person, but that is of no relevance to the fairy tale. The few or many features in the description of a character depend on the character's function in the action, that is, on his function with respect to the message. Woolf, for instance, gives us a thorough insight into Clarissa's personality because it is necessary for understanding her complicated situation and the complex issues it implies. We do not need as much information about Snow White's personality to infer the fairy tale's simple cognitive content.

Only if context indicates that a particular character is more complex than he appears to be in the mental model, can the reader know for sure that the representation of this character is deficient. Similarly, in order to make the reader interpret the simplicity as thematic, the context must show clearly that the character is really meant to be simple. Instances of such simple minds are Lennie in Steinbeck's *Of Mice and Men* (Steinbeck 2000) and the protagonist of the novel *Hersenschimmen* (rendered in English as *Out of Mind*) by the Dutch author J. Bernlef (Bernlef 1984). In the former, the prominent character Lennie is immensely large and strong but has limited mental abilities, and in the latter, the first-person narrator is increasingly affected by dementia. In such cases, the characters' simplicity is thematically important and sheds light on interesting psychological and ethical issues.

If the thematically relevant simplicity of a fictional character is worked out in sufficient detail, the depiction of the character is no longer simple, but complex; the flat character turns out to be round, rendering the terminology problematic. Forster, Ewen and Rimmon-Kenan all seem to have missed the distinction between reality-related and selective simplicity. Even though it may be convenient to characterize a character as flat or round and simple and complex, the terms become inadequate when we cannot infer from context whether they stem from the characters themselves (the referent) or the selective depiction of them (the signified). In case of doubt, we can always resort to terminology related to selection on the one hand and everyday psychology on the other. Instead of describing a character as flat or simple, we can say more explicitly that the depiction of the character is poorly detailed or oversimplified when referring to the mental model of the action, and that the character has a simple personality when talking of the action itself (the character himself).

When talking about selection, we deal with the narrator's reproduction of the action, often taking the reliability of the action for granted. However, the simple/complex dichotomy, in addition to referring to selection and the characters' qualities, may refer to the reliability of the action: whether the characters' qualities reflect conditions in the real world. The author may leave out aspects of the character's personality, but he may also give a distorted picture of it (and consequently of the action). It is essential to discriminate between these two possibilities. If the distortion consists in simplification, the term *flat* also covers this aspect. In that case, *flat* gets a negative meaning and comes under the evaluative criterion of *truth*, which will be dealt with in the chapter on evaluation.

The creation of black and white characters is a kind of flat simplification. We have already seen that the author can deviate from the patterns of the real world as long as the deviation is not thematically relevant. If the reader finds the depiction of the characters black and white, he may, depending on the context, consider it a pedagogically motivated or time-saving simplification, or interpret it as an assertion that such pure forms of good or evil really exist. The term *flat* (*simple*) has three meanings independent of the distinction between simplicity, development and internal viewpoint: (1) simplification of the fictional characters in comparison to real people (untruth), (2) selective rendering of the action (incompleteness) and (3) simple personalities.

The criterion of *development* can in principle refer to the level of the mental model (selective characterization), to the action (the character as a complete personality) and to mimetic veracity as well. In the real world, there are people who develop and people who hardly change apart from normal aging. Rimmon-Kenan mentions Miss Havisham in Dickens's *Great Expectations* as an example of the latter and assumes that development is related to the action itself and not to the way it is presented to the reader. Largely, she is right, but in principle, the characters' development may be rendered selectively. A character may display only his static aspects in the mental model but nevertheless develop in other respects without the narrator's reporting it in the text. This pertains especially to minor characters that appear sporadically in the mental model of the action. In addition, a fictional character's lack of development may in certain contexts seem unreliable and be the result of bad mimesis. Development as a criterion for flatness or roundness is therefore as ambiguous as complexity. To remedy this, the analyst scholar ought to state explicitly whether a character's development or lack thereof is mimetically convincing, along with whether it accounts for his 'real' personality in the action itself or only for the selective impression produced by the mental model.

The criterion of *inner life* is identical with *internal viewpoint* and is only related to the level of the mental model, for all human beings have a consciousness with emotions and thoughts, so the question of the characters' inner life is consequently a question of internal and external viewpoint. Therefore, there is no need for Forster's or any new terminology to cover this aspect.

The action as a vehicle for the message

The elements of the action are closely related to the cognitive content, the message. An analysis of the structures of the action is largely an analysis of the message, because it is difficult to analyse the structures of the action without simultaneously taking into account the general patterns of reality itself. This creates a hermeneutic circle in which the reader's psychological, sociological, philosophical and political knowledge about the existing world influences his interpretation of the elements of the action, which in turn affects his own understanding of reality. Although literary analyses are usually formulated as statements about specific fictional elements in the fictional world, creating the impression that the analyst intends to understand the fictional world for its own sake, someone who reads a literary analysis transforms immediately – and often unconsciously – the statements about specific elements into general insights about the extratextual world.

In reading *Mrs Dalloway*, for instance, we are witness to a selection of the two doctors' treatment of Septimus, without the narrator's telling us why they behave this way. Nevertheless we may discern a pattern of goal and means, cause and effect, interpreting for example their lack of understanding as professional incompetence or an egocentric exertion of power, and we realize that this kind of behaviour is inadequate in treating Septimus's psychosis. Drawing on our psychological and ethical knowledge, we may perceive the doctors' aggressive behaviour as stemming from a feeling of inferiority, which entails destructive self-assertion. Although the pattern of behaviour related to feelings of inferiority and self-assertion applies specifically to the two doctors, it also pertains by extension to similar cases in the real world, and even further to all kinds of interaction involving feelings of inferiority and self-assertion.

Setting

In addition to characters and events, the action includes a setting, which is the time, place and social environment in which the events take place. The significance of the action's localization may vary. If the focus is on the interaction between the characters, a play, for instance, may dispense with a realistic setting, as does Thornton Wilder's *Our Town* (Wilder 1989). Even if the social environment in many works is so characteristic as to seem indispensable to the action, it is often possible to transfer the whole action to modern society. Ibsen's social dramas, like *A Doll's House* and *An Enemy of the*

People, are typical examples of works that may be transposed into a modern setting. The film *Jaws* contains many elements of *An Enemy of the People*. On the other hand, time, place and social environment often play an active role in the action. In the film *Titanic*, the vessel, the sea and the icebergs are a prerequisite for the tragedy. World War I is the cause of Septimus's problems in *Mrs Dalloway*, leading indirectly to his suicide, and in *Cakes and Ale*, the prejudiced, moralist and bigoted post-Victorian society is the backbone of the action and constitutes the main theme of the novel.

9

Selection

Selection is such a comprehensive issue that it encompasses almost all aspects of the work. The selection of the elements that constitute the mental model of the action determines not only the action but also the way it is rendered by the mental model. Selection is relevant to duration, viewpoint, voice, frequency and perhaps also to metaphor and tropes.

Selection may occur at two levels; that is, it is formally linked to the author and the narrator, but both, of course, are ultimately rooted in the author himself. The first level, which we will call *thematic selection*, is linked to the author's choice of theme, the aspect of the existing world he wants to throw light on through the fictional action. Thematic selection compels the author to choose between themes like racism, love, generational or class conflict, feminism, social injustice, the aging process, the school system, religion, corruption and so on – an infinite number of general topics, which in turn may be specified as slavery in the United States before the Civil War, as problems related to the choice of a partner or the art of maintaining marriage, and so on. Thematic selection also comprises the choice of fictional events that exemplify the theme. Only after the theme and concrete fictional events have been selected can there be room for *tendentious selection*, which implies that the author relegates to the fictional narrator the choice of how many and which elements of the action are to be reproduced in the mental model. The fact that the author renders particular elements of the action at the expense of others necessarily makes the presentation more or less biased, and influences the reader ideologically.

We dealt with thematic selection in the previous chapter on the elements of the action. In this chapter, we are going to study tendentious selection, which is related to the narratological category of *duration*.

Theories about duration

Since 1900, literary theorists have taken an interest in the temporal aspect of the novel (Lämmert 1967, 257), but Günther Müller (Müller 1948, 195–212) was the first to compare the so-called *narrative time* or *discourse time (Erzählzeit)* with *narrated time (erzählte Zeit).* The idea was that the relationship between the time it takes to read a particular passage and the duration of the event described in that passage is interesting; the amount of time the author dedicates to the various events can throw light on his priorities. Lämmert adopted Müller's theory unchanged, and from him it migrated further to Genette (Genette 1972), who substituted *pages* and *lines* for narrative time, and *story time (temps de récit)* for narrated time, categorizing the phenomenon as *duration (durée)* and later *speed* and *rhythm (vitesse and rhythme).* It is obvious that narrative time is no ideal measure of the duration of the text, because different readers read at different speeds, whereas pages and lines are objective measures, at least as long as readers stick to the same edition.

In spite of Genette's improvements, the theory of duration has one serious flaw, an obscure conception of the primary goal of comparing narrative time and story time. To fully grasp the relationship between the spatial length of a text passage and the temporal length of the episode that the passage covers, we must distinguish clearly between text and mental model (signifier and signified) and have a sufficient idea of how literary fiction works.

What is it really we want to achieve by comparing narrative time and story time? Theorists take it for granted that this kind of comparison is meaningful and have failed to pose critical questions. It is revealing that both Genette and Chatman jump right into the discussion of the best way to measure the relationship between the two levels of time without considering the usefulness of such an analysis (Genette 1972, 122–3 and 1983, 22–3; Chatman 1978, 67–8). The Norwegian Petter Aaslestad tries to explain the goal of the procedure as a purely structural concern (Aaslestad 1999, 55, my translation):

> If you measure the story's length in chapters, pages or lines and compare the result with the story's extent in years, months, days and minutes, you find a *speed coefficient*, which we call speed for convenience's sake. Speed says something about the rhythm of the text, of the sort, "Three years are recounted in five pages."

He then proceeds to the technical aspects of the theory without asking what exactly the speed coefficient is supposed to show.

The theory of duration/speed only considers time, but in practice, at least unconsciously, narratologists also take into account that time is a measure of something. Lämmert, pointing out that the verbal reproduction of the action is based on selection, includes the action as an element of the theory (Lämmert 1967, 22–3): the story is an infinite whole which can only partially be rendered by the text, while the rest of it is left out. However, he does not specify what he means by *infinite whole* and *selection*. Similar views are expressed by later narratologists (Chatman 1978, 28–9; Rimmon-Kenan 1983, 2–3; Bal 1990, 18–19; Genette 1972, 72–6 and 1983, 10–11).

Bal has the clearest opinion, questioning the relevance of the theory and coming close to the point when she says that the analysis of rhythm, because it shows us the author's priorities, can shed light on the distribution of attention as well as authorial intention (Bal 1990, 81–2). In this way she includes a qualitative aspect, which becomes even more evident when she analyses concrete examples. In her account, episodes of short duration for which the author assigns many pages are important, in contrast to events of long duration that receive little space or are even omitted (83–6). She points out, however, that important events may also receive little or no space, because for instance it is so painful, difficult or embarrassing to put into words that it is better left suppressed or at least significantly reduced. Bal is clearly interested in the nature of the events rendered by the passage that is measured through narrative time.

Bal's application of the theory uncovers a prerequisite of which other theorists have not been consciously aware: if you want to measure the duration of the fictional elements, you must first identify them qualitatively to see what they are. In addition to the quantitative aspect, the theory of duration/speed has also a qualitative aspect: you have to know *how much* is rendered of *what*.

Unfortunately, narratology has not considered its primary goal in studying how much of the action is reproduced in the text (and hence in the mental model). Nevertheless, Bal suggests what it all comes down to when she points out that the attention drawn to the various elements reveals the vision of the story that is conveyed to the reader (81). 'The vision of the story' can only be the message, the cognitive content. In other words, Bal links the theory of duration to the message of the work.

Selection

We have already seen that the reader conceives of the fictional action as a complete world on account of the fiction/real world analogy, which also enables him to infer a general picture of the action. Although he cannot fill in the gaps of the mental model of the action with specific details, he can generally see what is missing. If he is not informed about a character's eye colour, he nevertheless infers that he must have had one. If the mental model does not detail a character's hygienic routines, the reader still knows that the character must use the toilet, bathe and brush his teeth, and if a dead body pops up somewhere, the deceased must have lost his life somehow.

The reader knows that there has to be an endless number of elements in the fictional world, just as in the real world, even if he cannot imagine them all in detail. Even the shortest episode is bound to consist of an infinity of elements and details that could have been described, and these elements are related to each other in a way that could also have been elaborated. If the author were to depict a square meter of lawn down to the tiniest detail, he could fill hundreds of pages without having accounted for every possible microscopic detail. The infinite number of possible details is deepened by the fact that the infinite details in a small area are part of an endless universe. A physicist or mathematician can perhaps on some level cope with this infinitude, but ordinary people have to develop strategies to comprehend the world we all live in. Through our intersubjective conceptual apparatus, we divide our surroundings into practical units, for instance various kinds of elements and properties, and above all, we are good at distinguishing the essential from the insignificant. In this way we reduce infinity into the practical minimum needed to handle a given situation. Leaving out an infinite number of elements, the author restricts his use of the fictional universe to a microscopic part of it, a limited selection of events: the action, which he subjects to a new radical selection. However, most of the time we do not miss these elements, on account of our very ability to sort essential from inessential.

The author's selection of elements and detail occurs at two levels. In the first place, it occurs outside the fictional world when the author chooses the material for the novel among the available topics and events of the existing world (*extratextual selection*). In the second, it occurs inside the fictional world when the fictional narrator selects the material for his story from the fictional world the author has made available to him by transposing material from the real world into fiction through the extratextual selection process (*intratextual selection*). Thus directed by the author, the narrator can choose which of the fictional (to him real) events he wants to recount and which of their aspects he wants to describe. He can leave out swaths of time, and because the author can make him omniscient, he can also reveal other people's minds. On the other hand, he cannot himself choose to be identical with a particular character and decide whether his story is first-person or third-person, nor can he decide to situate the action in his own past or present; such decisions belong to the author. Harriet Beecher Stowe chose, for instance, to write about the relationship between slave and owner in the United States, whereas her fictional narrator determines which parts of the corresponding fictional action are to be rendered and in what kind of formal structures they are to be presented, like viewpoint, voice, order, frequency and duration.

The author's choices, whether they occur in his own name or in that of the narrator, affect the reader ideologically. When the topic is slavery in America, and more specifically its negative impacts on human beings, this forces the reader to reflect on this particular problem at the expense of all the other problems he could have thought about. Since Stowe focuses on Uncle Tom's sympathetic qualities and the brutality of the evil slave owners, the reader is encouraged to identify with the slaves against the slave owners, and is likely to conclude that slavery and racism must be eliminated.

The study of speed/duration is meaningful only if the purpose is to shed light on the relationship between the mental model and the fictional world in order to show how the author's (and hence the narrator's) selective reproduction of the existing world (represented by the fictional world) affects the reader's attitude to the existing world. The problem of traditional narratology is its preference for objectively accessible structures, leading to the exclusion of the cognitive aspect of literature as too subjective for scholarly investigation. However, the novel's cognitive functions are a prerequisite for understanding the phenomenon of duration/speed, and Bal's crucial question about relevance has so far gone unanswered.

Time and its content

Besides giving little attention to the cognitive function of literature, the narratological theory of duration is marred by another flaw: its conception of time. Specifically, it does not set a sharp enough boundary between time as measurement (years, months, weeks, days and hours) and time as content. Years, months and so on are merely measurements of all the changes in space that create time, measurements of what happens: ways of measuring the content that takes place in the actual period. Narratologists overestimate the value of the clock's regular tic-tac as a measure of this content. A mathematical quantity like 365 days informs us as little about what happens in the course of the period as it is informative to know a woman's height of five feet two or that a man is 56 years old. The main thing is not the duration of an event but in what it consists: what happened. From the spectator's practical point of view, events consist of properties we can call *elements* or *details*. When we describe an event, the text (and its mental model) renders only a limited number of the various properties of the event: a certain amount of details which purport to convey a sufficient representation of the event. A detail is any information that increases our picture of the spatial and temporal properties of the event.

Instead of comparing the lines and pages of the text with the minutes, days and years of the action, we would do better to compare the mental model's selection of details with all the relevant details the narrator could have selected from the infinitely larger and more detailed fictional world if he had so wished. The elements the author prioritizes or omits indicate his ideological intentions.

Our comparison between the details of the text and those of the action has both a quantitative and a qualitative aspect: *how many* details and *which* details have been included or left out? The qualitative comparison concerns the kind of details the author includes or omits and sheds light on his thematic priorities. For example, if a novel contains an enormous amount of trivial details, this may express a wish to render reality realistically or to emphasize the important role trivial elements play in human life. The study of qualitative selection is closely related to the analysis of the cognitive content (the message) and must be dealt with accordingly. On the other hand, the quantitative comparison between the mental model and the fictional world it renders is useful for simplification and categorization and will be dealt with below.

Quantitative selection

Quantitative selection tries to measure how many of the action's elements have been included or omitted in the mental model. The elements or details of the mental model as well as those of the action must be quantified in some way. The narratologists' theory of duration/speed does not differentiate between the text and the mental model of the action; indeed, they overlook this distinction when grounding the comparison between text and story in the physical features of the text and the temporal duration of the story. In principle, the length of the text is related to neither the temporal extent of the action nor the mental model's richness of detail. It is possible to express the same content through verbal formulations of different length if one systematically replaces short expressions with synonymous longer ones. For example, 'The little Englishman suddenly sat in his chair' may be transformed into 'The man who was born and had grown up in England and was an English citizen and who was not particularly tall of stature, i.e. with respect to the number of centimetres one could count if measuring him from head to foot when he stretched himself at full length, bent his knees in such a way that the part of his body which he usually used for sitting purposes finally got into contact with the seat of the chair which had been assigned to him, and this movement occurred in such an abrupt way that it came as a surprise to those in his immediate social environment.' In this way, one line becomes seven without adding any new details to the mental model of the event. Stylistically there is, of course, an enormous difference, and it is debatable how this style affects the reader, but semantically the two versions are largely equivalent.

Even if the relationship between words, lines and pages on the one hand and the details of the mental model on the other is not one-to-one, in practice there is nevertheless a certain correspondence so that to some extent the details of the mental model can be measured in lines and pages. For the most part, every word corresponds to a detail. In the sentence 'He sat down slowly on the chair', we have for instance the following details: (1) he, (2) sit down + (3) past time, (4) slowly, (5) on, (6) chair + (7) definite article. At this micro level, it is difficult to count the exact number of details. Some details may be merely implied, while others may be redundant in the sense of being already implied and hence not needing to be mentioned explicitly. In the expression 'fall down', 'down' is more or less superfluous; hence you have two words, but in fact only one detail. In our example sentence above, it is also a question whether 'down' in 'sat down' consists of one or two details, because 'sit' needs the addition of 'down' to mean 'sit down', making 'sit down' only one detail. The measurement of details is therefore bound to be a little rough, but not so rough as to make it impossible to distinguish clearly between detailed and less detailed mental models. We may be in doubt whether a description of a particular object or event has 10 or 15 details, but it nevertheless is clearly less detailed than a description of a similar object or event that contains between fifty and sixty details.

We can also count the details of the fictional action (which are not to be confused with the details of the mental model), but in contrast, the number of details in the fictional world is in principle infinite, making a different strategy necessary. We count only the details needed for the comparison with those of the mental model, that is, the relevant details. In *Mrs Dalloway*, Clarissa's admirer Peter Walsh is described thus (Woolf 2000, 3):

> Until Peter Walsh said, "Musing among the vegetables?"—was that it?—"I prefer men to cauliflowers"—was that it? He must have said it at breakfast one morning when she had gone out on to the terrace—Peter Walsh. He would be back from India one of these days, June or July, she forgot which, for his letters were awfully dull; it was his sayings one

remembered; his eyes, his pocket-knife, his smile, his grumpiness and, when millions of things had utterly vanished—how strange it was!—few sayings like this about cabbages.

The narrator alludes to the millions of details about Peter Walsh that have vanished from Clarissa's memory, which can only cover a tiny part of the action. How infinitely many more details must have been left out if we consider the relevant parts of the action that she once must have perceived? At a glance we can ascertain that an infinite number of the details about Peter are omitted, but some of these missing details are more obvious than others, especially those that apply to objects that have already been mentioned (e.g. Peter's eyes, whose colour has been omitted, along with his general appearance at that). The description of Peter is restricted to Clarissa's limited memory, revealing her priorities in the process, but in addition to the filtering process performed by Clarissa's own mind, the narrator has left out an endless profusion of details that are still left to be omitted after Clarissa's own selection. For example, when mentioning Peter's eyes, the narrator opens Clarissa's mind to us but at the same time omits a closer description of these eyes. We get no description of the eyes' properties that have made such an impression on Clarissa – not to mention their colour.

If we go on enumerating a list of the details we lack, we end up establishing an alternative text and an alternative mental model of the action, with which we can compare the original text/model to find out how many and what kind of relevant details have been left out. The insight into the qualitative and quantitative selection in a fictional work enables us to expose the thematic and ideological priorities of the narrator – and by extension the author, not forgetting, of course, that the narrator's views do not always merge with those of the author (for instance in the case of an unreliable narrator).

A comparison of the above passage from *Mrs Dalloway* with a hypothetical, more comprehensive alternate text makes it clear that this description of Peter and of the scene he appears in is rather poorly detailed. This must absolutely not, however, be taken as a flaw: the important thing is that the amount of details complies with the cognitive content, the message. The description of Peter in the passage above fulfils the important function of revealing and explaining Clarissa's fascination with Peter.

The need for details depends on how complex the described object or event is. A complex object contains more details than a simple one, but we would not automatically call the description of it more detailed nevertheless. In a completely desolate desert at the equator where the only change is between day and night, very little happens in the course of a year compared to all that goes on in a big city in a couple of minutes. One or two pages suffice to depict in sufficient detail 1 year in the desert, whereas a hundred pages could easily be filled with what two million city dwellers experience over 5 minutes. The action in the desert is simple and contains few details, while the action that takes place in the city is complex and abundant in details.

Moreover, the reader's perception of details is relative, depending on his expectations. These expectations are based on his personal experiences with other literary texts, as well as his subjective views on what is important in the real world. However, there will always be similarities between different readers that allow for intersubjectivity, preventing the analysis of quantitative selection from becoming too personal and arbitrary. An intersubjective consensus among most readers about what counts as detailed is not inconceivable.

The relationship between the length of a particular text passage and the corresponding time of the action is meaningful only in the light of the way the text renders the fictional action and on the relationship between the details of the text and those of the action. Even if narratologists are not consciously aware of it, they too regard the selection of details as basic and tend to unintentionally use *detail* instead of *pages* and *time* (Genette 1972, 130, 142). The transition from counting pages and story time to a quantification of details entails a focus on details instead of speed or duration. How, then, does this affect the terminology?

Scene, summary, ellipsis, pause and stretch

The main 'classical' forms of duration or speed are *scene, summary, pause* and *ellipsis*, along with what Seymour Chatman calls *stretch*, where narrative time exceeds story time, which corresponds to slow motion in films (Genette 1972, 122–44; Chatman 1978, 72–3; Rimmon-Kenan 1983, 51–6; Bal 1990, 80–8; Herman and Vervaeck 2005, 60–2; Fludernik 2009, 32–3, 152–3). To what extent are these terms compatible with a theory of duration based on the content of elapsed time, or in other words, based on details?

The terms *scene* (called *isochrony* by Fludernik, a term that is derived from Genette), *summary* and *ellipsis* fit into the theory unproblematically. In my theory of quantitative selection, *scene* means a detailed re-creation of the action, *summary* designates a reproduction with few details, whereas *ellipsis* refers to a complete omission of details. The terms *stretch* and *pause* present more difficulties, however. The comparison between narrative time and story time implies obscurities that become obvious when we replace time with details, such as the temporal incongruence when narrative time is *longer* than story time. A typical example is a scene in the novel *Epp* by the Norwegian Axel Jensen in which the protagonist Epp boils and eats an egg (Jensen 1978, 9–13). It takes the narrator almost four pages to tell about this purely trivial event, which most narrators would have passed over. The reason for this extreme enumeration of details is to show the emptiness of Epp's existence. He has nothing meaningful to fill his time with any more, so he has to make the most out of his everyday routine.

Seymour Chatman introduces *stretch* for such cases where it takes more time to tell about an event than the event itself lasts, but it is not completely clear what the term is intended to cover. He uses it chiefly in relation to literary techniques that try to imitate filmic slow motion (Chatman 1972, 72–3), but he then extends it to other situations, mentioning especially the rendering of thoughts, which take longer to be written down and read than it does to think them. In such cases and in a case like the scene in *Epp*, there is, however, no slow motion effect, but Chatman does not elaborate on whether this ought to have terminological consequences. It is too bad, because here he is close to revealing the weakness of the theory: the fact that narrative time and story time are no satisfactory measure of the relationship between text and story.

If we disregard narrative time and story time, basing our definition of duration on *details*, the terminological problem solves itself. The exceeding of story time, as in the scene from *Epp*, would then of course be a *scene* instead of *stretch*, because the passage is rich in detail. A novel like *Mrs Dalloway*, which describes everyday life in detail, consists almost entirely of scenes. A passage rendered with few details is, on the other hand, a *summary*, as in the opening pages of *Gulliver's Travels* (Swift 1998, 5):

> My Father had a small Estate in *Nottinghamshire*; I was the Third of five Sons. He sent me to *Emanuel-College* in *Cambridge*, at Fourteen Years old, where I resided three years, and applied my self close to my Studies: But the Charge of maintaining me (although I had a very scanty Allowance) being too great for a narrow Fortune; I was bound Apprentice to Mr James Bates, an eminent Surgeon in London, with whom I continued four years; and my Father now and then sending me small Sums of Money, I laid them out in learning Navigation, and other Parts of the Mathematicks, useful to those who intend to travel, as I always believed it would be some time or other my Fortune to do.

Scene and summary are two extremes on a scale, with most text passages falling somewhere in between, being in other words more or less scenic or summarizing. To a certain degree, it may be useful to employ words, lines and pages as a rough measure of the detail in the description of the action in a particular passage. A necessary condition is that we link this measure to a concrete element and not to an abstract period of time. For instance, it is all right to say that Gulliver's youth and education are rendered in one and a half pages, whereas his stay with the Lilliputians takes 60 pages. This comparison tells us that the narrator finds Gulliver's youth and education much less important than his experiences in Lilliput, regarding Gulliver's youth as mere background material and his stay with the Lilliputians as the main event.

If we describe an object or a simple event with many words, the great number of words generally entails a corresponding richness of detail, as it demands more words to describe more details. Even here, however, we must be aware that there is no absolute correspondence between the number of pages and the number of details. I have already mentioned complex objects and events that require many words to describe, where we would not necessarily say the description is particularly detailed.

Basing our terminology on details in fact obviates the term *stretch*. The fact that narrative time exceeds story time is irrelevant, as the comparison between narrative time and story time does not provide us with reliable information about the way the text renders the action. If needed, *stretch* may be applied to text passages that try to imitate the effect of slow motion. Then the term would not refer to the relationship between narrative time and story time but to a special device that drags out the communication process. This pertains only to slowing strategies that do not interrupt the communication process by embedding irrelevant material.

Ellipsis means omission, and in our context it refers to the omission of relevant elements of the action. The text is bound to omit a major part of the countless elements and details of the action, and if *ellipsis* is to be useful, it can only refer to details that we miss in particular. *Details* covers complex elements (like events) as well as simple elements (like a single property of a thing or an event); hence, *ellipsis* does not only refer to the omission of events but also to the omission of small but important details.

One problem with *ellipsis* is its association with the psychological notion of absence, which depends on individual needs and hence brings a subjective element into the analysis. However, the fact that literary studies has to deal with this element of subjectivity does not automatically entail the chaos that many people associate with postmodernism (see Eagleton 1996, vii). The subjective feeling that something is missing may be shared by most readers, hence becoming intersubjective, which is the nearest we can come to objectivity as long as we want to say something interesting.

The problem *pause*

Genette's *pause* contrasts somewhat with *ellipsis*: in Genette's formulation, 'narrative time = n, story time = 0' (Genette 1972, 129). In principle, all text passages interrupting the action should be pauses, but Genette reserves the term solely for descriptions. Not all descriptions entail a halt to the action, and Genette is fully aware of this fact (Genette 1972, 133–8). If a description coalesces with one of the character's sensory impressions or thoughts, it becomes part of the action. Genette therefore defines *pause* as 'a description that interrupts the action and suspends the story time' (Genette 1983, 24–5), but in spite of this reservation, the term is problematic.

All writing is in fact description. Generally, we associate description with information about the properties of objects and characters. Descriptive passages usually interrupt the action, and one may be tempted to call them *pauses*. But then we are confronted with passages like this (Jensen 1978, 10, my translation):

> Then I went to the egg. I let Epp be Epp, forgot everything else, measured the egg by eye, touched it with my fingertips, weighed it in my palm, stood there with my eyes closed and somehow established contact with it before submerging it cautiously into the pan. But first I ensured that the water was right, that is, that it boiled but without boiling hard, for if I submerge the egg into a pan where the water is boiling hard, I subject the egg to the danger of cracking so that the white leaks out into the water.

These sentences consist of verbs, adverbs and objects and deal exclusively with activities, action, so according to Genette's definition, it is not a description and not a pause. Nevertheless, it is tempting to call the passage a description, on account of its detailed reproduction of Epp's trivial activities. We receive a lot more information about how the action transpires than what is strictly speaking necessary for visualizing it. The action is thoroughly *described*. In this case, we have a description but not a pause, for the trivial activities constitute an essential part of the novel's action. The final two lines of the passage do not describe the concrete action; they amount only to a general, hypothetical consideration, but because they express the protagonist's anxiety lest the action should fail, they are nevertheless part of the action.

The difficulty of distinguishing between description and action is even more evident when intense, thrilling activity is depicted through a mixture of action and description, as in the dramatic final scene of the short story *The Croton* by the Flemish Jos Vandeloo. The antipathetic protagonist H., an absolutist director of a firm, is sickeningly proud of a plant (a croton) he has made grow to monstrous dimensions in his own office. One evening it attacks him and devours him, and I quote the passage about his death struggle (Vandeloo 1972, my translation):

> Heavily and sensually its leaves are sweating out their inner life, its branches raising their arms femininely in the air, looking at their own reflections in the windowpane. The croton is a strange, charming, exotic beauty. It is a bisexual creature, floating around H. Hour after hour H. is working without noticing that the croton is taking possession of more and more of the room, its branches and roots creeping along in this oppressive greenhouse atmosphere, its leaves descending in the room like heavy, multicoloured curtains. He feels it only when the wet leaves reach his neck and the drops splash down on his paper. He looks a little distractedly around and discovers then the dark curtain with the glittering reflection of many colours. One moment he reflects. His eyes are shining feverishly as if observing a weird vision. The leaves nestle down on his shoulders as if the croton wants to caress him. H. feels strangely touched, but simultaneously he is seized by a strange uneasiness. The silence is heavy and ominous; only the croton is alive, moving, breathing, searching and groping its way forward. H. rises and wants to go to the door, but the croton holds him back with many arms. H. pushes the leaves aside. The twigs beat him in his face. He fights to reach the door; he struggles against these wet, obstinate walls. The leaves resist him elastically, the twigs waving jerkily around him. It is as if there are suddenly many sounds in the room, voices, music. As if the man becomes an animal and the plant a human being.
>
> H. stumbles over a root, he feels the twigs descend upon him, the leaves covering and burying him. He cries and defends himself obstinately, tearing the leaves and the twigs apart. Sticky sap is running down his arms, mingling with his sweat. Broken twigs are creaking with a loud, childish sound. But the croton smiles almost soundlessly. A fine drizzle fills the room, the light beam is obscured by leaves and invaded. Gradually H. feels the croton's stifling grip. Heavy like an animal the plant is lying on his chest. Once more H. screams desperately, but his resistance ebbs away and, defenceless, he becomes one with the croton.

Here the text repeatedly describes the plant and the atmosphere in the room, but these descriptions are unquestionably part of the action. The drizzle in the air, the plant's increasingly menacing appearance, the director's feverish eyes and so on contribute to a vivid mental model of the action. Description and action are as inseparable as they are in a film sequence, because in film, space and time constitute a unity. If two men fight in a film (which is part of the action), their movements consist of changes in the spatial relationship between the different parts of their bodies. So in order to perceive the movements (the action), we have to perceive their external appearance, which in a text would be accounted for only through description.

Language cannot render this unity simultaneously as film can. The text can only reproduce the simultaneity of reality by means of concepts, which are unavoidably linked to words, which are in turn linked to a space and a time of their own: the order in which they are presented in the text and the lapse of time it takes to read them. In this way, what was originally a unity is split into fragments: concepts related in part to time and in part to space. The fictional world is fragmented into elements that we classify as static or dynamic, as description or action, but in effect they are as inseparable as image and movement in film. When we separate description from action, we pretend to freeze time as a photo would, calling the resulting static image *description*, but the frozen situation inevitably implies action: the croton is lying on the chest of the director, who is lying on the floor, screaming with his mouth wide open, and so on. Verbs designating action imply description; it is impossible to imagine a movement without also imagining the space in which it takes place, and space demands and implies description. The sentence, 'He sat down', apparently refers only to action, but 'he' implies a character, an object to sit on and surroundings, which all of them have a particular appearance that is involved in and affected by the movement. Description only lends an explicit form to the implicit unity of time and space. Therefore, the distinction between description and action is artificial, a boundary that does not exist in reality and is more apt to cause confusion than further our understanding of how literary texts work. Hence, it would be better to drop the distinction altogether, or at least use it with caution, keeping its limitations in mind.

However, even if Genette's *pause* is no longer consistent with the differentiation between action and description, it may still be useful. Instead of linking *pause* to description, we can link it to the information provided by the various sentences and passages about the further development of the action. Some sentences and passages are more informative about the development than others. The fact that the reader often cheats, turning the pages to see how the story ends, demonstrates his interest in this kind of information. It is possible to investigate on a relatively low textual level how informative a given sentence or passage is with respect to the action's development. If a passage interrupts the information about the development of the events, we are dealing with a pause. The reader may perceive a purely aesthetic description of a town as a pause because the passage interrupts the development, whereas another description of a town might not seem as disruptive, because in this second case, a group of soldiers has to accomplish a particular mission in the town, making the description necessary for grasping their problems. So it is not, ultimately, a question of description or action but of the function of each passage with regard to the action. *Pause* may perhaps be a useful term in the study of slowing elements.

In my view, the primary goal of literary criticism and theory must be to understand how literary fiction works, that is, to understand the interplay between work and reader. Narratology has done an impressive job in identifying textual structures, but in its effort to achieve objectivity, it has neglected the cognitive functions of these structures. Unfortunately, if we want to say anything interesting about literature, we have to go beyond the objective facts. This also pertains to the theory of duration. Only when we realize that our study is concerned not with objective quantities like pages and periods of time but with the content they quantify, does the theory become interesting. However, then it is no longer a theory of *duration* but a theory of *selection*.

10

Voice

Genette's category of *voice* stems from the fact that the text is narrated, and describes how the narrator's voice is expressed by the various aspects of the text. Common issues related to *voice* are (1) the various levels on which someone is telling something (narrative levels), (2) the temporal relationship between the narrative act and the action (verb tense), (3) the relationship of identity between the narrator and the characters (grammatical person), (4) the way the narrator reproduces the character's statements (dialogue), (5) how the narrator influences the reader's reactions to the action by means of comments, humour, irony, emotive language and the like, and (6) to what extent the narrator makes his own presence conspicuous (*distance*).

In his account of *voice*, Genette intentionally disregards the author's voice, which he considers irrelevant to narratology, mainly because the author represents the cognitive content, which according to narratology is too subjective to be of relevance. Somehow, it looks as if the fictional narrator is responsible for the way the action is presented in the mental model, which Genette takes as sufficient to explain how the work affects the reader. The fictional narrator is, of course, the extended arm of the author and performs much of cognitive work on behalf of the author. The interplay between author and narrator may, however, be subtle; the relationship between their statements is not always one-to-one. Sometimes the author and the narrator simply disagree, for example when the author ironically lets the narrator announce views with which he obviously disagrees.

By determining the total framework of the work through his selection of genre, material and the fictional narrator's working conditions, the author takes full control of the work's cognitive functions, the latent message that is an echo of the author's voice: his intention. In terms of the cognitive functions of the work, the author also belongs to the category of *voice*, although I have dealt with this issue separately in Chapter 6.

The author is the work's almighty divinity that has been hovering above the waters long before the birth of the narrator, having determined the scope and content of the action before the narrator is allowed to make his own 'independent' choices, choices related to narratological and stylistic alternatives. The narrator selects the parts of the action he wants to reproduce and the way to render them, but he cannot change the chronology or content of the action. Because the narrator is the author's extended arm into the fictional world, we must distinguish clearly between the historical writer and the fictional narrator and strive to understand the distribution of the work between them. Although the fictional narrator and the mental model of the action can be considered independently of the author, their total function in the work can be understood only in terms of the author's primary ideological intentions. We have already dealt with the relationship between author, narrator and fictional world in Chapter 7. Our next task is to clarify the various ways in which the narrator's voice becomes audible in the mental model of the action.

Temporal relations

We have seen that there is no temporal relationship between the author and the fictional world (the fictional action). One cannot have a temporal relation to something that does not exist. On the other hand, by way of temporal adverbs and (in European languages) verb tense, the text indicates the temporal relationship between the narrator and the events he recounts. Verbal endings and adverbs distinguish inevitably between past, present and future time.

On the basis of the tense system in English, Chatman (1978) deals with the rendering of time in narrative fiction, adding anterior time (the past perfect), which is also past tense, but past tense with respect to a more recent time (the preterit). However, the linguistic differentiations between subordinate categories of the three tenses past, present and future differ enormously from language to language. Afrikaans, for instance, does not discriminate between past tense, perfect and past perfect. Afrikaans-speaking writers therefore write their novels in the present tense and only use the perfect where for example English uses the past perfect.

To describe the location of the narrator in relation to the action, Chatman reports the possibility of using the terms *anterior, simultaneous, posterior* and *inserted narration* (Chatman 1978, 80). In principle, posterior narration means a story in the past tense, simultaneous narration implies the present tense, and anterior narration refers to the future tense, while inserted narration is a combination of present and past tense, as in diary novels and epistolary novels. Superficially, the classification seems unproblematic, but it has aspects that need closer examination.

In fiction, the narrator has in practice the option between present and past time, that is, between the present tense, the past tense and the historical present. In principle, it is not impossible to write a novel in the future tense, concerning events that lie in the narrator's future. If the narrator is omniscient, he also knows, of course, what is going to happen in the future, but in this case, the narrative will sound like prophecy, along with the uncertainty that is normally linked to prophecies. Therefore, the future tense would give the reader a sense of something that might not happen, which may disturb his concentration and involvement. It is not as easy to be emotionally involved in something that is completely uncertain, which is probably why the future tense is not used extensively as a basic tense in fiction. On the other hand, the future tense is used in prolepses (flash-forwards and anticipation), as in the short story *To Kill a Child* (*Att döda ett barn*) by the Swedish writer Stig Dagerman (Dagerman 1992 [1948]), about a car accident in which a child is killed. The short story alternates between passages in the present tense describing the innocence and happiness of the characters before the tragedy and passages in the future tense that anticipate the accident and the situation afterwards.

Because the reader regards fictional events from the perspective of the real world, he expects the narrator to behave like a biographer or historian. Nevertheless, the reader allows for deviations, as we saw in the case of *Moby Dick* in Chapter 7. On account of the analogy with non-fiction, the reader tends to interpret the verb tense of the fictional text according to the rules that pertain to non-fiction. He interprets, for instance, the past tense as evidence that the action belongs to the narrator's past, and since we normally tell about events after they have taken place, the past tense presents no special problems.

Problems do arise when the narrator narrates in the present tense. The present tense means that things are happening in front of your eyes while you are telling about them, which is uncommon enough, and absolutely so in combination with written communication. If I am watching a tennis match, I can hardly sit with a notebook, taking notes on what I see. Normally, I will not describe the match to anybody either, as my fellow spectators do not need me to parrot what they can see with their own eyes. Live commentary belongs therefore principally to the radio, where the listeners cannot see what the commentator sees. It is different with television, because the viewers can see what is happening and only need explanations of what they do not know or understand.

On a basic level, we might say that readers imagine the present-tense narrator as a kind of radio or TV commentator, but the comparison with the real world and non-fiction indicates a more probable explanation related to the frequent use of historical present in everyday life. With the exception of the radio and TV commentary, it is highly unpractical, almost impossible for a narrator to write down or dictate a coherent text while dramatic events are taking place. As a consequence, present tense in a narrative comes across as illogical to the reader, which is only resolved by interpreting the present tense as the historical present, even if the present tense is used consequently throughout the work.

The historical present is probably to some extent an imitation of the present tense used in live commentary. We are all familiar with people who change abruptly from the past tense into the present tense when recounting a dramatic experience:

> I'd hardly opened the door when she comes out of the kitchen, screaming loudly . . .

Here the speaker pretends a moment to be reporting directly from the scene as an eyewitness, inviting the listener to step into the role of one who is listening to an on-the-spot reporter. The speaker is in fact asking the listener to participate in a role-playing game. The receiver may identify so strongly with the pretended situation that it even affects his emotions. The present tense reminds him of the intensity and strong emotional involvement of the reporter and of the suspense he has experienced in the past when listening to real on-the-spot reports, and he is influenced by the emotions of the speaker.

One important difference between the description of the present situation and a description of past events is that the narrator telling about the present does not know what is going to happen next, so he feels real suspense. The voice of the radio commentator in an ongoing football match expresses tension because he does not know what the final result will be. This tension is revealed by his way of speaking: voice rising and falling, interjections and so on. The listener is carried away by the emotions of the commentator and identifies with them. Although the receiver knows that the events belong to the past, he yields to the temptation of imagining them as if they happened here and now. The past tense implies a distance between the reporter and the events he is telling about, because he knows the story's further development and outcome. The future has for him become past. The voice of a radio commentator reporting a football match that is over does not have the same intensity as when he reported the same dramatic events that made him shout and scream a few moments ago. The narrator who tells his story in the past tense has had time to digest the past events, so the reader expects him to be calmer and more balanced. Therefore, the historical present seems more intense than the past tense.

Since the reading situation is a role-playing game, the reader knows that the present tense is only the historical present, and he is aware that there is no fundamental difference between the historical present and the past tense, as both refer to the past. Nevertheless, he reacts differently to the two tenses, because each of them entails a different role, each affecting him emotionally in a different way.

It is not certain that the reader is able to distinguish clearly between the historical and real present in narrative fiction. To be sure, on account of the analogy with reality and non-fiction, it is *probable* that the reader interprets the present tense in novels and short stories as the historical present. Nevertheless, we cannot preclude the fact that some readers may interpret the present tense literally, as a real present tense. This is possible if the reader imagines the narrator as omniscient. Omniscience may imply complete knowledge about everything that has happened in the past as well as about everything happening at present. In principle, there is an important difference between knowing and perceiving, but if you are omniscient, you have access to all the sensory impressions that were accessible during the events, so the difference between mere knowledge and direct perception is erased. Theoretically, this omniscience enables the fictional narrator to participate in the past and in the narrative act at the same time. As readers we may imagine an omniscient narrator peeping into past events as through a window or wormhole and telling us events as they happen, in the same way we were witness to the present-tense death struggle of the director in Jos Vandeloo's *The Croton*. In such cases, we visualize the narrator as an omniscient commentator. If he is writing, he has to write unbelievably fast, but we could perhaps better imagine him using a tape recorder and transcribing the recorded monologue later. The issue of how many readers would interpret the present tense as historical or real would then come down to personal preference.

In the case of the historical present, the reader would engage in a role-playing game as a listener to live commentary. With the real present tense, he would actually be reading a live commentary that is real within the fictional world. The difference between the two alternatives is, however, negligible, because in both cases the events are part of a fictional framework; the reader faces either a fictional narrator who tells events as he witnesses them here and now in the fictional world, or a fictional narrator inviting him to take part in fiction on a new level, in the role-playing game related to the historical present, a kind of fiction in the fiction. The fiction in the fiction does not amount to any change in the fictional events, only in a change of the framework in which they are experienced. To the reader of fiction, it is essential that he knows the events are fictional and that the future in it has already been determined by the writer. He is therefore unable to feel any real suspense related to the future, only the emotions evoked by the role-playing game.

In other words, reading a novel amounts to engaging in a role-playing game, inviting you to pretend as if you believe what is being told. In addition, the historical present makes you pretend to believe these events are happening before the very eyes of the narrator. As long as it is question of make believe, the reactions of the reader depend on his own ability to identify with the fictional situation and the feelings related to it. The reader feels real suspense only in relation to what he does not yet know but wants to know, and he feels this suspense whether the story is told in the present or past tense. The special suspense he feels with respect to the historical present is due to the contagious effect of the narrator's emotions.

Although narratives in the first-person are also told in the present tense, certain authors seem to dislike the combination of present tense and first-person narrative. This is in part due to the fact that the first-person narrator's active participation in the action makes it difficult for us to imagine him speaking or writing while taking an active role in the action. The present tense must at least be a historical present, but even then it is difficult for the reader to engage as a listener in the role-playing game, as even the role-playing game requires a logical narrative situation. It is conceivable that a person can be an omniscient witness to other people's experiences, but it seems rather illogical that he can both participate in an event and tell about it simultaneously as a witness on the outside. Epistolary and diary novels merely seem to be exceptions, because in these genres, only iterative events and the general situation of the protagonist are told in the present tense, whereas the events that led to the present-tense passages are recounted in the past tense.

Another problem with the combination of first-person narrative and present tense is that it is more difficult to distinguish between the voice of the narrator and the first-person character's internal point of view. This may be the reason behind the Flemish author Herman Teirlinck's unwillingness to combine the present tense with the first person in the novel *Het gevecht met de engel* (*The Struggle with the Angel*). In this novel, all the chapters dealing with third-person characters are told in the present tense, whereas the only chapter of the novel that has a first-person narrator switches to the past tense, which is maintained throughout the chapter (Teirlinck 1960–1969b, 229–352). The past tense makes it easy to sort out the passages in the present tense where we hear the first-person narrator's voice comment on the past events (Teirlinck 1960–1969b, 231; my translation):

> Alone I was not afraid. The window was almost always open. It was not big, big was the world outside. And once I saw a spider weave its cobweb. It was an enormous cobweb with nine arms, barring the

opening completely. Then the spider quietly sat down in the middle. I love spiders. There are neither animals nor plants nor any beings that I would not love.

The present tense marks the passages where we hear the narrator's voice comment on the action in retrospect. If we replace the past tense with the present tense, it becomes difficult to distinguish the comments of the narrator (his voice) from the thoughts of the first-person character (his internal viewpoint):

> Alone I am not afraid. The window is almost always open. It is not big, big is the world outside. And I see a spider weave its cobweb. It is an enormous cobweb with nine arms, barring the opening completely. Then the spider quietly sits down in the middle. I love spiders. There are neither animals nor plants nor any beings that I would not love.

Who is it now that loves spiders? The first-person narrator many years after the action or the first-person character at the time of the action? The ambiguity becomes evident if we rewrite the text yet again, replacing the original present tense with the past tense:

> Alone I was not afraid. The window was almost always open. It was not big, big was the world outside. And once I saw a spider weave its cobweb. It was an enormous cobweb with nine arms, barring the opening completely. Then the spider quietly sat down in the middle. I loved spiders. There were neither animals nor plants nor any beings that I would not have loved.

In this version, it is clearly the first-person character that loves spiders, and the whole passage is seen from his internal point of view.

Since the author invents the narrative situation as well as the action, he can allow the narrator to move freely in time with respect to the action without having to imitate the non-fictional narrative situation. Nevertheless, the author, influenced by non-fiction, tends to make the narrator as realistic as possible as long as it does not affect the informative and evocative value of the action. Most narratives are therefore written in the past tense in analogy with biography and travelogue. The present is used with reference to events that take place during the narrative act and last long enough to be told in the present, as with the sentence, 'My name is Dr Serenus Zeitblom, Ph.D.', the introductory words to the second chapter of Thomas Mann's *Doktor Faustus* (Mann 1967), or general information, like the opening line of *Anna Karenina* (Tolstoy 1960): 'All happy families resemble each other, each unhappy family is unhappy in its own way'.

Live commentary can be strongly emotional, like football commentary, but the strength of the emotions depends on the issue and on the uncertainty of the outcome. When romantic poetry renders events in the present, the narrator's feelings may be expressed by means of exclamation points and question marks, interjections and direct address, as in Shelley's 'Bereavement' (Shelley 1989–):

> How stern are the woes of the desolate mourner
> As he bends in still grief o'er the hallowed bier,
> As enanguished he turns from the laugh of the scorner,
> And drops to perfection's remembrance a tear;
> When floods of despair down his pale cheeks are streaming,
> When no blissful hope on his bosom is beaming,
> Or, if lulled for a while, soon he starts from his dreaming,
> And finds torn the soft ties to affection so dear.
> Ah, when shall day dawn on the night of the grave,
> Or summer succeed to the winter of death?
> Rest awhile, hapless victim! and Heaven will save
> The spirit that hath faded away with the breath.
> Eternity points, in its amaranth bower
> Where no clouds of fate o'er the sweet prospect lour,
> Unspeakable pleasure, of goodness the dower,
> When woe fades away like the mist of the heath.

In present-tense narratives, on the other hand, the tone is mostly quiet and the present tense often the only indication of live commentary.

In present-tense novels, the narrator frequently avoids deictic adverbs and pronouns that too obtrusively indicate his here and now as narrator. To *now*, *yesterday* and *today*, he prefers *then* (*when*), *the previous day*, *this day* and so on (Vandeloo 1972, my translation):

> He feels it only *when* the wet leaves reach his neck and the drops splash down on his paper. He looks a little distractedly around and discovers *then* the dark curtain with the glittering reflection of many colours.

We notice in particular the use of 'when the wet leaves' and 'discovers then the dark curtain' instead of, respectively, 'now the wet leaves' and 'discovers now'. In the present-tense narrative, the narrator tends to do the opposite of what he would do in a past-tense narrative, in which deictic adverbs would find their way in the form of characters' thoughts (Woolf 2000, 4):

> For it was the middle of June: The War was over, except for someone like Mrs Foxcroft at the Embassy *last night* eating her heart out because

that nice boy was killed and *now* the old Manor House must go to a cousin . . .

The attempt to relativize the here and now of the historical present through adverbs that indicate distance is evidence that the present tense only pretends to express live commentary, whereas the underlying structure is the past, including the adverbs indicating the distance of the past. The relativization of the historical present by the use of adverbs implying distance is also common in colloquial usage:

I was waiting at the bus station together with a couple of other people. *Then* suddenly we hear a horrible scream from behind . . .

The substitution of *now* for *then* would be felt as a grammatical error.

Identity and level

Since the fictional narrator belongs to the fictional world, he is necessarily related to the action in some way. We have already seen that the action can be defined both as an infinite fictional world and as the limited section of the fictional world rendered by the mental model. The narrator is automatically part of the endless fictional universe, whereas his relationship to the action in the narrow sense may vary from novel to novel. As we have seen, the narrative act is normally posterior to the action, and the action's anteriority may be expressed by the past tense as well as by the present tense, which we usually interpret as the historical present. In this way, the narrative process stands out as a level of its own that is independent of the action. The relationship between narrative level and action level is both *temporal* and *causal*: temporal because the narrative process occurs after the action is finished, and causal because the narrative process creates the mental model of the action.

In present-tense narratives where the present tense is literal, that is live commentary in which action and the narrative process are really simultaneous, the two levels coalesce temporally but not causally. There remains a narrative level that conveys the action (i.e. the mental model of it). As we have seen, narratives with a simultaneous level of narrative and action are relatively hypothetical and at any rate very rare. Even the literal present tense of epistolary and diary novels only applies in certain durative or iterative passages: 'Ever since the accident, I sleep very badly.' Moreover, such narratives do not deviate significantly from narratives with temporally separated levels, so we will here only consider literature where the two levels are both temporally and causally separated.

The fact that the narrator belongs temporally and causally to another level than the action necessarily places him outside it. As *retrospective narrator*, he cannot participate in the past action, because he cannot be in two places at the same time. This must not be confused with the fact that the narrator may nevertheless be *identical* with one of the characters of the fictional action, but in that case, we must distinguish between two different stages of his life: his previous character-self and his present narrator-self. The distinction between the narrator-self and the first-person character also remains intact in narratives told in a real present tense. Even if the narrative process and the action are simultaneous, the two roles do not merge. When a person involved in an event reports this event at the same time as he experiences it, the narrative act is still distinct from the action. Only in rare cases does the narrative act infiltrate the action, for instance if it prevents the speaker from concentrating on his other activities, but then the story is raised to a meta-level, where the influence of the narrative level on the action is reported on a new and higher level: the narrator's telling us that he is suddenly involved in the action by telling about it. This would be the case if the narrator informs us that he is being chased by a bull in a meadow and apologizes for momentarily postponing the story until he manages to jump over the fence 20 metres ahead.

It seems paradoxical to say that the narrator takes part in the action as one of the characters. This is due to an ambiguity of language with respect to the meaning of *identity*. The narrator's presence on the narrative level as well as that of the action does not mean he is in two places at the same time. As long as the two levels do not coincide temporally, the narrator is represented on each level by two different stages of his life, an earlier stage (the stage as character in the action) and a later stage (the stage as narrator). In a past-tense novel, an earlier version of the narrator participates in the action, while a later version of him tells about it by way of the text. The two stages are identical in terms of continuity but not in terms of simultaneity. We must therefore discriminate between *synchronous* and *diachronic identity*. Synchronous identity distinguishes one person from other contemporary persons, whereas diachronic identity differentiates between different stages of the same person's life. The narrator on the narrative level is therefore only diachronically identical with the *I* that takes part in the action. In other words, diachronic identity implies two different stages and a self linking them together. We can express this by differentiating between the *narrator-self* and the *first-person character*. The character called *I* in the action is then marked as diachronically identical with the narrator by the very term *I*.

In first-person narratives in the *real* present tense, the difference between the narrator-self and the first-person character corresponds to the time span of diachronic identity, but because the two *I*'s are simultaneous, the term *diachronic* ought to be replaced with another term that accounts for the distinction. The distinction here is not related to time but to function or role, and the *I* unites the two functions or roles into one identity. So there is identity, not across time but across roles.

A passage from *Three Men in a Boat* illustrates the different kinds of identity (Jerome 1957, 7):

> It is a most extraordinary thing, but I never read a patent medicine advertisement without being impelled to the conclusion that I am suffering from the particular disease therein dealt with, in its most virulent form. The diagnosis seems in every case to correspond exactly with all the sensations that I have felt.
>
> I remember going to the British Museum one day to read up the treatment for some slight ailment of which I had a touch—hay fever, I fancy it was.

In the first paragraph, the narrator-self is synchronous with the first-person character, but at the same time, they are causally distinct from one other. The narrator-self creates the text, in contrast to the first-person character, who may be occupied with such activities as reading and suffering from diseases, activities having no causal impact on the text (at least not in the same sense as writing it). In this particular example, it is especially easy to distinguish between the two roles of the narrator, because the present tense of the narrator-self is confined to a short and definite period of time (the moment of writing), whereas the first-person character occupies a much longer and more indefinite period of time that includes repetitions of a behavioural pattern. In the second paragraph, the narrator-self is not synchronous with the first-person character, and it is easy to distinguish between them temporally.

The narrator's participation on the level of the action – in terms of diachronic identity with one of the characters – is of the same importance to the action as the character with which he shares his identity. The first-person character may be a crucial or insignificant character, ranging from a protagonist to a minor character to an outside witness, like the narrator Zeitblom in Thomas Mann's *Doktor Faustus*.

As long as the narrator uses his own experiences (as a first-person character) at the level of action as his source, he may be interpreted as a character. However, one issue the terminology may need to confront is whether a first-person character on the action-level who is merely an outside witness without influence on the events may be said to be part of the action or not. The presence of this first-person character on the stage with the other characters is an argument that participation on the level of the action also means participation in the action, even if the involvement is peripheral. The fact that an element is not relevant to the development of the action does not necessarily mean it ceases to be part of the action, just as we cannot discount all the irrelevant elements that surround us in our real lives as non-existent.

Terminological problems

Traditional theory of the novel has tried to differentiate between the various relationships between the narrator and the fictional characters by way of the terms *first-person, second-person* and *third-person narrative* (or *I-, you-* and *he/she-narrative*). The use of grammatical person indicates that at least one of the fictional characters is represented in first, second or third person. In *first-person narrative*, one of the characters is identical with the narrator; *second-person narrative* means that one of the characters is identical with the narratee (the fictional listener or reader), and *third-person narrative* simply means that none of the characters is identical with narrator or narratee.

The distinction between first-person and third-person narrative is the most important, because most works of literature fall under one of these two alternatives. In principle, all texts in which the narrator is present on the level of the action (through diachronic identity) are first-person narratives, while he is absent from the level of the action in third-person narratives (or rarely, second-person narratives). In practice, however, the distinction between the first-person and third-person narrative is somewhat ambiguous. These terms traditionally go hand-in-hand with a definition of the action that distinguishes between the action and the level of the action. A character can be present on the level of the action without taking an active role in the action. First-person characters that do not participate actively enough in the action are not regarded as first-person characters, and the work itself is characterized as a third-person narrative. In Henry James's third-person novel *The Ambassadors*, the narrator is sometimes explicitly visible on the level of the narrative act when he mentions himself in the first person: 'The principle I have just mentioned . . ', 'Our friend . . ' (James 1992, 2, 19), but he is not present on the level of the action. In *Doktor Faustus*, the narrator Zeitblom explicitly announces his presence as an eyewitness (Mann 1967, 15, 399, my translation):

> Von dem Bilde dieser Vorgänger, die bald fast gleichzeitig wegstarben, ist mir wenig geblieben. Desto deutlicher steht mir dasjenige ihrer Kinder Jonathan und Elsbeth Leverkühn vor Augen.
>   Wir nahmen am einen Ende des wuchtigen Tisches Platz. . . . Adrian und ich nebeneinander.

(Of the picture of these predecessors, who soon died almost simultaneously, I remember little, while I have that of their children Jonathan and Elsbeth Leverkühn clearly in mind.

We sat down at the end of the massive table. . . . Adrian and I beside each other.)

In spite of regular contact with the protagonist, Zeitblom has no influence on the action, and *Doktor Faustus* has traditionally not been considered a first-person novel. How active the narrator must be to make it a first-person narrative is arbitrary, and the boundary between first-person and third-person novels is correspondingly blurred.

If the fictional reader or listener is identical with one of the characters in the action, the book is a second-person narrative, which is a relatively rare phenomenon. In second-person narratives, the fictional receiver's role may be as varied as in first-person narratives. In Camus's *La chute* (*The Fall*, Camus 1976), for instance, the second-person character is only a passive listener, whereas he is the protagonist in Michel Butor's *La modification* (*Second Thoughts*, Butor 1957). Just as it is a prerequisite for the first-person novel that a book must have a first-person character playing a sufficiently active role in the action, the second-person character of the second-person novel must also be actively involved in the action. Therefore, *La chute* is no second-person novel, while *La modification* is.

The same rational spirit that led to the terms *first-person*, *second-person* and *third-person narrative* also generated the corresponding *first-person*, *second-person* and *third-person narrator*. Since the narrator of all three narratives would speak of himself in the first person, it seems illogical to call him third-person narrator and so forth, as in principle all narrators are first-person narrators on the level of the narrative act (Genette 1972, 251–2; 1983, 65). The terms *first-person*, *second-person* and *third-person narrator* are, of course, contractions of *the narrator of a first-person narrative* and so on, and though unwieldy, the uncontracted terms avoid confusion with the narrator's own *first person*. In second-degree narratives (a narrative embedded in another [first-degree] narrative), it is common for a narrator in third person (or even second or first person) to tell a new, second-degree story, like Scheherazade in *One Thousand and One Nights*, and it is useful to reserve *first-person*, *second-person* and *third-person narrator* for such second-degree narrators, who may really narrate in first, second or third person: 'When we were together in Paris, I remember that Peter/you/I told the following story . . .'

The boundary between *first-person*, *second-person* and *third-person narrative* is in itself not always clear, but in addition, the author sometimes mixes the three genres intentionally, as in the novel *Aeneas, of de levensreis van een man* (*Aeneas, or a Man's Life's Journey*) by the Flemish writer Willy Spillebeen, where the protagonist Aeneas is alternately mentioned in the first, second and third person (Spillebeen 1992).

Gérard Genette eschews all three terms because, as mentioned above, the use of the first person in first-person narrative is ambiguous and may refer to narrator as well as character (Genette 1972, 251–2); all narratives are in some sense first-person on account of the narrator's *I*, and the variable factor is the relationship between the narrator and the characters of the action.

Instead of the traditional terms, Genette introduces completely new terms based on the Greek *diegesis* (story). Adding the prefixes *intra-*, *extra-*, *homo-* and *hetero-*, he creates the adjectives *extradiegetic* and *intradiegetic*, which refer respectively to the level of the narrative act and the level of the action, and *homodiegetic* and *heterodiegetic*, which refer to the relationship between the narrator and the characters with respect to identity. The narrator is extradiegetic, whereas the events and the characters are intradiegetic. When one of the characters in the action tells a story of his own, like Scheherazade in *One Thousand and One Nights*, he becomes a second-degree narrator and is called *intradiegetic*. The term *intradiegetic narrator* is therefore reserved for second-degree narrators, third-degree narrators and so on, that is, for the narrator of works where one story contains another, which in turn contains another and so on like Chinese boxes. A narrator that is absent from the scene of action is *heterodiegetic*, and if he takes part in the action, he becomes *homodiegetic*. Within the group of homodiegetic narrators, Genette distinguishes between peripheral and central roles in the action and reserves *autodiegetic* for the narrator who is identical with the protagonist. The first-degree narrator can never be intradiegetic according to Genette's terminology, except perhaps in relation to his own narrative act.

Genette's terms represent in some sense a departure from traditional terminology, which is based on grammatical person. While according to the traditional system, Zeitblom in *Doktor Faustus* features as a third-person narrator, he is homodiegetic according to Genette and ends up in the same category as Ishmael in *Moby Dick*, whom Käte Hamburger regards as a first-person narrator. Only autodiegetic narrators correspond to the first-person narrator who is diachronically identical with the protagonist. Facing criticism for his sharp distinction between narrator-as-protagonist and narrator-as-outside-witness, Genette later concedes that there are transitional forms (Genette 1983, 69–70).

By way of a cross-combination of the narrator's relationship to the two narrative levels (intra- and extradiegetic), Genette introduces the following diagram with *relationship* and *level* on the vertical and horizontal axes, respectively (Genette 1972, 256):

Relationship/Level	*Extradiegetic*	*Intradiegetic*
Heterodiegetic	Homer	Scheherazade
Homodiegetic	Gil Blas *Marcel*	Odysseus

According to the diagram, Homer is an extradiegetic narrator because he is situated on a level higher than the action, and heterodiegetic because he does not participate in the action. Similarly, Gil Blas is an extradiegetic narrator because he is on a level higher than the action, but homodiegetic because what he is relating is his own past. In *One Thousand and One Nights*, Genette has left out the real narrator (the first-degree narrator, who is, of course, both extra- and heterodiegetic like all third-person narrators). Instead he includes Scheherazade, who is the protagonist of the action and hence intradiegetic (as well as autodiegetic). But at the same time, she tells stories about other people and becomes therefore a second-degree narrator. As she does not relate her own past, she is heterodiegetic. Like Scheherazade, Odysseus is the hero of the action and hence intradiegetic and autodiegetic, but by telling the Phaeacians about his experiences after the fall of Troy, he becomes a homodiegetic second-degree narrator.

This diagram is not as unproblematic as it may seem. Genette's use of the real, biographical author Homer as an extradiegetic narrator is a serious flaw, for the author does not belong to the fictional world and is irrelevant to traditional narratology. Nevertheless, the mistake is not irreparable; it suffices to include the first-degree narrator in for example, the *Odyssey* or *One Thousand and One Nights*, which both belong to the fictional world they report from, being at the same time situated on another level of the action. The diagram could then be improved as follows:

Relationship/Level	*Extradiegetic*	*Intradiegetic*
Heterodiegetic	The first-degree narrator of *One Thousand and One Night*	Scheherazade
Homodiegetic	Gil Blas	Odysseus

Moreover, Genette's diagram disregards the fact that, in addition to being an outsider to the events she recounts, Scheherazade is situated on a level higher than these events and is hence an extradiegetic narrator in relation to this action level. She is simultaneously an extra-, intra- and heterodiegetic narrator, which is not reflected in Genette's diagram. Likewise, Odysseus is extra-, intra- and homodiegetic. The fact that the same narrator can be extra- and intradiegetic at the same time seems to be a paradox, making it necessary to add that the terms are related to two different levels, which is simply inconvenient. The fact that the second-degree narrator Scheherazade is heterodiegetic implies, however, that she is also extradiegetic, so the extradiegetic relationship is redundant.

One type of novel not mentioned in Genette's diagram is second-degree narratives with a first-person narrator, that is, first-person narratives where the first-person character tells a new story, either about himself or about others. In other words, the first-degree first-person narrator (*I* no. 1) relates that the first-person character (*I* no. 2) as second-degree first-person narrator has related a tale about a first-person character (*I* no. 3) or a third-person character on a still lower level. It might sound like this:

> When I lived in Paris, I was together with a couple of friends, to whom I told the following story: "Some years ago, I (or Peter) was taking a course in London, when suddenly . . ."

This would be similar to the *Odyssey* if we transformed it into a first-person narrative, letting Odysseus – now as a first-person narrator – (a second-degree narrative is a narrative embedded in another [first-degree] narrative), tell the Phaeacians about his experiences after the fall of Troy. According to Genette's terminology, the *I* no. 1 is extradiegetic/homodiegetic (like Gil Blas), whereas *I* no. 2 is intradiegetic like Scheherazade and Odysseus, and moreover, hetero- or homodiegetic in relation to the action on the lowest level. Now there are evidently too many levels and variables to be compressed into a diagram with four components.

Although Genette's terminology is meant to be an accurate scholarly instrument, it has several flaws in its original form, the least of which is the fact that the Greek terms are unfamiliar and take time to get used to. The prefixes at each end of his bipolar system are so closely related semantically that one easily confuses them. *Intra-*, *auto-* and *homo-* all refer to inclusion, and *extra-* and *hetero-* mean exclusion. In practical use, these terms also seem suspiciously synonymous. Both *intra-* and *homodiegetic* mean that the narrator is included in the action, while *extra-* and *heterodiegetic* mean that he is situated outside. The only difference between *intra-* and *homodiegetic* is that the former applies to the second-degree and third-degree narrator's presence on the level of the narrative act, while the latter refers to the first-degree narrator's presence on the level of his own narrative act – which is self-evident – as well as to his presence on the level of the action.

A similar, minimal difference pertains to *extra-* and *heterodiegetic*. *Extradiegetic* designates the level on which the first-degree narrator is narrating his story, while *heterodiegetic* means that the narrator is not present on the level of the action. Are these distinctions so important that we need to reserve special terms for them, and if they are, are Genette's almost synonymous terms a good way of doing so? The problem with these terms is that they must cover relationships in simple two-level narratives as well as in three- and four-level narratives. On account of this double function, his terminology is overloaded. We may first examine how it works in relation to the most common sort of text, the two-level narrative.

In the first place, we need terms to discriminate between the two levels, and for that purpose, we have the adjectives *extra-* and *intradiegetic*, which refer respectively to the level of the narrative act and that of the action. For example, the narrator's comments are extradiegetic, while the characters' statements are intradiegetic. The text, as a material phenomenon, is as a whole extradiegetic, whereas the action it reproduces is intradiegetic.

In the second place, we need terms to differentiate between first-person and third-person narratives where the narrator is diachronically identical with one of the characters and narratives where he is not. Here Genette introduces the terms *homo-* and *heterodiegetic*, but *intra-* and *extradiegetic* would also do the job without leading to misunderstandings. Genette's terminology needs simplification because all narrators are obviously extradiegetic, as their narrator-self is situated on the level of the narrative act, *outside* the action they recount. It is not necessary to use *extradiegetic* with reference to this matter of course. Consequently, this term is released for other use.

Since the narrator-self of the narrator is inseparably linked to the level of the narrative act, it is also a matter of course that the narrator-self cannot simultaneously take part in the action. Only an earlier version of him in a previous stage of development can have participated. Genette calls participation in the action and exclusion from it *homo-* and *heterodiegetic narration*, respectively, but because *extradiegetic* is now available, I prefer to use it here, with reference to the narrator who has not taken part in the action (the third-person narrator). Now, *extradiegetic* refers to the relationship between the narrator and the action. Correspondingly, it makes sense to term the narrator that has participated in the action (in an earlier stage of himself) *intradiegetic*. Genette applies this term only in relation to the multilevel narrative, and it remains available to us as long as we stick to two-level narratives. This makes *homo-* and *heterodiegetic* superfluous, at least with respect to two-level narratives.

What consequences, however, does discarding *homo-* and *heterodiegetic* entail for the multilevel narrative? When Scheherazade in the third-person narrative *One Thousand and One Nights* has to share *intradiegetic* with Gil Blas, we need a new term to express that Scheherazade is a third-person narrator and Gil Blas a first-person narrator. We can easily make up for this by calling Gil Blas an *intradiegetic first-degree narrator* and Scheherazade an *extradiegetic second-degree narrator*. *Extradiegetic* here means that Scheherazade is situated above the level of action she recounts, for it is a matter of course that as a second-degree narrator, she is *intradiegetic* in relation to the action on her own level. Correspondingly, it is obvious that as a first-person narrator, Gil Blas is extradiegetic with respect to the action level below him, while as a first-person character, he is intradiegetic with respect to the action level. Instead of using the Greek terms, we may also refer to Gil Blas as a first-degree first-person narrator and Scheherazade as a second-degree third-person narrator. After our adjustments, Genette's diagram looks like this:

Relationship/Level	*First level*	*Second level*
Extradiegetic (third-person narrative)	The first-degree narrator of *One Thousand and One Nights*	Scheherazade
Intradiegetic (first-person narrative)	Gil Blas	Odysseus

Although Genette's terminology is both inconvenient and abstract, it has been generally accepted and used alongside the traditional one based on grammatical person, although the two systems entirely coincide. I see no reason why we should not combine them, using whatever term we find most appropriate to the given situation. If we want to characterize narratives according to the relationship between narrator or receiver and the fictional characters, the grammatical terms are easier to understand, whereas Genette's terms are unwieldy and in some respects even inadequate. On the other hand, the distinction between *intra-* and *extradiegetic* is useful for describing how certain elements are related to the level of the narrative act or that of the action, such as comments and irony from the narrator or characters.

The significance of the author's choice of grammatical person

In creating his novel or short story, the writer can choose between first-, second- and third-person narrative. Genette points out that this is not primarily a choice between different grammatical persons but between different attitudes of the narrator, without elaborating on what he means by that (Genette 1972, 252). We will now turn to the impact of this choice of personal pronouns and narrative attitude on the reader.

The distinction between grammatical persons proves useful because the choice of personal pronouns affects the reader's understanding of the action. As second-person narratives are rare, first- and third-person narratives will require most of our attention. Because the first-person narrator is identical with one of the fictional characters, we encounter two stages in the narrator's life: his past as a participant in the action and his present life as the narrator writing down his reminiscences. These two stages of the narrator's life make the *I* ambiguous, obliging us to distinguish between the narrating *I*, *the first-person narrator*, and the *I* taking part in the action, *the first-person character*. The first-person narrator becomes conspicuous when the narrator comments on the past events from his retrospective position or says something about the narrative process.

Third-person narratives have a corresponding distinction between the level of the narrative act and the level of the action, and the narrator may comment on the action just as in the first-person narrative, but with a significant difference: the narrator of a third-person narrative is not identical with any of the characters involved in the action. In the first-person narrative, the narrator's identity with a character in the action makes the narrative act a continuation of the action. The first-person narrator's experiences during the narration extend the action, which becomes evident when he, for instance, turns out to be more mature than his former self in the action.

A first-person novel, in other words, consists of action plus a sequel to the action constituted by the narration of the story, whereas a third-person novel contains action that has no necessary connection with the narrative act afterwards. In the first-person novel, for example, the first-person character cannot in principle die, since he has to survive to tell the story afterwards. Nevertheless, the author may deviate from this convention if he finds it interesting, but the reader is so accustomed to the immortality of the first-person character so as to feel a certain security in this while reading a first-person novel. In a third-person novel, any of the characters may die without any consequences for the narrator's ability to recount the story afterwards, and the reader has to read the ending to know whether the protagonist survives.

Because the first-person narrator is identical with one of the fictional characters, there is a peculiar relationship between the first-person narrator and the first-person character. As the first-person narrator speaks about his own past, the way he is relating it can tell us something about him at the last stage of his life that we know. He can garner sympathy by being open and candid, particularly if he is able to adopt a critical attitude to his past actions, a sign of personal development and maturity. Of course, he can also show indifference and make a negative impression. In either case, the atmosphere is different from a third-person novel, where the narrator is diachronically identical with none of the characters. The first-person novel connotes confession, apology or defence, while the non-involved third-person narrator can at the most be an empathizing or critical stranger to the action. In effect, the first-person novel is always longer than the third-person novel, independent of pages, because the narrative process functions as an extension of the action.

As we have seen, second-person narratives are rare. It is not common for a first-person narrator to tell a second-person character what the latter has experienced, as the second-person character should know his own story best. Therefore one would expect the second-person narratee to perform the narrative act – in the first person – instead of the first-person narrator. This is exactly why the role reversal in the second-person narrative has an effect of its own. The narrator's voice comes across as an accusation or reproach because he is confronting another person with the latter's behaviour and experiences, especially if the confrontation has the character of criticism. The narrator may also, however, assume an advisory role, analysing the behaviour of the second-person listener.

The representation of a second-person human being as a thinking and feeling subject seems even more unusual than disclosing the thoughts and feelings of third-person characters. Internal focalization in the third-person narrative conveys an illusion of being in the mind of another person because the narrator can more easily avoid elements reminding of his own presence in the text. Symptoms of the narrative voice tend to disturb this illusion of direct contact with the focalized character. The direct address betrays more obtrusively the presence of the narrator than substantives and personal pronouns of the third person, because the addressee takes actively part in the communication. However unobtrusively the narrator deals with his own person, he cannot prevent the direct address from drawing attention to him as narrator: where there is an addressee, there has to be a sender, too.

In the novel *Zelfportret of het galgemaal* (*The Man in the Mirror*, Teirlinck 1973, 9) by the Flemish Herman Teirlinck, the narrator addresses the protagonist Henri in the second person, telling him in the present tense what he (Henri) is experiencing. The novel commences thus:

> In a few weeks you will be seventy, Henri, and you are still busy polishing away the fraud you are, the deceit you set out on half a century ago, seeking to give it a remarkable perfection. You know you can never

complete the job, that the work of perfecting will be endless. You are resigned to the inaccessibility of your goal. For lying has become your life's work, too exacting ever to be brought to a conclusion.

Here the narrator looks into the soul of his protagonist, criticizing his behaviour, and the hero has to listen whether he wants to or not. The narrator is not realistic; it seems rather as if Henri's conscience has taken the floor. The combination of direct speech and present tense gives the impression of the narrator confronting the protagonist with his own behaviour, making the protagonist responsible in a manner different from a third-person character, who is unaware of his own behaviour as taking place before an audience. Insofar as the second-person character hears the narrator's critical voice, he is challenged to improve. The difference becomes evident if we change the second person into third person:

> In a few weeks Henri will be seventy, and he is still busy polishing away the fraud he is, the deceit he set out on half a century ago, seeking to give it a remarkable perfection. He knows he can never complete the job, that the work of perfecting will be endless. He is resigned to the inaccessibility of his goal. For lying has become his life's work, too exacting ever to be brought to a conclusion.

In this version, the narrator conveys to the reader what is happening in Henri's mind, but Henri himself is not involved in the dialogue, and it is uncertain whether he understands his own behaviour himself.

In a past tense novel, the effect of the second person would be different still. The narrator would then be confronting the second-person character with events that are already past and hence no longer subject to change, perhaps in an attempt to instil some self-knowledge as part of a more general education process:

> In a few weeks you would be seventy, Henri, and you were still busy polishing away the fraud you were, the deceit you set out on half a century ago, seeking to give it a remarkable perfection. You knew you could never complete the job, that the work of perfecting would be endless. You were resigned to the inaccessibility of your goal. For lying had become your life's work, too exacting ever to be brought to a conclusion.

In order to understand the effects unique to first, second- and third-person narratives, one must understand the text as a verbal act: why does A tell B the story about A? Why does A tell B the story about B? Why does A tell B the story about C? The text's pragmatic function explains the special atmosphere the text conveys to the reader: confession, reproach, advice, exposure or example.

The report of speech and thoughts

When fictional characters speak, their statements can be rendered in various ways that are traditionally distinguished as *direct speech*, *indirect speech* and *free indirect discourse*, along with the more condensed way of reproducing speech, *speech report* (Fludernik 2009, 65). Corresponding distinctions apply to the representation of thoughts and feelings, which we can regard as a kind of unspoken interior speech. These terms are contracted forms of *direct rendering of speech*, *indirect rendering of speech* and so on, because the original literal statement or thought is of course not direct, indirect, free indirect or condensed. The modification of the original wording occurs only when the narrator renders it by way of one of the above-mentioned options.

1. *Direct discourse* means that the statement or thought is rendered unchanged, a literal copy of the original version:
   a. "Come here, darling! Oh God, I love you so much today!" said Paul.
   b. Peter stood at the window, looking down on the empty street and thinking, "Oh God, how lonely I am today!"

Since direct discourse accurately reproduces the statement, it preserves all the original features that exemplify the personality and mood of the speaking or thinking person. Such features are

1. verbal tense indicating the speaker's temporal position in relation to the object he is talking or thinking about
2. pronouns and verbal endings of the first or second person (I, you)
3. deictic adverbs (today, tomorrow)
4. interjections (Oh, ouch)
5. exclamation points
6. direct address (you, darling)
7. imperative (Come here!)
8. direct questions

Of course, direct speech can never account perfectly for the original utterance. As Fludernik points out, 'spoken language can never be faithfully represented in writing', and literature tends to stylize and simplify spoken conversation (Fludernik 2009, 65). However, the ability of fictional direct speech to represent real-life conversation is rather a question of realism and mimesis, and does not affect the usefulness of the term *direct speech*. In the fictional world, direct speech is meant to render the dialogue between characters in a way that accomplishes the communicative intention. As long as the author's main intention is not to give a scientific account of genuine everyday speech, the stylizations, simplifications, recurring clichés and formulaic phrases that characterize fictional dialogue are adequate enough for the communication of the cognitive content. Neither Racine's versified nor Ibsen's realistic dialogues purport to be material for sociolinguistic research. They are only intended to inform the reader in more general terms about important aspects of human interaction, and in that respect, direct speech is successful as long as it contributes to the characterization of the fictional characters.

2. In contrast to direct speech, *indirect speech* does not guarantee the preservation of the original wording. The statement or thought may be subjected to a process of interpretation, condensation or simplification, and words may be replaced by synonyms of another stylistic level or emotional value. Like direct speech, indirect speech leaves the message intact:
   a. Paul said that she should come to him and that he loved her so much (that day).
   b. Peter stood at the window, looking down on the empty street and thought of how lonely he was (that day).

Here the verbal tense and personal pronouns have been adapted to the frame text (Paul said; Peter stood). Distinctive features like deictic adverbs, interjections, direct address, imperative and exclamation points have been left out, giving the reader a less personal impression of the speaking or thinking character.

3. *Free indirect discourse* is a combination of direct and indirect speech, and like the two other forms, it preserves the message:
   a. Paul looked up as she entered the room. She had to come to him! Oh God, he loved her so much today!
   b. Peter stood at the window, looking down on the empty street. Oh God, how lonely he was today!

Verbal tense and personal pronouns are adapted to the frame text in the same way as in indirect speech, but some of the distinctive features (deictic adverbs and exclamation points) remain from the original version, revealing more of the speaking or thinking character's personality and mood. Since free indirect discourse dispenses with quotation marks, only the context reveals whether it refers to speech or thought. The sentences, 'She had to come to him! Oh God, he loved her so much today!' may report either speech or thought. To ensure the right interpretation, it is possible to attach a declarative verb to the free indirect discourse (Woolf 2000, 35):

> And she opened her scissors, and said, did he mind her just finishing what she was doing to her dress, for they had a party that night?

The past tense and use of third instead of first person indicate indirect speech, but the direct question and omission of the conjunctions *if* or *that* signal direct speech.

Free indirect discourse is above all used to render thoughts and feelings (Woolf 2000, 3):

> What a lark! What a plunge! For so it had always seemed to her when, with a little squeak of the hinges, which she could hear now, she had burst open the French windows and plunged at Bourton into the open air.

4. The term *speech report* should perhaps be modified as *condensed speech report* to avoid confusion with the rendering of speech in general. At any rate, *speech report* shortens the original statement so radically that it ceases even to be a sentence:

   a. Paul met her with an enthusiastic declaration of love.
   b. Peter stood at the window, looking down on the empty street, feeling awfully lonely.

Often the statement is reduced into a mere report of the speech act itself, while the message is left out:

> She did not respond to his proposal.

Whatever way the narrator renders speech and thought, it is the outcome of a process of selection and influences the reader's impression of the speaking or thinking character. Therefore, direct speech is the most informative and speech report the least informative rendering, with free indirect discourse and indirect speech somewhere in between.

As the rendering of speech and thought entails selection, it is to a certain extent related to the kind of selection that dominates the passage in which the utterance occurs. In scenic passages, direct speech and free indirect discourse are more frequent than in summary passages, where indirect speech and condensed speech report tend to predominate. Direct speech and free indirect discourse render the original statement in more detail than indirect speech and speech report, making it best suited for scenic representation, which tends to appear in the most important and emotionally gripping passages of the work where richness of detail is a prerequisite. Summary is generally meant to equip the reader with practical facts he needs to understand the scenic parts of the action, making indirect speech and speech report better suited to summary.

Although direct speech and free indirect discourse are more appropriate in scenic representation, their distribution in the text depends to a certain degree on the distribution of speech and thought. Direct speech more frequently renders speech, whereas free indirect speech tends to render thoughts and feelings. This is probably due to the fact that we do not conceive of thoughts and feelings as verbal in the normal sense of the word. Thoughts and feelings are by their very nature hard to pin down, composed of a stream of words, feelings, images, sense impressions and obscure forms of intuition. Nevertheless, a character's thoughts can only be rendered in words as if they consisted of speech; hence, the use of direct speech to reproduce thought seems artificial, an obtrusive reminder that the rendering is directed by a narrator. In *Mrs Dalloway*, where the action largely consists of the characters' thoughts and feelings, Virginia Woolf manages to dampen the artificiality in her oscillation between direct speech and free indirect discourse (Woolf 2000, 37):

> Stop! Stop! He wanted to cry! For he was not old; his life was not over; not by any means. He was only just past fifty. Shall I tell her, he thought, or not?

The imperative, 'Stop! Stop!' represents Peter's thoughts directly, as does the present tense ('Shall I tell her . . . or not?'), while the rest is free indirect discourse in the past tense. It is worth mentioning that Woolf does not use quotation marks when rendering thoughts in direct speech, although she always uses them when rendering speech in direct speech. Quotation marks are an explicit signal of direct speech, and by leaving them out when the direct speech renders thoughts, Woolf subdues the impression of artificiality.

Interference of the narrator

The narrator may supplement the representation of the action with comments that exceed the mere reproduction of it. Such comments may apply to the action itself or to the way it is rendered. The action itself as well as the material text and the mental model of the action may also be subject to comment, which can come in the form of values or information, and may be expressed directly or indirectly. The narrator can leave his imprint through personal comments, facts, evaluation, tendentious humour and irony, along with the use of metaphors, tropes and symbols.

Comments of the narrator

1. In the first place, the narrator may comment on the narrative process in order to help the reader orient himself in the work, as in the opening lines of Steinbeck's *Tortilla Flat* (Steinbeck 1950, 9):

> This is the story of Danny and of Danny's friends and of Danny's house. It is a story of how these three became one thing, so that in Tortilla Flat if you speak of Danny's house you do not mean a structure of wood flaked with old whitewash, overgrown with an ancient untrimmed rose of Castile. No, when you speak of Danny's house you are understood to mean a unit of which the parts are men, from which came sweetness and joy, philanthropy and, in the end, a mystic sorrow. For Danny's house was not unlike the Round Table, and Danny's friends were not unlike the knights of it.

The narrator's comments may also inform the reader about the relationship between the narrator and the work, as in the opening to Goethe's *The Sorrows of Young Werther* (Goethe 2002):

> I have carefully collected whatever I have been able to learn of the story of poor Werther, and here present it to you, knowing that you will thank me for it. To his spirit and character you cannot refuse your admiration and love: to his fate you will not deny your tears.

Such comments are not indispensable but contribute to building confidence between narrator and narratee, as well as the reader identifying with the role of narratee.

2. Second, the narrator may comment on the fictional world itself. Comments on the fictional world may be biological, geographical, historical, psychological, political, religious, scientific or philosophical in nature. It may also contain practical information about the fictional world, mostly in a present tense that refers to general insight or to permanent features of the fictional world, as in Sinclair Lewis's *Arrowsmith* (Lewis 1961, 10):

The state of Winnemac is bounded by Michigan, Ohio, Illinois, and Indiana, and like them it is half Eastern, half Midwestern. There is a feeling of New England in its brick and sycamore villages, its stable industries, and a tradition which goes back to the Revolutionary War. Zenith, the largest city in the state, was founded in 1792.

The famous opening to Tolstoy's *Anna Karenina* contains a reflection on life in general:

All happy families resemble each other, each unhappy family is unhappy in its own way.

3. The narrator may make modal statements like *maybe, perhaps, possibly, probably, hardly* and *seem*, which sow doubt into the text (from *Effi Briest*, Fontane 1969, 63, my translation):

Effi reichte dem verlegenen Eintretenden die Hand, die dieser mit einem gewissen Ungestüm küsste. Die junge Frau schien sofort einen großen Eindruck auf ihn gemacht zu haben.

Effi held out her hand to the embarrassed visitor. He kissed it rather intensely. It seemed as if the young woman had made a great impression on him at once.

This technique reminds the reader of how difficult it is to acquire reliable source material in the real world which has cognitive value in itself. Moreover, with such doubtful expressions, the narrator creates the impression of being realistic and serious, which reinforces his reliability within the fictional world (Booth 2005, 75–88; Nünning 2005, 89–107).

4. A more special form of comment is the expression of attitudes and values, often in the form of emotive words like *good, evil, naughty, kind, beautiful* and *ugly* (from *Max Havelaar*, Multatuli 1860):

The Controller Verbrugge was a good man. If one saw him there in his blue clothing, with embroidered oak and orange branches on the collar and the cuffs, it was hard to mistake the type which is common among the Hollanders in the Indies – a kind of man who is very different from the Hollanders in Holland.

Especially in older literature that predates naturalism, there are many instances of extradiegetic judgement (the narrator's judgement). From naturalism onwards, the narrator becomes less obtrusive and avoids judgement in the name of objectivity.

Humour as a manifestation of voice

Humour may be a manifestation of the voice of the narrator or author, especially when it functions as an indirect way of communication. But humour is a broad concept, and not all kinds of humour are equally representative of the narrator or author. Humour is generally a way of experiencing an object, an attitude linked to pleasure and laughter, which may be evoked by the things themselves (the comical) or the way they are presented (humour in the narrower sense). It is the latter type of humour that is relevant as a manifestation of the narrator's voice, and usually goes under the name of *joke*. The joke differs from usual communication in using an innocent surface structure to convey a taboo underlying structure:

> A young lady who wants to go to a carnival party, not knowing what disguise to wear, simply dons some pages of a newspaper. Over the course of the evening, she dances with a man, who after some time asks, "What are you in fact disguised as?" "As a newspaper," answers the girl. "That's funny," says he, "I have an article that I would very much like to get into it."

The surface structure of the punch line is a trivial statement about publishing an article in a newspaper, but the underlying structure is of course an invitation to sex. The two structures share the two-sided statement about the article; if the man had said the same thing to the female editor of a newspaper, the statement would no longer be ambiguous. In our example, however, the special context makes it ambiguous: (1) a woman and a man dancing together, that is, two potential sexual partners, (2) article's dual meaning as a written document and an object and (3) the woman wearing only a newspaper. These circumstances suffice to recast the whole as an invitation to sex.

In the above-mentioned context, an open invitation to sex is taboo and cannot therefore be expressed directly without being censored by the superego, which 'plays the critical and moralizing role' in the human mind (Wikipedia). With the invitation thus disguised as an innocent activity, the superego closes its eyes and pretends not to have noticed anything, allowing the deep structure to reach the id, the mind's 'set of uncoordinated instinctual trends' (Wikipedia).

Freud explains the humorous effect of the tendentious joke as the release of energy suppressed by inhibition (Freud 1958, 81, 85, 95–6). The misleading surface structure disengages us from the superego, releasing the suppressed energy and causing *relief* which expresses itself as laughter. While Freud bases his theory on relief, other theories link humour to *incongruity* or *superiority*. These three theories are not incompatible and shed light on different aspects of humour. The theory of superiority is based on an aspect of the releasing factor, the content of humour: the ridiculous is always in some sense negative, inviting a feeling of superiority. The incongruity theory concentrates on the structure of incongruity as the releasing factor (Dopychai 1988, 118). The relief theory foregrounds the joke's impact, on the other hand. The above-mentioned joke has several points reflecting these aspects of humour: (1) sex in the punch line (relief/release of accumulated energy), (2) a man outwitting a woman (superiority); (3) woman as sex object (superiority) and (4) a newspaper article signifying a sexual organ (incongruity).

Michael Mulkay's sociological explanation of humour as a special discourse is an important supplement to these three theories. While normal, serious discourse claims to be true and understands the world as a coherent and logical whole, the humorous discourse (or mode) allows for pluralism and incongruity (Mulkay 1988, 213–14). Laughter and smiling must be understood in terms of social processes: in addition to resulting from humorous stimuli, they are an interactional resource, a signal that communication is now transferred to the humorous mode, which exempts the participants from claims concerning truth, consistency and relevance (Mulkay 1988, 110). Humorous statements are ambiguous in that the one who utters them can always deny responsibility for the real content by saying, 'I was just joking.' As a consequence, one can permit talk about taboo topics and say things one would otherwise have refrained from saying. This also applies to literature, where the author or narrator uses humour to convey a taboo content.

The short story *Ballstemning* (*Ball Atmosphere*) by the Norwegian Alexander Kielland takes place in Paris at the time of the French Revolution. A beautiful but poor young girl is taken care of by a rich man, who later marries her and provides a good life for her. Driving through the mass of people on her way to a ball, the young lady is reminded of her own youth in poverty and the social injustice she escaped. At the ball, a young count flirts with her and compliments her beauty, to which she only draws his attention to the hateful crowd outside (Kielland 1897, my translation):

> The count stood perturbed on the balcony where she had left him, and threw a glance at the crowd. It was a sight he had often seen; he had made many bad and tasteless jokes about this many-headed monster. But only tonight had it occurred to him that this monster was in fact the most frightening environment one could imagine for a ball. Strange and disturbing thoughts were whirling in the count's brain, where they had plenty of space. He was utterly upset, and it took him an entire polka to regain his peace of mind.

Pointing out the ample room in the count's brain is of course a joke; to say that there is plenty of space in a brain is ambiguous and as innocent on the surface level as saying that there is much space in a room, but space also means *emptiness*, which here alludes to the count's vacuousness. Since it is somewhat taboo to denigrate others, a direct characterization of the count might have seemed offensive to the reader, whereas the humorous paraphrase suspends the critical influence of the superego, enabling the reader to receive the forbidden message without remorse. In this example, various factors contribute to the humorous effect: incongruity (a brain is no room), superiority (the count is characterized as stupid) and relief (the inhibition against denigration is suspended and energy is released). To a certain extent, humour exempts both the narrator and the reader from responsibility for the negative message, because they can counter any criticism by saying it was just a joke.

The sentence, 'It took him an entire polka to regain his peace of mind,' also has a humorous effect, but here it is related to irony. According to the surface structure, the count needs a lot of time to regain his composure (an *entire* polka), whereas the deep structure (*only* a polka) reveals the time involved as insignificant. In other words, the count's superficiality prevents him from grasping the basic problems in his own society.

In this example, the humour is extradiegetic (external), that is, a transaction between narrator and reader. Since literary fiction sheds light on the extratextual world by way of resemblance, it also contains intradiegetic humour, that is, humour between the characters. This humour is part of the theme and has cognitive significance, representing the function of humour in the existing world. In addition, intradiegetic (internal) humour has the same functions as it does extradiegetically, expressing taboo topics that might offend if stated explicitly. The humorous discourse suspends the censoring superego, allowing the reader to receive thoughts he would otherwise reject. This pertains especially to attitudes and prejudice he unconsciously entertains himself, which are reawakened by the indirectness of humour. By unmasking negative behavioural patterns by way of a humorous disguise, the narrator can more easily influence the reader's attitudes and opinions without his being aware of it. The use of humour to gain acceptance for controversial views is nevertheless a double-edged sword, because by exempting the sender from responsibility, it entitles the receiver to discard the deep structure by pretending it was just a joke.

All kinds of humour are used to sweeten potentially disagreeable passages, for instance when suspense or sadness in the action becomes unbearable. A typical example is the nihilist novel *De avonden* (*The Evenings*) by Dutch writer Gerard Reve (Reve 1947), which draws a depressing picture of the protagonist's monotonous, empty life. The author compensates for all the gloom with external and internal irony, comedy and internal jokes throughout the book. In it, however, humour is often no longer a manifestation of the narrator's voice (extradiegetic humour) but a quality of the action itself (intradiegetic humour).

Irony

Irony plays an important role in literature, but definitions of irony have often been too broad and ambiguous, as when Cleanth Brooks regards contrasts in general as ironic (Brooks 1962, 729–41, Booth 1974, 3, 7). This concept of irony departs from colloquial usage and is moreover too broad to be of any use. To be sure, the everyday notion of irony does not cover *situational irony* (including *irony of fate*), *dramatic irony* and *romantic irony* (*metafiction*). Situational irony and irony of fate consist in a disparity between actual and expected outcomes, for instance when King Oedipus brings about the oracular prophecy by trying to avoid it. Romantic irony is when the author breaks the fictional illusion by alluding to it external conditions, for instance by talking about pages or the stage as such. Dramatic irony consists in the reader's knowing more about the action than the protagonist. In all these cases, there is an opposition between entities, but ultimately, irony is more than that.

Irony has interested scholars from antiquity, and this interest shows no signs of diminishing in modern literary theory (for instance, Booth 1961, Muecke 1970, Lapp 1992, Hutcheon 1994, Colebrook 2004). It is often defined as saying the opposite of what you really mean but in such a way that the receiver catches the real meaning. Although irony is commonly associated with contradiction, it can also involve things other than opposites. It is sufficient that there is a clear contrast between what is said and what is meant. This definition of irony must not be confused with contrasts in general, like the contrast between black and white, good and evil and so on, which would be more in accordance with Cleanth Brooks's conception of irony, which we rejected above. For example, understatement can be ironic, as when one says of a person so drunk that he falls out of the back of someone's car:

I think he's had a little too much.

This understatement is ironic although there is no complete contrast, only a gradual difference between a little and far too much. But one may, perhaps, regard *a little* and *far too much* as opposites, which would make this statement ironic based on complete contrast.

Another example is a mother who tells her husband that their 19-year-old son was behaving strangely when he came home the previous night, and she wonders whether he could have been out drinking. Her husband answers:

I think not—look at how thirsty he was this morning!

In this case, the contrast is between thirst from having had too little non-alcoholic fluid to drink and thirst from drinking too much alcohol. The father pretends to be so naïve as to think alcohol works like water, but he effectively confirms his wife's suspicion that their son came home drunk. The little dialogue also, of course, works as a joke.

Edgar Lapp defines irony as a simulated verbal act, in which the sender *pretends* to be lying (Lapp 1992). In order to succeed, irony requires a context revealing the ironic intention. This context may consist in external or internal circumstances, for instance an extratextual situation or prior knowledge on the part of the receiver, or in exaggeration, understatement or euphemism. The sender says something different from what he means, and the receiver is aware enough to know that the sender wants the message to be exposed. The sender does not believe his actual statement and does not want the receiver to believe it either. The ironic father expects his wife to know the difference between the effect of alcohol and dehydration and to see through the apparent naïveté of his statement. The context reveals the irony: the couple shares the same general knowledge about the effects of alcohol, and both are familiar with the husband's personality.

Lapp points out that irony may occur on all levels of the verbal act. A part of a sentence, the whole sentence or the verbal act as such may be ironic:

May I read your masterpiece sometime? (when no great masterpiece is expected)

Only the word *masterpiece* is ironic here.

How well-prepared you've come today! (when the student turns up without having done his homework)

The entire sentence is ironic.

Could you turn it up a notch? (when the music is so loud, it's deafening)

The question is ironic. The sender pretends to ask a question in order to make an affirmative or imperative statement: 'The music is deafening' or 'Turn it down!' At the same time, the question expresses the opposite of what the speaker means: turn the music *up* instead of *down*.

Irony usually expresses a negative attitude, but it may also be positive, as when a girl admiring her friend's new dress says:

Oh, that doesn't fit you at all!

Or when someone says to a fellow student who always receives excellent marks but is worried before a particular exam:

Poor thing, you've never passed anything in your life!

Irony can also be without words, using signs like gestures and mimicry, for example, an ironic smile when you have obviously no reason to be smiling.

In spite of the broad scholarly attention devoted to irony, it is striking how little irony's psychological mechanism has been explored. Why do we use irony? Why do we make as if we mean something other than we really do? Why not say directly what we mean? If scholars have posed these questions at all, the answer has often been too superficial to reach the core of the problem (see Hutcheon 1994, 37–43). But to fully grasp the various functions of irony, it is necessary to identify the psychological mechanisms behind it, which we will attempt to do in this chapter.

In his analysis of the joke, Freud points out that irony shares many technical aspects with jokes (Freud 1958). In many jokes, an innocent surface structure conceals a taboo underlying structure, and although Freud does not explicitly say so, it seems natural to relate irony to the interplay between the joke's ambiguous structure and the mind's unconscious functions (superego, ego and id). The ambiguity is a Trojan horse, the surface only a means to smuggle the underlying structure past the censoring superego to the id. The superego sees only the innocent surface structure and unsuspectingly allows the Trojan horse passage, in which the underlying structure lies in wait until it reaches the id, which takes up and enjoys the forbidden content. According to Freud, the receiver's pleasure is due to relief and the release of energy: 'for erecting and for maintaining a psychical inhibition some "physical expenditure" is required'. The humorous technique deceives the superego into letting go of the inhibition in question (Freud 1960, 145). Thus the energy required for the inhibition is saved and can be released as laughter, a yield of pleasure corresponding to the physical expenditure that is saved (145). However, it seems plausible that the pleasure is more directly attributable to the satisfaction of giving expression to the sinful content. Whether the pleasure is due to the message or the violation of the taboo, it gives pleasure to express the true meaning, but also to provoke for the sake of provocation, as part of a power struggle.

It may also be possible that the superego sees through the trickery but allows itself to be deceived by the innocent surface structure. Then the surface structure works as an alibi or excuse so that the super-ego can counter any criticism by playing innocent, pretending not to have understood anything at all.

The double structure of irony corresponds to the ambiguity of the joke. The literal words are a surface structure, and the real meaning is an underlying structure (deep structure). In negative statements, the surface structure is friendly while the deep structure takes care of expressing the criticism. As criticism is a kind of aggression that is more or less taboo or can at least entail an unpleasant conflict, it is useful to dress up the intention to make it less overt. The surface structure reassures and distracts the superego so that the deep structure may pass.

Like the joke, irony makes bystanders laugh and hence belongs to humour. The expression of the repressed content engenders a feeling of pleasure, and if the irony is negative, both sender and bystander feel superior to the victim. Irony involves all three theories of laughter: superiority, relief and incongruity.

When the irony is positive, an apparently negative utterance conveys a positive assessment, admiration, affection and the like to the receiver. Why disguise a positive statement, when there is no taboo making a disguise necessary? It happens that there may be other reasons for obscuring expressions of sympathy and praise. Even if there are no clear restrictions, we are often for various reasons too shy or considerate to express positive emotions, perhaps for fear of embarrassing the receiver, who might feel obliged to return the compliment without wanting or being able to do so. If the receiver displays joy or gratitude, he risks becoming conceited, and if he protests in order to act modest, he may hurt the sender's feelings. This is a dilemma we often face in our culture, and irony offers a way around it.

Another reason may be the fear of being compromised. People who are in love often do not dare admit their feelings, for fear that their feelings will not be returned if they are exposed. If the person knew about these feelings, he might also take advantage of the other person. This fear can apply to other expressions of positive emotion, and irony offers a convenient way of disguising compliments and encouragement.

One final reason for masking positive feelings with irony is a kind of sadomasochistic game in which one *pretends* to hurt another person, without really meaning it. Some think it is funny to hide behind a door and jump out to frighten someone, and similarly, it may create a feeling of power or superiority to frame a compliment in negative terms that momentarily disconcert the receiver until he discerns the good intention. The negative surface structure may hurt a fraction of a moment before the receiver understands the irony, and so the sender is allowed to combine the nice gesture of giving a compliment with a sadistic game.

In literary fiction, irony may be intradiegetic (internal) as part of the interaction between characters, or extradiegetic (external) as direct communication between narrator and narratee or author and reader. Since fiction sheds light on the existing world through its mimetic function, irony is also a means of communication available to the fictional characters. In this case, it has a thematic function, showing the reader how irony is used and functions in the real world. The fictional characters, fictional narrator and author may all make use of irony; the characters can ironize themselves or other characters, the narrator can ironize himself and characters, and the author can ironize the narrator.

Internal irony corresponds to the irony with which we are familiar in everyday life, as in the above-mentioned examples. Jerome's *Three Men in a Boat* contains the following example of internal irony (Jerome 1975, 163):

> I am not a good fisherman myself. I devoted a considerable amount of attention to the subject at one time, and was getting on, as I thought, fairly well; but the old hands told me that I should never be any real good at it, and advised me to give it up. They said that I was an extremely neat thrower, and that I seemed to have plenty of gumption for the thing, and quite enough constitutional laziness. But they were sure I should never make anything of a fisherman. I had not got sufficient imagination.

In fishing, laziness is a positive quality if it means *patience,* and because the protagonist's constitutional laziness is mentioned in connection with several positive qualities, it is natural to interpret the word in its positive sense. However, in the previous events, he has shown clearly that he is lazy in the negative sense of *work-shy.* As readers we easily get the message about his serious fault which his fishing friends were trying to convey through the innocent surface structure.

External irony is frequently based on a disparity between the characters' and reader's values (i.e. the values the author expects the reader to have). The author can describe his characters' blameworthy behaviour without letting the narrator criticize it. The reader, who expects the author to share his own ideals, assumes that the author is only pretending to accept the negative behaviour. In other words, external irony presupposes that author and reader have the same basic values, without which the reader could not see the irony. In the opening lines of *Three Men in a Boat,* the narrator talks about his past hypochondria (on the level of the action) as if he, as retrospective first-person narrator (on the level of the narrative act) has not yet seen through his past self, the first-person character (Jerome 1975, 7):

> With me, it was my liver that was out of order. I knew it was my liver that was out of order, because I had just been reading a patent liver-pill circular, in which were detailed various symptoms by which a man could tell when his liver was out of order. I had them all.

The surface structure informs us about the first-person character's various ailments, while the underlying structure exposes him as a hopeless hypochondriac. The irony is revealed by the combination of exaggerations in the text and the reader's own general knowledge about hypochondriacs. The reader will be familiar with such abuse of medical literature, and in addition, it is suspicious that one single person should get all the symptoms of an illness at the same time and in particular after having read about them in medical literature.

Another example from the same book deals with the above-mentioned laziness of the first-person character. George, Harris and the first-person character (who is identical with the author) are on a boat trip up the Thames, taking turns rowing upstream, and they have the luck to be towed by another boat when it is the first-person character's turn. Of course, George and Harris count on his taking his turn afterwards, but he refuses (Jerome 1975, 159):

> This seemed to me most unreasonable. It had been arranged in the morning that I should bring the boat up to three miles above Reading. Well, here we were, ten miles above Reading! Surely it was now their turn again.

The first-person narrator pretends to agree with the first-person character's reasoning even though it is obviously wrong. As readers we cannot imagine the narrator having a more unfair view of the case than we do, so we take his apparent acceptance of his past self's bad behaviour as the surface structure of a self-deprecating irony that in reality criticizes the character's laziness and disloyalty.

Both of these examples are ambiguous as to the role of author and narrator. Which of them is responsible for the irony, the author or the narrator? Perhaps the narrator ironizes himself, but it is also possible that he agrees with his past self (the first-person character), neither being aware of anything wrong. In that case, it would be the author that ironized his own narrator, who is unreliable. The difference is not important, since the irony's effect is the same either way.

As we have seen, literary irony can have various functions. Since its ambiguity suspends the superego's resistance, the reader becomes open to negative statements he would otherwise reject. The threshold for what he can accept is lowered. Irony is a sneaky, indirect way of communication that brings the reader's dormant prejudices and negative attitudes to the surface. The same applies, of course, to criticism of a character, which is easier to convey in ironic disguise. By exposing the character's ridiculous qualities, the narrator can influence the unsuspecting reader's attitudes and views. The suspension of inhibition and guilt makes it easier for bystanders to join the harassment of the victim, so irony is at once socially inclusive and exclusive.

Since irony renders its objects ridiculous, making us laugh, it makes reading funnier. The entertaining effect of irony is therefore useful to create interest in the cognitive content, but may also be the end goal of the communication, as in popular literature, whose primary goal is entertainment.

Other kinds of indirect communication

Irony and humour are not the only ways of giving expression to taboo. Indirect communication may also use metaphors, tropes (of which irony is an example), allusions, puns, foreign words and so on. The statement by Kielland's narrator that the count's head afforded ample space for his whirling thoughts is not only an example of humour but also an example of metaphor. The metaphor of *empty space* means that the count has little to no brains: he is stupid. This is a negative description that normally exceeds the limits of decency, but the superego permits the metaphor on account of its innocent surface structure.

The ability of various stylistic devices to convey a message indirectly and more leniently does not mean that this comprises its only function, or even a great part of it. Metaphors, for instance, are mostly used to clarify, add variety or wonder, defamiliarize and the like, but even then they are manifestations of the narrator's voice, his choice of expression, and betray something about his personality.

11

Viewpoint, Focalization

Every perception has an observer and an object that is perceived, and the observer's spatial location determines how he perceives his object. Literary theory has taken up the relationship between observer and object under a variety of names: *viewpoint, perspective, aspect, vision, narrative situations* and *focalization*. The contributions of Genette, Chatman, Bal and Rimmon-Kenan to the field between 1970 and 1990 have undoubtedly clarified the issue in many ways, but there are still aspects to be elucidated.

Viewpoint or focalization?

The need to distinguish between viewpoint and voice is the impetus behind Genette's theory of focalization (1972, 204–20). Genette shows the extent to which previous theories have confused viewpoint (who sees?) and voice (who speaks?). Above all, the confusion results from the inclusion of grammatical person in the notion of *viewpoint*, as when Bertil Romberg discriminates between (1) narrative with an omniscient narrator, (2) narrative with viewpoint, (3) objective narrative and (4) first-person narrative. Here the fourth classification is based on a different principle than the first three (Romberg 1962, quoted by Genette 1972, 205). Genette does not reject the possibility of establishing a typology of narrative situations that includes both voice and viewpoint, as long as one explicitly calls attention to the combination and avoids lists where the two principles of determination compete confusingly with each other (Genette 1972, 206).

In order to avoid foregrounding the visual aspect at the expense of the other sensory aspects, Genette adopts Brooks and Warren's term *focus of narration*, which he translates into French as *focalization*, which has in turn been brought largely intact into English (*focalization*). Since then, most modern scholars have adopted Genette's term (Rimmon-Kenan 1983, 71–85; Bal 1990, 113–28; Herman and Vervaeck 2005, 70–9; Herman 2007, 94–108 and Abbott 2008, 73–4), with the exception of Chatman (1972), who prefers *point of view*, and followers of Stanzel (Stanzel 1965, 1985) who stick to *perspective*, like the Danish scholar Morten Nøjgaard (Nøjgaard

1996). Although *focalization* refers primarily to perception, both Bal and Genette include thoughts and feelings in it (Bal 1977, 38; 1990, 123–4; Genette 1983, 50).

Whether the term *focalization* is better than *viewpoint* is debatable. Rimmon-Kenan points out that *focalization* is not free of optical-photographic connotations (Rimmon-Kenan 1983, 71) but prefers it nevertheless because it 'has the advantage of dispelling the confusion between perspective and narration which often occurs when "point of view" or similar terms are used.' Her point is that terms like viewpoint are more easily associated with interests and worldview.

Focalization draws attention to the observed object (that upon which focus is drawn) and to how much and what kind of information the reader receives about it. The normal sense of *focalize* is to see, observe something, and does not automatically indicate internal or external focalization. If we focalize a wall, we see the wall. If we focalize a person in fiction, we must add *internally* or *externally* to clarify what we mean.

Viewpoint foregrounds the observer. It restricts his sensory impressions, for he is able to perceive only what is within the range of his senses. He cannot, for example, see behind himself or hear something beyond his scope of hearing. Since viewpoint determines how much and what kind of information the focalizer receives, it also determines the information that is channelled to the reader through the consciousness of the focalizer. The position of the focalizer in relation to his focal object reveals how much and what kind of information he receives. In practice, *viewpoint* is therefore equivalent to *focalization* as far as its relationship to the object is concerned. Both terms have advantages and disadvantages, and there is no good reason for not using them interchangeably.

Viewpoint in non-fiction, film and drama

In the existing world, the individual only has access to its own mind, and in non-fiction, only the mind of the sender is accessible to the receiver, and then only insofar as the former permits. All other beings are seen from the outside, whether they are humans, animals or plants, and only they know what is going on in their minds insofar as they have a mind or consciousness. Therefore, the perceiving, thinking and feeling human subject faces a closed social environment, where the only knowledge of other minds comes by interpreting external behaviour: speech, mimicry, movements and actions. As a consequence, the existing world is divided into the individual's sensory, intellectual and emotional world on the one hand and the inaccessible objects the individual confronts in his surroundings through the senses, thoughts and feelings.

Fictional film and drama mirrors the real world in that the spectator only has access to his own mind and confronts a fictional world of closed objects. Admittedly, the film can give him access to a character's visual and auditory apparatus, showing him what the latter sees and hears, but the other three senses and thoughts and feelings are still inaccessible to the audience. If the dramatist or filmmaker wants to enter a character's thoughts and feelings, he must resort to artificial devices like monologue and thinking aloud, or introduce an external narrator or voice in analogy with the novel. On stage and in film, point of view is restricted to the view from the theatre or the camera lens. Although the dramatist and filmmaker are not restrained by the laws of reality, their respective media do not convey characters' thoughts, feelings or perceptions, apart from what the audience can see and hear from their seats in the theatre or cinema. The barrier between fiction and reality becomes conspicuous when the actor perceives something outside the stage or the screen that the audience cannot see.

Viewpoint in the novel and short story

The situation is radically different in the novel, because the mental model of the fictional action is not limited by any particular location in time and space. Although the mental model reproduces the fictional action in time and space, it is remarkably versatile in terms of viewpoint and knowledge. The mind has the capacity to transfer our own experience to others; knowing how we perceive, think and feel, we are able to infer what goes on in other people's minds. Although we do not know for sure that their perceptions, thoughts and feelings resemble ours, we presume so because there are so many likenesses between them and us in other respects.

In fiction, the mind's ability to empathize and infer enables the author to invent a human world, giving the reader insight into the minds of others in a way that would be unimaginable in real life. The author's general knowledge about human beings and the world makes him an omnipotent god, but from the point of view of the reader, who as a witness to the one-way communication between narrator and narratee only comes into contact with the fictional narrator (and only indirectly with the author), the omnipotence of the author is transformed into omniscience of the narrator. What the narrator needs to know, the author invents.

Omniscience and perception

Being omniscient, the narrator can report all that happens in the fictional world. This does not require his presence when the events are taking place; if he is omniscient, his knowledge is equivalent to being on the spot, but he is not related to the events in time and space. The narrator can receive the information about the action in three different ways. First, he can be an eyewitness to past events, while second, he may simply look back into the past from his omniscient retrospective point of view. Finally, he may look into the memory of an eyewitness who was actually there. Omniscience can imply that the narrator knows everything that happened in the past, everything happening at present and everything that will happen in the future.

In principle, there is an important difference between knowing and perceiving, as Chatman points out (Chatman 1972, 155). He claims that the narrator telling about events from his retrospective perspective is never on the level of the action and cannot see anything there, as 'discourse-time is not a later extension of story-time'. Our discussion in Chapter 7 showed how, to the contrary, discourse-time is in fact a later extension of story time, because they both belong to the fictional world, and the narrator's very use of the past tense creates the temporal connection that Chatman denies. Nor is it strictly true that the narrator never perceives the events; for the omniscient narrator, the difference between knowing and perceiving disappears because he knows every detail of the past events *as if* he had seen them himself. Theoretically, the fictional narrator can at the same time be an eyewitness to the past events and tell us about them afterwards. As readers we may be able to imagine an omniscient narrator who observes the events of the past through a magic window, reporting them while they take place, just as we saw the death struggle of the protagonist rendered in the present tense in *The Croton*. We have to imagine the narrator as an omniscient and unimaginably fast reporter; if he writes, he has to write very fast, or we could imagine him using a tape recorder so he can write everything down later. Or perhaps the writing process occurs in some supernatural way.

Whether the narrator is on the spot when things happen, recording them in the present tense, has been on the spot and relates them later, or merely observes the past through his omniscient window, the result is the same: he knows everything as if he had experienced it himself. Nevertheless, there is a difference: if he tells about the events afterwards, he is, in the first place, aware of the entire course of events and, in the second, he is unable to influence what has happened. Since the events are completely accessible to the narrator in either case, the only difference is the intensity conveyed by the present tense, an intensity missing in the past tense.

Position: Internal and external viewpoint

On account of his omniscience, the narrator can be present everywhere. He can stand anywhere as an invisible spectator or he may look into the minds of the characters, describing what is going on there. He can show us the characters as perceiving, thinking and feeling individuals. His unlimited mobility allows him to move from one mind into another whenever it suits him. When his omniscience permits him to enter a third-person character's perceptions, thoughts and feelings, it is termed *internal point of view* or *internal focalization*. The narrator appropriates a fictional character's inner life and conveys them to the narratee (and hence to the reader), as in *The Ambassadors* by Henry James (James 1992, 2):

> After the young woman in the glass cage had held out to him across her counter the pale-pink leaflet bearing his friend's name, which she neatly pronounced, he turned away to find himself, in the hall, facing a lady who met his eyes as with an intention suddenly determined, and whose features—not freshly young, not markedly fine, but on happy terms with each other—came back to him as from a recent vision. For a moment they stood confronted; then the moment placed her: he had noticed her the day before . . .

This passage exemplifies how, in some supernatural way, the narrator gains access to the protagonist Strether's mind, reproducing Strether's mental experiences during his past stay in Europe. He can relate Strether's perception of and emotional reactions to Maria Gostrey at their first meeting. If the narrator shows us the characters only from the outside – the way we experience others in the real world – it is called *external point of view* or *external focalization*. When the narrator enters the mind of a character, the reader receives double information: internal information about what is happening inside the character's mind as well as external information about the object he is perceiving. Take the following example from *Mrs Dalloway* (Woolf 2000, 119):

> Rezia, sitting at the table twisting a hat in her hands, watched him; saw him smiling. He was happy, then. But she could not bear to see him

smiling. It was not marriage; it was not being one's husband to look strange like that, always to be starting, laughing, sitting hour after hour silent, or clutching her and telling her to write.

This example permits both an internal and external point of view. The third-person character Rezia is seen from the inside, because we get to know what she sees and thinks, whereas her husband Septimus is seen only from the outside.

Genette speaks primarily of *passages with internal* or *external focalization*, and when he is obliged to relate a particular character to focalization, he uses *foyer (focus)* as well as *personnage focal (focal character)* to refer to the character whose mind we are in, but no shorthand term for characters that are seen from the outside (Genette 1972, 206–7; 1983, 48–9). According to his terminology, Rezia is the focus or focal character and Septimus is simply a character observed from the outside. Genette tends to foreground the general viewpoint of a passage, mostly contenting himself with *internal* and *external focalization*, which do not specify the relationship between focalization and particular characters. Bal aims to remedy this by terming a character seen from the inside *focalizer* and the character or object seen from the outside *focalized object* (Bal 1990, 118–120). She later shortens the focalized object into *the focalized*.

However, whereas the terms *external focalization* and *internal focalization* are clear, the terms derived from *focalization* (Genette's *focus* and *focal character* along with Bal's *focalizer* and *focalized*) are basically ambiguous. *Focus, focal character* and *focalize* all stem from *focus*, meaning 'a central point, as of attraction, attention or activity' (the Random House dictionary, http://dictionary.reference.com/browse/focus). The natural meaning of *focus, focal character* and *focalized* is therefore only *the character that is the centre of our attention*, which does not by itself indicate whether the character is seen from the inside or the outside. The agent noun *focalizer*, on the other hand, is naturally associated with a person that focuses on something and is therefore an appropriate term for a character through whose mind the narrator observes the action. Genette shows little enthusiasm for Bal's terms, which are not in accordance with his original usage (Genette 1983, 48–9), but if we explicitly define *focalized* as a character or object seen from the outside, the dichotomy is undoubtedly practical. Used in this way the verb *focalize* means *perceive* or *observe*, and *focalizer* and *focalized* are equivalent to *perceiver* and *perceived*.

Unfortunately, perceiving does not automatically mean looking through the observer's eyes, listening through his ears and perceiving the world through his other senses. Bal tends to confuse perception and point of view, imagining that one focalizer focalizes another focalizer who focalizes another focalizer, like Chinese boxes (Bal 1990, 119–20). But, as Genette points out, there can only be one focalizer (or *viewpoint person*) at a time. Even in fiction, only the omniscient narrator is able to penetrate into the minds of third-person characters (Woolf 2000, 34):

> "And how are you?" said Peter Walsh, positively trembling; taking both her hands. She's grown older, he thought, sitting down. I shan't tell her anything about it, he thought, for she's grown older. She's looking at me, he thought, a sudden embarrassment coming over him, though he had kissed her hands.

Here Peter is focalizer or viewpoint person, and we hear his thoughts and see through his eyes that Clarissa is looking at him, whereas he cannot see himself through Clarissa's eyes. Omniscient third-person characters are impossible except if the author equips them with supernatural powers, making the following modified version of the passage impossible:

> "And how are you?" said Peter Walsh, positively trembling; taking both her hands. She's grown older, he thought, sitting down. I shan't tell her anything about it, he thought, for she's grown older. She's looking at me, he thought, a sudden embarrassment coming over him, *for indeed, she thought he had grown older, too.*

In this version, Peter feels embarrassed *because*, looking into her mind, he discovers that she finds him older, too. This is impossible as long as the author has not explicitly equipped him with the ability to read thoughts, which of course is not the case here.

Depth

Internal viewpoint may show us different levels of the focalizer's psyche, the most superficial of which consists in sensory perception: sight, hearing, smell, taste and touch. To make it clear that not only the narrator but also the character perceives the object, the author applies verbs related to the senses: to see, hear, feel and so on. He may also draw an associative connection between the perceived object and the observer thus:

> Peter stood in front of the window. Outside the sun was shining.

Due to his own experience or logical convention, the reader understands that the sensory verb is implied and that the sunshine reflects Peter's perceptions.

The focalizer's thoughts and feelings exist on a deeper level of his consciousness. Both Bal and Genette· include the characters' thoughts and feelings in the concept of focalization (Bal 1990, 123–4; Genette 1983, 49–50). In addition, Bal distinguishes between the perceptible and imperceptible. The depth of the viewpoint determines the reader's understanding of the character's situation and affects his sympathy or antipathy, which is in turn essential for his attitude to the inherent cognitive content.

The unconscious is a still deeper level than thought and feeling but is by definition not accessible to the character himself, whereas the narrator may penetrate into every corner of the character's psyche:

> Peter was intent on keeping this promise, but unconsciously he was already trying to find an excuse for not keeping it.

When the unconscious conflicts with conscious intentions in this way, it is a special case of what Genette calls *paralepsis*, which consists in the narrator's providing information that should have been omitted because the information exceeds what the character is supposed to know (Genette 1972, 211–3). In Genette's usage, paralepsis is a kind of *zero focalization*, in which the narrator knows more than the fictional character (we will have more to say about zero focalization below). On the other hand, the unconscious is part of the character's psyche and confirms its own existence by influencing his behaviour, and it would be wrong to define the unconscious as something the character cannot know. From one point of view, he knows it, from another, he does not; it is thus a question of definition whether the unconscious is included in internal focalization. At any rate, neither external nor internal viewpoint accounts satisfactorily for the unconscious processes, and *zero focalization* does not solve the dilemma as long as the description of the unconscious is a kind of internal viewpoint in at least one respect.

Breadth

Breadth denotes how the narrator distributes internal and external viewpoint among characters. On account of his potential omniscience, the narrator could tell the story from every possible point of view, informing us about all the involved characters' experience of the action, but such an objective description would be too comprehensive to be feasible, so normally the narrator contents himself with showing the inner life of only one or a few of the characters. If he nevertheless decides to show the same event from the point of view of two characters or more so that every moment is seen through two different pairs of eyes, the viewpoint (or focalization) is *multiple* or *many-sided*. *Single* or *one-sided viewpoint* means, on the other hand, that the narrator shows an event from only one character's point of view.

The idea behind the use of many-sided viewpoint is that different individuals experience the same thing in different ways and that multiple perspectives are not felt as repetition (Genette 1972, 211–3), as they yield two or more unique versions of the action. The following diagram shows how one-sided and many-sided focalization can be used in narrative. The numbers designate episodes according to their location in the chronology, and each letter indicates a fictional character:

Single or one-sided internal focalization

Episode:	1	2	3
Character:	A	A	A

Multiple or many-sided internal focalization

Episode:	1	1	2	2	and so on
Character:	A	B	A	B	and so on

Since one text cannot describe two different viewpoints at the same time, every episode must be told twice to represent the viewpoint of each character, a device that is inconvenient and therefore infrequent.

Many-sided viewpoint makes the story more objective because the information about the action is more balanced. When a conflict is reported from only one character's point of view, the reader is more inclined to sympathize with the focalizer (viewpoint character) than the characters he knows less about.

Stability

From one moment to the next, the narrator may move from one character's mind into another's, changing focalization or viewpoint, or he may stick to the viewpoint of one character. The period of time during which each character holds the viewpoint may vary. If the events are observed through the same person's mind through the whole action, the point of view is constant. If the internal point of view alternates between two characters or more, we call it *variable*. If A and B symbolize two different characters and the numbers from 1 to 5 represent the episodes they appear in, the following diagram represents how constant and variable internal viewpoint may be used in a narrative:

Constant internal focalization:

Episode	1	2	3	4	5
Character	A	A	A	A	A

Variable internal focalization:

Episode	1	2	3	4	5
Character	A	B	C	A	B

Mrs Dalloway has many instances of internal viewpoint shifting from one character to another. One moment one character holds the viewpoint only to become the object of another's viewpoint the next and so on (Woolf 2000, 101):

> "And it came over me 'I might have married you'," she said, thinking of Peter sitting there in his little bow-tie; with that knife, opening, shutting it, "Just as he always was, you know."
>   They were talking about him at lunch, said Richard. (But he could not tell her he loved her. He held her hand. Happiness is this, he thought.)

Variable viewpoint has approximately the same objectifying function as multiple viewpoint. Although variable viewpoint, in contrast to multiple viewpoint, never lets us see the characters' mental reactions to the same event, it gives us so much general information about their personalities that we understand why they think and act the way they do. Another advantage of variable viewpoint is that it avoids the repetition that is characteristic of multiple viewpoint. The repetition in multiple viewpoint serves the same functions as repetition in general, which will be dealt with in the next chapter on frequency.

Rewriting in the first person

In accordance with a proposal of Barthes, Genette suggests that the possibility of rewriting third-person narratives in the first person may serve as a minimal criterion for internal focalization. If one can replace third person with first person, the viewpoint is internal. To illustrate this,

Genette rewrites the sentence, 'James Bond caught sight of a man in the fifties who still seemed youthful . . .', as 'I caught sight of a man in the fifties who still seemed youthful . . .', showing that it has internal viewpoint. Genette points to the expression *caught sight of* as betraying the internal viewpoint, because it represents a sensory impression that only the character himself can know about.

The problem, however, is that it is also possible to revise sentences that do not describe mental experiences (and which therefore do not indicate internal viewpoint) in the first person: 'Peter stayed several years in Paris learning French before returning to his native country' becomes 'I stayed several years in Paris learning French before I returned to my native country.' Even passages with an obvious external viewpoint can be rephrased in the first person without evoking a feeling that something is amiss. The sentence, 'They saw him come out of the forest, a bunch of violets glowing in his hand', can be rewritten as, 'They saw me come out of the forest, a bunch of violets glowing in my hand.' The original, external viewpoint is here transformed into internal viewpoint precisely because of the substitution of the first person, not because the sentence was already internal to begin with. The substitution causes the reader to reinterpret the text accordingly: to him it seems that the first-person character, as he comes out of the forest, catching sight of the others standing in front of him, empathizes with their situation as witnesses of his own appearance. In the original sentence, there is no implication of this empathy, as the third-person character coming from the forest is seen entirely from the outside so that we have no indication of his thoughts. A further possible interpretation of the revision is that the first-person narrator has somehow acquired information about the others' experience of the episode so that he is able to recount how *they* experienced his coming from the forest that day in the past. Either way, rewriting in the first person is not a reliable criterion for internal viewpoint, because even sentences that clearly indicate external viewpoint can be rewritten in the first person, and then the very use of the first-person pronoun makes the reader reinterpret the viewpoint as internal.

The point of view in the first-person novel

By definition, the first-person character is always focalized internally. It is an *I*, and everything the *I* experiences is automatically part of its psyche. In the first-person narrative, everything that happens is interpreted as something the *I* perceives:

> I was ill, lying in bed. Outside the leaves were green and people in the street were dressed in light summer clothes.

In this text, the first-person character must either be lying in such a way that he can look out the window, or he must somehow have acquired information about the events outside, for instance by having stood up and looked out the window, by conferring with someone else who knows what is going on outside, or simply on account of his prior knowledge of what goes on outside at that time of year. Theoretically, it is possible that only the first-person narrator is aware of what happens outside, and tells the narratee something the first-person character does not know. However, to make the reader accept that interpretation, he has to add a clear context:

> I was ill, lying in bed. Outside the leaves were green and people in the street were dressed in light summer clothes, but luckily I knew nothing of this, chained to my bed by a hernia that hardly allowed me to turn around to change my position. Had I known about the summer delights I was missing, lying in bed would have been even more unendurable.

Thanks to the context, we understand that substantial parts of the text render only the first-person narrator's knowledge in retrospect, not the first-person character's own experience in the past. This statement of the narrator is primarily a manifestation of voice, not of viewpoint, but of course, the narrator must somehow have acquired the information about what was going on in the street at the time his sick past self was lying in bed. As we associate the first-person novel with the rules pertaining to autobiography, we avoid picturing the first-person narrator as omniscient, imagining rather that he has got his information in some natural way. In all likelihood, our conception of the narrator's sources is vague or even a complete blank, as the figure of the narrator is comparatively irrelevant in contrast to his past experiences, or in other words, the action. Hence, we are less interested in the angle from which the narrator's source observed the green leaves and the people in the sunny street: the first-person narrator could conceivably have been informed by the first-person character's wife (his own wife at the time of the illness) who looked out the window in the patient's room without mentioning what she saw to him, or by someone else who was in the street that day. What went on in the street this very day must have been reported by some witness who must have observed it from a particular position in space, but in our simple example, the witness is anonymous and the position from which the street was observed unknown.

On the other hand, all the sentences describing the first-person character's situation have internal focalization, showing us his perceptions, thoughts and feelings. The first-person narrator's only possibility of escaping the internal viewpoint of the first-person character (his past self) is explicit commentary at the external (extradiegetic) level of the narrative act, as in this example when he recounts information the first-person character does not know. Anything else in the first-person narrator's statement refers to the point of view of the first-person character (his past self).

Although the first-person narrative's single internal viewpoint is usually constant and only shows us the world seen through the first-person character's mind, this rule may be broken. We have already seen that in *Moby Dick*, the first-person narrator Ishmael tells us what Captain Ahab experiences in private. This is a deviation from the rule, which Hamburger condemned as a serious flaw, but as first-person narratives are fiction, after all, the narrator does not have to be a realistic character himself as long as his narrative function is not part of the theme (cognitive content). Melville does not attempt to convince the reader that real people can be omniscient, and the reader readily understands this. To the reader it is not important whether the narrator behaves realistically, only whether the information he offers is interesting.

The narrator's viewpoint: Double focalization?

We have seen that however covert and unobtrusive he tries to be, the narrator is always present in the text, because the existence of a text implies the existence of a sender. Ultimately, a narrator must perceive or have perceived everything, either from his own direct experience or omniscience. He may also base his story on another witness, but then the text mirrors the viewpoint of this witness, who must somehow have told the story to the narrator and who is therefore in effect the primary narrator of the text. Therefore, every story is necessarily perceived from the viewpoint of the narrator. Omniscience frees the narrator from the limitations of time and space, allowing him to perceive the events from outer space or at close range like a fly on the wall. At will he can read the minds of all the characters at the same time all the time. However, the fact that he always knows everything does not mean that it is technically possible to report everything simultaneously. Verbal communication requires that the material be spread out spatially on paper when written and extended temporally as phonetic sounds when read aloud, even if originally its elements are chronologically synchronous. If the narrator opts to show only what happens in one character or to alternate between different viewpoints from episode to episode, this constitutes a limitation with respect to his total knowledge, as Genette points out. Bal calls it *double focalization* when the narrator voluntarily restricts his knowledge to only one person, because we come to know both what the narrator perceives and what the character experiences. Nevertheless, double focalization is a misleading notion that can easily cause misunderstanding.

Specifically, it obscures the fact that we *always* experience the action through the eyes and the mind of the narrator, as the narrator cannot tell us anything he is not aware of. In the case of external focalization, the narrator sees the characters from the outside, as is normally the case in the real world, restricting himself to his own perception of the events. Again, take *Arrowsmith* (Lewis 1961, 11):

> Martin was twenty-one. He still seemed pale, in contrast to his black, smooth hair, but he was a respectable runner, a fair basketball center, and a savage hockey-player. The co-eds murmured that he "looked so romantic," but as this was before the invention of sex and the era of petting-parties, they merely talked about him at a distance . . .

The third-person character Martin and the co-eds are seen from the outside, because we have no information about their perceptions, thoughts or feelings. The verb *seemed* reveals a feeling of uncertainty that can only refer to a human consciousness observing Martin, so to a certain extent the observer is focalized internally. This witness is probably the narrator himself, who may have witnessed the action himself in the past or heard it from others in Martin's social environment, or is simply omniscient. In other words, the focalization is external with respect to the characters involved but internal as far as the narrator is concerned. However, since ultimately, every story is bound to focalize the narrator internally, it is absurd to take into account the narrator's internal viewpoint; instead of saying that the above passage has double focalization (internal and external focalization), we therefore leave out the self-evident internal focalization of the narrator and concentrate on the focalization of the characters, which in this case turns out to be external.

In passages with internal focalization, the omniscient narrator transfers his own consciousness into that of one of the characters, showing us simultaneously his own mind and that of the character, as in the scene where Septimus commits suicide in *Mrs Dalloway* (Woolf 2000, 126):

> Septimus could hear her talking to Holmes on the staircase.
>
> "My dear lady, I have come as a friend," Holmes was saying.
>
> "No, I will not allow you to see my husband," she said.
>
> He could see her, like a little hen, with her wings spread barring his passage. But Holmes persevered.
>
> "My dear lady, allow me . . ." Holmes said, putting her aside (Holmes was a very powerfully built man).

> Holmes was coming upstairs. Holmes would burst open the door. Holmes would say, "In a funk, eh?" Holmes would get him. But no; not Holmes; not Bradshaw. Getting up rather unsteadily, hopping indeed from foot to foot, he considered Mrs Filmer's nice clean bread-knife with "Bread" carved on the handle. Ah, but one must not spoil that. The gas fire? But it was too late now. Holmes was coming.

The narrator has perceived this event through the peephole of Septimus's mind, receiving exactly the same impressions as Septimus, all of Septimus's thoughts and feelings. He conveys not only Septimus's sensory impressions, thoughts and feelings but also his own experience of Septimus's experience. The action is therefore presented from two viewpoints that completely merge, at least as far as Septimus's experience is concerned. Septimus's experience is filtered through the mind of the narrator, who may supplement the action with elements from his own mind, for instance in the form of comments.

The narrator's viewpoint is inevitable, in other words, always present in the text, and the character's viewpoint can only be expressed through that of the narrator. Usually, however, only the character's viewpoint is thematically relevant. The mind of the narrator is primarily a vehicle for conveying the character's internal experience and is mostly of minor importance. This is reflected in the terminology: *internal viewpoint* or *focalization* as used by Genette refers only to the internal viewpoint of the character, not to that of the narrator. Since the internal viewpoint of the narrator is a self-evident constant property of the text and often thematically irrelevant, it is superfluous to mention it. Describing the focalization of a particular passage as internal refers explicitly to a character's inner life, and implicitly to the narrator's consciousness, as the narrator is also focalized internally.

By calling internal focalization *double focalization*, Bal gives the impression that the narrator's point of view is more relevant and less obvious than it really is, and the term is apt to entail misunderstandings. Double focalization implies that there is also something named *single focalization*, even if Bal does not introduce such a term. Single focalization would mean that only the narrator's internal experience is open to us while that of the characters is closed, but that would be *external focalization*, which is already a separate term we are familiar with (Steinbeck 1950, 55):

> The wine went down and down in the jug, but before it was gone the three friends grew sleepy. Pilon and Pablo staggered off to bed, and Jesus Maria lay comfortably on the floor, beside the stove.

The fire died down. The house was filled with the deep sounds of slumber. In the front room only one thing moved. The blessed candle darted its little spear-pointed flame up and down with incredible rapidity.

In *Tortilla Flat*, only the narrator (from his omniscient, retrospective position) observes what happens after the three friends have gone to sleep. Although the narrator is, of course, focalized internally (making it irrelevant), the viewpoint is external, because no character on the level of the action is described with internal viewpoint. As the narrator's point of view is irrelevant, there is neither double nor single focalization: the important thing is the scene's external focalization.

The terminology Bal introduces to explain *double focalization* is also confusing (Bal 1990, 119). To distinguish the narrator from the characters as focalizer, she calls him *narrator focalizer* (Dutch *externe focalisator*) and the characters *person focalizer* (*persoonfocalisator*). The confusion arises when Bal uses *narrator focalizer* in third-person narratives and *person focalizer* in first-person narratives (Bal 1990, 124–6). As long as *person focalizer* refers only to the characters on the action level, it indicates a distinction between levels of focalization – the narrator's viewpoint in contrast to the characters' viewpoint. But Bal also uses *person focalizer* to refer to the level of the narrative act in the first-person novel, making the terminology incomprehensible. Why is the narrator of the third-person narrative not a person focalizer like the first-person narrator? Is Bal insinuating that the third-person narrator is not a person (which he demonstrably is) in contrast to the first-person narrator, or has she overlooked the double nature of the narrator in first-person narratives, a split between the first-person narrator and his past self, the first-person character? Bal seems to infer that the first-person narrator is a person from his (diachronical) identity with the first-person character, who is a person, but it does not follow that the third-person narrator is less human because he is not similarly identical with one of the characters. The reader conceptualizes both narrators in analogy with authors of the real world; just as nobody would contend that the author of an autobiography is more human than that of a biography or travelogue, it is inconceivable that there should be such a difference between the first-person and third-person narrator.

Is there always a viewpoint (or focalization)?

The mental model of the action comprises normally at least one observer: it is perceived through the mind of at least one person. As a rule, the observer obtains insight into the action by observing it himself, but he may also acquire it in some other way, for instance by inference or the testimony of others. As long as the action is experienced or witnessed by a human being, it is linked to a particular viewpoint or focalization: the angle and point of view from which it was perceived when it happened.

There is only one case in which we can imagine events without any particular viewpoint: when something takes place in the empirical world without humans experiencing it. In this case, nobody knows about it, although sometimes it is possible to infer past events on the basis of circumstantial evidence. Such events are linked to no particular viewpoint, and stories about them cannot reduce them to a restricted angle or viewpoint. For example, when we visualize the big bang, we realize the inherent impossibility of an observer from whose limited angle the whole drama could be observed. Nevertheless, our way of thinking dictates that everything be perceived by someone, and this someone must observe the event from a particular angle. As a consequence, we cannot imagine anything without an observer and a point of view, not even the big bang. We regard any viewpoint that is not given to us as simply uncertain, whether fluctuating or showing the object from all angles at once.

Verbal communication does not necessarily indicate a particular angle or point of view. In spite of language's ability to indicate the angle from which a scene is observed, it is not obliged to do so, so the mental model of the action is not automatically linked to an explicit perspective. To be sure, apart from events that have to be inferred because there were no witnesses, the omniscient narrator (or his informer) is always present as a witness to the action, or else he would not be able to relate it, hence the action is always linked to a particular viewpoint. But because focalization is not an automatic property of language and the mental model of the action, the reader has to rely on context to infer the viewpoint of the narrator or his source.

When the mental model does not supply enough details to determine the viewpoint, the viewpoint (or focalization) is *indefinite* (Lewis 1961, 5):

> The driver of the wagon swaying through forest and swamp of the Ohio wilderness was a ragged girl of fourteen. Her mother they had buried near the Monongahela—the girl herself had heaped with torn sods the grave beside the river of the beautiful name. Her father lay shrinking with fever on the floor of the wagon-box, and about him played her brothers and sisters, dirty brats, tattered brats, hilarious brats.

In this passage from *Arrowsmith*, we do not know what goes on in the minds of the characters, and the angle and the viewpoint from which the scene is perceived is indefinite. The burial of the girl's mother may be part of the girl's thoughts or merely an explanatory comment on the part of the narrator. We do not know, so the focalization is indefinite.

Ambiguous viewpoint

In the example from *Arrowsmith*, the focalization is uncertain with respect to the angle from which the scene is perceived as well as the identity of the focalizer. Who perceived the event: the narrator or one of the characters or even all of them collectively? However, the focalization may also be indefinite in the sense of *ambiguous*. In that case, we cannot decide whether the narrator is relating his own knowledge or the perception of a particular character:

> Peter was ill, lying in bed. Outside the leaves were green, the people in the street dressed in light summer clothes.

Is this something Peter sees or something only the narrator knows? The ambiguity becomes apparent if we add context:

1. Peter was ill, lying in bed. Outside the leaves were green, the people in the street dressed in light summer clothes, but the curtain was drawn, concealing the bright summer day.
2. Peter was ill, lying in bed. Outside the leaves were green, the people in the street dressed in light summer clothes. The sight of happy passers-by made him even sicker.

In both cases, the context eliminates the ambiguity.

Mrs Dalloway affords another typical example; here we do not know whether we're reading only Richard's thoughts, or a comment on the part of the narrator (Woolf 2000, 97):

> And flicking his bowler hat by way of farewell, eager, yes, very eager, to travel that spider's thread of attachment between himself and Clarissa; he would go straight to her, in Westminster.
> But he wanted to come in holding something, Flowers? Yes, flowers, since he did not trust his taste in gold.

Does the sentence about the spider's thread express the thoughts of Richard or the narrator? Throughout the book, Richard seems to be a well-meaning but not very self-critical person, so he is unlikely to see himself as a spider preying on Clarissa. We are more likely to read the sentence as a critical comment on the part of the narrator, who informs the narratee (and consequently, us the readers) that the marriage between Richard and Clarissa is more a marriage of convenience than a genuine love affair. As an expression of the narrator's opinion, the spider's thread metaphor would be an example of voice, whereas it would be viewpoint if it expressed Richard's own thoughts.

Viewpoint and voice

Chatman extends Genette's perception-based notion of viewpoint, adding to it the terms *conceptual viewpoint* and *interest point of view*; to Chatman, *point of view* is ambiguous, having three different meanings (Chatman 1978, 151–2):

1. literal meaning: seen through the eyes of a particular person
2. figurative meaning: seen through a particular person's worldview
3. transferred meaning: seen in relation to a particular person's general, economic and personal interests

He gives three examples of each:

1. From John's point of view, at the top of Coit Tower, the panorama of the San Francisco Bay was breathtaking.
2. John said that from his point of view, Nixon's position, though praised by his supporters, was somewhat less than noble.
3. Though he didn't realize it at the time, the divorce was a disaster from John's point of view.

From these, Chatman distinguishes between *perceptual viewpoint, conceptual viewpoint* and *interest point of view*, including them all in his theory of point of view. In this way, he deviates from Genette's *focalization*, which is based on only the first kind, perceptual viewpoint. However, as mentioned above, both Bal and Genette include thoughts and feelings (Bal 1977, 38; 1990, 123–4; Genette 1983, 50), and since, on the level of the action, Chatman restricts his three types of viewpoint to the characters' viewpoint, his conceptual and interest viewpoints resemble Genette and Bal's emphasis on thoughts and emotions.

Rimmon-Kenan also distinguishes between three forms of viewpoint, adding to the conceptual viewpoint a psychological and an ideological aspect. The former she divides into a cognitive and an emotive component;

the psychological aspect corresponds to what I have called depth, that is, deeper level *thoughts* and *feelings*, and the ideological aspect is 'the norms of the text' and 'a general system of viewing the world conceptually' (Rimmon-Kenan 1983, 77–82). Although Rimmon-Kenan is aware of the difference between 'who speaks' and 'who sees' and consciously tries to avoid confusing viewpoint and voice, she follows Bal in including the narrator focalizer's ideological influence, whether it is implicit in the orientation he imposes on the story or formulated explicitly (81–2). Here she includes not only the voice of the narrator who formulates his norms explicitly, but also implicitly the voice of the author, which is linked to the characters' behaviour.

As almost everyone has pointed out, the difficulty in distinguishing between voice and viewpoint lies, of course, in the fact that just like the narrator's comments on the action, viewpoint is conveyed by the narrator's voice. It is not as simple as a distinction between 'who sees' and 'who speaks', as demonstrated by Genette and Bal's addition of thoughts and feelings to viewpoint's perceptual aspect. Chatman's differentiation between elements of the story and those of the discourse is more helpful. The narrator's voice has two separate functions: (1) the communication of the action and (2) the communication of the narrator's intellectual and emotional attitude to the action as well as to the communication process itself. Viewpoint is linked to the communication of the action, and concerns how the characters perceive the events and react to them mentally – regardless of whether we have access to their perceptions, thoughts and feelings (internal versus external focalization and depth) and of how the viewpoint is distributed among the characters (breadth, single versus multiple viewpoint, stability, constant versus variable focalization).

Of course, viewpoint is a kind of selection and is just as much a part of the discourse as voice. Since discourse is actually the voice of the narrator, viewpoint is a manifestation of the narrator's voice; hence, it might seem logical to equate viewpoint with voice, contending that they are indistinguishable, one and the same thing. This misunderstanding may arise from Genette's term *voice*, which, in designating a subordinate aspect of discourse, is more or less synonymous with *discourse*. Instead of concluding that *voice* is a subordinate aspect of *voice*, it becomes necessary to point out that in spite of the synonymy, there is a real difference. *Voice* is obviously meant to account for the features of the narrator's voice that are most closely associated with voice: verbal tense, grammatical person, irony, commentary, assessments and the report of speech and thoughts. Frequency, order, duration and viewpoint are presumably less associated with voice, although they undoubtedly give evidence of narration. Genette's delimitation of *voice* may be debatable, but the abovementioned definition in terms of tense, grammatical person and so on distinguishes it clearly enough from viewpoint, which we then define in terms of the reader's access to the perceptions, thoughts and feelings of the fictional characters.

Analysing a few text passages should help us clarify the difference between voice and viewpoint:

> Peter saw Elisabeth approach him with a smile on her face and felt warm and happy. "Oh, Elisabeth!" he exclaimed.

In this example, the narrator only recounts the action without commenting on it. Peter is focalized internally, Elisabeth externally. We may change the text a little:

> If Peter had seen the sly expression in Elisabeth's eyes as she approached him with a smile on her face, he would hardly have felt as warm and happy as he did. "Oh, Elisabeth!" he exclaimed, however.

While we see the character from the inside, we learn how the narrator assesses the scene perceptually as well as conceptually. He sees more than Peter (the sly expression in Elisabeth's eyes) and interprets what he sees, reacting intellectually and emotionally to it, inferring that the sly expression in Elisabeth's eyes betrays intentions that might make Peter's life difficult. Peter does not know what the narrator sees and thinks and hence cannot act on this information. The narrator, on the other hand, compares Peter's innocence to his own scepticism, and surmises how Peter would have reacted if he could see what he sees.

In the previous example, we can distinguish between the narrator's visual impressions and thoughts on the one hand and those of Peter on the other. The narrator's visual impressions and thoughts comprise those of Peter as a whole because of internal focalization, but in addition, the narrator sees more than Peter and has thoughts of his own about what he sees as well as about what Peter sees. On top of this, he recounts all these facts. In other words, the narrator (1) recounts (2) what Peter sees, (3) what Peter thinks and feels, (4) what Peter says, (5) what he sees himself, and (6) what he thinks and feels himself. The narrator's activities are parallel to Peter's except that by putting everything into words, the narrator conveys a mental model that comprises the entire episode, whereas Peter's exclamation is only a subordinate part of it.

As for the narrator, we can distinguish between narrative act, perceptual viewpoint, and thoughts and feelings (comments), whereas the character has perceptual viewpoint, thoughts and feelings (comments) and direct speech. The narrator's thoughts about the action are of a cognitive nature, consisting in an assessment and prognosis, which have nothing to do with perceptual viewpoint and focalization; rather, as an explicit comment on the action, they are a manifestation of the narrator's voice but differ from the verbal reproduction of the action in that they explain the action instead of rendering it. The distinction between perceptual viewpoint and comment parallels the differentiation between the action and the cognitive content that we have dealt with before. The commentary is the cognitive content that the narrator extrapolates from the action, and it influences to a certain extent the cognitive content that the reader extracts from the work.

Zero focalization?

Following Tzvetan Todorov, Genette distinguishes between three forms of focalization, which depend on the relationship between what the narrator says and what the character knows:

1. *zero focalization*: the narrator says more than the character knows
2. *internal focalization*: the narrator says only what the character knows
3. *external focalization*: the narrator says less than the character knows

Genette uses *zero focalization* with respect to two different situations (Genette 1983, 49):

1. as a synonym of variable focalization, where the narrator gives us access to the consciousness of several characters (multiple or variable viewpoint)
2. when the focal agent (*le foyer*, "focalizer") is situated far away or his location is uncertain

Genette's tripartition seems logical at first glance, but it has one major problem: *zero focalization* does not fit in with the definition of the two other forms of viewpoint. The obscurity of the term is highlighted by the fact that most narratologists after Genette avoid the tripartition altogether, contenting themselves with the distinction between internal and external focalization.

Bal is among the first to raise objections to the tripartition (Bal 1977, 28–9), later finding support from Rimmon-Kenan (Rimmon-Kenan 1983, 138–9). Bal criticizes Genette for basing the three forms of focalization on two different classification criteria. His distinction between zero focalization and internal focalization is based on a restriction of the perceptual field (*restrictions de champ*), while the distinction between internal and external focalization is based on an opposition between the functions: in the case of external focalization, the focalized character is seen from the outside instead of from the inside. The difference between internal and external focalization is that the one *sees* and the other *is seen*.

Bal is right that something is wrong with Genette's criteria, but it seems to me that her explanation is not clear enough. It seems that external focalization also represents a restriction of the perceptual field in comparison to internal focalization, as the narrator restricts the information to the lowest degree on Genette's schematic tripartition.

The chief flaw in Genette's tripartition is rather that he bases it on the relationship between what the narrator says and what the character knows, without discussing what kind of knowledge is relevant. Knowledge can be anything. For example, is it of importance that the narrator says more than, as much as or less than the character knows about mathematics or horticulture? The answer is, of course, no, because general knowledge is irrelevant. But other, more specific kinds of knowledge are also not necessarily relevant to the focalization. By defining focalization as *knowledge* without restricting the notion, Genette forgets what viewpoint or focalization really means: first, an observer's position in relation to the perceived object, and second, how the observer's position affects his experience of the object.

Literary fiction is mainly oriented towards human interaction, and therefore both writers and literary scholars are interested in how focalization affects the character's perceptual and conceptual experience of others. The internal viewpoint conferred by the narrator's omniscience is a unique addition to our own limited access to the mental experience of others. The author can show us how a particular character experiences his surroundings (internal viewpoint) or only confront us with the mysterious surface of life we are accustomed to in the empirical world (external viewpoint). This choice affects our understanding of the action; viewpoint is a question of the information the narrator conveys about the various characters of the action, that is whether we may look into their mental processes or not. This is a very limited form of knowledge compared to Genette's unrestricted concept.

In spite of its lack of precision, the notion of knowledge might shed some light on internal and external viewpoint if we restrict the concept to knowledge about the character's *perceptions, thoughts and emotions*. *Internal viewpoint* would here mean that the narrator recounts only what the character knows *about his own perceptions, thoughts and emotions*. In spite of this improvement, however, Genette's notion of knowledge is an inadequate criterion for focalization. Complete correspondence between what the narrator says and what the character knows only obtains insofar as the narrator recounts both the character's perceptions and the character's thoughts and feelings. But if the narrator only recounts what the character perceives, he says less than the character knows, as the character naturally knows his own thoughts and feelings. According to Genette's definition, this would not make the focalization internal, even though it evidently is. Ernest Hemingway's novels display internal focalization despite largely avoiding descriptions of thoughts and feelings. Likewise, a first-person novel would have internal viewpoint even if the first-person narrator never disclosed his thoughts and feelings. Genette's comparison between the narrator's statements and the character's knowledge does not account for such alternatives. The flaw of Genette's criterion of *knowledge* is especially evident when the character is a professor in quantum physics and the narrator a layman on the subject, in which case the focalization should be external even if the narrator shows us all the thoughts and feelings of the professor. What narrator and character know about such irrelevant issues does not, of course, affect focalization.

Knowledge is certainly no useful criterion as an argument for *zero focalization*, which is essentially meaningless. It can only mean that the text contains passages with no focalization, no viewpoint, which we have already seen cannot be the case. An indefinite or ambiguous viewpoint does not mean there is none. Either we are in the mind of a character or outside it; there simply is no other alternative. In the sentence, 'He sat down', the text does not indicate whether the description is an observer's testimony or information about the character's inner experience of the act. The viewpoint is uncertain, but not absent. What is absent is the information about the viewpoint. At best, *zero focalization* may be regarded as a contraction of 'zero information about the focalization' and serve as a synonym for indefinite focalization.

This, however, is not how Genette defines the term. According to him, zero focalization means that the narrator knows more than the character. About what? The only things of relevance in which the narrator can know more than his character are the events and objects the character is not able to perceive himself, like other people's thoughts and feelings and events beyond the scope of the character's senses. But Genette's one criterion is the characters' lack of insight into each other's minds, thus making zero focalization merge with variable focalization. Genette is aware of this, so he concludes that zero focalization in the meaning of variable focalization only applies to the text as a whole (Genette 1983, 49). Consequently, zero focalization in itself occurs simultaneously with external and internal focalization in the text. In *Mrs Dalloway*'s variable viewpoint, this would mean that the alternation between the viewpoints of Clarissa, Richard, Peter and Lucrezia as a whole constitutes zero focalization.

However, variable focalization is not focalization in the same sense as internal and external viewpoint. It is only a way of distributing external and internal viewpoint in relation to the various characters of an action.

It is therefore misleading to use *focalization* to refer to the distribution of external and internal viewpoint, for which we already have *variable focalization*. Moreover, the application of *zero focalization* as a synonym for *variable point of view* may create the impression that there is no focalization at all in alternating between different internal viewpoints, since the various internal viewpoints cancel each other out. But the intimate information internal viewpoint provides about Clarissa is not nullified by the fact that we receive similar information about Richard, Peter and Septimus.

Genette's second criterion for zero focalization is that the focalizer (*le foyer, focal agent*) is located far away or is difficult to locate. When focalization is panoramic, as when the narrator zooms into the action from the outside and successively describes the landscape, town, house and finally the room where the action takes place, the narrator of course says more than the character knows, who is not able to perceive himself and his own surroundings from a bird's eye perspective. But the viewpoint in such a zoom sequence is external even if the characters are observed from so far away that they are not even discernible. In such sequences, the characters are seen from a very distant external viewpoint; to say that such a passage has zero focalization would be as absurd as saying that viewpoint vanishes when a little child hides from his parents under the couch. It is in fact the very external viewpoint that prevents the parents from seeing the child.

Nor can an indefinite viewpoint be taken as *zero focalization*, except if we consider it a contraction as mentioned above. Moreover, Genette's application of the term to indefinite viewpoint also contradicts his conception of focalization as an expression of knowledge, as indefinite viewpoint does not imply that the narrator knows more than the character.

There are, in other words, only two alternate forms of focalization: internal and external. When viewpoint is unknown or unclear, it is not focalization that is absent but knowledge about it. Genette's attempt to nevertheless find justification for zero focalization as the third alternative probably stems from the tripartition as a logical consequence of Todorov's combination of focalization and knowledge. For the sake of the tripartition, Genette tries to find a viewpoint where the narrator says more than the character knows. There are examples in which the narrator recounts things that the character does not know, but these have no logical connection with focalization.

Internal viewpoint and subjectivity

Internal viewpoint is linked to a duality in which the reader receives information about the perceived object as well as about the observer. On the one hand, he receives a description of the object itself, while on the other, he learns what the observer is thinking and feeling with respect to the object. If the focalizer's sensory apparatus, thoughts and emotions are all accessible, the reader participates in his entire mental experience of the observed object. The focalizer's experience of the observed object is coloured by his perceptual and psychological background, and hence tells us as much about him as about the object (Woolf 2000, 97):

> But Hugh was on his legs again. He was unspeakably pompous. Really, after dealing here for thirty-five years he was not going to be put off by a mere boy who did not know his business. For Dubonnet, it seemed, was out, and Hugh would not buy anything until Mr Dubonnet chose to be in; at which the youth flushed and bowed his correct little bow. It was all perfectly correct. And yet Richard couldn't have said that to save his life! Why these people stood that damned insolence he could not conceive. Hugh was becoming an intolerable ass.

Richard is ambivalent to the way Hugh treats the clerk. According to the snobbish norms of British society, Hugh's behaviour is acceptable, but it is also humiliating for the young clerk and contradicts another, more human norm, which is more important to Richard. In this scene, we learn, first, what Richard sees and hears in the shop and, second, what he thinks and feels about it. The scene is seen exclusively and constantly from Richard's point of view and includes perceptions, thoughts and feelings. The facts seen and heard by Richard are in themselves sufficient to characterize Hugh as unsympathetic, but Richard's thoughts and feelings reinforce this impression and affect our reactions as well. The subjective colouring of this episode gives us information about the focalizer Richard's personality and shows him from a more sympathetic angle than other parts of the novel do. At the same time, it yields information about the object Hugh, of whom we come away with a rather negative impression.

Viewpoint and identification

The cognitive content is affected by the author's choice between internal and external focalization (whether he lets the fictional narrator focalize the individual character internally or externally). The use of internal focalization may have two goals, which are related to each other. It may encourage identification with the character as well as create a sort of virtual understanding. When the reader experiences the action through a given character's sensory apparatus, he identifies more easily with this character and makes a greater effort to understand him as a human being. This tendency is reinforced if the reader also gets insight into the character's thoughts and feelings. Whether the criminal is focalized internally or externally in a given crime story has consequences for the reader's sympathy or antipathy. However, although external focalization tends to evoke less sympathy than internal focalization, other devices can compensate for it, as we have seen in the subchapter on identification.

External focalization may cause suspense if it entails withholding essential information. If it is evident that the character knows more than the reader, the reader becomes curious to know what is hiding behind the façade. An example of this kind of external focalization may be found in H. G. Wells's *The Island of Doctor Moreau* (1896). After being shipwrecked and rescued, the protagonist and first-person narrator Edward Prendick lands on an unnamed island, where the island's owner, Doctor Moreau, reluctantly lets him stay. Strange happenings on the island warn Edward Prendick that Doctor Moreau has a terrible secret, but being locked up in Prendick's consciousness, the reader knows as little as Prendick about what is going on. Suspense mounts as little by little, through Prendick's viewpoint, the reader discovers Doctor Moreau's cruel experiments in animal vivisection.

An important effect of internal focalization is identification with the character. By regulating the amount of information, the viewpoint can put the reader in the character's situation, confronting him directly with the character's limitations, making him feel acutely his ignorance of the dangers lurking around him. The shared ignorance and suspense makes the reader identify with the character and makes it easier for him to comprehend his reactions and behaviour. *The Island of Doctor Moreau*'s combination of internal and external viewpoint is an example of this effect. From the internal viewpoint, the reader feels Prendick's fright and suspense and becomes a kind of fellow sufferer.

Conclusion

In the previous subchapters, by using *focalization* and *viewpoint* interchangeably, I have tried to show that both are useful for literary analysis. Viewpoint or focalization is only possible in narrative fiction, which allows us to view the minds of others in a way that is unthinkable in real life. The omniscient narrator receives his unique information from the author's general knowledge about human beings.

Viewpoint has four aspects: position (internal or external point of view), depth (perception, thoughts and feelings, the unconscious), breadth (single or multiple viewpoint) and stability (constant or variable viewpoint). As we have demonstrated, rewriting in the first person is not a reliable criterion for internal viewpoint, because all it does is induce the reader to reinterpret external viewpoint as internal.

The first-person character is by definition always focalized internally. Although the single internal viewpoint in first-person narrative is usually constant and only shows us the world through the first-person character's mind, this rule may be broken, as in *Moby Dick*. To the reader it does not matter whether the narrator behaves realistically or not, but whether the information he offers is interesting.

There is a clear distinction between viewpoint and voice, even though both aspects are conveyed by the voice of the narrator. *Voice* accounts for the features of the narrator's voice most closely associated with voice: verbal tense, grammatical person, irony, commentary, assessments and the report of speech and thoughts. Frequency, order, duration and viewpoint are not regarded as elements of voice, although they undoubtedly give evidence of narration. Genette's delimitation of *voice* may be debatable, but the definition of it in terms of verbal tense, grammatical person and so on distinguishes it clearly enough from viewpoint, which is related to the reader's access to the perceptions, thoughts and feelings of the fictional characters.

We have seen that the term *double focalization* is superfluous because the action is always seen from the narrator's viewpoint. Instead, the internal and external focalization of characters is the crucial issue. There is always a viewpoint (or focalization), and if we do not know whether it is internal or external, it is simply indefinite or ambiguous. There is no such thing as zero focalization, only internal and external focalization, and of course indefinite or ambiguous focalization.

Finally, the author's choice between internal and external viewpoint affects the reader's identification with characters and his understanding of their situation, along with creating suspense.

12

Frequency

Frequency is the relation between the number of times an event occurs in the action and the number of times the event is mentioned in the text (reproduced in the mental model). In order to understand the four different forms of frequency, we must first clearly define the difference between *the same* and *similar*, which are key terms. In colloquial usage, *the same* means *identical with* as well as *similar to*, but in our context this can cause misunderstanding. In a novel's action, an event can only take place *once*. If *the same event* happens more than once, we mean different events that are *of the same kind*, different events that *resemble* each other.

In a literary text, if an event is told once, it is called *singulative* (or *singular*) representation: 'On Monday, he went to the cinema.' If one and the same event is repeated in the text, we call it *repetition* or *repetitive* representation: 'On Monday, he went to the cinema. On Monday, he went to the cinema,' and so on. In practice, of course, repetitions seldom occur as close to one other as in this example. If several events that resemble one another are recounted individually, we call it *anaphoric* representation: 'On Monday, he went to the cinema. On Tuesday, he went to the cinema again, and Wednesday was no exception, and. . . .' Language can condense the representation of similar events into one statement: 'Every day, he went to the cinema.' This is *iteration* or *iterative* representation.

Following Genette, we can make the following diagram:

Singulative representation: telling once what has happened once.
Repetitive representation: telling *n* times what has happened once (one and the same event).
Anaphoric representation: telling *n* times what has happened *n* times (similar events).
Iterative representation: telling once what has happened *n* times (similar events).

Singulative representation is normal and requires no special comment (Wells 2010, 7):

The cabin in which I found myself was small, and rather untidy. A youngish man with flaxen hair, a bristly strawcoloured moustache, and a dropping nether lip was sitting and holding my wrist. For a minute we stared at one another without speaking. He had watery grey eyes, oddly void of expression.

Here, in *The Island of Doctor Moreau*, every detail is reported only once, and there are no similar events that are told individually or condensed.

Anaphoric representation is also a kind of singulative representation, except that the events so resemble each other that narrating them feels repetitive. In Grimm's fairy tale, the wicked stepmother visits Snow White three times, trying to kill her in three different ways, first by suffocating her in tight clothes, then by combing her with a poisoned comb, and finally with the poisoned apple. The three events are all alike with the exception of the choice of murder weapon, a resemblance close enough to make possible a single, condensed account: 'In varying disguises, the wicked stepmother went to Snow White three times to try and kill her, and each time Snow White fell to the ground as if dead.' Twice Snow White is saved by the dwarfs as soon as they return from work, and the third time is a departure in that the recovery occurs only when the dwarfs have given up hope, and that the circumstances are more romantic, with a prince's kiss reviving her. The three murder attempts and the first two recoveries are recounted anaphorically, and only the third instance breaks up the impression of repetition.

Indeed, anaphoric representation is a kind of repetition and serves partially the same functions: reminding the reader of facts he already knows but needs to reassess in the light of new facts, or emphasizing important events or facts. In addition, anaphoric representation can create suspense, as in *Snow White* and other fairy tales where similar events are repeated three times, usually with a deviation in the third anaphoric repetition. The likeness of the anaphorically represented events increases the reader's fear of a bad ending or his hope for a good one, depending on the developmental trend of the action. In *Snow White*, each new 'repetition' (introduction of the next link in the chain of the similar events) includes a slight reinforcement of the negative elements: the queen's rage increases with each failed murder attempt, causing her to introduce ever more lethal methods. Her cunning also increases, so that the third time, she eats a non-poisonous part of the apple to convince Snow White that the apple is safe. This successive enlargement of the action's crucial elements reinforces the suspenseful impact of the anaphoric representation and is part of the anaphoric scheme. In other words, anaphoric representation does not require complete likeness to be anaphoric. On the contrary, when used to create expectations and suspense, it tends to go hand in hand with an increase of stimuli.

In fairy tales, threes occur in many contexts, as when Norwegian ogres have three heads, but the number's frequent appearance in anaphoric representation has a rational explanation. Three is the first number that is felt as many, so three repetitions have a stronger effect than only two but are at the same time less unwieldy than four, which would feel somewhat fatiguing. Also, two repetitions may be a coincidence, whereas three repetitions are often taken as a rule.

In *Mrs Dalloway*, Peter's habit of playing with his pocket knife is an anaphorically repeated element that has no intensifying effect. In a crime novel, it might make us expect an imminent attack, but here the text provides no elements to encourage such negative inferences. The knife may be interpreted in various ways, as a distraction, a sign of insecurity, a symbol of masculinity and so forth. The knife episodes could have been condensed into one single presentation of Peter's habit, but the anaphoric repetitions have a foregrounding effect that condensation lacks.

In connection with *Snow White*, I demonstrated the possibility of condensing anaphoric elements. *Iteration* or *iterative representation* is the condensation of anaphoric elements into one report. Iteration saves space and reading time and is a useful device to avoid boring the reader with unnecessary repetitions of information. As summary has a similar function, iteration and summary are frequent companions. An example of summary which was cited earlier is the passage from *Gulliver's Travels*:

> My Father had a small Estate in *Nottinghamshire*; I was the Third of five Sons. He sent me to *Emanuel-College* in *Cambridge*, at Fourteen Years old, where I resided three years, and applied my self close to my Studies: But the Charge of maintaining me (although I had a very scanty Allowance) being too great for a narrow Fortune; I was bound Apprentice to Mr James Bates, an eminent Surgeon in London, with whom I continued four years; and my Father now and then sending me small Sums of Money, I laid them out in learning Navigation, and other Parts of the Mathematicks, useful to those who intend to travel, as I always believed it would be some time or other my Fortune to do.

A clear example of iteration is the sentence, 'My Father now and then sending me small Sums of Money, I laid them out in learning Navigation.' Instead of recounting every single time Gulliver ever received money from his father, the first-person narrator compresses them into one statement. The iterative condensation serves the same purpose as the summary as a whole: saving time and space. Verbal economy is essential to this passage, which is merely meant to provide the reader with the necessary background for understanding the much more important subsequent events.

Not only is the receiving of money iteratively condensed, but also Gulliver's stay and studies in Cambridge and London, even though the similar events that constitute a study or a stay tend to merge into one continuous line of development that is difficult to dissect into discernible individual elements. However, the separate days and periods of study are individual events summed up as a three-year stay and so on.

Nevertheless, scenic representation may also be combined with iteration if the action contains many similar scenes, like Clarissa's daily pleasure of bursting open the French windows when she was young (Woolf 2000, 3):

> What a lark! What a plunge! For so it had always seemed to her when, with a little squeak of the hinges, which she could hear now, she had burst open the French windows and plunged at Bourton into the open air. How fresh, how calm, stiller than this of course, the air was in the early morning; like the flap of a wave; the kiss of a wave; chill and sharp and yet (for a girl of eighteen as she then was) solemn, feeling as she did, standing there at the open window, that something awful was about to happen; looking at the flowers, at the trees with the smoke winding off them and rooks rising, falling; standing and looking until Peter Walsh said, "Musing among the vegetables?"—was that it?—"I prefer men to cauliflowers"—was that it?—He must have said it at breakfast one morning when she had gone out to the terrace—Peter Walsh.

The condensing adverb *always* betrays the iterative character of the description, which does not refer to a single event but to a series of similar experiences. Only Peter's statement about the vegetables breaks the iteration, signalling singulative representation.

Repetition is a more problematic form of frequency, as Genette, along with later scholars, has been aware (Genette 1972, 145–6; Rimmon-Kenan 1983, 56–7; Bal 1990, 89–90). Repetition may refer to many kinds of elements and is not always felt as repetition. For instance, any text of some length is bound to use particular words again and again without it feeling repetitive. The repeated occurrence of the pronoun *I* in a first-person novel is normally not considered repetitive at all.

In poetry, linguistic elements are often used in a figurative sense, and repetition may serve a deeper function than reminding the reader of something or putting a known fact into a new context. The repetition may have a reinforcing and emphatic function, or carry emotional weight, like the mysterious 'nevermore' in Poe's *The Raven*.

In a narratological context, repetition becomes interesting when the narrator repeats events he has already related about. Here it becomes necessary to distinguish between different levels of repetition. Repetition may occur on the level of the text, that of the mental model of the action and that of the referent. In *The Raven*, the repetition of 'nevermore' is a repetition on the level of text. Such a repetition is naturally also a repetition of the same mental model, 'nevermore' inevitably repeats the same mental model, the meaning of the word. However, it is possible to repeat the (approximately) same mental model (signified) by way of different words. The sunset on a particular Monday evening is a unique event and can never repeat itself (as referent), but I can think about it as often as I want to afterwards, repeating the thought of it, that is repeating the mental model of it. If I tell a friend about it, I can share the essence of my own mental model of the sunset:

> On Monday there was a fantastic sunset. You should have seen it! The sky was blazing red!

If I later forget telling him about the sunset and repeat the same sentence verbatim, he will, of course, remind me that I have already told him. But even if I were to present a slightly modified version, he would accuse me of repeating the same story:

> It's too bad you weren't there to see the fantastic sunset Monday evening—it was like the entire sky was set ablaze!

Although the wording is different, he recognizes this new version as a repetition of the first, because the mental model is approximately the same. In other words, even though two texts are clearly different, the mental model that each conveys may be so similar that we recognize them as one and the same. In this case, only the mental model is repeated, whereas the text is not. Nevertheless, most of us would probably regard the second version of the text as a repetition of the first, because we are more interested in the mental model than in the text that conveys it and do generally not distinguish between the text and its meaning. Only a scholar scrutinizing the language of the two texts would be aware of the difference between them and be able to explain why two so different texts can convey approximately the same content. Theoretically, someone might object that neither the texts nor the mental models are sufficiently alike to be called repetitions, but even then no one could deny that the referent, the sunset, is repeated.

To a certain extent, accounts of repetitive frequency have been aware of the distinction between different levels, but not systematically, so far as I know. At any rate, it will be easier to analyse texts in terms of repetition if we are consciously aware of the importance of the three levels *text, model* and *action* to repetition.

The definition of repetition encounters various problems depending on the level of communication. On the level of the text, any change means that we face a new text, at least as long as we disregard meaning, making it easy to agree about what can be called repetition. The fact that the letter and phoneme *s* is repeated so and so many times in the text of a novel is a repetition everyone can agree about. Still, such repetitions are interesting only when they have an impact on the cognitive content. This function is not semantic in the primary meaning of the word, as it depends on the context and not on linguistic conventions. In the Disney film of *The Jungle Book*, the repetition of *s* is striking and interesting when the python Kaa says: 'I can't eat, I can't sssleep, ssso I sssing to myssself.' Here the fricative alludes to the hissing sound of snakes, linking Kaa's anthropomorphic properties to his original animal nature so that this snake functions as human and animal at the same time. In poetry, the repetition of the same rhythm often has an iconic function, as when trochee is used to connote sorrow and fear in *The Raven* (Poe 2006):

> Once upon a midnight dreary, while I pondered, weak and weary
> Over many a quaint and curious volume of forgotten lore—
> While I nodded, nearly napping, suddenly there came a tapping,
> As of someone gently rapping, rapping at my chamber door.
> "'Tis some visitor," I muttered, "tapping at my chamber door—
>   Only this and nothing more."

The example of repetition that I gave at the beginning ('On Monday, he got up at seven o'clock. On Monday, he got up at seven o'clock') is farfetched, of course; in normal texts, the same event is not repeated at such short intervals unless there are special stylistic or pragmatic reasons for doing so. On the other hand, after a certain distance in pages and time, it may be meaningful to repeat the same thing to remind the reader of it or put it into a new context:

> I suppose you still remember that I went to the cinema on Monday.

Or:

> When I told you that I went to the cinema on Monday, I forgot to mention who was sitting beside me . . .

This kind of repetition has no thematic function in the deeper meaning of the word and is hardly interesting for literary analysis. On the other hand, repetition becomes interesting when it serves a thematic function. It may then have various functions, primarily to emphasize and reinforce, like the word 'nevermore' in *The Raven*.

Repetition normally occurs extradiegetically (on the level of the narrative act): the narrator repeats events in order to influence the reader's reactions. In Robbe-Grillet's present-tense novel *La Jalousie*, extra- and intradiegetic repetitions coalesce in an interesting way. With frequent repetitions of the same events in the present tense, this novel reproduces the sensory impressions of a consciousness. These repeated impressions are a manifestation of a jealous husband's attempts at reconstructing and interpreting recent episodes in order to discover his wife's feelings for a friend of theirs, and the action consists in the act of memorizing itself, with all its repetitions.

13

Order

Genette and later narratologists like Bal, Chatman and Rimmon-Kenan treat *order* with varying thoroughness. Bal devotes a separate chapter to the functions of order (Bal 1990, 72), but Lämmert's account of the functions of flashbacks and flashforwards is especially thorough and clarifying (Lämmert 1967, 100–94). Since *order* is an uncontroversial issue and has been well accounted for by others, this chapter will be restricted to a short survey of the most important issues.

By definition, the omniscient narrator knows everything that has happened. When telling a story that is finished and in the past, he may choose to tell the events in their natural *chronological order*, but he may also start from a later point than from the beginning of the action and go back to give the reader the previous events. This device is called *flashback* or *analepsis*. By the same token, the narrator may skip ahead, which is called *flashforward* or *prolepsis*.

Such deviations from the chronological order (*anachronies*) may be used to create expectations or suspense, or to place an explanation in a context that makes it easier for the reader to understand the action. For the reader, it is more difficult to discern the connection between two things that are far apart than when they are closer to each other.

If the reader rereads the text, he is less dependent on the order of the elements and can browse back and forth as much he wishes. The mental model of the action renders the events in chronological order, but as the ordering of events in the text determines when the reader learns about them, it also leaves traces on the mental model. To a certain extent, this effect is renewed every time the reader consults the text, depending on how much he browses back and forth. Contexts which the textual order revealed to him in his first reading are a permanent part of his reading experience, and contexts that the textual order has concealed remain difficult to discern. His first emotional reaction to the book also influences his later contact with it.

Chronology, flashback and flashforward are illustrated in the following diagrams. The numbers indicate the chronological position of the events in the action, while the textual ordering is indicated by their order from left to right:

Chronological order	1	2	3	4	5	6	7	8
Flashback	3	4	*1*	*2*	5	6	7	8
Flashforward	1	2	3	*8*	*4*	*5*	*6*	*7*

The numbers indicating flashback and flashforward are italicized. The position of the flashback or the flashforward may vary, of course, and the diagram shows only one alternative. Another alternative might be:

Flashback	8	*1*	*2*	*3*	*4*	*5*	*6*	*7*
Flashforward	*8*	1	2	3	4	5	6	7

In the last two examples, flashback and flashforward seem to be completely alike, as the chronological position and textual ordering of the elements are the same. Only the italics are different, indicating that the diagrams are different along a third axis, an axis of verbal tense, which it is difficult to express graphically. The two diagrams are different with respect to the temporal relationship between action and narrator. The flashforward is linked to the future and expresses this by using the future tense, whereas the action before the anticipated episode is rendered in the present or the past tense (Dagerman 1992, *To Kill A Child*, my translation):

> It is a gentle day, and the sun is shining diagonally above the plain. Soon the bells are going to toll, because it is Sunday.
>   Between a couple of rye fields two youngsters have found a path they have never taken before, and in the three towns of the plain, windowpanes are flashing. Men shave themselves in front of the mirrors on the kitchen tables, and humming women cut bread for the coffee, and children are sitting on the floor, buttoning up their shirts. It is the happy morning of an evil day, because today a child is going to be killed in the third town by a happy man.

In this short story, about a child killed in a car accident, the action itself is rendered in the (historical) present, while the anticipated accident and the death of the child are rendered in the future tense.

Flashbacks, on the other hand, are recounted in the past perfect or the past tense, depending on the context. In principle, flashbacks should be rendered in the past perfect in past-tense narratives and in the past tense in present-tense narratives, but the past perfect is often inconvenient and replaced by the past tense. In *Mrs Dalloway* the action covers one day and is told in the past tense, whereas events from 30 years back are rendered as flashbacks (Woolf 2000, 50), also in the past tense:

> "Lord, Lord!" he said to himself out loud, stretching and opening his eyes. "The death of the soul." The words attached themselves to some scene, to some room, to some past he had been dreaming of. It became clearer, the scene, the room, the past he had been dreaming of.
>
> It was at Bourton that summer, early in the 'nineties, when he was so passionately in love with Clarissa. There were a great many people there . . .

The flashbacks are embedded in the action in the form of thoughts (internal monologue) and do not therefore interfere with the development of the action, as the internal monologue *is* the action.

A common device for arousing the reader's interest is omitting the beginning of the action, instead starting at a more advanced and captivating point in order to grip the reader from the very first. The historical background of the events is then presented afterwards in flashback. This mode of narration is called *in medias res* (Latin: in the middle of things) (James 1992, 1):

> Strether's first question, when he reached the hotel, was about his friend; yet on his learning that Waymarsh was apparently not to arrive till evening he was not wholly disconcerted.

In this first sentence from James's *The Ambassadors*, the pasts of Strether and his friend Waymarsh along with the immediate background to their meeting at the hotel are suppressed and will only be subsequently delivered little by little in flashback.

Another technique involves starting at the end and showing the reader the background of the situation and causes of the events in flashback. In Maugham's *Cakes and Ale*, the text starts at a late point in the action, arousing the reader's curiosity about the main theme: the heroine's questionable morals. The subsequent chapters disclose the woman's secrets little by little.

Anachronies may be embedded in the mental model of the action in two ways: intradiegetically as integrated parts of the action or extradiegetically as independent information directly from the narrator to the reader. *Embedded anachronies* unite the past or the future with the present by embedding the flashback or flashforward in the dialogue or in the characters' thoughts and dreams. An embedded flashback is doubly linked to the action, by reproducing the past event and by being part of the present action. Reporting the past through the characters' dialogue is a way of including the past in the present time of the stage without breaking the unity of time and action (a move characteristic of Ibsen's retrospective technique). The same technique may be used in novels and short stories, but as narrative literature also has access to the characters' minds, the anachrony may consist of thoughts as well as speech, as is the case with *Mrs Dalloway* and *The Ambassadors*. Embedded anachronies are dynamic parts of the action which drive it forward. Therefore, we do not feel them as delaying or disruptive elements. What Ibsen's characters tell each other about the past affects their present relationships with each other, resolving conflicts and problems or giving rise to new ones.

Independent anachronies do not have the same double bond with the action as embedded anachronies. They do not affect the action, as they render only a bit of it and have a delaying effect since they interrupt the narration of the present action.

When it comes to flashforwards, Lämmert distinguishes between *certain* and *uncertain flashforwards*. Uncertain flashforwards may consist in dreams, omens, prophecies or simply an object that creates fear of the future, like a knife on the table. In *The Island of Doctor Moreau*, the strangeness of the inhabitants of the island makes the reader anxious and makes him wonder what is going on.

The certainty of independent flashforwards, on the other hand, consists in our trusting the narrator's omniscient memory (Tolkien 1981, 282):

> It is true that for ever after he remained an elf-friend, and had the honour of dwarves, wizards, and all such folk as ever passed that way . . .

This also pertains, in fact, to flashbacks. Embedded anachronies are always uncertain, as they are linked to the characters' subjectivity. A character may be wrong not only about the future but also about the past due to memory lapses or misinterpretation, so that embedded flashbacks may also be uncertain. Strictly speaking, the embedded flashbacks in *Mrs Dalloway* and *The Ambassadors* are uncertain, but the uncertainty is irrelevant (as in most novels) because there is nothing in the action to indicate their unreliability.

In addition to promoting or counteracting particular associative connections, anachronies may have pragmatic or thematic functions. Flashbacks may, for instance:

1. change the reader's curiosity from 'How does it end?' to 'Why did it end like that?'
2. create suspense by postponing information, which is provided later in flashback
3. clarify or solve mysteries
4. provide the right information at the right time
5. enable *in medias res* narration
6. delay the further development of the action
7. summarize

Flashforwards allow the author to

1. create suspense by hinting at the future
2. change the reader's curiosity from 'How does it end?' to 'Why did it end like that?' (when the ending is revealed at an early stage)
3. prepare the reader for a particular issue

14

Suspense

Except when it is caused by clearly structural devices, suspense has largely been neglected by narratology. This is probably due to the structuralists' general lack of interest in the content and functions of literature. For instance, Eric Rabkin's *Narrative Suspense* (Rabkin 1973) turns out to be a study of narrative structures instead of an exposition of suspense in the traditional meaning of the word.

Scholars have defined suspense in various ways, though they often foreground the reader's need to know how the action develops. Suspense therefore has been formulated as uncertainty with respect to development of the action (Lothe et al. 2007, 213), as stimulation of the reader's engagement by the interplay between factors of the story (Gorp et al. 1991, 376–7), as 'wanting to know what happens next and what will happen ultimately' (Hawthorn 2000, 350–1), and as uncertainty 'often characterized by anxiety. . . . Suspense is usually a curious mixture of pain and pleasure' (Chatman 1978, 83–4, who quotes Barnet et al. 1960). Several theorists distinguish between *result-oriented suspense*, which is directed towards *what* is going to happen, and *process-oriented suspense* directed towards *how* it happens (Lugowski 1990, 37; Brecht 1963/64, 117).

One common feature in these various definitions is the association of the receiver's excitement with knowledge and ignorance or expectations. Although knowledge/ignorance and expectations are crucial to suspense, this is nevertheless too narrow to fully account for how suspense works.

What is suspense?

Suspense is created through an interplay between the reader's mind and the structure of the work, a fact that literary theory has not ignored. The definition of suspense must consider the reader's whole personality and range of interests and give more than a one-dimensional account of the reader's experience, for suspense is not always a simple reaction. It may be complex and even somewhat self-contradictory, as when I continue to read a novel even though I find the action boring or unpleasant. The distinction between result-oriented (ending-oriented) and process-oriented suspense may too easily be interpreted as two mutually exclusive alternatives that turn on whether we know the end of the story or not, when both kinds of suspense can be felt simultaneously, even in action presented chronologically so that the outcome is not known until the end of the text.

Suspense is better explained not in terms of knowing and expectations, but rather in terms of needs in general (which of course include knowing and expectations). Suspense is an emotional state caused by a need, and ceases when the need is satisfied. Since we can have various and partially conflicting needs at the same time, we can also feel various forms of suspense simultaneously. Suspense is therefore not simply one effect of the reading process: it is rather a combination of various effects, which we have to distinguish from each other. The suspense we feel from a novel is due to various needs that are either already there or arise during the course of reading. Every need causes suspense of its own, for we feel not only the suspense engendered by the need but also suspense concerning the probability of the need's being met. Hunger causes a state of tension due to the need for food, but in addition to the feeling of hunger, the hungry person also needs to know *how* he can get food and *whether* he will get food at all, thus linking various other needs to the primary need. The same complexity pertains to literary needs: when I pick up a novel, I do it because I need entertainment or information or both, but at the same time I am anxious to know whether the book will satisfy my needs.

Various forms of suspense

We start reading because we feel the need for it: indeed, reading is only a means of fulfilling various needs, which are related to the functions of fiction. The needs that make us read a fictional work entail suspense until they are satisfied. The suspense we feel in advance before opening the book may simply be termed *interest*. A particular book piques our interest for one reason or another, for instance because someone recommended it, because people are talking about it, or because we are interested in its theme. Our interest is automatically accompanied by another kind of suspense: will our interest be rewarded? Will the book satisfy our needs or not, that is, will it be good or bad? We can call the latter kind of suspense *benefit-oriented*. If the interest vanishes, for instance because the reader is disappointed with the content of the book, uncertainty becomes certainty, and both kinds of suspense vanish, being instead replaced by satisfaction or frustration.

Thus, suspense is already there when we start to read. The reader's interest and uncertainty last as long as he expects to find material suited to satisfying his needs. His interest is maintained by the content of the text: to some readers the satisfaction of needs implies learning something from the action and the mental model of it, while to others it may mean finding confirmation for particular views (for instance, that the weak may win in the end through perseverance), which makes the reading agreeable as well as entertaining. Suspense related to learning may be termed *cognitive* or *intellectual suspense*, in contrast to *emotional suspense*, which aims to entertain based on the confirmation of an (often unrealistic) optimistic view of life. Both cognitive and emotional suspense depend on the information the reader receives through the action (and the mental model of it), and they increase or decrease according to the quality of the information. The difference between the two kinds of suspense lies in the attitude of the reader: the intellectually oriented reader accepts all kinds of information as long as it seems objective and true, whereas the emotionally oriented reader only wants information that presents the world in an optimistic light. Cognitive suspense is primarily accompanied by feelings like interest and curiosity, with excitement and pleasure being secondary, whereas emotional suspense is primarily associated with pleasure. Both forms of suspense represent a kind of interest and are accompanied by benefit-oriented suspense. Interest and benefit-oriented suspense occur on many levels of the novel.

Most people associate suspense with emotional suspense. Even the most intellectual reader is subject to this kind of suspense, because whether he likes it or not, he is affected by the picture the action draws of reality. He interprets the fictional events as a manifestation of laws that apply to the real world. As we have seen above, such a law may be the belief that virtue is always rewarded, which of course is a subjective belief that depends on one's values and worldview. Its subjectivity is revealed by the fact that it is possible to assert the contrary: virtue is often not rewarded. However, most people like virtue to be rewarded and wish it were a natural law in the real world, even if they understand that it is not realistic. We welcome any real or fictional example that seems to confirm such rosy hopes, disliking anything that contradicts them. Intellectually we may disapprove of such mental opportunism displayed by many books, but nobody is exempt from it.

Emotional suspense manifests itself largely as hope and fear. While reading the text, we understand little by little why the action develops as it does. The characters' actions are means or causes that produce effects or consequences, forming patterns we can learn something from. We have already mentioned *process-oriented* and *result-oriented suspense*. Emotional suspense is as a rule also result-oriented, whereas process-oriented suspense is primarily cognitive (intellectual), but there is no necessity to these connections. The suspense we feel when we only want answers we like is purely emotional. If the reader wishes an effect to have a particular cause, the suspense he feels may be emotional and process-oriented at the same time. This would be the case if he wishes the bad guy to meet his end through his own treachery and not because of an evil act on the part of the hero. On the other hand, it is process-oriented and intellectual to want to know the end of the action if the goal is primarily to understand the dynamics of the development. But if, at the same time, the reader prefers a particular outcome, usually a happy one, emotional suspense comes in addition to the cognitive (intellectual) suspense.

In principle, the ending answers all the reader's questions and resolves all suspense, confirming or contradicting the message that the reader is looking for. Of course, the ending may be complex, confirming or contradicting only part of the message, leaving other parts uncertain. The reader is then left with a mix of emotions, as his satisfaction has been only partial. Suspense pertaining to the action as a whole, which only the ending resolves, may be termed *global* or *principal*.

In principle, the reader reaches the end of the action after having read the preceding episodes. These episodes illustrate causal relationships and values by way of forces that promote or deny a happy ending. As long as all goes well, the reader feels optimistic and rejoices at the turn of events; if there are problems, he becomes nervous and ill at ease. As a whole the action raises one principal question (or at least a limited number of principal questions), while the individual episodes and subordinate elements raise subordinate questions of a more limited scope. Every question creates suspense of its own until it is resolved. This kind of subordinate suspense is *episodic suspense*.

We have already discussed the possible coexistence of cognitive and emotional suspense; the objective need for learning does not prevent the reader from wishing the information he receives to turn out a particular way. All the common contradictions and conflicts that characterize the human psyche are also involved in the reading process. The reader may therefore find a tragic novel cognitively interesting and at the same time emotionally unbearable. Some readers may only feel emotional suspense, such as those who read only for pleasure. On the other hand, it is less likely that a process-oriented reader would feel no emotional suspense in addition to cognitive suspense.

The understanding of suspense as an emotional manifestation of unfulfilled needs sheds light on the so-called paradox of suspense (Wikipedia):

> Some authors have tried to explain the "paradox of suspense," namely: a narrative tension that remains effective even when uncertainty is neutralized, because repeat audiences know exactly how the story resolves (see Gerrig 1989, Walton 1990, Yanal 1996, Brewer 1996, and Baroni 2007). Some theories assume that true repeat audiences are extremely rare because, in reiteration, we usually forget many details of the story and the interest arises due to these holes of memory (see Brewer); others claim that uncertainty remains even for often told stories because, during the immersion in the fictional world, we forget fictionally what we know factually (Walton) or because we expect fictional worlds to look like real world, where exact repetition of an event is impossible (Gerrig). The position of Yanal is more radical and postulates that narrative tension that remains effective in true repetition should be clearly distinguished from genuine suspense, because uncertainty is part of the definition of suspense. Baroni (2007, 279–95) proposes to name *rappel* this kind of suspense whose excitement relies on the ability of the audience to anticipate perfectly what is to come, a precognition that is particularly enjoyable for children dealing with well-known fairy tales. Baroni adds that another kind of suspense without uncertainty can emerge with the occasional contradiction between what the reader knows about the future (cognition) and what he desires (volition), especially in tragedy, when the protagonist eventually dies or fails (*suspense par contradiction*).

Why do we feel tension when rereading the same text? In their knowledge-based accounts of suspense, Brewer, Walton and Gerrig try to explain the suspense in repeat readings in terms of knowledge: because we forget the action (Brewer 1996), because we forget fictionally what we know factually (Walton 1990), or because we expect fictional worlds to look like the real world, where events cannot be perfectly duplicated (Gerrig 1989). Brewer's argument is the most plausible, in that insofar as we forget, we need repetition. But this does not explain why repeat readers still feel suspense regarding details they still remember. Walton's and Gerrig's explanations are not convincing: our identification with the fictional world does not affect our memory, and although we do not expect repetitions in the real world, we never expect the ending to change in a novel.

Yanal's distinction between genuine suspense in a first reading and the narrative tension that remains effective in repetition is interesting, on the other hand (Yanal 1996), because he reserves uncertainty for the definition of suspense, implying that the narrative tension repeat readers feel is not related to uncertainty. However, he does not explain the nature of this special tension further.

Baroni seems to offer two different explanations, to which he attaches two different terms: *rappel* (reliving) and *suspense par contradiction* (suspense related to contradiction). The former is exemplified by children's listening to the same fairy tale repeatedly, and the latter is a contradiction between what the reader knows about the future (cognition) and what he desires (volition) (Baroni 2007, 279–95). However, the suspense children feel when hearing the same story over again is related to neither knowledge nor contradiction. Children are thrilled not because they do not remember what is going to happen but precisely because they know it. When they hear for the umpteenth time that Snow White is rescued by the prince and that the evil queen is punished, they learn nothing new. The reason for their suspense and subsequent pleasure is the anticipation of a pleasure to come and the fulfilment of anticipation. In other words, the pleasure they derive from repetition reaches them in two stages: first in anticipation and then in the pleasure of seeing their hero succeed and the antagonist lose. Only anticipation, a general uncertainty of future events, contains an element of suspense, and a moderate suspense at that, because the goal is certain to be reached.

Baroni's *suspense par contradiction* is akin to the thrill children feel when hearing the same fairy tale again, but in contrast to that of the children, it is accompanied by negative feelings, as Baroni links it to tragedy. With children, there is no contradiction between their desire and the development of the action, whereas tragedy thwarts the reader's desire for pleasure. While children listening to fairy tales look forward to the ending, the repeat reader (or theatre audience) dreads it, a difference due to their respective motives for reading (or listening). While the children want a repetition of the fairy tale to achieve pleasure, readers and audiences usually reread (or watch again) the tragedy for intellectual reasons, in order to improve their wisdom about the world. Therefore, the feelings evoked by the tragedy are mixed: readers and audiences enjoy the wisdom inherent in the drama while disliking the ending, which is ironically part of the wisdom: tragic experiences are part of life and a risk we have to live with.

Consequently, Baroni's contradiction is not between what the reader knows about the future and what he desires but between two different aspects of this future: between the cognitive and the emotional aspect of the cognitive content. Moreover, the contradiction between the cognitive and emotional aspects of the cognitive content has little to do with suspense. Baroni confuses suspense with the emotions the reader entertains: the satisfaction of receiving information and dissatisfaction over the information's unpleasantness. Suspense when rereading a tragedy is as moderate as that of children listening to fairy tales, and it is linked to a kind of uncertainty that the future always entails: uncertainty whether the work will prove to be as good this time as the first, whether there remain interesting structures to be discerned and so on.

A reason for rereading novels may be a need to check whether the work is still the same as the first time we read it. Just as we sometimes recheck the front door although we clearly remember having closed it, or just as a lottery winner needs repeated confirmation of the prize because he really cannot believe it, rereading a book is a kind of rechecking the facts that entails suspense. This suspense is not very strong, however, or at any rate only as strong as the reader's need to recheck the facts of the action.

Our discussion has revealed several possible reasons for rereading fiction:

1. We have forgotten important details we need to remember.
2. We want to check that we remember the important facts correctly.
3. We want to re-experience pleasant moments of the action.
4. We want to scrutinize the elements of the action in order to understand it better, that is, in order to enhance the cognitive content we extrapolate from it.

Each of these is related to needs, which create suspense, whose strength depends on the strength of the needs arousing it. If we have just finished reading a novel, rereading it will probably cause little suspense if the reason behind it is the fear of having forgotten details. If we reread it many years later after forgetting most of the action, we may perhaps feel the same suspense as the first time. On the other hand, if we reread the work in order to study its structures more closely, the interval between the first and the second reading is of little importance, because the scholarly pursuit ensures plenty of suspense of its own: how is this work constructed, and how do its elements work? The wish to re-experience pleasant moments of the action is better suited to engendering pleasure than creating suspense, because when rereading a book, we are fairly certain of achieving the pleasure we are looking for, and delight over the protagonist's successes must not be confused with suspense. Nor must we confuse the conflict between intellectual and emotional desires with suspense.

Suspense in *Effi Briest*

I will try to illustrate the above-mentioned types of suspense by way of a concrete text, Theodor Fontane's *Effi Briest* (Fontane 1969). This novel is about a young woman's marriage and divorce in Germany at the end of the nineteenth century. At age seventeen, Effi Briest is already married to a much older man, whom she does not love but respects highly. She expects him to make a career and give her a life full of pleasures, but his career causes him to neglect her. Her boredom drives her into the arms of a womanizer, an affair she repents bitterly afterwards. Only many years later does her husband discover her infidelity. Afraid of social opinion, he throws her out even though it happened a long time ago and he still loves her. Effi dies shortly after of tuberculosis, while his life is ruined.

Suppose the reader chooses this book because it is a renowned work of high quality, expecting to find true, important information about life, literary naturalism or Fontane the novelist. This *interest* lasts until the end of the book, unless the reader somehow finds it disappointing. He may have imagined Fontane's literary style to be different, perhaps he does not find the novel typical of naturalism, or maybe he is unable to identify with the worldview inherent in the action and the mental model of it. The suspense connected with these aspects – interest and result-oriented suspense – is so individual and subjective that it is useless to elaborate on it. As for the emotional suspense, on the other hand, different readers are perhaps more likely to have approximately the same reaction, so that one reader's emotional response to the text may be representative of other readers' reactions.

Fontane's novel starts with a detailed description of Effi's home that fills about one page. Some readers may find such descriptions boring and wish instead for some action. Of course, it is debatable how concrete the reader's mental model of the physical environment must be so that he may identify with the action. Different literary movements have different views of how to depict setting and events. If the description is clearly separated from the action, giving the reader the impression of nothing happening, he may become impatient unless he feels that the description is necessary for appreciating the action. This of course is a dilemma the writer faces when rendering events by way of language. The sentences take time, and you cannot convey the sensory experience of a scene as directly as in a film or on the stage. The author has to leave a lot to the reader's imagination to prevent the text from becoming too comprehensive and fatiguing. But how much and which elements? The author can avoid this by starting in the middle of the action (*in medias res*), where more things are happening. Then the necessary descriptions are postponed until the reader has become so interested that he willingly puts up with static descriptive passages.

But Fontane does not employ *in medias res*; he forces the reader to get acquainted with the action's physical framework before he lets him know the purpose of this framework. He details even the sunshine and depicts an idyllic environment that evokes no apprehension or suspense. Except for the interest he may have had already at the outset, the reader feels only moderate curiosity: what is the intention behind this description of the manor house in Hohen-Cremmen? The action, too, is rather insignificant in the beginning and arouses merely cognitive suspense: Effi is chatting peacefully with her mother or playing quietly with her friends. During these first pages, emotional suspense may at most arise if the reader wonders how long this idyll will last.

As readers we nevertheless expect a novel to present conflicts and problems, so we are more sensitive to symptoms of them than in real life. We prick up our ears when Effi tells her friends that her mother is expecting a visitor, an old admirer of hers, for although visits do not have to mean anything particular in the existing world, in a novel they may signal something important about to happen. We know that in fiction, all superfluous elements are normally omitted, leaving only the essentials.

Fontane incrementally increases both the cognitive and the emotional suspense by providing the reader with apparently insignificant but ambiguous information. First the reader wonders what this visit may mean to Effi, because at the outset it seems to concern only her parents, perhaps a conflict around jealousy involving her mother, her father and the old admirer. We do not expect this man to come to propose to Effi. Effi has no inkling of what will happen and shows no interest in her mother's ex-admirer. Moreover, her childish qualities are repeatedly emphasized, so the reader is not likely to think of marriage for her.

The surprising offer of marriage resolves the modest cognitive and emotional suspense created by the ex-admirer's presence and engenders instead a strong cognitive and emotional suspense:

1. What issues will this marriage shed light on (cognitive suspense)? What kind of information will it give us?
2. How pleasant or unpleasant will this information be for us (emotional suspense)?

This suspense lasts until the end and is, in other words, global or principal suspense.

The readers soon identify with Effi and regard her as the protagonist of the story. Their sympathy and the identification are due to various causes. The action is mostly seen from Effi's point of view, through her mind, and deals chiefly with her. She is endowed with sympathetic features of personality and appearance. Her destiny exemplifies something that might happen in our own lives in some form or another. To exaggerate slightly, a happy ending will strengthen the readers' general optimism towards life, whereas a sad one will make them more pessimistic. Of course, one book has only a limited impact on the readers' worldview, but its influence is nevertheless strong enough to affect their emotions. The wish for a happy ending constitutes both result-oriented and emotional suspense, which manifest themselves as curiosity, hope and apprehension.

The action of *Effi Briest* is rendered in chronological order, so the readers feel mostly result-oriented suspense: what will happen when Effi's husband reads the old letter from her lover? Another question that creates suspense in retrospect is why she had the love affair in the first place. Although several facts explain why (boredom, a lack of attention from her husband), when her husband reads the letter we still lack information about the exact circumstances. This is not revealed until a later report of her thoughts: she did not love the seducer, it was just a whim. When we combine this information with the already known external circumstances, we understand why it happened (which we had already suspected), and the process-oriented suspense is resolved.

Artificial suspense

Up to this point, we have dealt with forms of suspense created by the action itself, but the author can also create suspense by way of literary devices. When a novel starts with the ending, and the events that led to it are recounted in retrospect, the narrator resolves the result-oriented (ending-oriented) suspense, replacing it with process-oriented suspense. The reader's curiosity is directed more towards causality than towards the result. We can term suspense created through literary devices *device-related*, as opposed to the natural *action-related* suspense engendered by the action itself. Alternatively we may call them *artificial* and *natural suspense*. Device-related/artificial suspense may be created with devices like selection, viewpoint and anachrony (deviations from strict chronology – flashbacks and flashforwards), which create gaps that need to be filled in. Natural suspense is a prerequisite for artificial suspense; if the action does not grip the reader, he does not care how the gaps are filled.

One simple way of creating suspense is to leave out information, which can be done in a number of different ways and theoretically applies to all the details of the action. If the reader misses a detail and waits for it to be filled in, he already feels suspense. A typical example is beginning *in medias res*, where the reader does not yet understand what is going on and wants to know both the continuation of the action (result-oriented suspense) and the background (process-oriented suspense).

Viewpoint is another kind of selection well-suited for creating artificial suspense. By presenting the action from a particular point of view, the author omits information in order to trigger the reader's curiosity and fear. Bal exposes the relationship between focalization and suspense in the following chart, in which minus and plus indicate whether the reader or the actual fictional character knows something important or not (Bal 1990, 128–9):

Person	Knowledge	Person	Knowledge	Kind of suspense
Reader	−	Character	−	Mystery
Reader	+	Character	−	Threat
Reader	−	Character	+	Secret
Reader	+	character	+	No suspense

As the chart indicates, mysteries operate by concealing important facts from the reader as well as from the character, for instance, in the traditional detective novel, where neither the reader nor the protagonist knows the killer's identity until the very end ('Whodunit' mysteries). If the reader finds out the killer before the character, the question is whether the character will discover the *threat* in time. If the character knows more than the reader, he has a *secret*.

There is no suspense at all, according to Bal, if both reader and character know who the killer is. This applies, however, only to this particular aspect of suspense, for independent of what the reader and the character know, the action itself still evokes plenty of suspense. What further atrocities is the killer capable of? Will they catch him before it's too late? How? Even if the reader has a sense of how it will all turn out, there is at least still suspense in terms of what exactly will happen and how.

Information can also be withheld by way of a flashforward that hints at future events. We can distinguish between two types of omission: the *transparent* and the *non-transparent hint* (Lämmert 1967, 139–40). The transparent hint is uncertain and gives only as much information as necessary to give rise to different alternatives. Small but ominous details like a knife on the table, a storm or two strangers in front of the house may create suspense in the right context, and sometimes such details are misleading, sometimes not. The non-transparent hint only indicates enough to arouse the reader's curiosity without suggesting different possibilities. For instance, the reader notices Effi's repeated absence for a certain period of time from her meetings with the house maid. This is, of course, the period of her affair with the other man, but the reader is not yet informed about this and as yet has no intimations of what her absence may mean. The hint is too vague to lead his apprehension in a particular direction.

The title of a work or the chapter headings may be another form of flashforward that causes suspense. Some narrative techniques are used so often to introduce exciting episodes that they have almost become conventions. When a scene follows a summary passage, the reader expects something important to happen and therefore already feels suspense. Symbols, too, may create suspense. In addition to symbols that the characters use in speech and in thoughts, symbols may occur in the action itself without the characters being aware of it. Such symbols are direct signals from the author to the reader, and can be weather, season, the hour of day and colours. Storms, autumn and winter, evening and night, black and grey are bad omens, whereas sunshine, spring and summer, light or pure colours are good signs.

Furthermore, correlative events may give rise to suspense on account of likeness or contrast. Even extratextual factors like literary conventions may arouse suspense, because they create expectations. The reader knows in advance that the hero in popular literature always succeeds, which is nevertheless not strong enough to reduce the result-oriented suspense. The action in popular literature is constructed so that the reader is continuously afraid the rule might be broken this once. The convention of the happy ending becomes a sort of comfort when the suspense becomes too intense: 'Don't despair, it ends well!'

All in all, suspense is a complex phenomenon that cannot be described with a single curve of development; different kinds of suspense have different curves of development. *Interest* is a kind of suspense that is relatively constant, a straight line. *Benefit-oriented suspense* may, on the other hand, vary from moment to moment, but it may be difficult to measure how intense it is at each individual moment. It is easier to see where the benefit-oriented suspense arises and where it ceases than to describe all the variations in between. Nevertheless, particular factors reinforce or weaken benefit-oriented suspense. When the author introduces factors that contradict the result the reader wants, he increases the benefit-oriented suspense, and this suspense increases with the number of obstacles. The more obstacles there are, the greater the reader's apprehension that the story will end badly. But if the obstacles become so enormous that the reader loses his faith in their solution, he may become so resigned to the bad outcome that the suspense vanishes. This may happen when the hero catches a lethal disease for which there is no cure; the reader endures the rest of the story to receive the rest of the information inherent in the action, but the emotional suspense is gone.

In theory, it should be possible to physically measure the reader's suspense at the various stages of the reading process, for instance by feeling his pulse, measuring perspiration and so on. This might seem to be an interesting, objective way of measuring suspense, but the question is whether such data would tell us anything of value as long as it does not distinguish between the various impulses that the measured amount is composed of. The most plausible method for studying literary suspense is therefore probably the method that literary studies cannot avoid in the long run: introspection and exchanging observations. Literature is, after all, something that occurs exclusively in the mind of the individual', in spite of the apparently objective existence of the material text.

15

The Functions of Literary Fiction

Up to now we have investigated the basic aspects of the fictional communication process and seen how fictional literature works. We have implicitly touched on the functions of literary fiction in analysing the interplay between its structures and effects. Now it is time to elaborate on fictional communication's primary and secondary functions.

In terms of reception, literary function has three aspects: the effect intended by the sender, the effect the receiver expects, and the actual effect. We have treated all three aspects, but mainly in terms of what I take to be the primary function of literary communication: giving insight into the problems of the real world and their possible solutions, in other words, the cognitive content.

I have already argued for this mimetic-cognitive vision of literature, while also to some extent taking it for granted. A problem in dealing with complex issues is of course choosing the order of the various items. Because so many elements are based on one another, you risk treating prerequisites too early or too late. I have tried to resolve this dilemma by making certain compromises: anticipating issues when necessary by dealing with them provisionally in order to elaborate on them later. This has the drawback of repetitiveness, but repetition does yield certain pedagogical advantages. Although I have often touched upon – and in various contexts also argued for – a mimetic and cognitive view of literature, some aspects still remain to be discussed. This chapter is therefore devoted to a thorough discussion of literary fiction's primary and secondary functions.

Two prominent theories do not share the mimetic-cognitive vision of literary fiction I have been advancing. The first (especially French narratology) is based on Saussure's linguistic theories and limits its research to literature's objective linguistic aspects, excluding the cognitive, mimetic aspects as too subjective. My description of the literary communication process thus far ought to be a sufficient argument for a broader approach.

The other anti-cognitivist theory does not deny the importance of the cognitive content, but considers the fictional work an autonomous universe to be enjoyed for its own sake with no relevant connection with the extratextual world. New Criticism is a typical proponent of this view (see Abrams 1989,

25–6). However, an autonomist view of literature is not necessarily opposed to mimetic cognitivism. Some readers identify so strongly with the fictional world that they nearly forget their own real world. This fictional dream world becomes a surrogate for real life and seems to be autonomous because the real world is temporarily excluded. Nevertheless, even under such circumstances, the fictional world is not autonomous, because its elements are still more or less imitations of elements of the real world and would be incomprehensible without this connection. Therefore, on account of the likeness between the two worlds, the fictional action would still shed light on the structures of the real world and vice versa, however distorted the fictional work's picture of the real world may be. It seems unlikely, however, that the autonomists are referring to this experience of apparent autonomy, but there is stronger evidence against literary autonomy.

In previous chapters, I have shown that the fictional work inevitably exerts a significant cognitive influence on the reader, and up to now I have taken it for granted that this is its primary function. But the cognitive impact of fiction does not alone prove that this influence is really an important function, let alone the primary function. *Impact* does not automatically mean *function*. Function depends on volition: the reader must want literary fiction to have this impact on him. Hence, the question is: does the reader want the fictional work to give him insight into the mechanisms of the existing world? Many readers do not read primarily in order to learn something, instead seeking only entertainment or to pass the time; do entertainment and passing the time have anything to do with receiving information and learning? This is the crux of the discussion since antiquity about the role of learning and pleasure in literature (see Abrams 189, 3–30).

By living our own lives, we learn an infinite amount of facts and general insight into numerous aspects of the existing world. This learning process is, however, only a means that helps us live in a good way; the experience itself – life itself – is the real goal. We do not live in order to learn but learn in order to live. Is this also the case with literature? Is the reading experience itself the ultimate objective, whereas the cognitive effect (learning) is just a side effect? Is there a parallel between living and reading, or are they different? Is it possible that cognitivism promotes a secondary function of fiction as its main function?

The autonomist view of the fictional world is based on certain superficial facts that we must see through in order to expose the weaknesses of the theory. It *looks* as if we read for pleasure, and we *apparently* enjoy the fictional action for its own sake, just as it may seem as if we enjoy language for its own sake (which we argued against in Chapter 4, on the aesthetic). To penetrate beneath the surface, we must analyse what happens to us when we read a novel. Is there a complete analogy between the way we experience the fictional action and the way we experience our own lives?

A decisive difference is the fictionality of the novel's action, which contrasts with the reality of our own experiences. We experience life's events directly, whereas the fictional action is only indirectly accessible through the verbal mediation of another person's experience. The fictional grass has no perceptible scent and does not expose us to hay fever; it merely reminds us of the fragrance of real grass and its unpleasant effects on those with allergies. It is a characteristic feature of the fictional world that we cannot sense it, but even more important is the fictionality of the action: that the fictional events and characters have never existed and never will. Why should we take so much interest in something that does not exist and allow ourselves to become as emotionally involved as we do when we read fiction?

To say that our emotional involvement could be a kind of illusion would hardly suffice as an explanation, because at no point are we under any illusions that the mental model is anything but the product of the author's imagination. We do not lose touch with reality the way mental patients do. The readers of Goethe's day who wept over *The Sorrows of Young Werther* knew all the time that Werther was a fictional creation (even if they were aware of the story's roots in Goethe's own life). If some readers committed suicide in response to the book, as history attests, they did not do so on account of Werther's fictional suicide per se but because Werther represented attitudes and values that were valid in their own lives.

The reason fictional characters and events evoke such strong emotions is that we regard them as representative of our own real world. The action tells us something about the world of the past, present and future we continually confront. It is hence not difficult to see how Werther's hopeless infatuation, though fictional, could have induced inexperienced youths to find so much tragedy in their own love lives that they ended up taking their own lives. It is of little avail to assert that Werther's tragedy could just as well be taken as a warning against sentimental suicides, when the reader is not mature enough to understand that very message.

When we identify with fictional events and characters, the identification has no pragmatic impact on our own lives, as it would if one of our friends suffered or died. When one of my friends is depressed, it affects my own behaviour, whether I decide to avoid or help him. Septimus's depression and suicide in *Mrs Dalloway* has no influence in the reader's everyday life, and the sorrow or anxiety the reader feels reflects only the pessimistic insight into real life that the fictional suicide conveys. Through the fictional action, Woolf tells the reader indirectly about the dangers human beings in general (including the reader himself) have to face in the extratextual world. The two doctors' lack of understanding for Septimus gives rise to anxiety, since the reader realizes that the same can happen in his own life. What stirs the reader's emotions and grips him is the cognitive content that is inherent in human behaviour and human experiences, in fiction as well as in real life.

This applies not only to negative, cautionary experiences but also to positive ones. When the poet describes his love and tenderness for his beloved, we do not know whether the person he is addressing is real or fictional, and it does not matter, for what really grips us is the observation of people in love along with the virtual experience of the possibility that love, tenderness and kindness may exist in the real world.

The difference between real and literary experience is that, in addition to the cognitive value they have in common, real experiences have a value of their own because they consist of direct sensory impressions that can be enjoyed for their own sake: the scent of grass, the feeling of fear or tenderness. When you kiss someone you love, it is an autonomous experience, and it is this autonomous value that fiction lacks. Only the cognitive dimension is left; the observation of two lovers kissing in a novel or film does not give the reader or spectator a feeling of being loved himself by one of these persons, only the pleasant confirmation or hope that he may one day be so lucky as to get kissed himself.

One important reason reading fiction is not experienced as a cognitive activity is that it happens under the same conditions as playing, a voluntary act without pragmatic consequences. In contrast to normal learning processes, when we read the cognitive process absorbs us so completely that we do not associate it with learning at all. Reading a novel for fun and not because one must is like taking an adventure trip without being aware that it is essentially a trip of discovery. We may compare it to tourists on safari on the savannas of Africa, enjoying the excursion as pure entertainment, unaware that they are continuously learning something about animals, people and the country. Readers are like adventurers that are not aware they are taking part in of serious exploration.

Just as playing seems to be a goal in itself but is essentially a way of gaining skills and maintaining body and mind, reading is an activity that trains our mental adaptation to life in a pleasant way. By reading about human behaviour and how humans experience reality, we are confronted directly with realistic problems, which we have to handle intellectually and emotionally as if they were real. Because reading is as voluntary and safe as playing, we find it entertaining even though it has a pragmatic function. In fact, we like to be challenged intellectually and emotionally, just as it is pleasant to go exploring in the forest and to run when you play football. To run in order to catch a tram or to walk from house to house on a paper delivery route is less amusing even though the activity is the same as when you do it for pleasure. It is less pleasurable to read as a duty, for instance, reviewing novels or reading a drama in preparation for an exam. To most readers reading fiction is free from obligations and utility, and becomes a game even though the content that is prerequisite to the game is cognitive and demanding.

To the reader it seems as if he likes observing fictional characters for the sake of the observation; the abstraction and generalization process itself is invisible, and he is not consciously aware of the fictional/real-world likeness providing him with insight into the problems and values of the existing world. Consciously occupied with the aspect of play, he forgets fiction's much more important function, by which the work grips him and without which reading novels and attending plays would lose most of their attraction.

But as long as the reader remains unaware of acquiring knowledge about human existence, how can we say that fictional literature has cognition as its main function? As we said, function is linked to volition: a human will that wants the actual effect. Can we say that the reader *wants* to be influenced cognitively? Yes, even if the reader is not fully aware of what his activity really consists in, the cognitive content that allows the enjoyment. Unconsciously he wants the cognitive influence; without it, he would lose interest in the work. Even if he is not consciously aware of it, he knows deep in his mind that the fictional world is representative of the existing world and that this is the real reason for reading. If the fictional action is unreliable as a source of general information about the existing world, he will blame the author. This does not imply that the fictional world must be in every respect realistic, only that the work must somehow shed useful light on reality.

The reader's deep awareness of the cognitive function of literature is also evidenced when he comments on real people and events by referring to fictional characters and events. People often refer to a split personality as a Dr Jekyll and Mr Hyde or use Aldous Huxley's *Brave New World* as an argument against electronic surveillance. To some extent reading may be compared to eating: the meal may be felt as a pleasure in itself, while its real function, feeding the body, is invisible. Literary fiction is food for the mind, but the primary function is invisible, and the enjoyment itself dominates. In the case of eating, it is easier to prove its impact on us because it often makes us gain or lose weight. Literary fiction influences our understanding of life, people and the world around us, but its long-term effects are difficult to prove because we cannot easily compare people before and after reading a particular novel.

Didactic literature and simplification

One reason for some of the resistance to cognitive literary theory may be the association of cognition with school education and didacticism. Concepts like *message* and *cognitive content* may be easily confused with reducing the ideological and artistic scope of literature to a pool of psychological, sociological, political, ethical, philosophical, moral or religious slogans. In *Theory of Literature*, Wellek and Warren say that 'the reduction of a work of art to a doctrinal statement – or even worse, the isolation of passages – is disastrous to understanding the uniqueness of a work: it disintegrates its structure and imposes alien criteria of value' (Wellek and Warren 1954, 110–11). But simplifying in the course of understanding the main tendencies of a work does not amount to forgetting the limitation of our analysis, nor does it claim to have exhausted the ideological and artistic scope of the work. Simplification is simply necessary to understanding complex structures. A complete analysis of a work would have to describe the structure and functions of every single element and the interplay between all elements, and would further have to register and comment on every possible cross-reference between elements within and outside the work. This task would be impossible, not to mention extremely tedious. The analyst has to foreground particular structures at the expense of others, and the different priorities among different scholars is a problem of interpretation and does not prove that the work has no cognitive function.

We have already mentioned Beardsley's distinction between *theme* and *thesis* (Beardsley 1981, 404). Themes delimit actual issues (for example jealousy, the horrors of war, how to get a partner), and theses represent claims about the theme ('Exaggerated jealousy may destroy a relationship'). Themes and theses are rough simplifications and are only instruments that help describe the work. They are not meant as exhaustive explanations about what makes the work valuable. Otherwise, the author could simply have published a less time-consuming pamphlet of abstract wisdom. Any analysis implies a certain amount of simplification, and Beardsley's concepts of *theme* and *thesis* are useful for understanding the functions of a literary work. This does not mean that the analyst ignores or disregards the multitude of the other aspects of the work, much like the physician who must scrutinize the skeleton in isolation in order to better understand the human mind and body as a whole.

Result- and process-orientation

The cognitive influence may have various objectives: the author may provide the reader with clear solutions to the problems in the action, or he may confront him with a set of unresolved problems. In the latter case, the author tries to start an intellectual and emotional process in the reader's mind that may lead to solutions or may be valuable in itself in contributing to intellectual and emotional development. The cognitive function may, in other words, be result- or process-oriented or both. Process-orientation may be a significant reason why readers (and the theatre audience) may feel attracted to texts (or plays) they understand but dimly or perhaps not at all. In extreme cases, the text and the action may be entirely incoherent, as in a lot of modernist texts. Then the receiver feels the incomprehensibility as a challenge, a mystery to be solved. This process-oriented cognitive function corresponds to puzzle-solving in general, like crossword puzzles, mathematical problems or chess problems, and is not literary in the traditional sense of the word. However, there is a gradual transition from pure puzzle-solving to the analysis of causality and ethical, psychological, sociological, political, philosophical and religious problems, and it is difficult to draw the precise boundary between literary and non-literary cognitive activity.

Even in works where puzzle-solving is of minor importance, intentional ambiguity or vagueness may serve a positive purpose, for instance in the gaps that appear when a sentence is followed by an unexpected continuation (Iser 1976). According to Iser, the unexpected is something positive, for if the expectations are too easily granted, the text becomes too predictable and didactic. A text presenting a harmonious world without contradiction or conflict should therefore not deserve to be called literature. Iser does not elaborate on why the didactic is negative and why contradiction and obscurity are necessary ingredients, but it seems that he considers process-orientation more valuable than result-orientation.

The idea that process-orientation may serve a stimulating and constructive function does not nevertheless mean that result-orientation is inferior. This is more a question of personal taste and subjective needs than 'objective' quality. A novel is not necessarily better because it is more obscure than another, and vice versa. We will come back to this issue in the chapter on evaluation, but for now, we have to content ourselves with the fact that some literary works are more result- or process-oriented than others. The result-oriented cognitive function may be objective or tendentious, and through didactic literature, realism and documentary novels, it ranges from propaganda to various forms of literature with a more open content, like symbolism and surrealism.

Non-cognitive functions

In Chapter 4, on the aesthetic, we saw that in addition to a cognitive function, aesthetic objects can have a separate aesthetic function. The action may comprise other elements that have a non-cognitive function in addition to their cognitive function. When people in the real world are fascinated by watching others, the reason may be cognitive, social or sexual. One may become wiser by observing others, or feel less lonely and isolated, and it can also be exploited as a source of sexual excitement. Similarly, the fictional characters in a novel or a drama may evoke corresponding feelings. It is possible to read a novel with the sole aim of sexual arousal, as in pornography, or to feel the human presence of the fictional characters, perhaps out of the feeling that they are, to some extent, rooted in the author's own soul, mediating contact with the author himself. This feeling of interpersonal contact may be termed the *phatic function*, in accordance with Roman Jakobson's phatic linguistic function, and is particularly strong in confessional poetry, where the lyric subject and the author are more likely to be identical than in other kinds of poetry. Humour may also be a goal in itself, in addition to its cognitive function, as in humorous literature, jokes and stand-up comedy.

However, even if the phatic, sexual, humorous or aesthetic effect has its own value, this is normally only a side effect of the action, which rather confirms its mimetic function, just as a tourist inadvertently addressing one of the wax sculptures in a museum confirms its likeness to real persons. In a general context, these functions play a subordinate role. In literature, however, they play a thematic part, as in pornography and jokes, but even then they inevitably have a cognitive function in addition to their special function.

Besides boosting the reader's self-confidence and optimism, fiction engenders a range of other feelings that may be felt as valuable in themselves: pleasure, disgust, sorrow, frustration, joy, fear, hope, boredom, suspense and so forth. The release of accumulated emotions also belongs to this category (catharsis). All these emotions are manifestations of the reader's reactions to the cognitive content and are therefore closely related to the cognitive function, but they may also have a value of their own. Our excessive focus on the feelings that the cognitive content evokes is akin to certain drivers' use of cars as a way of experiencing speed and thrills instead of as a mode of transport. The functions we have already mentioned allow also for a therapeutic function, for both author and reader. The author may benefit from talking about his problems (albeit in an indirect, fictional manner), and the reader may likewise in learning about the situations of others (even if they are fictional). Moreover, the activity of writing or reading may have a therapeutic function, and if phatic, sexual, humorous or aesthetic elements are embedded in the action, these may also have some kind of therapeutic impact in addition to their other functions. An inevitable side effect is biographical information about the author, because the work indirectly provides information on the personality of its creator.

As long as the cognitive process interests the reader, it helps him pass the time, which is another side effect. Of course, nothing can prevent the reader from transforming this secondary function into a principal goal, but it is still the cognitive content that allows for such use of the work. We have seen how the reader's self-confidence is bolstered when fictional characters he identifies with succeed. Even unsuccessful characters can boost the reader's ego if they make him feel superior.

One last function can be held by meaningless texts, which the reader interprets as a protest against the yoke of reason that provides security and satisfaction. Although the primary function of fictional literature is cognition, the cognitive basis gives rise to a number of other secondary functions. The following list comprises both primary and secondary functions:

1. indirect information about general aspects of the existing world
2. intellectual and emotional development through learning
3. intellectual and emotional development through problem solving
4. direct information about specific phenomena in the existing world (history, geography, philosophy, science and so on)
5. ideological influence
6. passing the time
7. entertainment, suspense, laughter
8. escape from reality
9. boosting the reader's ego
10. releasing accumulated emotions (catharsis)
11. therapy for reader and author
12. sexual arousal
13. aesthetic pleasure
14. the phatic function (a feeling of social contact)
15. a protest against rationality
16. indirect biographical information about the author

Although the list is comprehensive, additions are still possible, but because the cognitive function of literary fiction is so basic, it is likely that the items already in the list will remain so in the future. New forms of literature with goals other than the purely cognitive may arise in the future. As long as the fictional action is sufficiently similar to the patterns of the empirical world, cognitive functions will be an inevitable part of the fictional communication process. It is at least arguable that literature with no cognitive function should not be termed literature at all.

16

Evaluation

On account of its subjective and relative character, modern literary scholarship tends to regard literary evaluation as an activity that should be left to popular criticism and individual readers. Luxemburg (Luxemburg et al. 1988, 120) holds that literary scholarship does not evaluate at all. It is characteristic that Jørgensen's *Litterær vurderingsteori og vurderingsanalyse* (*Literary Theory of Evaluation and Analysis of Evaluation*, Jørgensen 1971) from 1971 is still a standard work on evaluation and that modern theorists neglect the issue (Chatman 1978, Rimmon-Kenan 1983, Bal 1990, Herman and Vervaeck 2005, Phelan and Rabinowitz 2005, Herman 2007, Davies 2007, Abbott 2008, Fludernik 2009, Vermeule 2010). Two exceptions are the Danish scholar Morten Nøjgaard's chapter on evaluation in *Det litterære værk: Tekstanalysens grundbegreber* (*The Literary Work: The Basic Concepts of Textual Analysis*, Nøjgaard 1996) and the Norwegian scholar Erik Bjerck Hagen's *Literaturkritikk* (*Literary Criticism*, Hagen 2004), which perhaps signal an increasing interest in evaluation. To be sure, neither of them tries to reform the traditional theory, but their critical attitude to it clears the way for new ideas.

To what extent is evaluation inevitable?

In spite of the general scepticism to evaluation, Nøjgaard holds that literary science cannot avoid it, because an evaluative understanding is prerequisite to the literary work (Nøjgaard 1996, 277–8). Hagen is of the same opinion (Hagen 2004, 20, my translation): 'Whether we like it or not, the phenomenon of quality is central to all activity related to literary scholarship.' Nøjgaard argues (Nøjgaard 1996, 278, my translation):

> In order to understand the work I have to evaluate it. But as evaluation is a purely subjective process, my analysis of the work cannot involve the value aspect, because then the analysis becomes as subjective as the assessment. . . . On the other hand, analysis without evaluation is false, for in all my interpretations my view of the values of the work is hidden.

However, this paradox is not real, because it confuses two kinds of evaluation, evaluation at two levels. Nøjgaard does not distinguish between the reader's ethical, psychological, sociological, philosophical and political assessment of the characters' behaviour on the one hand (internal evaluation) and the evaluation of the work as reading material on the other hand (external evaluation). Internal evaluation means that the reader assesses the characters' behaviour on a scale from good to bad (ethical judgement) and from wise to unwise (pragmatic judgement), whereas external evaluation means assessing the work according to criteria like truth, importance, relevance, novelty and entertainment value. There is no necessary connection between internal and external evaluation. However well or badly, wisely or stupidly the characters behave, it does not affect the value of the work. The unwise behaviour of Effi and her husband that ruins their marriage does not reduce the novel's value, and the literary scholar does not have to assess the value of a work in order to judge the behaviour of the characters and understand the cognitive implications of the action. Nøjgaard's assertion that one must evaluate the work to understand it is therefore wrong; it is not the evaluation of the work but that of the characters' behaviour that is important for understanding the work.

The work's value may be of importance for the literary scholar's choice of research object, but evaluation does not infiltrate the analysis. Meaningful literary analysis cannot be value-neutral, but the values in question here are internal and have nothing to do with the evaluation of the work as literature, so they cannot be used to prove that evaluating literary works is inevitably part of literary studies.

Nevertheless, there are better arguments for including evaluation in literary studies. Literary evaluation is important to society because it helps consumers orient themselves in a complex market, and not only private readers are consumers of fiction, but also publishers, critics, librarians, booksellers, institutions assigning awards and grants and so on: everyone who comes in touch with literature. Moreover, literary evaluation gives important feedback to authors and has a normative effect. On account of the consumer groups, literary evaluation should have a solid professional, scholarly basis.

How subjective is evaluation?

The principal argument against including evaluation in literary studies is the subjectivity inherent in the pursuit. Literary evaluation depends on an interaction between the objective structure of the work and the subjective influence of the reader. The object of evaluation, the structures of the work, are only accessible after they have been filtered through the reader's mind, through the reader's interpretation. Evaluation must therefore be based on the reader's subjective interpretation of the work, so the evaluation is bound be subjective. Hagen 2004 (20) objects that literary evaluation is at least no more contingent and subjective or less subject to scholarship than interpretation and analysis. Jørgensen 1971 (41, 81) defends literary evaluation by pointing out that the critical reference systems used for evaluation can to some degree be empirically and logically corroborated and allow for intersubjective review (a view endorsed by Nøjgaard 1996, 278, 288). The idea is to make the basis of one's evaluation as accessible as possible to other readers in order to establish an intersubjective platform for critical dialogue between readers. According to Nøjgaard, a prerequisite for dialogue is knowledge about the interplay between the structure of the work and the reader's mental qualities, that is, an understanding of how fiction works; 'a theory of evaluation presupposes a theory of function' (283). In the previous chapters we have provided such a theory of function.

Literary evaluation means evaluating the work's capacity to satisfy the reader's relevant needs, that is, those needs that the work can be expected to satisfy within reason. I have argued that literary fiction lends itself primarily to satisfying the reader's cognitive needs and that ironically, its entertaining effect is due to its cognitive function. We have also mentioned aesthetic, social, sexual and humorous needs, which can dominate certain passages or even the entire work (nature poetry, confessional poetry, pornography and jokes). Literature that is intended to fulfil these special needs must also, of course, be evaluated, and this activity belongs to literary evaluation. In serious literature (as well as popular literature, paradoxically), however, the cognitive function dominates, and cognition is also unavoidable in nature poetry, confessional poetry, pornography and jokes. Therefore, cognition must dominate our further discussion of literary evaluation.

As stated above, the cognitive content manifests itself in various versions: the message of the author, the latent message and the received message. Which of these messages is to be evaluated? We want to evaluate neither the author's nor the reader's personality, only the impact of the work itself, so the answer must be the *latent message*. Although it is interesting to study the empirical effects of the work on particular readers, we wish primarily to evaluate its potential with respect to readers in general. Unfortunately, the interaction between the literary work and its different readers is extremely complex, and there are often significant differences between the various received messages according to the reader's background, qualities and interests. The problem in identifying the latent message becomes apparent: there is no shared entity to evaluate.

The latent message can only be reached through the received message, leaving us two alternatives:

1. to infer the latent message from the received message, that is, from the enormous amount of messages that actual and possible readers have extrapolated or may extrapolate from the work, including the author's own message, because his interpretation is also a kind of received message

2. to disregard the latent message and evaluate only the received message

If we opt for the second alternative, we seem to have abandoned the evaluation of the work itself, but the evaluation of the work's cognitive impact on the individual reader reflects necessarily the qualities of the work since they are the cause of the reader's experience. A steak may be prepared in various ways, but in whatever way you do it, it remains a steak, and the quality of the meat always determines the taste. The reader's evaluation of his own literary experience is therefore partially an evaluation of the latent message of the work.

If we try instead to infer the latent message from the received message, we repeat in principle what we did when we decided to disregard it: we still scrutinize the received message, but because we are now consciously looking for the latent message, we may choose strategies for reducing subjectivity. We may compare the cognitive benefit of different readers in the same way a linguist compares related words across different languages in order to reconstruct their common root. Among a sufficient amount of reader experiences, we will find common features that can without question be identified with the latent message. Other features are found only in a lesser amount of interpretations but may still be representative of the latent message, whereas some features are limited to so few interpretations that it is uncertain whether they are due only to idiosyncrasies of the reader or constitute a feature of the latent message that all others have overlooked. When we take many readers' interpretations into account, we choose a broad approach that increases the probability of uncovering the properties of the latent message.

If we are not dependent on one single, random reader experience, we can also reduce subjectivity by going more deeply into the work. Ingarden has drawn attention to the distinction between what he calls *passive* and *active reading*. There is a great difference between reading a work inattentively and scrutinizing it thoroughly. If you read with attention, perhaps taking notes, you will notice more details and discover more connections, even more so if you read the book twice. Nevertheless, it is not likely that one single scholar can discover all relevant structures and cognitive impulses. If we combine the breadth method with the depth method by comparing the analyses of several scholars, we ought to gain valuable insight into the work's cognitive potential.

It is now important to recall that the latent message is not a complete message, only properties of the action and the mental model of it that are suited for conveying a particular message to the reader, that is, it exists merely as potential. To uncover this potential, we need to know in general terms how variations in the structures of the action and the mental model on the one hand and variations in the properties of the reader on the other influence the reader. In other words, we need general knowledge about the interplay between the structures of the work and the properties of the reader. This, of course, becomes a circle: in order to know in general terms how the structure of the work influences the reader, we have to know in general terms how readers react to such structures, but in order to know why readers react as they do, we must find out why the structures elicit such reactions, and so forth. This is obviously a hermeneutic circle but in more general terms. By studying both readers and literary structures, we acquire little by little general insight into the interplay between them and discover causal relationships, understanding how the fictional action and the mental model are likely to influence the reader and how the latter is likely to react to the former. General knowledge about the reader is available from the social sciences but also from our own experience. Human beings have a lot in common, especially within their own cultural community, and in addition, they are more or less familiar with the horizon of understanding of other communities. As long as the discussion partners are familiar with each other's intellectual and ideological backgrounds, they can have a fruitful dialogue, because they know the basis on which they disagree. A racist and an anti-racist can both read *Uncle Tom's Cabin* and understand the author's message, even though their ideologies differ. Nevertheless, although global understanding is a human ideal, intersubjective consensus about values across cultural boundaries is not unproblematic. This is also reflected in literary evaluation, as both post-colonialism and feminism can attest.

On account of the subjectivity of the message, narratology has intentionally disregarded the novel's cognitive function and instead concentrated on the relationship between story and discourse, that is, between the action and the mental model of it, because this relationship can be described more objectively than that between the action and the message. As long as one disregards the functions of the action, this too can be described objectively.

Although narratologists analysing the structure of the mental model of the action to a certain extent draw attention to functional aspects (for instance Genette 1983, 104–5), their tepid interest in function has itself been noted (see Booth's criticism of Genette, quoted in Genette 1983, 104–5). The reason for this reluctance is probably that narrative structures have a cognitive function of their own, and affect the angle of the cognitive content of the action and the reader's reactions to the action. Hence, we can only understand the function of literary devices (i.e. viewpoint, voice, frequency etc.) in terms of the message to which they contribute.

The contributions of the text and the mental model to the message are an inevitable factor in literary evaluation, and because these structures create the message in conjunction with the action, the evaluation of their functions also depends on their interplay with the reader. The reader's background and interests may influence his evaluation of the structures of the mental model. As long as different readers extrapolate different cognitive contents (differently received messages), any variation in interpreting the cognitive content will affect their interpretation of the literary devices' function. For example, a constant one-sided internal viewpoint contributes to identification and sympathy, and if a character presented with internal viewpoint expresses values and attitudes the reader dislikes, he may find fault with the choice of viewpoint, because it promotes interpretations of the action he disagrees with.

Even if the communicative functions of the narrative and stylistic elements may seem obvious and objective, we must recognize that even these may be subject to disagreement. It is not certain that everybody will find a particular metaphor successful or that a given viewpoint or voice is the best vehicle for the cognitive content, but our prior general knowledge of literature and readers makes evaluating the structures of the mental model less subjective. Such prior knowledge derives from literary studies as well as from our own experience as readers. With respect to the functions of the action, the mental model and the text, we have intersubjective prior knowledge that counteracts subjectivity. If we add to this knowledge a broad, representative selection of reader experiences and individual analysis, we are able to establish a rich variety of interpretations that can be considered representative of the work's cognitive potential. Future readings may extend and alter this impression, but this provisional picture enables us to evaluate literary works in a way useful to our own time.

Before we can evaluate, in other words, we must identify our object of evaluation. In fiction, the object is relative because it depends on the interplay between the work's structures and the reader's background and personality. But the reader's intersubjective knowledge about readers, reading and literature offsets the subjectivity so that his reactions to the work are not entirely accidental and unpredictable. If we base evaluation primarily on its cognitive function, the problem of evaluation is not a purely subjective question of taste that is beyond discussion but an intersubjective question of values.

Which aspects of the work are subject to evaluation?

The fictional action is dependent on the text and the mental model in order to reach the reader and cannot help being coloured by their structures. A symbiotic whole comes into being where the structures of the different levels contribute together to the cognitive content. Although theorists have been reluctant to distinguish between content and form (see Aarnes 1965, 60), structuralism and narratology have shown the possibility of distinguishing the action from the devices that convey it, which amounts to a distinction between content and form. Although the action can only reach the reader through the text and the mental model, we discern enough of the action behind the text and mental model to isolate it from their devices (viewpoint, voice etc.).

It is in fact feasible to reconstruct the original structure of the action, peeling away viewpoint, voice, duration, frequency, order, metaphors, symbols etc. and using our general knowledge about the extratextual world to fill in all relevant gaps. We finally face the action itself as we would have perceived it if it were unmediated empirical reality. Booth 1983 (437) argues against narratologists' distinction between story and discourse (or text):

> Unfortunately, our contemporary tendency to reduce all questions to questions of language frequently has the effect of turning this distinction into one of *content* as opposed to *form*, or *raw events* as opposed to *language* or discourse. This suggests that the events somehow remain unchanged, while the language is being doctored to surround them with something either less real or more important. But what a novelist does in transforming chronologies—playing up some moments and telescoping entire decades, suppressing some motives and playing up others—is to transform one kind of event into another kind: the characters and actions that emerge from the process of "realizing" a plot, a full "narrative," are not the same as the characters and events that much more vaguely "exist" in the raw chronology.

Booth is naturally right that the action and the mental model are created more or less simultaneously when the author plans and writes the book, and in the creative process, the action emerges probably first as a mental model. Indeed, the distinction between action and mental model has nothing to do with the process of creation. It is instead a purely theoretical distinction related to the analogy with non-fiction. Our knowledge about the difference between signified and referent in non-fiction makes it possible to discriminate in a similar way between action and mental model, for we know in general terms what the fictional action (the referent) must comprise to be complete (for instance, the characters' eyes having a colour although it is not mentioned in the text). By virtue of this distinction we can study how viewpoint, voice, selection, frequency and order affect the presentation of the action, *without changing the action itself* (as we picture it before it is rendered by the model). Booth does not differentiate between two different meanings of *raw events*: (1) the raw material the author works on during the writing process; (2) the complete action as it would have been according to the analogy before it is rendered verbally.

The reconstruction of the original action implies, of course, that the text and the structure of the mental model are separated from the original action so that the narrative and stylistic devices can be evaluated apart from it. We have seen that it is also possible to distinguish between the interplay of text, action and mental model on the one hand and the extrapolated message on the other. Here there is also a symbiosis: the message is inseparably linked to text, action and mental model, but it is at the same time possible to isolate it for evaluation. Literary evaluation hence comprises three areas: the cognitive content (the message), the impact of the action on the message and the influence of text and mental model on the message.

On account of the symbiosis between action and message, it is in principle impossible to evaluate the former without automatically including the latter. If we find the action interesting, for instance, we have effectively also said the same for the message. This is due to the fact that the action has no value on its own, only as a vehicle for the message. The action cannot be changed in any important respect without a corresponding change in the message.

This is nevertheless a truth with some reservations, for the message is abstract, and its level of abstraction may vary according to the degree of generalization. If the reader generalizes minimally, the fictional action and the message go hand in hand so that the message only pertains to cases that are almost exactly alike. As long as it does not affect the truth value, however, it is appropriate to increase the level of abstraction so that the message obtains broader validity. Although Septimus's mental problems in *Mrs Dalloway* stem from his experiences as a soldier, his destiny throws light on the problems of other kinds of psychiatric patients, too, and the arrogant manner of the two doctors sheds light on the relationship not only between doctor and patient in the broadest sense but also between people in a position of power and their victims.

Depending on the level of abstraction, different actions can cover the same message; the higher the level of abstraction, the more actions will cover that message. If we reduce the thesis of Shakespeare's *Romeo and Juliet* as, 'Enmity between two groups should not prevent the innocent among them from having contact', not only do all the novels and dramas and poems about Romeo and Juliet fit in but also a lot of other works. However, it is the reader who generalizes, and if he moves too far away from the original action, his evaluation of the action as a vehicle for the message becomes correspondingly unrepresentative of the action's original potential. Ultimately, the reader may impose an almost random message on the action, and then criticize the action for not conveying the message in a good way. In other words, it is important to generalize within limits, and the criterion for sensible abstraction is the degree of intersubjective consensus.

The action may have flaws, for instance improbable patterns of behaviour or unconvincing events, banal passages, omission of necessary elements etc., which, of course, entail similar weaknesses in the message. To expose such defects, the reader needs a basis of comparison, which he already has in his own general knowledge of the world and of literature. By comparing the mental model of the fictional action with his own general knowledge, he reconstructs the original action as he thinks it would have been (had it been real). The reconstruction is also influenced by the reader's idea of what kind of message corresponds to the reconstructed action.

Symbols and allegories present their own interesting situation, in which the action splits into a symbolic or allegorical surface structure and a realistic underlying action. The underlying action is the real vehicle for the message. As a vehicle for the underlying action, the value of the symbolic or allegorical action can be evaluated separately from that of the underlying action, as the interplay between them is not as tight as the symbiosis between action and message. The same action could be represented by various symbolic actions as long as the common features they share with the underlying action are sufficient to symbolize it.

When we evaluate the message, it is essential not to confuse the message (the thesis) with the *topic* or *theme*. As we know, the message is a more or less coherent multitude of insights and problems, which we can simplify by using Beardsley's *thesis*. Theses are linked to particular themes or subjects, but themes and theses must be evaluated separately. The message may have an interesting theme without being interesting itself if the theses are uninteresting or false. On the other hand, the theses may be interesting and the theme uninteresting, such as when the action of a novel exemplifies in an insightful way a theme that has become dated (Lamarque and Olsen's example is a novel about the generation of 1968).

The ties between the action and the form imposed on it by text and mental model are not as tight as the symbiosis between the action and its cognitive content, the message. Changes in the text and the model do not entail corresponding changes in the action; the action is only viewed from a new angle, certain parts of it more or less foregrounded, for instance by omission or elaboration. Therefore, there is in principle no necessary connection between the value of the message and the action on the one hand and the devices of the mental model on the other. Nevertheless, as a property of the mental model and the action, selection occupies an intermediate position between the action and the mental model. If, for example, an element of the model is left out, a corresponding gap appears in the action and hence also in the message, unless the reader can fill in the missing element by virtue of the analogy with the existing world. The question may arise as to how we discover such an omission. The old adage that whatever you don't know can't hurt you may not be altogether inaccurate here, since as we have seen, gaps in the mental model are normally not sensed by the reader. A gap may become noticeable if it has ideological consequences, for instance if a problem is dealt with in a biased way. If Harriet Beecher Stowe had left out all violence and injustice in her story about Uncle Tom, readers would probably find it to be a misleading picture of slavery in nineteenth-century America.

Although the cooperation of the different levels and all their elements is indispensable for communication, it is not of course necessary that all the factors of communication function equally well. Just as the different organs of the body need not be equally healthy in order to keep us alive, parts of the literary work can be less successful than others without disrupting the communication. We are familiar with literary critics applying their nuanced evaluations to different aspects of the work; even with respect to one and the same aspect, the evaluation may vary, such as when a critic finds flaws in action he otherwise finds good, and an almost perfect work may be marred by some banal metaphors or a confusing order of elements. Not everything, however, has to function perfectly in a work to make it valuable enough to be published. Just as in many other areas of life, one has to make a calculation between the positive and negative aspects of the work.

Evaluation criteria

Once we have ascertained the relevant aspects of the message and analysed how the structures of text, action and mental model contribute to the message, we can evaluate the work as a whole and its individual elements. Michael Kienecker points out that evaluation by way of words like *good, bad, nice, beautiful, ugly* etc. implies two components, one *emotive* and the other *semantic*. The emotive component has the pragmatic role of distinguishing, recommending, praising etc., while the semantic is related to function: the capacity of the object to fulfil certain criteria or needs. An object is, in other words, good or bad depending on whether it satisfies particular criteria or needs. In everyday parlance, for example, a 'good car' is one that is safe, comfortable and dependable. Using criteria in the same way, one can substantiate literary judgements and perhaps achieve intersubjective consensus, even though the criteria themselves are subject to endless discussion (Kienecker 1989, 64). If two readers disagree on the plausibility of the action, for instance, they may work out a definition of *plausibility* that allows them to explain and defend their opinions.

Traditionally, literary criticism has used a wide range of criteria for value: universality, mimesis, cognitive depth, pleasure, sentimental value, originality, peculiarity, wholeness, unity, coherence, consistency, simplicity, complexity, diversity, conformity to literary conventions, classicism, formulaicness, openness, closedness, sincerity, sensitivity, intensity, realism, morality, quality of language, elegance and sentimentality. In addition, there are a lot of criteria pertaining to communicative ability, like clarity, to name just one.

Most of the above-mentioned criteria apply both to the cognitive content and to the structure of the text, mental model or action. The quality of language refers only to the text and mental model of the action, whereas universality, mimesis, cognitive depth, morality and pleasure are related to the cognitive content (message). I will provide some comment on the various criteria.

Evaluation criteria for the cognitive content

Since I do not recognize the aesthetic as a general literary function, we can exclude obscure aesthetic criteria from evaluation in order to concentrate on the cognitive function. We devoted sufficient attention to the message to see that it can largely be treated as a form of information, with the reservation that it does not have to consist in complete insights and attitudes, perhaps also consisting of hints and pointers towards starting an informative process.

Having a cognitive function has been regarded as a value criterion, but if the cognitive function is already the work's primary function, this criterion becomes self-evident and irrelevant, like praising a car for having four wheels. However, for those who mean that the cognitive function of fiction is equivalent to its aesthetic function or even inferior to it, the cognitive aspect is not a matter of course and may therefore be a criterion for value. *Universality*, *mimesis* and *cognition* have been used as synonyms for cognitive value (Jørgensen 1971, 111), but when the cognitive content becomes the main function of literature, one must evidently also evaluate the cognitive value of the cognitive content.

Nøjgaard points out that we characterize literature as *boring* or *interesting* rather than as *bad* or *good*, but these terms are not incompatible. In order to be good, literature must be interesting; interest is a specification of what we mean by *good*: *gripping, consuming, absorbing, thrilling, exciting, engrossing*, all of which are, however, as obscure as *interesting*. Traditionally, five more precise terms have been used: *truth, importance, relevance, novelty* and *entertainment value*.

Truth

The criterion of *truth* refers to the message, or the cognitive content we extrapolate from the action and the mental model of it. The message consists in general knowledge about the existing world and must be true to be of value. Since the message is inherent in the action, the truth criterion also pertains to the action, but we cannot say that the action is true, because that would mean that it is not fictional. Instead we have to resort to words like *lifelike, faithful, true-to-life* or *authentic*, which stress likeness instead of identity with reality. As we have repeatedly pointed out, the likeness between fiction and reality does not mean the fictional action must be *realistic* and must not deviate from the patterns of the real world, but thematically relevant elements must conform to the general patterns of reality. Symbolic structures symbolize real events, exaggerations can reveal the truth, and unrealistic auxiliary structures make insightful thought experiments possible. Saint-Exupéry's *The Little Prince* employs symbols to draw a revealing picture of the real world in spite of the action's fairy tale structure.

The precise meaning of a 'faithful recreation of reality' will always be subject to discussion. The reliability of the fictional action can only be verified by a reader who can attest that there are parallels in the real world and similar things that have really happened, or who compares the message with his own general knowledge about the real world. In areas where the reader does not have prior knowledge, this filtering process may admit false information that is integrated in the reader's worldview as truth. Anyway, literary fiction contributes to the reader's general conception of the world. Although there is no objective truth, it is at least possible to establish an acceptable degree of probability by intersubjective consensus.

Among the various literary movements, *realism* is most closely associated with the truth claim. Realism tries to create fictional characters that resemble living people as much as possible, along with a fictional world that parallels the general patterns of the existing world. This technique requires solid general and specific knowledge about reality or drawing on living humans as sources of inspiration. In both cases, the author must be a keen observer, able to discern the essential aspects of reality and human behaviour. If his observations or psychological knowledge are inexact, it affects the cognitive value of the work, and the reader may reject the work as unrealistic. To what degree the truth value of the work is reduced depends on the importance of the deficient detail. The message is a complex system, so a minor detail need not affect the value of the work as a whole. A character dressed in clothes from the wrong period does not ruin a historical novel if the main facts are correct.

If essential aspects of the action of a novel are implausible, however, the reader is inclined to lose interest. Popular literature is nevertheless largely an exception. Much popular literature draws a false picture of the existing world without the readers finding fault with it, and what would be a serious flaw in other works is popular literature's forte. The entertaining effect of popular novels is based on the success of characters with whom the reader sympathizes, whether or not the action complies with reality.

Several traditional criteria for literary value that seem to stand on their own feet prove to be subordinate to the truth criterion. This applies to *sincerity*, which in addition to meaning *reliability* and *truthfulness* also has a *phatic* function, which will be dealt with later. Another criterion related to truth is *realism*, which we have already dealt with. Criteria with negative connotations like *sentimentality*, *melodrama* and *formulaicness* are also related to truth. Both *melodrama* and *sentimentality* mean an abuse of strong emotional expressions, that is, emotional reactions that are exaggerated or inadequate in relation to the events that evoked them. Melodrama more strongly emphasizes that the action is not true to life, for instance because of exaggeration or a breach of causality, but both concepts imply a false conception of reality. Both may be used to lend an appearance of significance to uninteresting action, but they may also have a political or ideological function. By making the characters' reactions stronger than is justified by the situation, the author may try to unambiguously brand the behaviour that elicited the reactions as morally wrong, for instance.

Hagen (2004, 74–6) has convincingly argued that sentimentality has undeservingly become a negative concept on account of 'an ascetic and now slightly dated modernist aesthetics of impersonality'; as long as the strong emotions comply with the releasing factor, he claims, it is justified to depict them. He mentions Jane Tompkins's rehabilitation of sentimentality in her renowned article on *Uncle Tom's Cabin*, which prompted a revaluation of the novel (Tompkins 2002). At any rate, *sentimentality* is a concept that calls for a thorough discussion and re-evaluation.

What in English is commonly called *formulaic* or popular fiction is in German *Trivialliteratur*; 'trivial' does not refer to the subject of the action but to the sociological function of the cheap, mass-market books sold at newsstands or supermarkets that are considered trivial in comparison to so-called serious literature. The criticism of popular literature is largely directed at the cognitive value of the genre: 'The work is merely reproductive and draws a picture of a past world. . . . It impoverishes and makes stupid on account of its reductive psychology and worldview' and 'avoids conflict; instead of solving the psychic and social tensions one flees into a utopian world of happiness, whereby the reader is kept in his false consciousness' (Nøjgaard 1996: 287–8, my translation). Nøjgaard does not question this criticism but finds fault with the lack of interest in the positive functions of popular literature. Although popular literature has evident cognitive flaws, it still contains elements of cognitive value that make it important to evaluate as a genre.

Importance

The cognitive content we extrapolate from the action, the message, must be important, that is, provide us with information (or prompt us to acquire information) about things we find useful to know something about. This is often information about how people react in difficult situations, which is what most fictional literature is about.

Analysing a work in terms of importance requires our discrimination between theme and thesis, between the subject and what is said about it. As mentioned above, an action may have an important theme even if the thesis is unimportant (for instance, because the action is superficial and makes it difficult to identify and explain the problems) and vice versa. Therefore, to be important, both the subject and the information about it must be so. The concept of *cognitive depth* is useful in this context, as it implies that the author furnishes the reader with so much information about a particular subject that the reader is more likely to understand its cognitive implications. If the information does not delve deep enough into the problems, the information becomes less important, because the reader is less able to profit from it.

Like truth, importance is a subjective criterion dependent on the situation and background of each individual reader, but as people in addition to purely subjective needs also share needs with others, importance has an intersubjective aspect that makes exchanging judgements meaningful. If different readers explain the basis of their subjective interests, they can understand each other's values and discuss the importance of literary works from this intersubjective perspective.

Lamarque and Olsen hold that literary value is linked to the great, recurring universal themes in canonical literature (Lamarque and Olsen 1994). The practices of universities, schools, publishers and the media obviously reflect this conception of literature, but that does not preclude other themes from being important. A discussion about who is entitled to evaluate literary works is obviously relevant, and nobody can deny a particular reader or particular groups of readers the right to have their own opinion based on their own background, situation and interests. The continual discussion among the established literary elite reveals that even they have widely diverging notions of importance. Importance is therefore in the last resort a question of the subjective needs and interests of each reader. As we have seen, this does not exclude intersubjectivity, which must be based on theoretical insight into the structures and functions of the literary work and their interaction with readers, as well as on a sufficient understanding of the interests of different readers.

Sensitivity is related to importance, as it too pertains to the depth of the cognitive content. It means *susceptibility to impressions* and refers to the author's ability to perceive and describe nuances and details that help the reader understand the action and its cognitive implications. In this way, the sensitivity of the author bears on the importance of the action and message.

Another of the above-mentioned criteria, *morality*, is more or less tantamount to *important cognitive content*.

An interesting example of how the criterion of *importance* comes into play is the novel *Twee vrouwen* (*Two Women*) by the Dutch writer Harry

Mulisch (Mulisch 1980). When the book came out in 1975, the reactions were extremely divided. A recurring criticism was that the action gives too vague a picture of the characters and does not explain their somewhat dramatic behaviour.

The plot is in principle simple. The 35-year-old Laura is divorced from Alfred because she is sterile. Though she is not a lesbian, she falls in love with the far younger Sylvia, who moves into her flat. Sylvia, however, makes the acquaintance of Laura's ex-husband and leaves Laura to live with him. This is a terrible shock to Laura, but gradually she recovers. Then Sylvia returns, pregnant, and it turns out that she has used Alfred only in order to give Laura the child she has always yearned for. Alfred shoots Sylvia in revenge, and Laura is unable to recover from this new shock. She goes to Nice to attend the funeral of her mother, but suffers a breakdown on the way. As she writes the story from a room in Avignon, the ending suggests that she is going to end her own life.

The selection of elements in this novel reveals peculiar priorities. At 126 pages, the book is already relatively short, but only about a third of the text deals with the interaction between the two women and shows how they spend their time together. Moreover, the depiction of the relationship is superficial, mostly recounting practical activities and trivial conversations. Small everyday problems and conflicts, touching scenes of reconciliation, common experiences and pleasures, tenderness and little signs of affection and love – all the details that confirm a relationship and involve the reader emotionally – are very scarce. It is hard to identify with the two women, which explains why several critics find the characters vague or empty. The author uses a little more than a third of the text to describe Laura's grief after the two times Sylvia leaves her, but it is difficult to fully understand her strong emotions and suicidal feelings, because we know so little about them. Hence, some readers evaluate the selection of elements in *Two Women* negatively, judging from the reviews.

Selection is related to importance; with respect to *Two Women*, it implies that important elements have been left out, elements that could have created a vivid representation of the two protagonists. The omission entails that the reader is left on his own to determine the values tying the two lovers together, and the information about interpersonal relationships in general is too superficial to be of great value, even if the issues the novel highlights are themselves important.

This novel also throws light on melodrama, given that Laura's reactions to Sylvia's death seem out of proportion to the relationship's shortness and superficial nature. The substantial space devoted to Laura's desperation and suicidal inclinations may be seen as a ploy to compensate for the deficient selection; if the description of the love affair alone does not convince the reader, perhaps Laura's strong reactions might.

Relevance

Relevance may seem like another word for importance, but things that were once important may lose their relevance by becoming dated. We already mentioned Lamarque and Olsen's example of the novel about the generation of 1968; in *Don Quixote*, Cervantes parodies a genre of chivalric novels that had lost its relevance at the time of his writing around 1600. Today, that kind of chivalric literature is almost unknown, but *Don Quixote* continues to be read not for its no-longer-relevant parody of medieval chivalric literature but for the still relevant themes of misunderstood idealism and the confrontation between escapism and hard reality.

Novelty and difference

Novelty can mean various things and effectively represents different criteria. It can mean that something is of recent date, as when a renowned writer publishes a new novel, but as long as the new object brings nothing new, this meaning of the word has nothing to do with value. *Novelty* can mean that something has not existed before, for example when a writer introduces a topic that has never been treated in literature before. When realism began bringing up social issues in literature, such themes were new to readers and theatre audiences. Hence, what was being said about the new themes was also new, not only because the subject was new but also because the message expressed progressive opinions that had not been widely aired at that point.

However, novelty is a property that can easily be misunderstood and abused. In advertising, novelty is frequently employed to create new needs among consumers, playing on the notion that new is better. However, there is a rational reason why literature must always bring something fresh and new. Fiction is a kind of information, and information is expected not to repeat what the receiver already knows. Unnecessary repetition is boring, so the message in literature must bring in something new enough to make the communication interesting. The novelty may consist in an extension, rejection, revision or reinforcement of the reader's previous knowledge. Although reinforcement may look like repetition, it adds something new by repeating in a *different* way.

The message may have varying degrees of abstraction which can affect its novelty. The more general the message, the less likely it represents something new. Superficially, it may look as if literary works' cognitive content seldom brings anything that is truly new, and that also pertains to the great classics, with the same old themes and theses recurring in literature and new literature rarely introducing anything new. Literary history even has many examples of the 'same' story being told in different versions, like all the versions of the Faust legend that culminated in Goethe's *Faust* and Mann's *Doktor Faustus*, or the tales of Romeo and Juliet before and after Shakespeare's drama like Gottfried Keller's *Romeo und Julie auf dem Dorfe* (*A Village Romeo and Juliet*).

If it really were true that literary works kept returning to the same small number of themes and theses, it would deprive novelty of its value as a criterion for evaluation. However, the recurrent themes and theses in literary analyses are only the tip of the iceberg, as a great variety of thoughts and ideas are hidden beneath the surface. The impression of paucity is due to the fact that interpreters render the message at such a high level of generalization that it becomes banal. Beyond infrequent theses like Ibsen's 'The minority is always right' and 'If you deprive an average human being of his illusions, you take away his happiness', it is not earth-shattering news that people ought to be kind to each other, that it is important to be open and talk about problems and so on.

It is not the most general theses that make the cognitive content valuable, but the complex network of subordinate theses embedded in the numerous details of the action: the wisdom inherent in the concreteness and authenticity of the action, which involves the entire psyche intellectually and emotionally and gives the message a persuasive power a single thesis lacks. The concrete individuality of the action makes it possible to convey a cognitive content that is different from the messages of other literary works in spite of the similarities it shares with them at higher levels of abstraction. Even in works based on the same plot, like the literature about Romeo and Juliet, it is not the same action that is repeated, only the skeleton around which the different actions are constructed. The different actions built around this skeleton, which may be rather simple, deviate strongly from each other in terms of individuality and richness of detail and generate different messages in spite of their common denominator.

In addition to the charge that fiction keeps recycling the same themes and theses, the criterion of newness encounters the objection that what seems new one day is old the next. How can Ibsen's *An Enemy of the People* lay claim to our attention when its message has become so well-worn and familiar that it is readily transferred to a blockbuster film like *Jaws*? Again, it is generally only the diluted ideological content at high levels of abstraction that is propagated in this way and becomes commonplace. The more profound basis of the ideas, which is inherent in the virtual world of the fictional action, is too complex and requires too much intellectual and emotional work to lose its novelty. Even when you reread it for the second or third time, Ibsen's play offers new information.

In this context, it is important to remember that newness is relative and varies from person to person. The knowledge a society possesses does not necessarily reach all of its members, and the arrival of new generations renews the need for this information. What is well-known to some will therefore always be new to others. Even if novelty is transitory, the complexity of the action and symbiotic message along with the arrival of new readers will always prolong the newness of literary works.

The notion of novelty also includes *difference*. When a cognitive content is new, this implies, of course, that it is different from knowledge we are already familiar with, but difference may be more profound, consisting in permanent deviation. Within this type of novelty, we can distinguish between *originality* and *strangeness*.

It is not easy to define originality in a precise way. A message's originality means that it is different in a relatively consistent, characteristic way. It must be different from other messages and perceived as special or even weird, but what is special or weird is debatable. Contrary to the novelty criterion, the criterion of originality seems dubious. If originality were an absolute condition for literature to be good, a lot of acclaimed literature would be excluded, and it would be impossible to draw the boundary between original and less original works. If originality means anything more than novelty in the usual sense of the word, the criterion has the flaw of being either obscure or – if originality can be defined as weirdness – of hardly being a prerequisite for good literature. This naturally does not preclude the fact that weirdness can be charming, and may add value to the other qualities of the work.

The criterion of strangeness, if valid, would belong under the criterion of novelty. In his famous article on art as device, Victor Shklovsky asserts that defamiliarization is the criterion that makes literature art (Shklovsky 1990). In everyday life, we tend to take things for granted, not really perceiving them, and when talking about them in everyday speech, we economize expression by using well-known words and sayings – clichés – which the receiver understands immediately. By using unfamiliar, strange words and constructions, art tries to prolong and deautomatize the process of perception in order to make 'a stone a stone again' – make it as if you were seeing it for the first time. Defamiliarization draws the reader's attention to aspects of reality he is otherwise inclined to overlook. Shklovsky does not distinguish between the different levels of the communication process and gives examples of defamiliarization in the text, mental model and action. Defamiliarization may consist in whatever deviates from the usual. For instance, in a period where rhyme is common, rhymeless poetry becomes strange, and vice versa. On the level of the message, defamiliarization would mean that the action would somehow force the reader to think differently.

Shklovsky's view of defamiliarization as a criterion for art has proved to be inadequate. In his article about what he calls the poetic function of language, Roman Jakobson shows that defamiliarizing devices can be found anywhere from advertising to everyday language, even if it is more frequent in poetry, and that it may be absent altogether in realistic novels (Jakobson 1960). Therefore, defamiliarization alone is not a sufficient criterion of literary value.

Elegance has been postulated as an independent criterion, but it is effectively subordinate to the criterion of *novelty* in the sense of *difference*. The word has a purely emotive meaning and positive connotations, but distinguishes itself from words like *good* by indicating something special in the appearance of the object, but what that special something is is not specified. Elegance expresses merely, in other words, a positive kind of difference. Language has a rich vocabulary of more or less synonymous words to express favourable strangeness: *fantastic, exquisite, fine, exclusive, refined, smart* and so on. The feeling of difference is often based on intuition and may be so subtle that it is hard to tell whether it consists in properties of the text, mental model or action. In some contexts, *elegance* adds to its purely emotive sense a semantic reference to the ease with which an action is performed. A text is elegant if it seems to have come off effortlessly. When an artefact is perfect, its perfection does not reveal whether it was easily made or not. Only if the perfection reveals minimal traces of imperfection is it possible to infer that the author toiled over it, but then the text would not be elegant. However, the effort that went into the work is immaterial to the reader as long as it does not affect the result, and whether the minimal traces of concentration and hard work degrade the work or not, elegance in this sense would be tantamount to perfection and belong under our own five criteria of truth, importance, relevance, novelty and entertaining effect.

Entertaining effect

When novels draw a picture of reality that conforms more to how we wish it than how it really is, they are called *escapist literature* and are classified as popular literature. Examples are detective stories, science fiction, Western novels, love stories, mysteries, erotic literature, etc.

Escapism is not necessarily the only reason a novel can be entertaining. For one thing, true-to-life action may include an optimistic view of life; not all high literature ends sadly. For another, some readers feel pleasure even if the action conveys a pessimistic worldview. Receiving useful information may be pleasant in itself regardless of its emotional effects. What we find entertaining depends of course on our own predilections. A masochist may like sad or unpleasant stories because of the very pain it causes to read them. On the other hand, humour may make even sad action entertaining or at least less depressing. In contrast to the first four criteria, which are often imprecisely condensed under 'interest', the adjective *entertaining* does not have *interesting* as a synonym. The reason is probably that entertainment exploits cognition for its own purposes, whereas serious literature seeks cognition for its own sake.

Evaluation criteria for form alone and form and content as a whole

It is to some extent possible to distinguish between action and form. If we think of the action as a given structure with its own cognitive effect, literary form is everything that influences the reception of the action without modifying the action itself: order, frequency, voice, viewpoint, selection, rhyme and rhythm, hypotaxis and parataxis, metaphor, symbols and so on. Such formal elements cannot be evaluated separately, only together with the action and the work's total cognitive function, and the possibilities of cross-combining the various formal elements with the various elements of the action is so enormous that it is impossible to say anything general about their effects and the evaluation of them within the framework of this book. Nevertheless, literary theorists have traditionally occupied themselves with certain evaluation criteria that include formal aspects or deal exclusively with form. We will now take up these criteria.

Of the five criteria for the message, only novelty applies also to the formal elements of the mental model. Fictional works may increase the reader's interest in an familiar issue by presenting the action in a new way, that is, changing the structure of the text and mental model in comparison to previous versions, because it may be interesting to hear the same thing over again if it is presented in a different and perhaps more appropriate way. When the same issue emerges in new contexts, the action must nevertheless be more or less modified in order to arouse new interest. It is hardly enough to change the order of elements, shift from third-person to first-person or second-person narration or substitute verse for prose. On the other hand, changes in viewpoint or selection may in general entail the omission of essential elements of the action, playing up others in the new picture of the action the reader receives.

In addition to the above-mentioned criteria of the message, literary criticism has traditionally used many others. Apart from affective value, which excludes itself in advance because of its subjectivity, the following are in current use: wholeness (coherence, consistency, unity and closedness), complexity (variation), simplicity, openness (ambiguity), compliance with conventions, classicism, permanence, sincerity, sensitivity, intensity, realism, elegance, sentimentality, formulaicness and professional competence of the author. In addition, there are several other criteria pertaining to the ability to communicate, like clarity and beauty of language.

Wholeness

The criterion of *wholeness* has also been termed coherence, consistency, unity and closedness and refers to every aspect of the work. Like its synonym of *unity*, the term *wholeness* itself is relatively vague, because simply by virtue of being collected between two covers the elements of a work constitute a whole or unity. It is a task for the reader to find out the purpose of this wholeness/ unity: why have these events been put together in this text? If he does not see the utility of the wholeness or unity, it may be due to a deficiency of his own as well as to a flaw of the work.

Defining *wholeness* as *coherence* only shifts the problem from the need to define *wholeness* to a need to define *coherence*. There are many kinds of coherence, and the likelihood is great that the reader fails to see some of them. A serious challenge for coherence is the relationship between the elements of the action. We have differentiated between causal, consecutive, correlative and facultative relationships. The facultative relationship effectively legitimizes a lack of coherence, but the thematic aspect of the work opens for many other relationships than for causality, consecutiveness and correlation. Heterogeneous elements may become related by each in its own way shedding light on the same theme. If the theme becomes sufficiently general, any element will be relevant in the end, for instance if the theme is life's infinite variety. Moreover, the human ability to find coherence where least aspected is amazing. It is up to the individual reader to decide what is meaningful and how general and vague the theme may be. A group of readers may agree on fixed rules, but these rules are an obligation they assume voluntarily, and it has no natural bearing on the function of literature.

As for the interplay between form and content, there is always a functional connection between the text, structure of the mental model, action and message so that every change in one element entails corresponding changes in the total effect. The claim concerning coherence is here automatically met and thus becomes meaningless. On the other hand, it may make sense to evaluate the cooperation between the elements of the work in terms of their impact on the final cognitive result of the communication.

The substitution of *consistency* for *coherence* reduces the scope of the concept a little more. Consistency is the quality of being the same overall, being uniform but also reliable, logical, not contradictory. In the sense of logical, it implies the fulfilment of expectations: there must be a logical relationship between what we expect and what really happens. If a novel's causal chain that clearly seems headed for a tragic ending instead ends happily, this inconsistency affects the reliability of the action and elicits a negative evaluation in this respect. In the sense of similarity, consistency entails that heterogeneous elements should not be added when we expect homogeneity. For example, we expect the language in the various parts of a novel to have approximately the same stylistic features, and we do not like unrealistic events to appear in realistic action. Whether consistency means logical coherence or homogeneity, it is synonymous with unity.

But the expectations linked to consistency are largely based on conventions and may also be a kind of prejudice, because the decisive criterion is what the reader himself finds interesting. We already mentioned Hamburger's criticism of *Moby Dick* for breaking first-person narrative conventions, and we saw that inconsistency cannot as a rule be rejected as a flaw. One must evaluate each individual case in terms of the overall cognitive goal.

A text's consistency has also been interpreted in terms of no word being *superfluous*, which may however be tantamount to coherence. The notion that every element of a text should be functional imposes a kind of coherence that superfluous words would break.

Closedness is a metaphorical usage and as such invites too many interpretations. Something being closed may mean that it forms a unity, but at the same time closedness excludes contact between inside and outside elements. Does this imply that all gaps that cannot be filled by means of natural implication within the work are deficiencies? What about elements the reader is unable to integrate into his own interpretation: are they deficiencies of the work or the reader? Is it a flaw if some sequences of the action do not lead to a clear ending? Or does closedness imply no connection between the fictional and existing world? The criterion of closedness is in itself too obscure to be useful, but in addition, it is difficult to imagine any kind of closedness as an obligatory quality of the work. We have mentioned how realism uses seemingly functionless elements to create an illusion of reality, and Iser even considers it a flaw if a text meets too many of the reader's expectations. On the contrary, Iser claims, the action attains its dynamic strength when we are led in unexpected directions that allow us to use our own imagination (Iser 1974).

In order to be meaningful, the claim concerning wholeness and coherence must have a cognitive function, which may be related to economy of time as well as to the communication itself. Irrelevant elements take up valuable time and disturb comprehension, as the reader assumes at the outset that they have a function and tries to interpret the whole in such a way that they fit in. It is a convention of non-fiction to contain only relevant elements, and traditional views of literature have transferred this convention to literary fiction. We crave logical coherence and relevance because we do not want to waste time on something that is unnecessary. However, fictional literature leaves room for other priorities, for we read not only to receive information but also for entertainment or to pass the time. Although entertainment and the passing of time are products of the cognitive content, the reader often regards reading primarily as a way of passing the time and not as cognition. Consequently, independent of coherence and relevance, he is ready to accept every aspect of the work that makes time pass in an agreeable or at least meaningful way.

The work may also, however, contain irrelevant elements for cognitive reasons, which follows from Iser's positive attitude towards elements that do not apparently fit in. The author may, for instance, embed irrelevant and confusing elements in order to strengthen the feeling of unedited, authentic reality (see Barthes 2006) or even as part of his message that the world is not coherent and consistent. Irrelevant elements can also be intended to stimulate the reader's imagination.

Complexity and simplicity

Complexity may concern the structure of the action as well as that of the mental model. Simple action may be wrapped in a complex mental model, whereas complex action may be presented in a simple way through a simple mental model. According to this criterion, which Nøjgaard rejects as false (Nøjgaard 1996, 285–6), complex actions and complex mental models should be preferable to simple ones. A reason for this criterion may be the conviction that greater professional competence is required to create something complex than produce something simple. Another reason, applying only to the quality of the action, may be the belief that complex events are better suited to understanding the empirical world than simple ones, given the complexity of events in the real world.

There is nevertheless a problem with this criterion: even if it may be artistically impressive to master complex content, a complex form or the interplay between them, complexity is not per se a prerequisite for literary value. The proof is all the simple works that literary history has rated highly despite their simplicity, like Goethe's *Wanderers Nachtlied* (The Wanderer's Night Song). And, whether a work is complex or simple, it does not become good unless its complexity or simplicity works well. Both condensation and elaboration can enhance the literary quality of a work if used correctly, but they hamper understanding if they are brought into play in the wrong place. The literary canon affords examples ranging from the very simple to the very complex, and therefore neither complexity nor simplicity can be a valid criterion for literary value.

Openness

One definition of *openness* has been as *ambiguity* (Jørgensen 1971, 114). Jørgensen considers poly-interpretability a symptom of high quality and regards less ambiguous works as 'less important'. In this respect, he is in tune with Iser, who emphasizes the reader's freedom to interpret the work in his own way, but neither explains whether the ambiguity resides in the text itself, in the mental model of the action or in the message.

First, obscurity of the text obscures the corresponding details of the mental model. While the novel and the drama usually prefer clear, unambiguous language, modernist poetry's tendency is towards textual ambiguity, whether from a desire to provoke, initiate unpredictable reactions in the reader or express the inexpressible.

Second, obscurity in the mental model is due to gaps, which may affect the coherence of the action and may make it difficult to understand the characters' motives. Here, too, the author's intention may be to activate the reader's creativity.

Finally, obscurity in the message is due to a corresponding obscurity in the mental model of the action but also to the poly-interpretability of even clearly coherent events: even if the action is clear, the interaction between characters and between characters and environment may be open to multiple interpretations.

By way of elements embedded in the action, like symbols, extradiegetic comments, irony, intradiegetic statements and a tendentious structure of the action, the author can exert a marked influence on the received message, making it less open. Like Jørgensen, Iser criticizes such literature as too didactic, which applies to much children's and youth literature as well as to works like *Uncle Tom's Cabin*. Revealing basic differences between men's and women's ways of thinking, Jane Tompkins has defended such novels as a feminist literary response to the traditional male-dominated canon (Tompkins 1985). The use of strong, clarifying devices like sentimentality was more or less an implicit part of women's literary strategy at the time of Harriet Beecher Stowe, and I think it is difficult to prove that clarity and sentimentality per se are reprehensible, in spite of modern literary criticism's aversion to it. Clarity must also be understood in relation to the primary goal of fictional literature and the interests of different groups of readers.

Openness may become so complete that it becomes a problem, of which poetry consisting of empty pages is an extreme example. Jørgensen points out that there are limits to openness and to how poly-interpretable the text can be before it affects the value of the text, and he mentions symbolism as a negative example of poly-interpretability. Ultimately, it is up to the readers to determine the limits of what is interesting.

Criteria related to phatic function

One group of criteria stands out as being linked to manifestations of the author's personality in the work and having to do with the reader's need for human contact. Such criteria are *sincerity*, *sensitivity* and *intensity*, in which we are not concerned with the qualities of the fictional narrator, who is merely a fictional character without connections to reality apart from likeness, but with the personality that the reader intuitively infers from the work as a whole and which he feels is a genuine expression of the human behind the text. As expressions of the author's personality, sincerity, sensitivity and intensity are primarily linked to Jakobson's *expressive* or *emotive* linguistic function, but from the reader's point of view, the feeling of contact is essential. Jakobson terms the function of language that seeks to establish contact ('Hello', 'Can you hear me?') *phatic*, and the term is also used with reference to verbal communication having primarily a social instead of informative function, like small talk (see Malinowski in Ogden and Richards 1969, 315–16). In fiction, the phatic function is derived from the expressive function of language, as the sound of the author's voice evokes a feeling of contact: the reader feels that the author himself is speaking directly to him and sharing his private thoughts and feelings with him. As mentioned above, this feeling is stronger in confessional poetry, but it may also be present in other genres if the reader can discern the voice of the author behind the voice of the narrator and behind the action.

Sincerity belongs in many respects under *truth*, but carries an additional meaning of the *desire* to tell the truth. Sincerity in a text means that the author sounds sincere, signalling a wish to confide in the reader. The reader feels that the author is forming a private alliance with him by telling *him* the truth.

Sensitivity was dealt with under *importance*, as it pertains chiefly to the author's ability to perceive nuance and details. Hence, sensitivity is related more to the author's understanding of what happens around him than his relationship to the reader. Nevertheless, the reader may interpret the author's sensitivity as the expression and result of vulnerability, or on the contrary, his sensitivity may be a defence mechanism caused by his vulnerability. Most readers are likely to interpret works with a sad or bitter undertone as an expression of the author's own feelings. Vulnerability appeals to the reader's sympathy and compassion and makes him feel less alone with his own problems. Although there is no hope of direct contact between the reader and the author, the reader is nonetheless left with a feeling of social contact.

Intensity may refer to strong suspense in the fictional action, whether it be in the thrill of events or in strong emotional bonds between characters. If the thrilling action or the emotional relationship suggests the author's emotional involvement, the reader may perceive this as a kind of contact with the author's own feelings. However, the level of involvement implied by intensity, whether on the part of the author or the reader, is above all a symptom of the important events going on in the action. Only important events evoke such strong emotions, so intensity as well as sensitivity belongs chiefly under the criterion of importance.

Insofar as sincerity, sensitivity and intensity are felt as direct contact with the author, these properties of the work are of course valuable to the reader and are relevant to his evaluation of the work. Their phatic function may also be of intersubjective interest. Nevertheless, it is only a side effect of structures whose function is primarily cognitive, which is measured by the five principal criteria of truth, importance, relevance, novelty and entertainment.

Professional competence

Another possible criterion for literary value might be the author's competence; a work is good because it gives evidence of good craftsmanship. This is however an unnecessary detour, as competence is measured in the quality of the work, and in that case, we may as well evaluate the work itself, which leads us back to our five principal criteria.

Criteria linked to time

Literary history has clearly shown how literary trends and conventions arise and disappear. In accordance with shifting literary movements, literary critics advance and dismiss claims concerning the functions of literature. The claim that literary works should fulfil given conventions is so closely linked to particular trends and periods that it must be discarded as too unstable a criterion. There is only one stable claim concerning the functions of literature, but it is so general that it is of little value to evaluation: the literary work must satisfy the reader's needs, which may vary, because the reader who formulates his needs may be any individual or group at any point in the past, present or future.

Criteria linked to language

An old criterion for literary value has been the quality of language in the text. Of course, the language of the text must be good in the sense of being an adequate vehicle for the mental model of the action (the signified: the primary meaning of the text). That is, the language must convey a proper idea (mental model) of the events, avoiding misunderstandings and unintentional ambiguities, expressing efficiently the author's intention. If we prefer to disregard the author's intention, then the language must at least create a mental model that the reader finds attractive. As we have pointed out multiple times, language and meaning (text and mental model) are inseparably linked so that any change in the language implies a corresponding change in the meaning (mental model). Language has no value of its own, only as a vehicle for the corresponding meaning. As a means of communication, language must have qualities that make communication possible and (within reason) easy, so it must, for instance, be sufficiently clear (if that is what the author or the reader wants) and (preferably) vivid and evocative.

However, traditional literary criticism often seems to regard language as having a value independent of meaning; language should be original, good, beautiful, elegant and so on. As we have seen, another claim has been that language should have a deautomatizing, defamiliarizing effect; clichés should be avoided. However, what is original, good and beautiful language is subjective and debatable, and even if we were able to define these criteria, we would still have to discuss whether they are a prerequisite for good literature. Some works of canonical literature have neither original nor defamiliarizing language but nevertheless have a cognitive content capable of gripping readers. Clichés are not necessarily harmful, unless they present obstacles to understanding the work; quite often they are a quick and safe means of communication. It is impossible to pass general judgement on them, and each cliché must be evaluated in its full context. Innovative and challenging language may be useful for communication, but it is no prerequisite for good literature. The same pertains to language that has a personal tone, which may evoke a feeling of social contact but again is not necessary. Anything that draws attention to the essential goal of literary communication – the cognitive content – is useful, but that does not mean that it is essential. As a consequence, linguistic factors must be evaluated together with all the other aspects of the work.

Extratextual factors

In addition to criteria related to the structure of the work, several sociological criteria have been used as indicators of literary value: the number of copies printed, sold or in circulation at libraries, number of editions, number of reviews and other kinds of publicity, inclusion in university and school curricula and literary canons etc. Adorno, for instance, considers success a criterion for art: 'the concept of the work of art implies the notion of success. Botched art is no art at all' (Genette 1999, 219; Adorno 1983, 269). Such criteria show how much interest various social groups take in the work, but they reveal neither the reasons for their interest nor the potential of the work with respect to future readers.

A literary work's value depends on several external factors, such as its relationship to the society in which it is read, and evaluation may vary from one period to another according to the needs and interests of readers at any particular time. The Czech structuralists distinguish between short-term *actual value* and long-term *general value*. Certain writers, like Ibsen and Shakespeare, are considered to have high general value, whereas others have been entirely forgotten, having, in other words, low general value despite having had high actual value in their own time (see neglectedbooks.com).

The general value of a work is, of course, no more objective than its actual value, although the ability of the work to evoke long-term interest is more dependent on intersubjective consensus and is therefore considered a more reliable criterion for the value of a work. But many works of the past are kept alive by a cultural elite, which largely consists of scholars, teachers, authors, critics and publishers, who all belong more or less to the same social milieu, such that it is disputable of whom their opinion can be said to be representative. The fact that affiliation with given social, cultural and geographic groups affects evaluation is a problem that has occupied feminism and post-colonialism. I already mentioned Jane Tompkins's rehabilitation of *Uncle Tom's Cabin*; Edward Saïd's criticism of the Western attitude to Eastern literature is also relevant in this connection (Saïd 1984).

There is no objective measure for the value of a literary work. As long as readers feel they benefit from reading a book, it is valuable to them, if not to anyone else. To playful readers, a poem composed of meaningless syllables may be valuable, whereas readers who want a clearer cognitive content will reject it.

Who is entitled to evaluate?

Who is entitled to evaluate a work of fiction? Scholars, publishers, critics, pollsters, religious or political censors or the individual reader? In every society there will always be individuals and groups who consider themselves better qualified than others. Some claim to be experts, others simply have extraordinary self-esteem, and some of them carry weight by virtue of their position in society. Nevertheless, it is not certain that their opinions are any more relevant than those of others. In principle, every user of something is entitled to have an opinion about how the thing works for him. Different readers may have different interests and needs that affect their evaluation of a given work. Factors like geographic and cultural background, age, gender and profession influence the interests and needs of the readers and, consequently, their evaluation. The philosophical definition of objectivity as intersubjective consensus among presumptively competent persons solves the problem only partially, because even the evaluation of presumptively competent persons is valid only with respect to those who agree.

Even though literary evaluation is relative, the existence of literary criticism, referees, awards and canons proves its social importance. However, there is no consensus about the functions of literary fiction, and there is always the risk that the critics do not consciously know which group they are addressing and are not aware of their own authority's limitations. An important issue related to evaluation is therefore not only the relationship between author, work and reader but also their social context. Who has the competence to evaluate and in terms of which group of readers?

Film critics generally take into account the various audiences that belong to each genre, while literary critics often seem to judge literature from a more elitist point of view. What kind of authority is the power of the individual critic based on and what responsibility does this power entail? Literary evaluation is important because in terms of status as well as economics it affects the production, distribution and reception of literature and its influence on readers.

A solution to the problem of evaluation that has frequently been discussed is the critic's imagining an ideal reader as his target group, at the risk of the ideal mirroring in practice his own personality, but insofar as he is representative of readers in general, this is not necessarily a drawback. It seems at least useful to elucidate the potential of the work as broadly and deeply as possible, meeting the needs of as many groups of readers as possible. This kind of evaluation does not shed light on the experience of particular readers, only on the kind of experience they may have if they use the work in the way indicated by the critic.

Conclusion

I have tried to show that the value of literary fiction is chiefly related to cognition, even when it is at its most entertaining, but the action may contain elements that have an aesthetic, phatic, sexual or humorous effect in addition to its cognitive value. These side effects also require evaluation, and in genres where they are dominant, as in confessional poetry, nature poems, jokes and pornographic literature, they constitute, of course, the main object of evaluation. Most of the criteria for literary value are not only too subjective and relative, but also irrelevant, and should not be taken into account when we evaluate literary works. The five criteria of truth, importance, relevance, novelty and entertainment are exceptions, for in spite of their subjectivity, they are pertinent and allow for intersubjective discussion.

The structure of the text and the mental model of the action have functions that influence the cognitive effect of the action and must be evaluated together with the action in each individual work in terms of the interplay between the different levels of the work. Although the choice between equivalent devices (for instance different kinds of viewpoint) alters the total effect of the work, it is not certain that one alternative is necessarily better than the other. The evaluation of such devices must take into account the whole context, and an attempt to find general criteria must be based on a large and varied pool of literary material. Such a study exceeds the scope of this book.

The literary establishment tends to focus only on the literature it finds worthy of the literary canon, for which it has itself stipulated the criteria. This elite's competence, versatility and tolerance are bound to vary according to time and place, which entails that its evaluation of literary works is bound to be correspondingly unstable and unreliable, not only to readers outside the group but also even to its own members. The more homogeneous the literary establishment, the greater the danger that evaluation takes place within a closed circle of insiders. The negative stance towards popular literature may be a symptom of the elite's inability to understand the needs and interests of the outside majority. When critics praise literature that hardly anyone reads, their criteria may still be defensible, but it is tempting to question their ability to adjust their criteria to the needs of different people.

The ambiguity of the concept of *aesthetic* is an obstacle to understanding the functions of literary fiction and invites misunderstandings. If we deny or underestimate the cognitive function of fiction, we deprive ourselves of the key to understanding how fictional literature works and risk equating literary fiction with other art forms like music and abstract art, as Ingarden does. This sort of misunderstanding has entailed misunderstood criteria like complexity, wholeness, intensity and ambiguity, which may be useful to understand certain works but are not prerequisite to literary value. Confusion with respect to the functions of literary fiction may lead to false values and blind incompetence, so that writers create empty literature that profits nobody but which nobody has the courage to speak up about. This does not mean we should forbid experimentation, but experimental literature must also be evaluated according to criteria that reflect the real needs and interests of the reader, even if it is a question of only a few readers. Even if the author subjects the different levels of the work to radical experiment, the cognitive function is likely to remain intact (even if reduced to a protest against rationality) and is still the factor that makes the work meaningful. The value of the cognitive content and what kind of readers it appeals to, on the other hand, is bound to vary.

Both because the literary establishment tends to appoint itself and because it is always exposed to insularity, we must take its evaluations with a certain amount of scepticism. On the other hand, the literary establishment represents a great range of human experience and insight, which makes its judgements valuable even to outsiders. Even though canonical literature is undoubtedly valuable, it has no right to reject all other literature as worthless. The boundaries between valuable and less valuable are blurry, and neither now nor in the future will there ever be consensus about value, not even among the members of the literary establishment.

On account of the connection between literary value and the reader's needs, it is impossible to state in general terms that particular literary works are more valuable than others without characterizing some people as worth less than others. Literary value is a private question after all, but it may be raised to an intersubjective level, provided that the attempt at intersubjectivity is accompanied by humility towards the relativity that is always associated with literary evaluation.

17

Conclusion

In the previous chapters, we have dealt with a series of issues related to the way literary fiction works, and I have tried to find new and clearer answers. My guiding star has been a mimetic, cognitive view of literature and a practical model of the fictional communication process that distinguishes between the material text, the mental model of the action, the action itself and the cognitive content that the reader extrapolates from the work. I have tried to prove that a deeper understanding of the different levels of the communication process can shed light on a series of theoretical problems and counteract misunderstandings and prejudice.

In spite of the existence of the material text, literature is primarily something that occurs in the mind of each reader, and therefore introspection is the most important gateway to understanding literature. Literary theory and criticism are consequently a question of observing and interpreting what happens in our mind when we read and after reading. But what we observe in our own mind resembles to some extent what happens in the mind of other readers, and is more or less intersubjective depending on which aspects of the work are involved. Consequently, the text and the action (as manifested in the signified, the mental model) are in principle shared by all readers, whereas the cognitive content or message (the individual reader's interpretation of the text and the action) is subjective. Different readers will find it difficult to agree about all the aspects of the message, depending on the properties of the action and the latent message. It is probably easier to agree on the interpretation (the message) of *Uncle Tom's Cabin* than *Waiting for Godot*. This does not preclude that the cognitive level may also allow for intersubjectivity, and even if what different readers can agree about will vary from work to work, there is at least the possibility of explaining and understanding each other. Although literary criticism and theory are based on the subjective experience of the individual reader, the intersubjective community (by virtue of linguistic conventions, common concepts and cultural communities) ensures that it is possible and interesting to conduct a dialogue about theoretical problems in general as well as about individual literary works.

As readers and theatre audiences, we interpret our observations in terms of our prior knowledge and our own mental background and capacity. If these conditions change, our experience will change. Our background and capacity are individual but also partially collective, as a product of our environment and external influences. What we experience is therefore not only a question of *who* experiences but also of *when* and *where* we experience.

In this book, the well-known distinction between signifier, signified and referent together with the structuralist differentiation between story and discourse (text) has been a decisive source of inspiration, but because *discourse* is associated with *text* and straddles the boundary between signifier and signified, it has been necessary to link it clearly to the signified and detach it from the material text (the signifier).

The signified is an abstract entity that is difficult to grasp apart from its intermediate position between signifier and referent. It is difficult to see the relationship between the abstract signified and the concrete action clearly and discriminate clearly between the concepts of text, discourse and action (as we saw when defining the action). Since we are already familiar with various kinds of models, the practical concept of *mental model* has the advantage over the abstract *signified* in facilitating the distinction between the different levels of the reading process and the understanding of their interaction. Transparency also becomes easier to understand in relation to the concept of model and explains why we so easily confuse the signified with the referent (or, in my terminology, the model with the action itself). The distinction between model and action is a prerequisite for understanding selection, duration, viewpoint, the rendering of speech and thought, and iteration, whereas the differentiation between model and message is necessary for understanding the delimitation of the work itself, the message and the importance of cognition, along with the problems related to intention, suspense and entertainment. The comprehension of the message (the cognitive content), on the other hand, is a prerequisite for understanding the functions of literary fiction and the limited role of the aesthetic in fiction, and furthermore, the mimetic relationship between the fictional and the existing world explains the relationship between author, implied author and narrator.

Because this book's various attempts to explain and solve problems of literary studies are all based on the human ability to perceive and interpret, the solutions proposed are, of course, linked to the same uncertainty as all other theories of literature. The truth is at best a question of intersubjective consensus, and indeed, literary theory and criticism are characterized by disagreement in most areas. Disagreement is a negatively loaded word that connotes conflicts, lack of cooperation and inefficiency. When literary scholars are unable to so much as agree over whether language works as a means of communication and whether literary studies is justified at all, the hope of future consensus is perhaps illusory.

The situation may be softened by renaming disagreement *diversity* and regarding the chaos of literary scholarship as a charming and exotic element in the colourless world of academia. It does not matter which solution we opt for, for there are no consequences; no bridges collapse, nobody dies, and the lack of consensus affects neither the ozone layer nor the Gulf Stream. It does not matter what literary scholars are doing in their little playpen, and none of their activities face the threat of extinction. As an important branch of cultural life, it is sealed off, exempted from control and claims concerning material results. It seems not to matter *what* scholars deliver as long as they deliver.

And nevertheless, literary criticism and theory may be meaningful, may have an important social function, provided literature has a cognitive function and influences readers and society by virtue of its content, its cognitive content. The Catholic Church's index of forbidden books and interference with published literature, the fatwas against writers and publishers that have come into conflict with Islam, the censorship and banning of books in dictatorships and all periods in which books have been banned and burned through the ages are evidence that society takes the cognitive function of fiction seriously. To a great extent, literary criticism also assigns importance to the cognitive content. I hope society's interest in literature and its material support for it are due to a conscious or unconscious understanding that fiction can contribute to a better world by influencing the individual's as well as society's understanding of human behaviour and values. If literature has such a function, it is essential for us to understand fully our own relationship to it in terms of both production and reception. In this context, literary theory is useful and necessary.

Bibliography

Aarnes, Asbjørn. 1965. *Litterært leksikon*. Oslo: Johan Grundt Tanum Forlag.

Aaslestad, Petter. 1999. *Narratologi: En innføring i anvendt fortelleteori*. Oslo: Landslaget for Norskundervisning (LNU)/Cappelen Akademisk Forlag.

Abbott, H. Porter. 2008. *The Cambridge Introduction to Narrative*. Cambridge: Cambridge University Press.

Abrams, M. H. 1989. 'Types and Orientations of Critical Theories'. In *Doing Things with Texts: Essays in Criticism and Critical Theory*. New York: Norton, pp. 3–30.

Adorno, Theodor W. 1983 (1970). *Aesthetic Theory*. Translated by C. Lenhardt. London: Routledge & Kegan Paul.

Anderson, Amanda. 2006. *The Way we Argue Now. A Study in the Cultures of Theory*. Princeton, NJ.: Princeton University Press.

Baker, Carlos. 1972. Hemingway: The Writer as Artist, 4th edn. Princeton, NJ: Princeton University Press.

Bal, Mieke. 1990. *De theorie van vertellen en verhalen*. Muiderberg: Coutinho.

Barnet, Sylvan, Norton Berman and William Burto. 1960. *A Dictionary of Literary Terms*. Boston: Little, Brown and Company.

Baroni, R. 2000. *La tension narrative: Suspense, curiosité, surprise*. Paris: Seuil.

—. 2009. *L'oeuvre du temps: Poétique de la discordance narrative*. Paris: Seuil.

Barthes, Roland. 1977a. *Poétique du récit*. Paris: Seuil.

—. 1977b. 'The Death of the Author'. In *Image-Music-Text*, edited by Stephen Heath. London: HarperCollins, pp. 142–8.

—. 2006 (1968). 'The Reality Effect'. In *The Novel: An Anthology of Criticism and Theory, 1900–2000*, edited by Dorothy J. Hale. Oxford: Blackwell, pp. 229–34.

Beardsley, Monroe. 1981 (1958). *Aesthetics: Problems in the Philosophy of Criticism*. Indianapolis: Hacket.

—. 1982. 'The Aesthetic Experience'. In *The Aesthetic Point of View: Selected Essays*, edited by Michael J. Wreen and Donald M. Callen. Ithaca and London: Cornell University Press.

Beckett, Samuel. 2008. *Waiting for Godot*. New York: Bloom's Literary Criticism.

Bernlef, J. 1984. *Hersenschimmen*. Amsterdam: Querido.

Booth, Wayne C. 1974. *The Rhetoric of Irony*. Chicago: University of Chicago Press.

—. 1983. *The Rhetoric of Fiction*, 2nd edn. Chicago: University of Chicago Press.

—. 2005. 'Resurrection of the Implied Author'. In *A Companion to Narrative Theory*, edited by James Phelan and Peter J. Rabinowitz. Oxford: Blackwell, pp. 75–88.

Brecht, Berthold. 1963/64. 'Anmerkungen zur Oper *Aufstieg und Fall der Stadt Mahagonny*'. In *Schriften zum Theater*, edited by Werner Hecht, vol. 2. Frankfurt am Main: Suhrkamp.

Bremond, Claude. 1973. *Logique du récit*. Paris: Seuil, 1973.

Brewer, W. 1996. 'The Nature of Narrative Suspense and the Problem of Rereading'. In *Suspense. Conceptualizations, Theoretical Analyses, and Empirical Explorations*, edited by Peter Vorderer, Hans Jürgen Wulff and Mike Friedrichsen. Mahwah: Erlbaum.

Brinker, Klaus. 1992. *Linguistische Textanalyse. Eine Einführung in Grundbegriffe und Methoden*, 3rd revised edn. Berlin: E. Schmidt.

Brooks, Cleanth. 1962. 'Irony as a Principle of Structure'. In *Literary Opinion in America: Essays Illustrating the Status, Methods, and Problems of Criticism in the United States in the Twentieth Century*, edited by Morton Dawen Zabel. New York: Harper, pp. 729–41.

Brown, Roger. 1965. *Social Psychology*. New York: The Free Press.

Bunyan, John. 2009. *The Pilgrim's Progress*. New York: W. W. Norton.

Butor, Michel. 1957. *La modification*. Paris: Minuit.

Camus, Albert. 1976. *La chute*. Paris: Gallimard.

Capote, Truman. 1966. *In Cold Blood*. Harmondsworth: Penguin.

Carroll, Lewis. 1996. *Alice in Wonderland*. Harlow: Longman.

Carroll, Noel. 1996. 'Moderate Moralism'. *British Journal of Aesthetics*, 36: 223–38.

Chatman, Seymour. 1978. *Story and Discourse*. Ithaca: Cornell University Press.

Cohn, Dorrit. 1999. *The Distinction of Fiction*. Baltimore: Johns Hopkins University Press.

Colebrook, Claire. 2004. *Irony*. London/New York: Routledge.

Conrad, Joseph. 1996. *Heart of Darkness*. Boston: Bedford.

Culler, Jonathan. 1997. *Literary Theory: A Very Short Introduction*. Oxford: Oxford University Press.

Dagerman, Stig. 2012 (1948). *Att döda ett barn*. Translated by Steven Hartman. 'To Kill A Child'. In *Stig Dagerman. To Kill a Child*. New Hampshire: David R. Godine.

Davies, David. 2007. *Aesthetics and Literature*. London/New York: Continuum.

De Man, Paul. 1989. *The Resistance to Theory*. Minnesota: Minnesota University Press.

Dohrn, Wolf. 1907. *Die künstlerische Darstellung als Problem der Ästhetik*. Hamburg: L. Voss.

Dopychai, Arno. 1988. *Der Humor: Begriff, Wesen, Phänomenologie und pädagogische Relevanz*. Bonn: Rheinische Friedrich-Wilhelms-Universität zu Bonn.

Eagleton, Terry. 1990. *The Ideology of the Aesthetic*. Oxford: Blackwell.

—. 1996. *The Illusions of Postmodernism*. Oxford: Blackwell.

Eco, Umberto. 1994. 'Interpretation and history', 'Overinterpreting texts', 'Between Author and text'. In *Interpretation and Overinterpretation*, edited by Stefan Collini. Cambridge: Cambridge University Press, pp. 23–43, 45–66, 67–88.

Eeden, Frederik van. 1973. *De kleine Johannes*. Brussels: Manteau.

Falk, Eugene H. 1981. *The Poetics of Roman Ingarden*. Chapel Hill: The University of North Carolina Press.

Fietz, Lothar. 1976. *Funktionaler Strukturalismus: Grundlegung eines Modells zur Beschreibung von Text und Textfunktion*. Tübingen: Niemeyer.

Fish, Stanley. 1980. *Is there a Text in this Class?* London: Harward University press.

Fludernik, Monika. 1993. *The Fictions of Language and the Languages of Fiction: The Linguistic Representation of Speech and Consciousness*. London: Routledge.

—.1996. *Towards a 'Natural' Narratology*. London and New York: Routledge.

—. 2009. *An Introduction to Narratology*. London and New York: Routledge.

Fløgstad, Kjartan. 2009a. *Grense Jakobselv*. Oslo: Gyldendal.

—. 2009b. 'Har Tore Pryser copyright på krigen?'. *Dagbladet* (15 July 2009).

Fontane, Theodor. 1969. *Effi Briest*. München: Max Hueber.

Forster, E. M. 1927. *Aspects of the Novel*. London: Edward Arnold.

Foucault, Michel. 1981. *Power/Knowledge*. Brighton: Harvester Press.

Freud, Sigmund. 1958 (1940). *Der Witzund seine Beziehung zum Unbewussten*. Frankfurt a. M./Hamburg (London): Fischer Bücherei.

—. 1960 (1940). *Jokes and Their Relation to the Unconscious*. Translated by James Strachey. New York: Norton.

Friedemann, Käte. 1965. *Die rolle des Erzählers in der Epik*. Darmstadt: Wissenschaftliche Buchgesellschaft.

Gaarder, Jostein. 2007 (1991). *Sophie's World*. Translator Paulette Møller. New York: Farrar, Strauss, Giroux.

Gaasland, Rolf. 1999. *Fortellerens hemmeligheter*. Oslo: Universitetsforlaget.

Gass, William. 1970. *Fiction and the Figures of Life*. New York: Knopf.

Genette, Gérard. 1972. *Figure III*. Paris: Seuil.

—. 1983. *Nouveau discours du récit*. Paris: Seuil.

—. 1997. *Paratexts: Thresholds of Interpretation*. Cambridge: Cambridge University Press.

—. 1999. *The Aesthetic Relation*. Ithaca and London: Cornell University Press.

Gerrig, R. 1989. 'Suspense in the Absence of Uncertainty'. *Journal of Memory and Language*, 28: 633–48.

Goethe, Wolfgang von. 1985. *The Sorcerer's Apprentice*. In Sämtliche Werke, Briefe, Tagebücher und Gespräche: vierzig Bände/Johann Wolfgang Goethe. Frankfurt am Main: Deutscher Klassiker.

—. 2002 (1774). *The Sorrows of Young Werther*. Translated by R. D. Boylan and Thomas Carlyle. Mineola, New York: Dover Publications.

Goodman, Nelson. 1988. *Languages of Art: An Approach to a Theory of Symbols*. Indianapolis: Hacket.

Gorp, Hendrik van, Dirk Delabastita and Rita Ghesquiere. 1991. *Lexicon van literaire termen*. Groningen: Wolters-Noordhof.

Grammer, Karl. 1993. 'Gesichter und Schönheit, Partnerwahl und sexuelle Selektion—ein Blick in die aktuelle Forschung'. In Terry Landau: *Von Angesicht zu Angesicht*. Heidelberg: Spektrum Akademischer Verlag.

Greimas, A. J. 1966. *Sémantique structurale*. Paris: Presses universitaires de France.

Hagen, Erik Bjerck. 2003. *Hva er litteraturvitenskap*. Oslo: Universitetsforlaget.

—. 2004. *Litteraturkritikk*. Oslo: Universitetsforlaget.

—. 2006. 'Teori, metode og vitenskapelighet i litteraturforskningen', *Norsk Litteraturvitenskapelig Tidsskrift*, 1: 37–49.

Hamburger, Käte. 1953. *Deutsche Vierteljahrzeitschrift*. Stuttgart: Metzler Verlag, p. 27.

—. 1968. *Die Logik der Dichtung*. Stuttgart: Klett.

Hawthorn, Jeremy. 2000. *A Glossary of Contemporary Literary Theory*, 4th edn. London: Arnold.

Hemingway, Ernest. 1999. *The Old Man and the Sea*. London: Vintage.

Herman, David. 2007. *The Cambridge Companion to Narrative*. Cambridge: Cambridge University Press.

—. 2009. *Basic Elements of Narrative*. Oxford: Wiley-Blackwell.

Herman, Luc and Bart Vervaeck. 2005. *Handbook of Narrative Analysis*. Lincoln and London: University of Nebraska Press.

Hirsch, E. D. 1967. *Validity in Interpretation*. New Haven: Yale University Press.

Hutcheon, Linda. 1994. *Irony's Edge*. London: Routledge.

Huxley, Aldous. 1977. *Brave New World*. London: Grafton.

Ibsen, Henrik. 2006 [1884]. *The Wild Duck*. Translated and introduced by Stephen Mulrine. London: Nick Hern Books.

Ingarden, Roman. 1968. *Vom Erkennen des literarischen Kunstwerks*. Tübingen: Niemeyer.

Iser, Wolfgang. 1974. 'The Reading Process: A Phenomenological Approach'. In *The Implied Reader: Patterns of Communicationin Prose Fiction from Bunyan to Beckett*. Baltimore: The Johns Hopkins University Press.

—. 1989. *Prospecting*. Baltimore. The Johns Hopkins University Press.

Jakobson, Roman. 1960. 'Closing Statement: Linguistics and Poetics'. In *Style in Language*, edited by Thomas Sebeok. New York and London: The Technology Press of Massachusetts Institute of Technology and John Wiley & Sons, pp. 350–77.

James, Henry. 1992. *The Ambassadors*. Hertfordshire: Wordsworth.

Jensen, Axel. 1978. *Epp*. Oslo: Cappelen Damm.

Jerome, Jerome K. 1975 (1889). *Three Men in a Boat*. London: Penguin Books.

Juhl, P. D. 1980. *Interpretation: An Essay in the Philosophy of Literary Criticism*. Princeton, NJ: Princeton University Press.

Jørgensen, John Chr. 1971. *Litterær vurderingsteori og vurderingsanalyse*. Copenhagen: Borgen.

Kayser, Wolfgang. 1948. *Das sprachliche Kunstwerk*. Bern: Francke.

— (ed.), 1958. 'Wer erzählt den Roman?'. In *Die Vortragsreise*. Bern: Francke, pp. 82–101.

Keller, Gottfried. 1953. *Romeo und Julia auf dem Dorfe*. Stuttgart: Reclam.

Kielland, Alexander. 1897. 'Ballstemning'. In *Novelletter*. Copenhagen: Gyldendal.

Kienecker, Michael. 1989. *Prinzipien literarischer Wertung*. Göttingen: Vandenhoeck & Ruprecht.

Lamarque, Peter and Olsen, Stein Haugom. 1994. *Truth, Fiction and Literature*. Oxford: Clarendon Press.

Lämmert, Eberhart. 1967. *Bauformen des Erzählens*, 2. durchgesehene Ausgabe. Stuttgart: J. B. Metzlersche Verlagsbuchhandlung.

Lanser, Susan S. 2005. 'The "I" of the Beholder: Equivocal Attachments and the Limits of Structuralist Narratology'. In *A Companion to Narrative Theory*, edited by James Phelan and Peter J. Rabinowitz. Oxford: Blackwell, pp. 206–19.

Lapp, Edgar. 1992. *Linguistik der Ironie*. Tübingen: Gunter Narr Verlag.

Lawrence, D. H. 1977. 'As Far as I am Concerned'. In *The Complete Poems of D. H. Lawrence*. Collected and edited with an introduction and notes by Vivian de Sola Pinto and Warren. Roberts New York: Penguin Books.

Lewis, Sinclair. 1961. *Arrowsmith*. New York: Signet Classics.

Lothe, Jakob, Christian Refsum and Unni Solberg. 2007. *Litteraturvitenskapelig leksikon*. Oslo: Kunnskapsforlaget.

Love, Harold. 2002. *Attributing Authorship*. Cambridge: Cambridge University Press.

Lugowski, Clemens. 1990 (1932). *Form, Individuality and the Novel: An Analysis of Narrative Structure in Early German Prose*. Translated by John Dixon Halliday. Oklahoma: University of Oklahoma Press.

Luxemburg, Jan van, Mieke Bal and Willem G. Weststeijn. 1988. *Inleiding in de literatuurwetenschap*, 6th edn. Muiderberg: Coutinho.

Mann, Thomas. 1967 (1947). *Doktor Faustus*. Frankfurt am Main: Fischer.

Maugham, Somerset. 1960 (1930). *Cakes and Ale*. London: Penguin Books.

Melville, Herman. 2005. *Moby Dick*. Irvine: Saddleback Educational Pub.

Milton, John. 1968. *The Poems of John Milton*, edited by John Carey and Alastair Fowler. London: Longmans, Green.

Muecke, Douglas Colin. 1970. *Irony and the Ironic*. London: Methuen.

Mukařovsky, Jan. 1970. *Aesthetic Function, Norm and Value as Social Facts*. University of Michigan: Ann Arbor.

Mulisch, Harry. 1980. *Two Women* (*Twee vrouwen* 1975). London: Riverrun Press.

—. 2001. *Siegfried*. Amsterdam: De Bezige Bij.

Mulkay, Michael. 1988. *On Humour*. Cambridge: Polity Press.

Müller, Günther. 1948. 'Erzählzeit und erzählte Zeit'. In *Festschrift für P. Kluckhohn und H. Schneider*. Tübingen: J. C. B. Mohr, pp. 195–212.

Multatuli. 1860. *Max Havelaar*. Translation Wikisource, Chapter 9.

Nünning, Ansgar F. 2005. 'Reconceptualizing Unreliable Narration: Synthesizing Cognitive and Rhetorical Approaches'. In *A Companion to Narrative Theory*, edited by James Phelan and Peter J. Rabinowitz. Oxford: Blackwell, pp. 89–107.

Nøjgaard, Morten. 1996 (1993). *Det litterære værk*. Odense: Odense Universitetsforlag.

Ogden/Richards. 1969. *The Meaning of Meaning*. London: Routledge and Kegan Paul.

Orwell, George. 2008. *Nineteen Eighty-Four*. London: Penguin Books.

Phelan, James and Peter J. Rabinowitz (ed.), 2005. *A Companion to Narrative Theory*. Oxford: Blackwell.

Pirandello, Luigi. 1995. *Six Characters in Search of an Author*. In *Six Characters in Search of an Author and Other Plays*. Translated by Mark Musa. London: Penguin Books.

Poe, Edgar Allan. 2006. 'The Raven'. In *Collected Stories and Poems*. London: CRW Publ.

Propp, Vladimir. 1968 (1928). *Morphology of the Folktale*. Translated by Laurence Scott, revised Louis A. Wagner. Austin: University of Texas Press.

Pryser, Tore. 1994. *Fra varm til kald krig*. Oslo: Spartacus.

—. 2001. *Hitlers hemmelige agenter*. Oslo: Universitetsforlaget.

—. 2009. 'Hjelperytter for Fløgstad'. *Dagbladet* (14 July 2009).

Rabkin, Eric S. 1973. *Narrative Suspense*. Michigan: Michigan University Press.

Reve, Gerard. 1947. *De avonden: een winterverhaal*. Amsterdam: De Bezige Bij.

Richards, I. A. 2001 (1926). *Principles of Literary Criticism*. London: Routledge.

Riffaterre, Michael. 1990. *Fictional Truth*. Baltimore and London: The Johns Hopkins University Press.

Rimmon-Kenan, Shlomith. 1983. *Narrative Fiction: Contemporary Poetics*. London and New York: Routledge.

Robbe-Grillet, Alain. 1963. *Pour un nouveau roman*. Paris: Gallimard.

—. 1957. *La jalousie*. Paris: Editions de Minuit.

—. 1966. *French Short Stories: Nouvelles Francaises*. London: Penguin Parallel Texts.

Roberts, Thomas J. 1972. *When is Something Fiction?* Carbondale: Southern Illinois University Press.

Romberg, Bertil. 1962. *Studies in the Narrative Technique of the First-Person Novel*. Stockholm: Almqvist & Wiksell.

Rommetveit, Ragnar. 2005 (1972). *Språk, tanke og kommunikasjon*. Oslo, Bergen, Tromsø: Gyldendal.

Ryan, Marie-Laure. 1991. *Possible Worlds, Artificial Intelligence and Narrative Theory*. Bloomington: University of Indiana Press.

Ryle, Gilbert. 1971. *Collected Essays 1929–1968*. London: Hutchinson.

Saïd, Edward W. 1984. *The World, the Text and the Critic*. London: Harvard University Press.

Saint-Exupéry, Antoine de. 1997. *Le petit prince*. Paris: Gallimard.

Shelley, Percy Bysshe. 1989–. 'Bereavement'. In *The poems of Shelley*, edited by Geoffrey Matthews and Kelvin Everest. London: Longman.

Shklovsky, Victor. 1990 (1925). *Theory of Prose*. Elmwood Park: Dalkey Archive Press.

Simpson, Louis. 1972. *An Introduction to Poetry*. New York: St. Martin's Press.

Spillebeen, Willy. 1992. *Aeneas, of De levensreis van een man*. Antwerpen: Manteau.

Stanzel, Franz. 1965. *Typische Formen des Romans*, 2nd edn. Göttingen: Vandenhoeck und Ruprecht.

—. 1985. *Theorie des Erzählens*. Göttingen: Vandenhoeck und Ruprecht.

Starobinski, Jean. 1970. 'Le progrès de l'interprète'. In *La relation critique*. Paris: Gallimard, pp. 86–110.

Steinbeck, John. 1950 (1935). *Tortilla Flat*. Harmondsworth: Penguin Books.

—. 2000. *Of Mice and Men*. London: Penguin Books.

Stifter, Adalbert. 1978. *Brigitta*. Stuttgart: Reclam.

Stowe, Harriet Beecher. 1910 (1852). *Uncle Tom's Cabin*. New York: Norton.

Swift, Jonathan. 1998. *Gulliver's Travels*. New York: Oxford University Press.

Teirlinck, Herman. 1960–69a. *Zelfportret of het galgemaal* (*The Man in the Mirror*). *Verzameld werk*, vol. 1. Brussels: Manteau.

—. 1960–69b. *Het gevecht met de engel* (*The Fight with the Angel*). *Verzameld werk*, vol. 7. Brussels: Manteau.

—. 1963. *The Man in the Mirror*. Translated by James Brockway. London: Heineman.

Tennyson, Alfred. 1938. *The Charge of the Light Brigade*. In *The Poems and Plays of Alfred Lord Tennyson*. New York: The Modern Library.

Timmermans, Felix. 1950 (1916). *Pallieter*. Amsterdam: P. N. van Kampen & Zoon.

Todorov, Tzvetan. 1973. *Poétique*. Paris: Seuil.

Tolkien, J. R. R. 1981. *The Hobbit*. London: Carpenter.

Tolstoy, Leo. 1960. *Anna Karenina*. Translated by Joel Carmichael. New York: Bantam Books.

—. 2006. *War and Peace*. New York: Viking.

Tomashevsky, B. 1965. 'Thématique'. In *Théorie de la littérature*, edited by Tzvetan Todorov. Paris: Seuil, p. 293.

Tompkins, Jane (ed.), 1985. 'Sentimental Power: *Uncle Tom's Cabin* and the Politics of Literary History'. In *Sensational Designs: The Cultural Work of American Fiction, 1790–1860*. New York: Oxford University Press, pp. 122–46.

Vandeloo, Jos. 1962. *De croton*. Brussels: Manteau.

Vermeule, Blakey. 2010. *Why Do We Care about Literary Characters?* Baltimore: The Johns Hopkins University Press.

Walsh, Dorothy. 1969. *Literature and Knowledge*. Middletown, Conn.: Wesleyan University Press.

Walsh, Richard. 2005. 'The Pragmatics of Narrative Fictionality'. In *A Companion to Narrative Theory*, edited by James Phelan and Peter J. Rabinowitz. Oxford: Blackwell, pp. 150–64.

Walton, K. 1990. *Mimesis as Make-Believe*. Cambridge: Harvard University Press.

Weinsheimer, A. Joel. 'Theory of Character: *Emma*'. *Poetics Today*, 1 (1–2): 185–211.

Wellek, René and Austin Warren. 1954 (1949). *Theory of Literature*, 2nd edn. New York: Penguin Books.

Wells, H. G. 2010. *The Island of Doctor Moreau*. London: Kessinger.

—. 1985. *The Days of the Comet*. London: Hogarth Press.

—. 2001. *The Invisible Man*. London: Gollancz.

Wilder, Thornton. 1989. *Our Town*. New York: Mastervision.

Wimsatt, W. K. and Monroe Beardsley (eds), 1954. 'The Intentional Fallacy'. In *The Verbal Icon: Studies in the Meaning of Poetry*. Lexington: University of Kentucky Press, pp. 3–18.

Wittgenstein, Ludwig. 1967 (1953). *Philosophical Investigations*. Translated by Anscombe, G. E. M. Oxford: Blackwell.

Wood, James. 2008. *How Fiction Works*. London: Jonathan Cape.

Woolf, Virginia. 2000. *Mrs Dalloway*. Oxford: Oxford Paperbacks.

Wyndham, John. 1954. *The Day of the Triffids*. Harmondsworth: Penguin Books.

Yanal, R. 1996. 'The Paradox of Suspense'. *British Journal of Aesthetics*, 36(2): 146–58.

Author Index

Aaslestad, Petter   178
Abbott, H. Porter   2, 26, 32, 39, 72
Abrams, M. H.   42, 287
Adorno, Theodor W.   325
Anderson, Amanda   44

Baker, Carlos   143
Bal, Mieke   31–2, 35, 179–81, 232,
   236–8, 243, 245–6, 249, 252–3,
   267, 283, 297
Barnet, Sylvan   273
Baroni, R.   277–9
Barthes, Roland   111, 158–9, 240
Beardsley, Monroe   53–5, 79, 89,
   111, 114, 122, 292, 305
Berman, Norton   273
Bernlef, J.   173
Booth, Wayne C.   2, 111, 115, 117,
   219, 223, 302–4
Brecht, Berthold   273
Bremond, Claude   160, 167
Brewer, W.   277
Brinker, Klaus   35
Brooks, Cleanth   126, 223, 231
Brown, Roger   50, 52
Burto, William   273

Capote, Truman   7
Carroll, Lewis   153
Chatman, Seymour   2, 31, 34, 143,
   147–8, 154, 169, 178, 185–6,
   194, 231, 234, 249–50, 267
Cohn, Dorrit   5, 9, 11–12
Colebrook, Claire   223
Conrad, Joseph   11
Culler, Jonathan   1, 38

Dagerman, Stig   195, 268
Davies, David   44, 75

De Man, Paul   3, 25
Dopychai, Arno   221

Eagleton, Terry   75, 186
Eco, Umberto   94, 109

Falk, Eugene H.   29–30, 106
Fish, Stanley   27, 63, 94, 98, 109
Fløgstad, Kjartan   7
Fludernik, Monika   6, 22, 31, 34, 42,
   115, 134, 154, 185, 214, 297
Fontane, Theodor   219, 280–1
Forster, E. M.   30, 170–4
Foucault, Michel   111
Freud, Sigmund   69, 220, 225

Gaarder, Jostein   11
Gaasland, Rolf   53
Gass, William   168
Genette, Gérard   2, 5, 10, 31, 34,
   38, 47, 62, 75–81, 88–9, 143,
   147–8, 178–9, 188, 190, 193,
   206–10, 231–2, 236–41, 243,
   245, 250, 252–8, 262, 267, 302
Goethe, Wolfgang von   26, 83, 218,
   289, 314, 321
Goodman, Nelson   8, 27, 61, 68, 95,
   102, 106
Gorp, Hendrik van   273
Grammer, Karl   79
Greimas, A. J.   35, 143, 160, 167

Hagen, Erik Bjerck   76, 297, 299, 310
Hamburger, Käte   8–12, 59, 133–9,
   206, 243, 319
Hawthorn, Jeremy   30, 111
Herman, David   7, 32, 39, 72,
   231, 297
Herman, Luc   2, 69, 154, 231, 297

Hirsch, E. D.   4, 94, 107–14, 119–26
Hutcheon, Linda   223, 225

Ingarden, Roman   4, 29–30, 35–6,
    42, 56, 75, 85, 87, 89–90, 105–6,
    300, 328
Iser, Wolfgang   29, 42, 56, 65, 75,
    106, 113, 141, 293, 320–2

Jakobson, Roman   28–30, 294,
    316, 322
James, Henry   204, 235, 269
Jensen, Axel   186, 188
Jerome, Jerome K.   20, 97,
    203, 227–8
Jørgensen, John Chr.   91, 297, 299
Juhl, P. D.   111–14, 119–20, 124–6

Kayser, Wolfgang   2, 133
Kielland, Alexander   221, 229
Kienecker, Michael   307

Lamarque, Peter   10, 27, 44, 54–5,
    92–3, 127, 306, 311, 313
Lämmert, Eberhart   163
Lanser, Susan   141–2
Lapp, Edgar   223–4
Lewis, Sinclair   218, 244, 247
Lothe, Jakob   273
Love, Harold   115
Lugowski, Clemens   273
Luxemburg, Jan van   297

Mann, Thomas   140, 199, 203–4, 314
Maugham, Somerset   94, 157,
    159–60, 269
Milton, John   63, 98
Muecke, Douglas Colin   223
Mukařovsky, Jan   77, 94,
    107, 109–10
Mulisch, Harry   45, 151, 312
Mulkay, Michael   68, 221
Müller, Günther   177
Multatuli   154, 219

Nøjgaard, Morten   25, 75–7, 92, 231,
    297, 299, 308, 310
Nünning, Ansgar F.   11, 219

Ogden   28, 35, 323
Olsen, Stein Haugom   10, 27, 44,
    54–5, 92–3, 127, 306,
    311, 313

Phelan, James   69, 297
Propp, Vladimir   143, 160, 164–7
Pryser, Tore   7, 14, 16–19

Rabinowitz, Peter J.   69, 297
Rabkin, Eric S.   273
Reve, Gerard   222
Richards   28, 35, 323
Richards, I. A.   93, 109
Riffaterre, Michael   43
Rimmon–Kenan, Shlomith   2, 31,
    143, 148, 154, 161, 168–9, 171,
    173–4, 231–2, 249–50, 252,
    262, 267
Robbe-Grillet, Alain   137, 145, 265
Roberts, Thomas J.   10–13
Romberg, Bertil   231
Rommetveit, Ragnar   36, 43
Ryan, Marie–Laure   40, 69
Ryle, Gilbert   44

Saïd, Edward W.   326
Shklovsky, Victor   85, 153, 315–16
Simpson, Louis   103
Spillebeen, Willy   206
Stanzel, Franz   2, 134, 231
Starobinski, Jean   60
Steinbeck, John   173, 218, 245
Swift, Jonathan   153, 162, 186

Teirlinck, Herman   15, 198, 212
Timmermans, Felix   145
Todorov, Tzvetan   143, 252, 255
Tolkien, J. R. R.   270
Tolstoy, Leo   11, 199, 219

Tomashevsky, B.   154
Tompkins, Jane   54, 101, 199, 219,
    310, 322, 326

Vandeloo, Jos   188–9, 197, 200
Vermeule, Blakey   297
Vervaeck, Bart   2, 69, 154,
    231, 297

Walsh, Dorothy   21, 44
Walsh, Richard   43
Walton, K.   277
Warren, Austin   2, 4, 25, 100, 292

Wellek, René   2, 4, 25, 100, 292
Wells, H. G.   45, 257, 259
Weststeijn, Willem G.   297
Wimsatt, W. K.   111, 114, 122
Wittgenstein, Ludwig   77, 89, 166
Wood, James   158, 168
Woolf, Virginia   11, 15, 63–5, 96,
    120, 122–4, 137, 146–7, 163,
    173, 183, 200, 216–17, 234,
    237, 240, 244, 248, 256, 262,
    269, 289

Yanal, R.   277

Subject Index

action   35–8, 143–55 *see also* story
aesthetic, definition of   76
ambiguity   102, 321
anachronies   267
analepsis   267
anaphoric representation   259
anti-intentionalism   111
author   115, 127, 135, 150
autodiegetic   206

biography   169

causal elements   162
character   154–8, 168, 170, 315
chronology *see* order
closedness   319
cognitive content   40, 53, 87, 89–90,
     307 *see also* message
cognitive depth   311
coherence   318
communication process   25
complexity   321
compliance class   68
condensed speech report   216
consecutive elements   162
consistency   307, 318
correlative elements   163

defamiliarization   85, 153, 315–16
detail   181
diegesis   206
discourse   31–5, 38, 62, 66, 72–3, 85,
     148, 214–17, 221, 250
distance   48, 193
documentary novel   11, 14, 16
drama   26, 67, 93, 99, 101, 232
duration   177

elegance   307, 316
ellipsis   185

embedding   7, 10, 19, 83,
     187, 270
emotive components   83, 193,
     249, 307
entertainment   25, 52, 90, 146, 229,
     288, 295, 308, 317
epic preterite   59, 134, 138
escapism   52, 317
evaluation   91, 297
events   154, 303
external text   135
extradiegetic   206

facultative free elements   60, 318
feigned non-fiction   9
fiction   5–24
film   232
flashback   267–8
flashforward   267
flat characters   170
focalization   231
frequency   259
function   287

gaps   56, 61, 67, 101, 143, 179, 282,
     293, 303, 321
genre   26
grammatical person   193, 210

heterodiegetic   209
historical present   137, 195–201, 268
homodiegetic   209
humour   220

identification   48, 256
identity   142, 193, 201–4, 248
implied author   111, 115,
     117, 141
implied reader   141
importance   310

in medias res   269
indirect communication   27, 108,
        112, 114, 229
indirect speech   214
intention   111
intentional fallacy   111
interest   274
interest point of view   249
internal text   135
interpretative strategies   130
intradiegetic   206
irony   223
isochrony   185
iterative representation   259

levels   28
literature   27
lyric poetry   5

material text   35
melodrama   309, 312
mental model of the action   35
message   99
mimesis   41, 54, 307
morality   307, 311

narratee   50, 140
narration   31–4, 232
narrative   20
narrative, first-person, second-person
        and third-person *see* voice
narrative function   133
narrative situations   231
narrator   135, 201–14, 218, 246
non-fiction *see* fiction
novelty   313

omniscience   197, 234, 253
openness   321
order   267
originality   315

paratexts   10
past tense   138, 194–200

pause   185
person focalizer   246
plot   30
popular literature   52
possible worlds   69
present tense   194–201
prolepsis   267

rappel   277
realism   309
receiver   112, 140
reference   25
referent   25
repetitive representation   259
rhythm   177–8
round characters   170

scene   185
selection   177
sender   28, 115, 119–29, 133,
        138, 243
sentimentality   307, 309–10
setting   175
signified   28, 31
signifier   28, 31
simplicity   320
sincerity   309, 322–3
singulative representation   259
speed   177–8
static situation   161
story   30–4, 38, 52, 58, 62, 65, 71–3,
        137, 143–9, 178
strangeness   270, 315–16
stretch   185
subjectivity   5, 21, 110, 187, 255, 270,
        275, 298–303, 318
summary   185–6, 217, 261
suspense   273
symbol   28

text   25, 30–5, 38, 42, 55, 63, 66, 71,
        81, 99, 117
theme   41, 53–4, 165, 177, 292,
        306, 310

thesis   54, 292, 310
transparency   57, 67, 70, 332
truth   308

unity   92, 318
universality   92, 307–8

viewpoint   231
vision   231
voice   193
volition   136, 277, 288, 291

wholeness   318, 320